PARANOIA

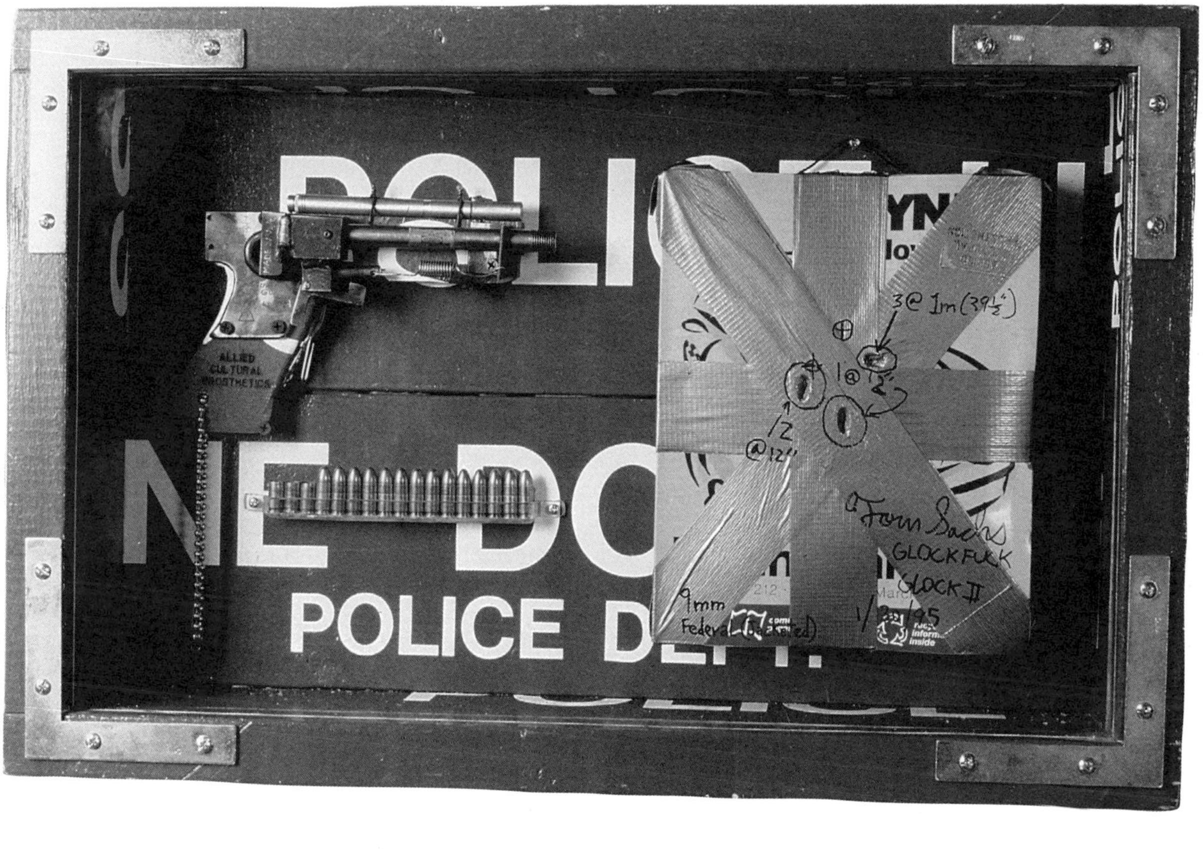

GRAND STREET 60

DAVID FOSTER WALLACE
Death Is Not The End
6

JAMES LAUGHLIN
Three Pentastichs
10

SALVADOR DALÍ
The Rotten Ass
12

TOM SACHS
Cultural Prosthetics (PORTFOLIO)
(introduced by WILLIAM T. VOLLMANN)
16

ROBERT MCLIAM WILSON
From Ripley Bogle
26

DAVID CRONENBERG
From Shivers (PORTFOLIO)
50

JOHN WATERS / ANNE DORAN
On Shivers
58

D. NURKSE
Two Poems
62

DANIIL KHARMS
A Man Came Outside
(introduced by VICTOR PELEVIN)
64

HEINRICH ANTON MÜLLER
Mobiles and Machines (PORTFOLIO)
76

JEFF CLARK
St. Nemele
83

DANIEL LEE ANDERS
Letters from the Hole
(introduced by MIKE DAVIS)
84

MICHAEL HOFMANN
Four Poems
102

VLADIMIR KOVENATSKY
The Way It Was (PORTFOLIO)
105

EINAR MÁR GUDMUNDSSON
Angels of the Universe
114

LARISSA SZPORLUK
Holy Ghost
135

ADRIAN PIPER
Decisions, Decisions (PORTFOLIO)
136

FANNY HOWE
The Wreck of the 737
146

FIONA SHAW / JEAN STEIN
Illusions and Delusions
150

DAMON KRUKOWSKI
Caresse Crosby Dreams a Dream
169

MELVIN WAY
Untitled (PORTFOLIO)
170

NORA OKJA KELLER
From Comfort Woman
178

PARANOIA

PAUL LAFFOLEY
Speculations in Mind-Physics: Work in the Visionary Genre (PORTFOLIO)
200

FORREST GANDER
Two Poems
210

SURVIVAL RESEARCH LABORATORIES
(PORTFOLIO)
214

LAWRENCE FERLINGHETTI
Two Poems
219

LÁSZLÓ DARVASI
Stories of Kisses, Stories of Tears
221

JORGE GUILLÉN
Six Poems
230

PETER FEND
Chernobyl Solutions (PORTFOLIO)
233

CLAYTON ESHLEMAN
Spectator, Specter, Sitter
241

ANTONIN ARTAUD
Untitled
245

**SYLVÈRE LOTRINGER /
DR. JACQUES LATRÉMOLIÈRE**
I Talked About God With Antonin Artaud
251

CONTRIBUTORS
261

ILLUSTRATIONS
270

FRONT COVER AND BACK COVER Tom Sachs, 12 ga. @ 3 m 1/6/97 9:46 p.m., 1997.

TITLE PAGE Tom Sachs, *Glock Box*, 1995.

TABLE OF CONTENTS Film still from *Shivers* by David Cronenberg, 1975.

"Angels of the Universe" is excerpted from *Angels of the Universe*. Copyright © 1996 by Einar Már Gudmundsson. Translated from the Icelandic by Bernard Scudder. Reprinted with permission from St. Martin's Press.

"The Rotten Ass" by Salvador Dalí. Copyright © Demart Pro Arte B.V.

Grand Street (ISSN 0734-5496; ISBN 1-885490-11-9) is published quarterly by Grand Street Press (a project of the New York Foundation for the Arts, Inc., a not-for-profit corporation), 131 Varick Street, Room 906, New York, NY 10013. Tel: (212) 807-6548, Fax: (212) 807-6544. Contributions and gifts to Grand Street Press are tax-deductible to the extent allowed by law. This publication is made possible, in part, by a grant from the New York State Council on the Arts.

Volume Fifteen, Number Four (*Grand Street* 60—Spring 1997). Copyright © 1997 by the New York Foundation for the Arts, Inc., Grand Street Press. All rights reserved. Reproduction, whether in whole or in part, without permission is strictly prohibited. Second-class postage paid at New York, NY and additional mailing offices. Postmaster: Please send address changes to Grand Street Subscription Service, Dept. GRS, P.O. Box 3000, Denville, NJ 07834. Subscriptions are $40 a year (four issues). Foreign subscriptions (including Canada) are $55 a year, payable in U.S. funds. Single-copy price is $12.95 ($18 in Canada). For subscription inquiries, please call (800) 807-6548.

Grand Street is printed by Hull Printing in Meriden, CT. It is distributed to the trade by D.A.P./Distributed Art Publishers, 155 Avenue of the Americas, New York, NY 10013, Tel: (212) 627-1999, Fax: (212) 627-9484, and to newsstands only by B. DeBoer, Inc., 113 E. Centre Street, Nutley, NJ 07110 and Fine Print Distributors, 6448 Highway 290 E., Austin, TX 78723. *Grand Street* is distributed in Australia and New Zealand by Peribo Pty, Ltd., 58 Beaumont Road, Mount Kuring-Gai, NSW 2080, Australia, Tel: (2) 457-0011, and in the United Kingdom by Central Books, 99 Wallis Road, London E9 5LN, Tel: (181) 986-4854.

GRAND STREET

EDITOR
Jean Stein

MANAGING EDITOR
Deborah Treisman

ART EDITOR
Walter Hopps

POETRY EDITOR
William Corbett

DESIGN
J. Abbott Miller, Luke Hayman, Paul Carlos
DESIGN/WRITING/RESEARCH, NEW YORK

ASSISTANT EDITOR
Julie A. Tate

ASSISTANT ART EDITOR
Anne Doran

ADMINISTRATIVE ASSISTANT
Lisa Brodus

INTERNS
Layla Hearth, Rachel Kushner, Christina Persico, Joanna Yas

ADVISORY EDITORS
Hilton Als, Edward W. Said

CONTRIBUTING EDITORS
Dominique Bourgois, Colin de Land, Mike Davis
Raymond Foye, Jonathan Galassi, Stephen Graham
Dennis Hopper, Hudson, Jane Kramer
Erik Rieselbach, Robin Robertson, Jeremy Treglown
Katrina vanden Heuvel, Wendy vanden Heuvel
John Waters, Drenka Willen

FOUNDING CONTRIBUTING EDITOR
Andrew Kopkind (1935–1994)

PUBLISHERS
Jean Stein & Torsten Wiesel

DEATH IS NOT THE END

DAVID FOSTER WALLACE

The 56-year-old American poet, a Nobel Laureate, a poet known in American literary circles as "the poet's poet" or sometimes simply "the Poet," lay outside on the deck, bare-chested, moderately overweight, in a partially reclined deck chair, in the sun, reading, half supine, moderately but not severely overweight, winner of two National Book Awards, an American Book Critics' Circle Award, a Lamont Prize, two grants from the National Endowment for the Arts, a Prix de Rome, a Lannan Foundation Fellowship, a MacDowell Medal, and a Mildred and Harold Strauss Living Award from the American Academy and National Institute of Arts and Letters, a president emeritus of PEN, a poet two separate American generations have hailed as the voice of their generation, now 56, lying in an unwet XL Speedo-brand swimsuit in an incrementally reclinable canvas deck chair on the tile deck beside the home's pool, a poet who was among the first ten Americans to receive a "Genius Grant" from the prestigious MacArthur Foundation, one of only three American recipients of the Nobel Prize for Literature now living, 5' 8", 181 lbs., brown/brown, hairline unevenly recessed because of the inconsistent acceptance/rejection of various Hair Augmentation Systems–brand transplants, he sat, or lay—or perhaps most accurately just *reclined*—in a black Speedo swimsuit by the home's kidney-shaped pool,[1] on the pool's tile deck, in a portable deck chair whose back was now reclined

---

[1] Also the first American-born poet ever in the Nobel Prize for Literature's distinguished 94-year history to receive it, the coveted Nobel Prize for Literature.

four clicks to an angle of 35° w/r/t the deck's mosaic tile, at 10:20 A.M. on 15 May 1995, the fourth most anthologized poet in the history of American belles lettres, near an umbrella but not in the actual shade of the umbrella, reading *Newsweek* magazine,[2] using the modest swell of his abdomen as an angled support for the magazine, also wearing thongs, one hand behind his head, the other hand out to the side and trailing on the dun-and-ocher filigree of the deck's expensive Spanish ceramic tile, occasionally wetting a finger to turn the page, wearing prescription sunglasses whose lenses were chemically treated to darken in fractional proportion to the luminous intensity of the light to which they were exposed, wearing on the trailing hand a wristwatch of middling quality and expense, simulated rubber thongs on his feet, legs crossed at the ankle and knees slightly spread, the sky cloudless and brightening as the morning's sun moved up and right, wetting a finger not with saliva or perspiration but with the condensation on the thin frosted glass of iced tea that rested now just on the border of his body's shadow to the chair's upper right and would soon have to be moved to remain in that cool shadow, tracing a finger idly down the glass's side before bringing the slightly moist finger idly up to the page, occasionally turning the pages of the 19 September 1994 edition of *Newsweek* magazine, reading about American health-care reform and about US Air's tragic Flight 427, reading a summary and favorable review of the popular nonfiction volumes *Hot Zone* and *The Coming Plague*, sometimes turning several pages in succession, skimming certain articles and summaries, an eminent American poet now four months short of his fifty-seventh birthday, a poet whom *Newsweek* magazine's chief competitor, *Time* magazine, had once rather absurdly called "the closest thing to a genuine literary immortal now living," his shins nearly hairless, the open umbrella's shadow distending slightly, the thongs' simulated rubber pebbled on both sides of the sole, the poet's forehead dotted with perspiration, his tan deep and rich, the insides of his upper legs nearly hairless, his penis curled tightly on itself inside the tight swimsuit, his Vandyke neatly trimmed, a clean ashtray on the iron table,

---

[2] Never the recipient of a John Simon Guggenheim Foundation Fellowship, however: rejected thrice early in his poetry career, he had determined that something personal and/or political was afoot with the Guggenheim Fellowship committee and had decided that he'd simply be damned, starve utterly, before he would ever again hire a Graduate Assistant to fill out the tiresome triplicate Guggenheim Foundation Fellowship application and go through the tiresome contemptible farce of "objective" consideration again.

not drinking his iced tea, occasionally clearing his throat, at certain intervals shifting slightly in the pastel deck chair to scratch idly at the instep of one foot with the big toe of the other foot without removing his thongs or looking at either foot, seemingly intent on the magazine, the home's blue pool to his right and the home's thick glass sliding rear door to his oblique left, between himself and the pool a round table of white woven iron impaled at the center by a large beach umbrella whose distending shadow now nearly touches the pool, an indisputably accomplished poet, reading his magazine in his chair on his deck by his pool behind his home. The home's pool and deck area are surrounded on three sides by a dense tangle of trees and shrubbery. The trees and shrubbery, planted years before, are densely interwoven and serve the same essential function as a privacy fence or a wall of fine stone. It is the height of spring, and the trees and shrubbery are in full leaf and are intensely green and still, and are complexly shadowed, and the sky is wholly blue and still, so that the whole enclosed tableau of pool and deck and poet and chair and trees and home's rear façade is very still and composed and very nearly wholly silent, the gentle gurgle of the pool's pump and drain and the occasional sound of the poet clearing his throat or turning the pages of Newsweek magazine the only sounds—not a bird, no distant lawn mowers or hedge trimmers or weed wackers, no airplanes overhead or distant muffled sounds from the pools of the homes on either side of the poet's home, nothing but the pool's respiration and poet's occasional cleared throat, wholly still and enclosed, not even a hint of a breeze to stir the leaves of the trees and shrubbery, the silent living nastic enclosing flora's motionless green vivid and inescapable and not like anything else in the world in either appearance or suggestion.[3]

---

[3] That is not entirely true.

JAMES LAUGHLIN

THREE PENTASTICHS

THE DISCOVERY

When will he discover that he's a joke, that the
smiles that greet him in the post office are really
hidden laughter, suppressed by politeness, that
when he leaves they laugh about him and his
pretensions to being an important poet and big brain.

THREE PENTASTICHS

IN MEMORY OF ROBERT FITZGERALD

> O best of friends it's years since you crossed
> the Lethe but still you often visit me in happy
> memories: how you cocked your head when you were
> talking, how you helped me with my Greek, and
> our battles as Achilles and Hektor on the links.

THE SURYA (THE SUN)*

> His bright rays bear him up aloft, the god who
> knoweth all that lives. The constellations pass
> away, like thieves, together with their beams,
> before the all-beholding sun. Swift and beautiful
> art thou, O Surya, maker of the light.

---

*A hymn from the Rig Veda (1200 B.C. or earlier), edited from the Sanskrit by Nicol Macnicol (abridged).

The Rotten Ass

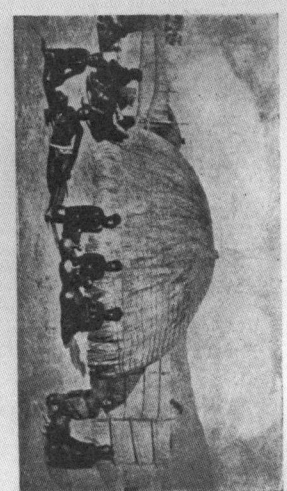
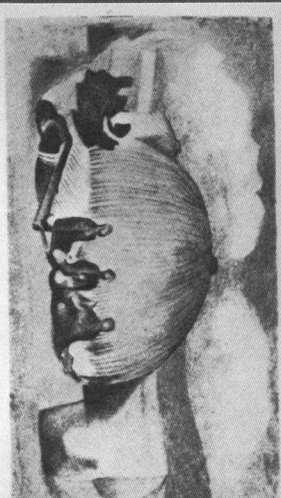
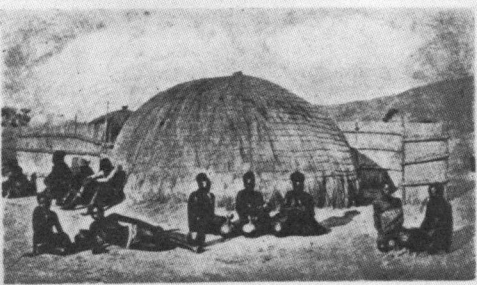

COMMUNICATION : Visage paranoïaque.
 A la suite d'une étude, au cours de laquelle m'avait obsédé une longue réflexion sur les visages de Picasso et particulièrement ceux de l'époque noire, je cherche une adresse dans un tas de papiers et suis soudain frappé par la reproduction d'un visage que je crois de Picasso, visage absolument inconnu.
 Tout à coup, ce visage s'efface et je me rends compte de l'illusion (?) L'analyse de l'image paranoïaque en question me vaut de retrouver, par une interprétation symbolique, toutes les idées qui avaient précédé la vision du visage.
 André Breton avait interprété ce visage comme étant celui de Sade, ce qui correspondait à une toute particulière préoccupation de Breton quant à Sade.
 Dans les cheveux du visage en question Breton voyait une perruque poudrée, alors que moi je voyais un fragment de toile non peinte, comme il est fréquent dans le style picassien.

Salvador DALI

SALVADOR DALÍ

A morally-inclined action could be provoked by the violently paranoid wish to render confusion systematic.

Paranoia itself, especially when seen as a mechanism of strength and power, leads us to the possibility of a mental crisis that is perhaps as serious as, though diametrically opposed to, the crisis induced by hallucination.

The moment is near, I believe, when, by means of a deliberately paranoid thought process (as through automatism and other passive states), it will be possible to systematize confusion and contribute to the total discrediting of the world of reality.

The new simulacra that paranoid thought could suddenly reveal will not only have their roots in the unconscious—more importantly, the strength of paranoid power will be placed at the service of the unconscious.

These threatening simulacra will act cleverly and corrosively with the clarity of everyday physical forms, in such a way that our minds, with their distinctive capacity for self-censorship, will dream of the old machinery of metaphysics and almost willingly confound this with the very essence of nature, which, according to Heraclitus, likes to hide.

As far removed as possible from the sensory phenomena that can be thought of as more or less connected to hallucination, paranoid activity always makes use of verifiable, recognizable materials. It is enough for someone in the grip of an interpretive delirium to link the meanings of heterogeneous paintings that happen to hang on the same wall for the real existence of such a link to become undeniable. Paranoia uses the external world to validate an obsessive idea, with

LEFT Salvador Dalí, *Paranoiac Visage*, 1931. "Following a period of study during which I had been obsessed by a long reflection on Picasso's faces . . . I was looking for an address in a pile of papers when I was suddenly struck by the reproduction of a face I thought was by Picasso, an absolutely unknown one. Suddenly, the face disappeared and I realized my illusion. The analysis of this paranoid image allowed me to discover, with a symbolic interpretation, all the ideas that had preceded the vision."

the troubling result of validating its reality to others. The reality of the external world serves as illustration and proof of the paranoid idea and is subservient to the reality in our minds.

Physicians uniformly acknowledge the quickness of mind and incomparable subtlety of many paranoiacs, who, by seizing on themes and facts with a finesse that escapes normal people, often reach conclusions that cannot be dismissed or contradicted and which almost always defy psychological analysis.

It is a clearly paranoid process that has made it possible to achieve a double image—that is, a representation of an object which becomes, without the slightest figurative or anatomical modification, the representation of another, absolutely different object, it too devoid of any distortion or abnormality that could indicate some sort of manipulation.

This double image was made possible by the violence of paranoid thought, which cunningly and skillfully availed itself of the requisite number of pretexts, coincidences, and so forth in order to reveal the second image, which in this instance takes the place of the obsessive idea.

The double image (an example of which might be an image of a horse that is also an image of a woman) can be extended, following the paranoid process—the existence of another obsessive idea being sufficient cause for the appearance of a third image (of a lion, for example), and so on, with the total number of images limited solely by the paranoid capacity of the individual's thought.

I subject to materialist scrutiny the sort of mental crisis that such an image can provoke. I subject to the same scrutiny the still more complex problem of determining which such image is most likely to exist if one allows desire to intervene, as well as the more difficult and more general problem of determining whether the series of such representations has a limit or whether, as we have every reason to believe, such a limit either does not exist or whether its existence depends solely on the paranoid capacity of each individual.

Assuming that no other considerations intervene, the foregoing allows me at the very least to assert that images of reality itself depend on the magnitude of our paranoid faculty. Theoretically, moreover, an individual endowed with a paranoid faculty of sufficient magnitude might at will perceive a series of changes in the shape of a real object—as in the case of voluntary hallucination—but with the more destructive peculiarity that the various forms assumed by the object can be seen and verified by anyone, once pointed out by the paranoiac.

The paranoid mechanism, which gives rise to the multiple figurative image, is the key to understanding the nature and origin of simulacra, whose fury dominates the disguise beneath which the manifold appearances of the concrete conceal themselves. Indeed, it is the fury and traumatic nature of simulacra vis-à-vis reality and the absence of the slightest osmosis between reality and its simulacra that lead to the conclusion that *comparison* of any sort is a (poetic) impossibility. It would be possible to compare two things only if it were possible to conceive of a lack of any type of conscious or unconscious connection between them. Made tangible, such a comparison would clearly embody our idea of the gratuitous.

Because simulacra are inconsistent with reality, and because the gratuitous can exist in their presence, they can easily take the form of reality, while reality can in turn adapt itself to the violence of the simulacra, which one form of materialist thought stupidly confounds with real violence.*

Nothing can prevent me from acknowledging the multiple presence of simulacra in the example of the multiple image, even if one of its states takes on the appearance of a rotten ass, and even if this ass is truly and horribly rotten, covered with thousands of flies and ants; since in this case, moreover, one cannot assume that the distinct states of the image have any intrinsic significance apart from the notion of time, nothing can convince me that this cruel putrefaction of the ass is anything other than the harsh, blinding reflection of new precious stones.

And there's no way to know that the much-desired "treasure island" isn't hiding behind the three major simulacra—shit, blood, and putrefaction.

As connoisseurs of simulacra, we have long since learned to recognize the image of desire behind the simulacra of terror and even the dawn of "golden ages" behind ignominious scatological simulacra. The acceptance of simulacra whose reality painstakingly strives to imitate appearances leads us to *desire* ideal things.

Perhaps no simulacrum has created structures to which the word *ideal* applies more exactly than the great simulacrum that constitutes the disruptive ornamental architecture of the Modern Style. No collective effort has managed to create a dream world as pure or as disturbing as these modern-style buildings that stand on the fringes of architecture as true realizations of solidified desire, in which the cruelest, most violent automatism achingly reveals a hatred of reality and a need to seek refuge in an ideal world that is common in childhood neurosis.

This is what we can still love, this imposing mass of cold, maniacal buildings scattered across Europe, scorned and neglected by anthologies and studies. This is all we need to combat our piggish contemporary aestheticians, who defend execrable "modern art." Indeed, this is all we need to combat the entire history of art.

Art critics, artists, and so forth need to be told once and for all that they should expect nothing from the new surrealist images but disappointment, disagreeableness, and repugnance. Far removed from all "plastic investigations" and other such imbecilities, the new images of surrealism will increasingly take on the forms and colors of demoralization and confusion. The day is not far off when a painting will have no value other than that of a simple moral yet gratuitous act.

The new images, as functional forms of thought, will freely follow the penchants of desire, even as they are violently repressed. The mortal activity of these new images can still, along with other surrealist activities, contribute to the destruction of reality for the benefit of those who, in opposition to infamous and abominable ideals of every sort, aesthetic, humanitarian, philosophical, and so forth, are leading us back to the limpid sources of masturbation, exhibitionism, crime, and love.

Idealists without sharing in any ideal. The ideal images of surrealism in the service of the imminent crisis of consciousness, in the service of the Revolution.

Translated from the French by Arthur Goldhammer

---

* Here I am thinking in particular of the materialist ideas of Georges Bataille, along with all the old materialism that Bataille pretends to bring up to date with the gratuitous support of modern psychology.

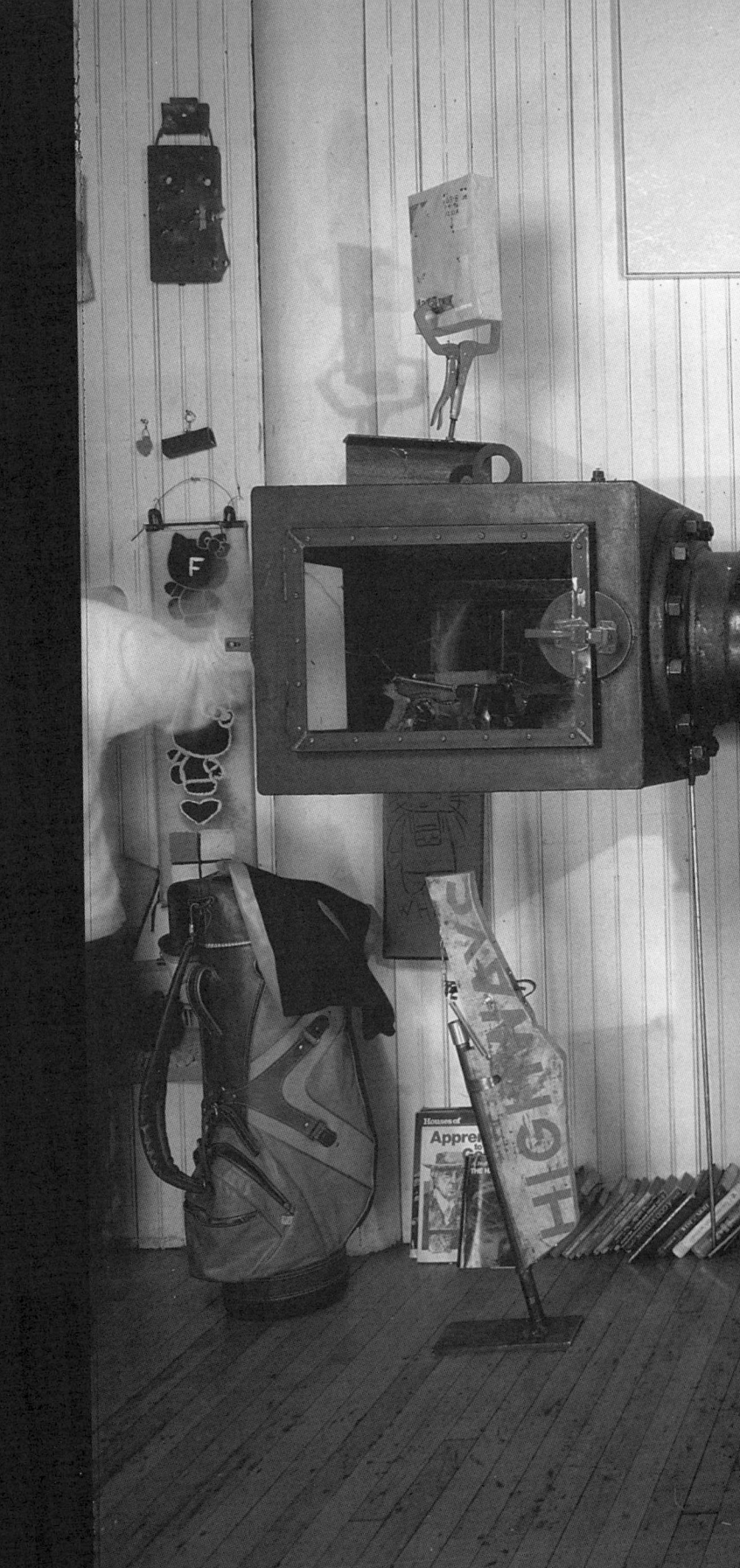

TOM SACHS
CULTURAL PROSTHETICS

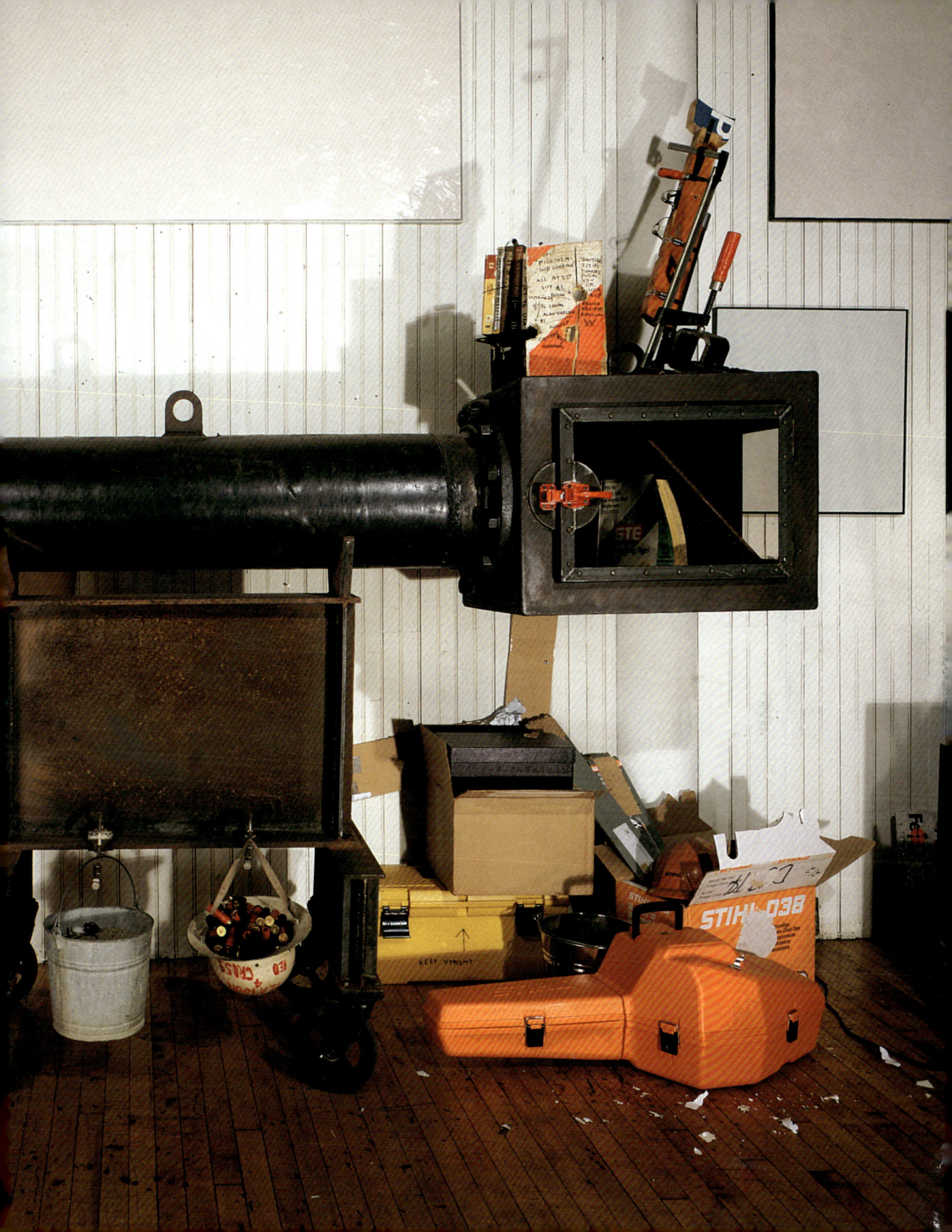

PAGES 16–17
View of Tom Sachs's studio with test firing chamber, January 1997.

BELOW
Untitled (Yellow Gun), 1995.

RIGHT
Valise, 1996.

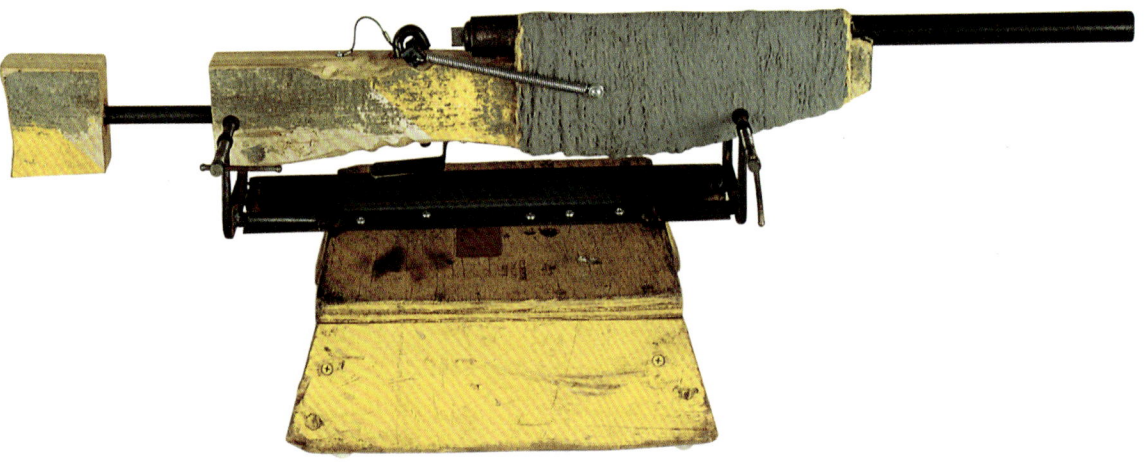

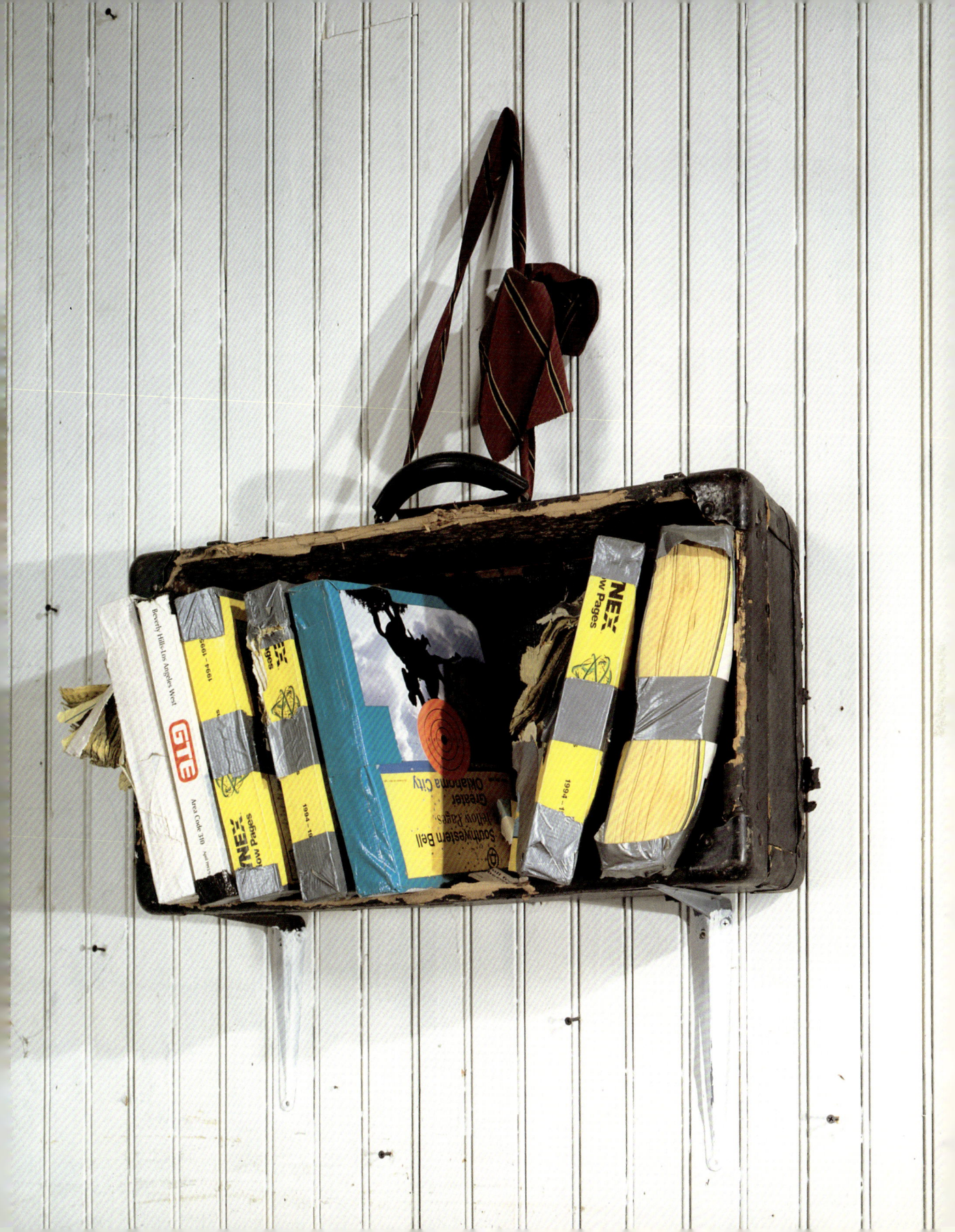

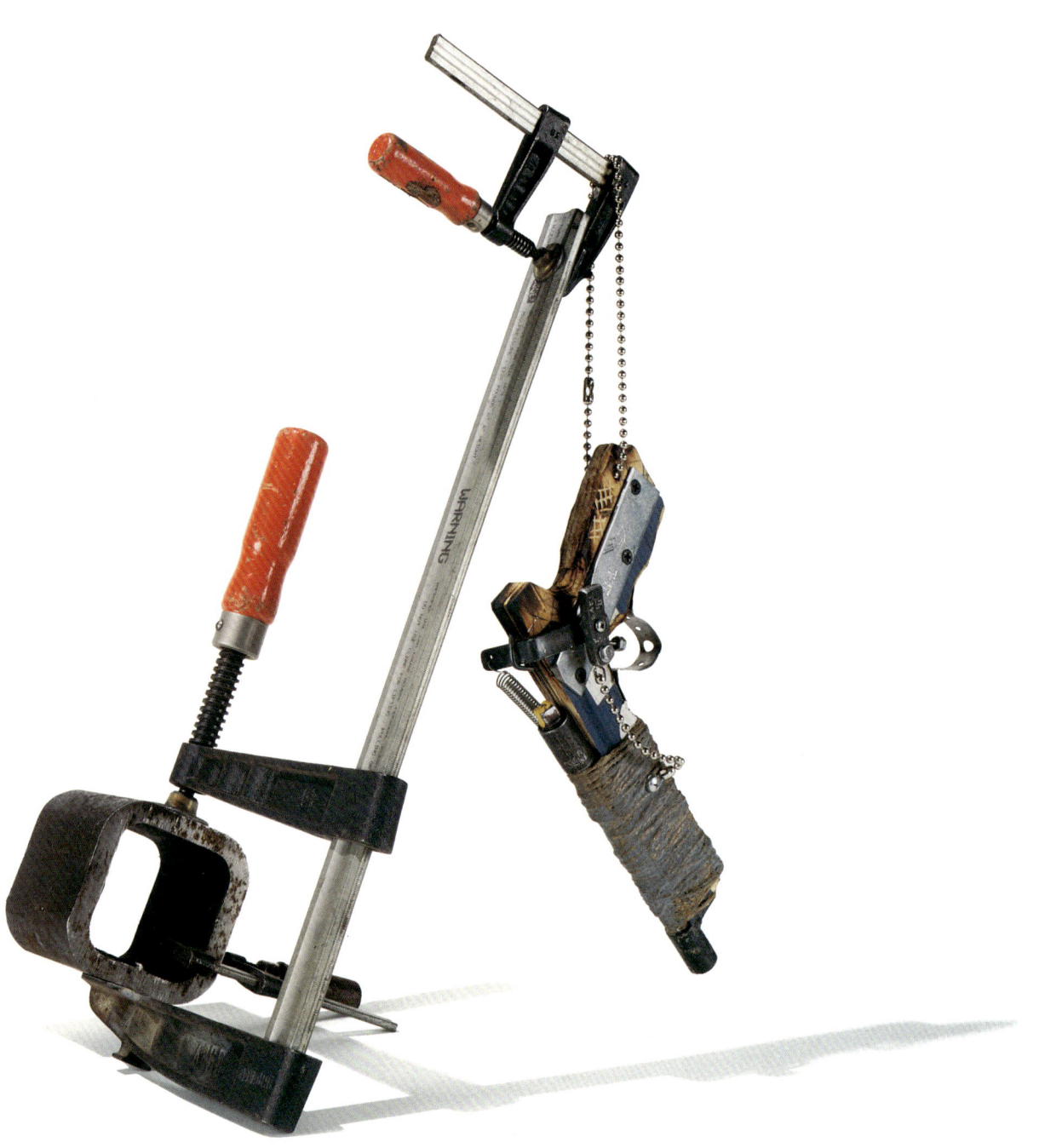

ABOVE
Two Women Under One Roof Equals Danger (in Chinese), 1996.

RIGHT
9-mm Glock with Laser, 1996.

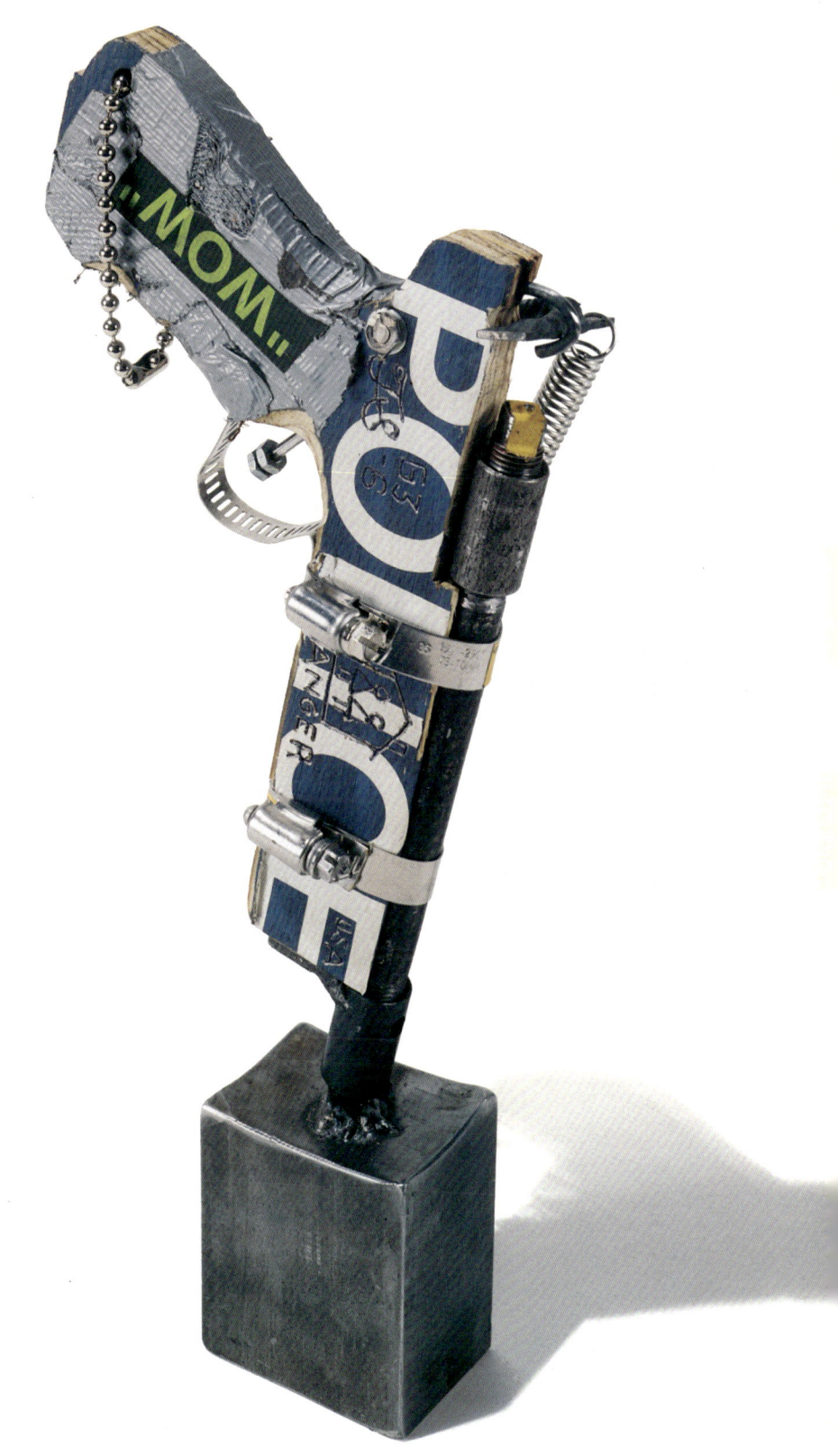

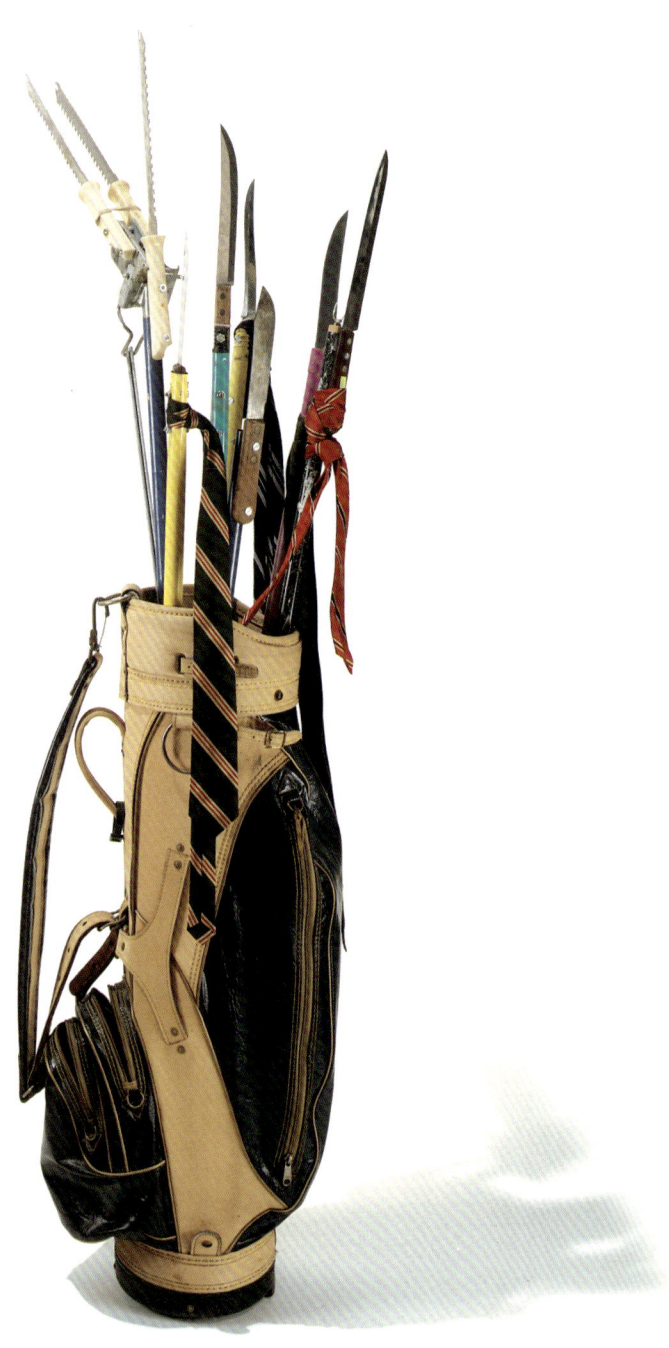

BELOW
Neckties and Steak Knives, 1997.

RIGHT
Hermès 9-mm Glock, 1996.

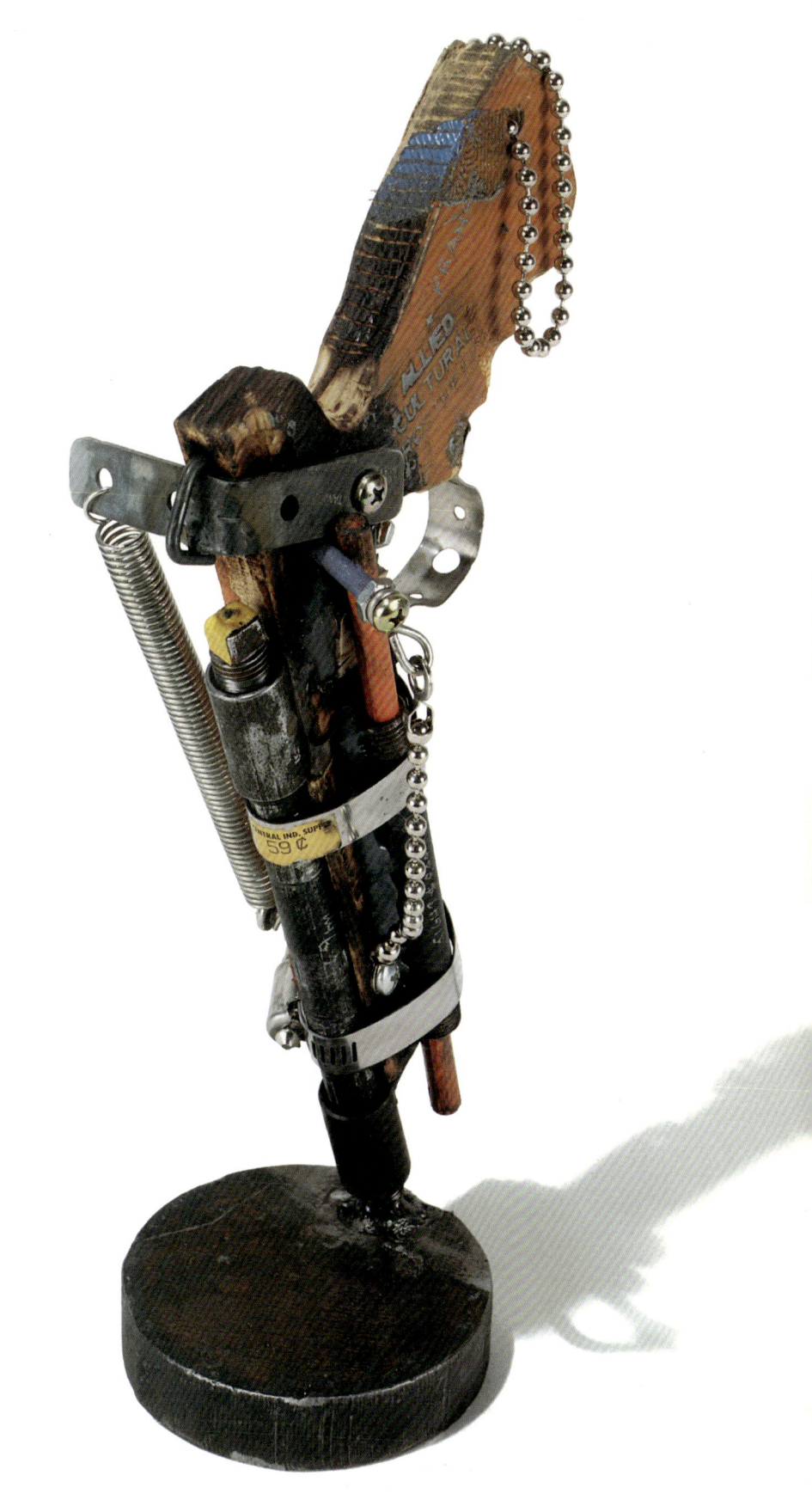

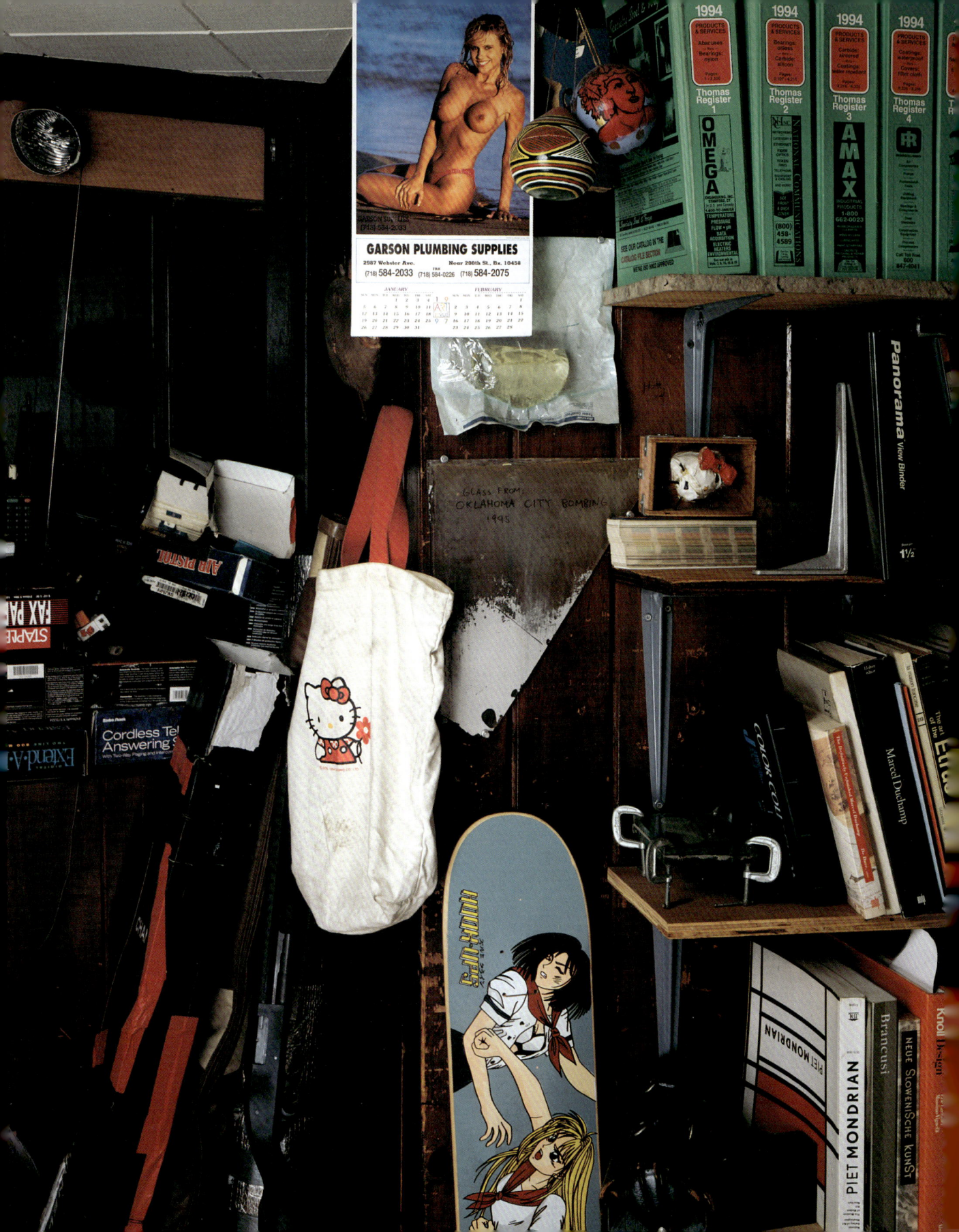

TOM SACHS

As objects, Tom Sachs's guns are pleasing in color and shape, with the exception of the duct-taped models. I have not seen one close up or handled one, but I would guess that they are single-shot items, for I see no evidence of a magazine either in the grip or in the body of the gun proper. Depending on the amount of work Sachs devoted to the barrels, these guns might be somewhat accurate at close distances.

The verticality of each pistol as it literally stands above its metal base, inviting, "presents" it, as a woman is said to "present" herself sexually when she wears high heels. There is a deliberate crudeness to these pieces, in particular to the slapdash coloring of the grips, by means of which criminal virility is sometimes excessively privileged at the expense of craftsmanship. However, the general impression given is one of spontaneity and vitality. These pieces would do credit to any improvised police or customs museum of confiscated zip guns.

As is the case with many venomous tropical snakes, their bright colors pleasingly complement their lethality.

WILLIAM T. VOLLMANN

LEFT
View of offices of Allied Cultural Prosthetics, January 1997.

FROM **Ripley Bogle**

ROBERT McLIAM WILSON

> One potato
> Two potato
> Three potato
> Four;
> Jamsticky fingers wiped on the door.

By all accounts I was an intrepidly repulsive infant. Apparently, even the most philanthropic onlooker could scarce suppress the yawing horror that tended to greet the first sighting of my infant self. It has been reported that a prodigious proportion of the nursing staff on the ward I occupied went on to change their careers or at the very least to require psychiatric care. There were nervous whispers about misbirth, lycanthropy, experimental subatomic detonations, and the like. I can't help feeling that this was all a ploy, a stream of hyperbole meant to mitigate my parents' immediate and lasting hatred for me.

> Five potato
> Six potato
> Seven potato
> Eight;
> I like the things I like
> And I hate the things I hate.

After my birth, my mother, Mrs. Betty Bogle (can you believe that?), was assailed with guilt. She had been married but one month before I was born, prematurely ending a promising and suitable career as a low-rent prostitute, and she considered that my illegitimacy was a contributing factor to my grotesquerie. My father, Mr. Bobby Bogle (it gets worse), was prone to agreeing with old Mumsy. He was a resolutely unemployed ex-baker with a miraculously inexhaustible supply of alcohol and rather felt that he had married beneath him. Well, that's the Welsh for you.

> Nine potato
> Ten potato
> Eleven potato
> Twelve;
> I'm sure I'll wet the bed tonight
> I hope I do it well.

Indeed, as my mother continued to parturate with dazzling regularity, her erstwhile profession and my own dubious pedigree became severe trials to Mr. Bogle's feelings. The resulting tempestuous brawls form some of my earliest and fondest memories. These scenes delighted me. Far from having any infantile intuition of conflict or trauma, I was intoxicated by the rapid, acrobatic brawls and operatic verbals. And soon, amidst the parental yelling, screaming, and screeching, there would be heard the unmistakable sound of my own gurgles and babyish cries of appreciation and encouragement. A good early example of a basic want of tact that has remained with me ever since.

Ah, my childhood! The mornings bowed and greeted my childishness, honoring it with their own day's infancy. My early life seemed to be composed of eternal mornings, greening trees and hedges, the verdant kiss of child's grass and the beaming wink of the paternal sun. My endless energy, health, and indestructible self-confidence stretched timelessly before and behind me.

All good things, however . . .

"Ripley . . . ?"

(Picture it—happy Bogleian breakfast, brats and bubs everywhere.)

"Yes, mam?"

"Ripley—I've got something to tell you. Do you know what school is?"

I well remember that when I heard the word "school," I felt a curious mixture of dread and excitement. I wondered briefly which sensation to adopt as policy but stuck to form and opted for dread.

"Well, do you know what school is?"

"No."

"Well, school is where everybody has to go to learn."

Fucking brilliant, eh? There was a brief pause of boyish assimilation.

"Why?" I squeaked.

That spannered her a little.

"Well, so as you'll be able to know how to read and write just like your father and me."

(Dubious at the best of times.)

"Why?"

"Because you'll have to be able to read and write when you grow up . . . or else nobody'll like you."

After this Malthusian definition, I calculated briefly before pressing on with my ploy of cute and bewildered child buggering boorish adult about with adorably precocious and unanswerable questions. It had served me well thus far.

"Why?" I repeated. (Though perhaps I could have varied it a little.)

"I told you why, ya cheeky wee bastard!"

I tried to regroup and lead a cavalry charge on the flank of her maternal tendernesses.

"Will you be there, Mummy?"

"Don't be stupid. Of course I won't be!"

I was a little bruised by this but I was in a sanguine mood and considered this bluntness merely a screen for the true turmoil of her conflicting emotions. I gave my pause all the doe-eyed charm of early boyhood before bleating piteously.

"I don't think I want to go to school, Mummy."

By Christ, I was a jerk even then! Needless to say, this didn't wash with old

Mumsy and, after putting her boot up my arse, she laid it on the line, so to speak.

"Well, tough titty! And don't get your trousers dirty today, because . . . " she had been a little lax in informing me in advance of the beginning of my educational career, " . . . because you're going to school tomorrow."

"Oh," I said, reasonably enough.

And so to school. From the intimate improvisation of familial neglect to the more organized version of primary education. I was a child unpunctured. No BCGs, no wimp's immunizations, no forms, no certificates, no doctors, and no dentists. Disease could have had me if it had wanted me. (Like everyone else, it didn't.) I had to muck along very much under my own endocrinal steam.

I hate to admit that I wasn't, generally speaking, actively abused. This costs me. I would dearly love to spin out a series of wild, schlocky tales about the mental tortures, the sexual eccentricities, and physiological experiments visited upon me in my boyhood. All those character-forming vilenesses that, strictly speaking, I deserved. Unfortunately, however, I can lay no valid claim to these incontrovertible qualifications for sympathy. I was merely ignored, neglected, edited, tippexed really. From all I had no word of tenderness, encouragement, or pity. I wasn't even worth the effort needed for cruelty or contempt. I made do with optimism and it made do with me.

I trudged trampishly to school on that first day, I seem to remember. All morning my brothers had been indulging in a spectacular riot of mewling and puking and my father had been discovered, dead drunk, in the coal shed. Subsequently, diplomatic beyond my years, I had made no further appeals to my mother's clemency.

I recollect that, as I was dragged toward the end of my innocence that morning, I wondered whether the people who passed us in the street could tell that I was a poor maltreated boy with a wicked mother. I fully anticipated that some gruff, balding, old man with kindly eyes and a nice-smelling pipe would stop us forcibly in the street, chastise my unnatural mother, and whisk me off to his bright-stoned castle where I would be able to eat marshmallows all day and have beautiful lady servants to play with.

(Vomacious, eh?)

Well, I was winked at a couple of times and even saw one or two faces with kindly eyes but there was bugger all in the way of bright-stoned castles for me that day.

That was it. Finis. Nadir.

I've said before that my childhood seemed to be all sunny morning. Well, from now on it seems to have been all hazy, anxious afternoon. At the time I wasn't quite sure what it was that I had lost but I was certain that whatever it had been I missed it very badly already.

I learnt of a great many things on my first day at school. I tasted the sour joy and disillusion of knowledge. It was pretty tough going. Christ, if you think I'm looking rough these days, you should have seen me back then! I was practically crook-backed with age and care.

I discovered that I lived in Belfast and that Belfast lived in Ireland and that this combination meant that I was Irish. The grim young bint we were loaded with was very fervent on this point. She stressed with some vigor that no matter what anyone else were to call us, our names would be always Irish.

Wishing to please, I spent most of the morning wondering which arrangement of nomenclature would placate the silly cow best. I felt that "Irish Bogle" didn't scan, and that Mommie Dearest wouldn't be too keen on "Ripley Irish," obscuring as it did my familial identity. Being at all times a witty and all-inclusive type of chap, I plumped in the end for "Ripley Irish Bogle." I remember being highly chuffed with that.

This temporary solution was, however, shattered when little Miss Trotsky herself told us that the occasional Misguided Soul would try to call us British but that of all the wrong things to call us—this was the wrongest. No matter how the Misguided Souls cajoled, insisted, or pleaded, our names would remain Irish to the core, whatever that meant.

Well, as you can imagine, this buggered me up no end. I was dazed and anxious. I was worried and confused. But with a precociously fine critical instinct and a juvenile distrust of pedagogical fervor, I decided to consult the maternal oracle upon my return home. In the meantime, in the spirit of compromise (ever with me even then), I dubbed myself "Ripley Irish British Bogle."

So, there I was, poor little sod, almost wiped out by the startling array of difficulty and consequence that I had suddenly been lumbered with. Predictably, when I quizzed old mater on the titular proprieties of my situation she tried to stick the kitchen table up my bum. She railed at God above for presenting her with such a misshapen blight as my good self. I tended to agree. On reflection, it might have been kinder in this God-above guy to have kept me for Himself.

(Should I show a little more clemency to the past? A little generous revision? No, I don't think so. I hate to think of it getting away with anything.)

In my boyhood, the sky was bright and clear, spilling its jeweled smiles into my widening windows. Mad September wasps fought lunatic dogfights in my days and suffered frenzied deaths at my experimental hand. The harbored dust of graveled paths sprinkled my classroom steps. The Sacred Heart Primary School for Catholic Boys—wood-brown and sun-pale. Old blackboards, chalked and musty. The venerable breadth of childhood. The tributes of the many wandering boyhoods that had been tricked out in this place. What gutsy scenarios I played out there! Lulled by the delicious boredom of school. Mind tickled by the once wordly figures of antiquity and legend (I had a youthful crush on Demosthenes for some obscure reason).

The sum of boyhood is always elegiac and patchy. Half-held traces of cloudless aspiration. Quick pictures. Same for me. Dusty days in granite playgrounds when I tried to understand the passing of time but gave myself a headache, so big and strange it seemed. Playing football after school while light grew dim and cast dramatic shadows on those walls. Grit-bound lanes where I waited for my life to form; events to come from uneventful haze of childhood wonder and confusion. Boy oh boy, the endless possibilities and comeliness of inexperience. Epiphanies galore!

You know, it took years for them to discover what a fucking genius I was! Hard to believe but true. I managed to bullshit my way up to the age of eight before they found me out. They were fooled by my adroit assumptions of righteous idiocy, my well-researched autistic eccentricities, my stalwart bed-wetting, and judicious charades of illiteracy. They despaired at the impenetrable slate-mist of my abnormality. They plotted, they planned. Briefly, they sent me to a special school for the Educationally Disadvantaged.

I wasn't clever enough and was sent back almost immediately.

It goes without saying that my lice-ridden ratbag of a mother couldn't give a toss. Imbecility was not something to bother Betty Bogle. She had a cloudy presentiment that I was perpetuating clan traditions.

Needless to say, I was a genius all the while. I had read the entire works of Dickens and Thackeray when I was five years old and had spent the rest of that year taping up most of the literary output of the nineteenth century. (Perhaps that's why my style is so florid, so rotund, so fucking courtly.) Then I throttled Shakespeare, Webster, Marlowe, and Spenser (propping them up on my nappy while I read). I moved on to that Hellenic thing before dipping into a little amateur astrophysics. My baby teeth were still going strong when I began to investigate Nihilism. Orwell, Camus, Sartre, Mann, and Eliot depressed me a little I admit, but I was only six years old so I recovered. I had already researched the Epicureans pretty thoroughly anyway, so I was laughing hedonism-wise! Higher Math caused me one or two problems, I concede, but I decided that it could wait until I was, say, ten. I mean, I had to pace myself. As a seven-year-old I laughed at Freud, giggled at Jung, sniggered at Lawrence, guffawed at Woolf, cackled at Barthes, and gave Bertrand Russell a pretty hard time of it.

Perhaps I was precocious.

Explanations? Yes, I think you deserve some of those. Perhaps my prodigious intellectual gifts do indeed merit a little casual background information. There are two. Explanations, that is.

One

As a child I suffered from a complete inability to ignore the written word. It might have been some quirky visual defect or wily kink in the smooth surface of my brain but whatever it was—I read *everything*. *Tout!* The whole lot. Shop signs, newspapers, posters, timetables, instruction manuals, cornflake packets, jam-jar labels, scraps of magazines rescued from the dusty greed of the street. Everything. I had this febrile, insatiable hunger for script and my mind would bubble and race horribly if I had nothing to read. Perhaps I was potty after all.

Two

The second cause is much simpler. First we had the demand, then we had the supply. My thirst for words led me to the Public Library on the Lower Falls Road (a surprisingly imposing building). There my literary needs and the light-fingered dexterity that I claimed as a family right combined. Now, I couldn't steal from the Children's Section. No chance! The psychotic hag librarians there were well onto that one. However, in the Adults' Section it was a vastly different story. There, I was above, or rather below, suspicion. What could be less worthy of vigilance than a stunted, noisome ghetto-urchin *comme moi* wandering aimlessly through wooden-shelved avenues bordered with all that's weighty in Literature and Philosophy? You get the picture? Easy pickings. With all my Bogleian adroitness and tenacity, I practically emptied the shelves. By God, what an education that place gave me! Illegal but extensive. When I had read these tomes I would bury them in a neighbor's garden with the aid of a soup ladle and an old, splintered cricket bat. Miraculously, no one ever discovered me in the midst of this operation and I was able to proceed with my underground educational dealings, more or less unmolested. And so I improved myself—which was a bloody good job as no one had the remotest intention of doing it for me. (Gripe, gripe, grizzle, grizzle.)

So, you'll say, if I was such a colon-bursting prodigy, why did I take all that trouble to hide it? Why did I pursue this policy of demonstrative imbecility? Why didn't I come out of the closet, do a few game shows, win awards, and make a little dosh?

Well, it occurred to me that if they ever discovered what a genius I was, they'd stomp my head off, they'd boil my balls and roast my bottom off. Yes, yes, I know I was a paranoid infant, I know all that—but guess what! Mmm? I was right. When they did find out, they *did* try to do all those things to me. Christ, they hated me. Now, just why was that?

This is what happened.

Classroom. Late morning. There we were, thirty-four assorted hunchbacks, cripples, and idiots learning to read under the pedagogical eye of the aptly named Mr. Samson. Dear God, that man was a brute! He used to arm wrestle us for our pocket money, cheat openly, and then threaten to twist our heads off if we told anyone. He was a complete bastard. Anyway, there we were, boiling in the microwave splay of our basement classroom, trudging through some goggle-eyed kiddies' book when all of a sudden the word "copper" came up. It happened. Mr. Fate came a-calling. Samson decided to open up the debate, the bastard.

SAMSON: Does anyone know what copper is?
(Expecting the answer, "Brown stuff, sir."— "What you use in pipes, sir."— "A coin, sir."—"A policeman, sir.")
BOGLE *(brightly)*: A mineral, sir.
SAMSON *(patronizing)*: No, Bogle. It's a metal.
BOGLE: It's a mineral, sir.
SAMSON: Bollocks!
BOGLE: It's not bollocks, sir.
SAMSON *(apoplectic)*: Don't you back-answer me, you little shit, you don't even know what a mineral is!
BOGLE *(insanity gripping)*: A mineral is a naturally occurring, chemically and physically homogenous, inorganic substance in a solid or liquid state, having a definite, defined atomic structure. They arise as a result of geological processes unaided by . . . man . . . sir . . .

My voice trailed into silence. There was a soft, rumorous hush as my classmates patiently awaited his verdict. I knew what I had done. I shouldn't have let my secret out like that. Adult censure and distaste were going to come round and sort me out now. Samson himself was gazing at me with distended nostrils, popping eyes, and gaping mouth (very unattractive). I felt the control of my life's events slip inexorably away. It was all out of my hands now. Samson vented a wild, blood-curdling screech and charged at me with thunder in his eyes and rage in his heart.

(Hackneyed but true. My life's like that. It has no subtle irony, no gloved wit, no satirist's intent. No dash and little flair. I have to settle for the capitals. Writ in large. Brute broad patches of character and discontent.)

Believe it or not, I was whopped into an ambulance and rushed to the Royal Victoria Hospital! Harper, the boss kiddie shrink (consultant child psychiatrist), just loved me to death. He congratulated my school for their prompt action. I was a bad case and worsening. A highly disturbed child. Obviously my unwonted intellectual precocity was just the tip of the jolly old iceberg as far as my neurotic disorders went (which was quite a long way according to him). With pearly eyes and smiling teeth, he began to make therapeutic plans for me.

I was sent to another special school once a week. Here the educationally subnormal and the exceptionally gifted were taught together in a fever of experimental egalitarianism. There we were, morons and geniuses, kicking the shit out of each other whenever possible. Great things were achieved. Kierkegaard was debated with illiterates and precocious polyglots were taught about the English alphabet with the aid of picture cards. All good stuff.

When Mumsy heard about this novel talent of mine she refused to believe it. She had enough humility to be astonished that a product of her low-grade womb could be anything other than troglodytic. When she eventually accepted it, she persisted in seeing it as lasting proof of my reasonless enmity and defiance. Naturally (and perhaps commendably) she used this new grievance as the excuse for a whole new series of vilifications and enthusiastic beatings.

In addition, there were hazardous diplomatic implications at school. I had always been popular on account of my ugliness and this was fading (the popularity, that is, the ugliness seemed there to stay). No one likes a genius. I began to get into fights which, to my surprise, I usually won. Exhibiting pugilistic skill on top of my mental gifts was tactless. I was due for a fall. I was challenged by D. Stark.

D. Stark was the best fighter in the school. Though barely twelve years old, he was already five feet nine inches tall. He had started shaving (I swear, honestly!) and even had a respectable number of hairs on his chest about which he affected a great lack of concern. He was big cheese and he felt that he could scarcely afford to ignore my new fame. There was room for only one School Phenomenon. There would have to be a contest of arms.

So D. Stark delivered his gage in the traditional manner of the warriors of our school, i.e. by gobbing thickly and wetly on the crown of my skull. D. Stark's mastery of this form of challenge was abetted by the fact that he had been smoking forty cigarettes a day since he was seven years old. His goads were always distinctive and marvelously adhesive.

On the day, I suspect that D. Stark had some qualms about tackling an opponent so much younger, smaller, and less psychopathic than himself. As he watched me in my tininess, dancing and weaving, his scruples dissolved. His honor was at stake. With heavy heart and weighty executioner's hand, he moved in.

It was a debacle. D. Stark was a monster. Even Samson was scared of D. Stark. It was rumored that he used to hang his father out of an upstairs window when he wanted fag money. The man was a brute. He mashed me. He minced me. He bounced me off walls and tarmac. He cracked my ribs like cardboard and punched my gob into a pulp. He went to town and back again. I was off school for three weeks.

To do him justice, my dad was actually pretty impressed. He felt that this was more like the manly order of things and even Big Betty was less violent than usual. When they learnt that in the middle of all the Bogle-butchery I had, by some incredible fluke, managed to dislodge one of D. Stark's teeth, a little parently pride managed to bluff its way into their grimy breasts.

Back at school, it was more of the same. Standing toe to toe with D. Stark was seen alternatively as the pinnacle of human courage or the very nadir of imbecility. On either count, my peers felt, that made me worthy of note. Even D. Stark himself grew rather friendly. He would give me cigarettes at breaktime and there we would sit—me green-faced and choking, him serenely smoke-soiled.

(I suppose at this point I should say something like— "My word, I wonder whatever happened to old D. Stark"—but that's easy and trim in the telling. After a short but successful life of trouble, crime, squalor, and a halfhearted association with Sinn Fein, D. Stark was shot dead by an army foot patrol in the Ardoyne. Like I always say—people shouldn't knock me about.)

Oh yes, those Troubles! Those nasty Irish things! The Northern Irish Conflict certainly did its bit for the decoration of my early years. I made damned sure that I got a good seat. I needed the material and it came to me early and gratis (mostly). They served it up to me and I fell to with a will and a half.

I spent a great deal of my childhood seeing things that I shouldn't have seen and making the acquaintance of uncomfortable notions that certainly could have waited a decade or so for their entrance. Murder, violence, blood, guts, and sundry other features of Irish political life tend to telescope one's development a little as you can imagine. You zip along to cynicism—blink and you'd miss it. For me, the beginning was Internment Night.

You've heard of Internment, I presume. No? Well, look it up. It's a good one. I must say, I had a hugely profitable Internment Night one way or another.

In common with the majority of the Catholic working-class population of the city of Belfast, we Bogles were raided on Internment Night. Just before two o'clock in the morning, the front door of our squalid little house was kicked in by four hard-faced, anxious, young soldiers. (At least, I presume they were hard-faced and anxious—I was in bed at the time.) Apparently, these soldiers were polite, even slightly diffident as they separated in order to ransack our ghastly, microscopic hovel. Daddybuns was as usual elsewhere and probably pissed and thus the Bogle materfamilias was able to give free rein to her violent indignation. Naturally, she did this with all her accustomed verve and gusto. The unfortunate militia hadn't really banked on this frothing harpy and they seemed distinctly less than chuffed to be there. A miserable young lieutenant was left to deal with the by now apoplectic Betty, while the others hurried off to search round the old homestead.

When the combined might of Her Majesty's Armed Forces crashed into my bedroom, my excitement knew no bounds. I looked up as the light was switched abruptly on. Imagine my amazement and joy when I beheld a massive West Indian corporal standing at my bedroom door brandishing a large automatic rifle. My untutored blood raced with elation. I had never seen a real black man before and now I had one standing, albeit rather sheepishly, in my own tiny and familiar bedroom. Boy, was I chuffed or what! He brought a breath of exotic and dangerous glamour to me. The man remained motionless and embarrassed for some moments while I felt my eyes grow moist with love. Uncertain, he tried a feeble wink and his teeth smiled whitely in his tactile, ebony face before he abruptly disappeared from view.

Well, after all this excitement I could hardly try to sleep now. I slithered toward my still-open door. I could hear shouts coming from downstairs, the business-like grunts of the soldiers mingling with the insistent bellow of my deranged mother. I felt an instant's pity for the unsuspecting soldiers. Then I heard my little brothers begin to screech and wail in remarkable unison and my pity doubled. Poor old Brits. Not the sort of palaver you expect when you're trying to suppress the natives a little. However, this was all much too good to miss. I slid furtively down the little staircase leading to the tumult.

I paused in the hall. My ragged pajamas were but thin and the cold air was blowing harshly through the large hole where our front door had once been. I crept toward it. To my joy, I could see the cul-de-sac outside, a swelling hive of activity. The whole string of tawdry little houses that were Monagh Parade were lit up by the implacable glare of the headlights of the army jeeps and Saracens that were lined up at the bottom of the cul-de-sac. And there were soldiers everywhere. Soldiers with blackened faces running into unlit, sleeping houses and dragging half-dressed men out into the waiting Saracens; soldiers crouched behind walls and lampposts, rifles poised and aimed; soldiers shouting; soldiers punching; soldiers kicking; lots of soldiers doing their soldierly thing while the screams and execrations of frenzied women dinned the tepid night air.

I sneaked gladly into that curtain of din, bustle, and glaring light. I crawled along, underneath the little fence of our tiny front garden. I felt a thrill of illicit freedom, never having been outdoors quite so late before. The air and sky seemed foreign to me, nocturnal inhabitant of my own daytime garden. Keenly, I watched the churning maelstrom of arrest and protest through the gaps in the little fence, feeling well-hidden and marvelously secure. It was almost cozy.

Abruptly, the blissful secrecy of my hiding place was in peril. A young soldier ran up to my fence and crouched down on the other side, hugging close to its flimsy white planks. Though he could easily have stretched his hand to touch me, he seemed unaware of my presence. My hardy blood checked still and frozen-calm. My face was scarcely inches from the massy, fatigue-clad figure, weighted and bulky with a vast array of curious, nameless military equipment. I could see the inarticulate knobs and catches on his dull black-and-brown rifle as it was aimed at Sean O'Grady's house on the far side of the open square. We both watched as Sean's father was dragged out to the Saracens. I knew that it was an SLR that the soldier carried because I had heard some boys at school discussing the merits of the British Army's

Small Firearms Issue:

"Nowhere near as good as an armalite!"

"Yes, it is."

"Come on, an armalite can blow your head right off, like squashing an apple!"

"But the Paras put dum-dums in their SLRs. Cut you in half as quick as look at you!"

I wondered if the young man whose cold, acrid breath whipped my face was a "Para." I wasn't as adept as the other boys in distinguishing the various regiments but many were the tales of relished atrocity that I had heard of these Paras. I trembled violently. The walkie-talkies clipped on the soldier's breast suddenly erupted into a dry cackle. I started violently, as one might, very nearly disclosing my presence. As the young soldier listened to the inarticulate sounds issuing tinnily from his chest, I was overwhelmed by the strangeness of crouching in the dark so close yet unknown to this man. I peered at this supposed enemy of mine. As the mysteries of war and hatred welled in my boy's mind, I felt a dreamy, veiled tenderness for the youth whose soft breath moistened my face. Close enough to kill, I could sense the birth of power and fear in my own warrior's heart. (I think I'd just been checking out D. H. Lawrence again.)

Suddenly I heard a muffled noise coming from the Ginchys' house next door. I turned quickly to see a small, ghostly female figure disappear into the long striped shadows that ran along the side of the Ginchy house. I knew that this would be Muire Ginchy and I knew what she was going to do. Walk her tightrope of barbed wire. Her party piece. She was always showing off to me by walking along the barbed wire on her father's fence. She had never done this in the dark.

The soldier's ears twitched with a doggy alertness when he heard the sound. He froze in fear and shouted to his sergeant. Suddenly, two huge soldiers vaulted out of the darkness over my head, crashing noisily to the ground in front of our parlor window, their guns and boots clattering in a loud, confused hymn of danger and fear. They crouched warily while my soldier joined them. I hid still, undiscovered, inches away from their sturdy, threat-blackened boots.

"What is it?" the sergeant asked.

The young soldier answered with an obviously burgeoning sense of his own importance.

"I saw one of them trying to get away. He went along the side of the house next door. I think he had a gun."

The sergeant took over quickly.

"Right, you go on through the back door of this place. Take the lads inside with you. We'll go round the side . . . we'll give you about forty-five seconds."

My soldier clattered enthusiastically into the Bogle domicile. I felt sick with panic. Forty-five seconds. It was only Muire Ginchy walking her tightrope of fence and gate. Showing off, that was all. All those soldiers and guns! I realized with reluctance that I would have to speak. I couldn't just leave her to them. I couldn't do that.

"Excuse me, mister . . ." I squeaked.

"Christ!"

An angry torch was flashed onto my terrified face and a panicked rifle butt was thrust into my minor chest. One of the soldiers yelped in terror. However, luckily for me, the nimble sergeant quickly perceived my extreme youth.

"Catch a grip of yourself, for Christ's sake! He's only a kid." He turned toward me. "What are you up to, sonny?"

Fear and horror seemed to melt my bowels and I could feel the first warm trickle of urine greeting my thigh.

"It's only Muire, mister."

"What?"

"It's only Muire."

"What are you talking about?"

"Round the back there. She's only a wee girl."

Again the burly sergeant was quick to comprehension and he reacted sharply. He shouted into the open doorway of our house.

"Wilson! Wilson! It's just a little girl . . . Wilson? Oh, shit."

He careered round the side of the house followed by the other soldier and myself. As we reached our large back garden there was a wild burst of confusion as bright torch shafts streaked the moonless black of the scene. Knowing my own garden well, I was able to cut through the stumbling mass of soldiers to where I knew Muire would be. I saw her. Standing high on the fence, her tiny draped figure stamped against the vague, looming glow of the Black Mountain. I saw Wilson just beneath her, gun raised. For a moment they were both still, their silhouettes framing a slow tableau of weird dusky beauty. Then I heard the soldier's rifle click and shunt, ready to fire, and I rushed madly toward him, bellowing with fury. Muire screamed, her body seemed to twist in terror, and she slipped, dropping straight down, her open legs straddling the barbed wire.

Of course, because of Internment, the ambulance was a long time in coming. Or so they said as we waited. At least Muire had stopped screaming by this time. Now the only sounds were Mrs. Ginchy's dead voice telling her daughter that it was going to be all right and the agonized sobbing of the soldier called Wilson.

"I'm sorry. I'm sorry . . . I'm so sorry."

His face was spattered with tears, black camouflaging grime, and smears of the bright blood of the child he had cradled when she had fallen. The other soldiers were quiet. They stood apart, feverishly waiting for the ambulance to come so that they could leave. One squaddie cradled a furtive cigarette in the crook of his hand.

A captain had arrived on the scene. A handsome young man, crested by the impossible glamour of a peaked cap. He stood near me, whispering to the attentive sergeant who still kept his firm grip on my shoulder. I somehow understood that the nature of little Muire's injuries in some way appalled these men, investing them with a helpless kind of chivalry. I tried to mirror their reactions though in truth I could not see what was so very terrible about it. I felt sorry for Muire and all the wet, red blood that she had dripped. Very sorry. But I was confused. I wondered why her mother wasn't angry. Why was she smiling at her daughter like that? No bitterness.

By the time the ambulance had taken Muire and her mother away, the commotion in the cul-de-sac had died down and I could see, to my great excitement, paleness begin to seep across the sky from behind the mountain, signaling my very first witnessed dawn. The soldiers had drifted off apologetically, depressed and shaken. Already I missed their brief glamour. In a wonderful moment, the sergeant had told my raging mother that I was a good brave lad and he had even given me a pound. Pride had swelled in my Irish heart though I still felt rather subdued about Muire. When the soldiers had finally left, my mother took the pound from me and threw it away hurriedly. Wisely, I said nothing. Dawn grumbled and spread across the sleepless city, bleating new life into the ragged dustbin-clanging protests of the night. Internment had begun.

I wonder what old Muire Ginchy is doing these days. She's no record-breaking matriarch, for sure. I think we can definitely rule that one out, gynecologically speaking. Sad—when you think about it. She's probably just a rancid, hard-eyed Irish tart like the rest of them now. Belfast does that to you. Thickens your body and your brains. Chases your soul away.

    Pity though. I liked Muire. I even had a vague prepubescent crush on her. She was a nice kid—and cute too. A show-off, true, but she didn't deserve the humbling she got.

    Who do we blame for that? Young Wilson? Me? Anyone? No, I don't think any of those fit this bill. I prefer to blame Belfast. It's all Belfast's fault. Something should be done. Belfast shouldn't be allowed to get away with this kind of thing. Belfast has to be stopped. Its time will come.

                                I hope.

I remember that when I was a brat I once saw a soldier killed on the Falls.* I was about ten. It was my first death and I have since grown attached to it.

    My deranged mother was dragging me along to consult the various vampiric shrinks whom I still had to attend at the RVH. It was a typical day on the Falls Road. The dusty squalor of that street cooked in an end-year haze of dirt and cold. The usual Falls stuff—arrests on spec, public strip searches, and halfhearted riots. All good fun for me.

    Anyway, as my mother and I neared the old hospital we heard several bursts of tinny gunfire. Everyone dived for cover in the generally accepted tradition for these occasions. An army foot patrol had been tortoise-trailing its way up the Grosvenor Road and now split, panicked, in all directions. A couple of massive squaddies huddled under the wall of the Eye, Ear, Nose,

---

* The Falls Road, center of a Catholic neighborhood in Belfast, formerly a Catholic ghetto.

and Throat Clinic with my mother and myself. There was a sniper on top of the Divis Flats at the bottom of the road. It was obviously perfect sniping ground, giving the perceptive bastard a marvelously unrestricted view of the entire length of the Lower Falls. There was a brief pause while my mother harangued the two soldiers for endangering her with their proximity. Patriotically, she felt that they should present a target less inimical to her own life (and mine too, doubtless). A few speculative volleys zinged harmlessly into the brickwork punctuating the wait nicely. The Brits had radioed for a helicopter and seemed well content to wait it out in the interval. Several minutes passed in blissful silence, apart from an occasional sanguine report from the persistent sniper. I was having a fucking brilliant time and keenly awaited some carnage.

Suddenly, this fat nurse came trundling down the Springfield Road on her bicycle. The traffic had all stopped and there were scores of pedestrians lying flat beside walls and doorways, but this obviously didn't say a lot to the silly cow!

The soldiers shouted for her to take cover but the fat-arse was wearing a pair of huge, furry earmuffs and obviously couldn't hear a thing. They shouted again, the silly sods. She heard this time, but panicked and came to a wobbly, rabbit-blind stop, slap bulls-eye in the middle of the crossroads. There were more frantic shouts and a few shots ripped into the tarmac close to her bicycle. He'd have been doing us all a favor if he had hit her.

One of the prepubescent squaddies near us chucked his rifle away and set off in a great, loping, weaving run toward the terrified nurse. Another rifle crack and he was flung, sprawling backward through the air at a tremendous height. He crashed to the pavement, many yards from where he had been hit. He was screaming in agony, not really wanting to die. I was surprised and ghoulishly disappointed that I could see no gouts of blood and organ. That sniper must have been some kind of fucking rifle genius. What a shot! Fully three-quarters of a mile away and at a moving target. Boy, was I impressed!

The choking nurse crawled unethically away from the dying man, her eyes wide and incredulous. The soldier's colleagues couldn't go to his aid. They were still pinned down by the invisible sniper and probably thought that he had proved his marksmanship sufficient to the task. So we waited. Soon we heard the fatuous grumble of distant helicopters. The soldiers brightened at this and advised their chum to take it easy and hang on in there and similar tactless nonsense.

The sniper evidently noted the arrival of the helicopters and more shots zipped into the walls. The wailing soldier gurgled briefly deep in his chest and tried to raise himself. There was another shot, his body kicked back into the tarmac and flopped still.

He should have stayed where he was, the jerk.

Later, I learnt that they had shot the sniper when he was trying to make his getaway. The Security Forces were rather embarrassed by the fact that he was only thirteen years old. A talented kid.

You know, I always felt rather sorry for the British in Ireland. They didn't want to be there. The Protestants had originally wanted them there but got browned off when their presence began to interfere with traditional Loyalist rites of Catholic killing. It wasn't strictly Britain's problem though, to be fair, they had committed some worthy cock-ups in the preceding four hundred years or so and Bloody Sunday *had* been a little tactless. Still, it was no reason to have to keep dying all the time.

The British were onto a very bad thing in Ulster. They couldn't win: if they left there was civil war and if they stayed they got crapped on from all sides. It couldn't have been much fun.

They were always getting into this kind of trouble, the British. In India, those Indians and Pakistanis were always kicking the dung out of each other as the dear old Brits tried to pull out. They were asked to stay a little longer. They did and got crapped on some more and slagged well off for their trouble. It was the same with Palestine after the war. The Jews and the Arabs have never really been the best of buddies. So who suffers? Trying to keep the peace. Trying to play the game.

Let's face it. Most European countries have had their empire at some time or another. Eventually, they crumble and another one comes along. This is what interregnums are—brackets of history. The British got it wrong. They grew all philanthropic and noble. They were the only imperial power ever to try giving their empire back. That was their mistake. We wogs, us wogs, we didn't like that. Not at all.

Of course, little hiccups like Amritsar, Bloody Sunday, and the Velt Camps didn't help. But nobody's perfect. It's hard to like the British, but I try.

I've seen someone tarred and feathered as well. It was about the same time, though this was a little strong even for my steel-plated stomach. My boyish voyeurism didn't extend this far. The victim of the tarring was a girl. (Most of them were.) Mary Sharkey. Apparently, Mary was having a little lamb through the fructile offices of some corporal from the Royal Engineers. The folk of Turf Lodge were jolly peeved. (I must have been a clever little sprog to winkle out all that strictly adult truth.)

Some patriotic young bloods decided on punitive action. They nabbed young Mary and tied her to a lamppost at the bottom of our cul-de-sac. They stripped her and shaved her head. To my surprise, I wasn't enjoying it at all. Mary had very small breasts which seemed to make it worse for some reason. I wasn't prepared for this. It was a Sunday and I'd been reading Trollope all afternoon! The bastards actually boiled the tar in front of her. Even I could see that this was undiplomatic.

To give them their due credit for philanthropy, the locals thought that this had gone far enough. Public humiliation was enough. Brutality was overdoing it. The neighbors stood at their doors in their Sunday suits and dresses, uneasy and reluctant. Of course, none of them had the bollocks to try to stop it but at least the thought was there. The women were weeping bitterly and the men stood, mumbling together, in anxious little groups. Mary was utterly still and completely silent.

Soon the tar was ready and two of the men simply chucked the nasty stuff over her. Now, human screaming can be horrible. Not like the cinegenic, kinky stuff you get in the movies. Real throttled-cat belches of outrage is what I'm talking about. Mary was well up there in the screaming league. She was first division and pushing hard for the championship. The deathly wails that she set up had a bad effect upon my youthful sensibilities and I became hysterical. My mother chucked me, screeching and choking, into the back garden to cool off a little.

For ten minutes I had a quiet and rather enjoyable little fit to myself.

When I came back to the scene a startling development had occurred. Bobby Bogle, my nominal father and actual scourge, had got in on the act. He made his entrance.

Goodness, would you believe it but my old arsehole papa, that wicked Welsh wanker, looked as if he was going to make a stand on behalf of the now sizzling Mary. My mother was bellowing at him in an access of fury and contempt but on he strode, my old dad, to the astonishment of the neighborhood and, no doubt, himself.

In a surge of filial pride, I escaped the bony grasp of my witch mother and belted on after him.

Mary was in bad shape now. Her hair, now matted and clogged, had been roughly shorn into violent, spiky tufts. On the few patches of visible skin between the steaming great gouts of tar, I could see that her flesh had already blistered and cracked horribly. She had stopped screaming and was now weeping inaudibly to herself. The ragged feathers that still dotted her head obscured her face but I could sense that she was having a bad time.

I watched my father approach the little group of young men around Mary. Anger and rage-judged pride burnt hard in my boy's heart. One of the youths called something to my dad and he stopped just short of them. I couldn't see his face but I saw that his great, lazy shoulders were trembling uncontrollably as if he were trying to hide secret, swelling laughter. The same youth spoke again. He was about twenty years old and had a sly, handsome countenance. Unlike the others, he was well-dressed in a vulgar manner and his sleek black hair was combed back carefully over his small neat ears. A wispy mustache disfigured his upper lip like a little strip of fluff or smut. He touched it often, as if to ensure that it was still there.

"Now then, Bobby. Just you go back up there to your own house. This here doesn't have anything to do with you."

Bogle didn't answer. Creeping closer, I noticed that he was carrying a short plump lath, like a baseball bat. I saw him grip it tighter and stiffen and ease the vibration of his shoulders.

"C'mon now, Bobby, you know we don't have any quarrel with you. Go home like the wise man you are."

Again there was no answer. I was shitting myself with terror but it was undeniably exciting.

Now, the other men began to lend their voices to the weight of friendly advice being meted out to my da. One of them, a big bastard with a harelip, was in his element. Oily and repulsive, he seemed to have a grudge against my poor pops and saw the time for a spot of retribution.

"Go on, Bogle, fuck away off! What do you think you're going to do with that wee stick? Mmm? Fuck off, you don't want the kind of trouble we can give you."

My father spoke for the first time as he moved slowly toward the sobbing girl.

"I swear to Jesus, if you open your mouth again, little boy, I'll break your fucking back, big as you are."

Thrilled to the new power and danger in my sire, I saw the jaundiced arrival of fear in Harelip's ferrety eyes. The men exchanged uncertain glances. The youth who had spoken first barred my father's way. Bobby stopped again. This youth was different. He threatened less but promised more. I felt (correctly as it turned out) that he was dangerous. He spoke softly, almost reasonably.

"Look, Bobby, stop this nonsense. You know what she did. Don't get yourself into any old trouble for her sake! She's not worth it, Bobby."

Still grasping the sliver of timber, my father stepped past him and began slowly to untie Mary. Gently, gingerly, he whisper-touched her tarred and wounded flesh, hopelessly struggling against the heat and the smell. Silence. Icy fear. His bent and ministering back was blind and unprotected against any onslaught the young men cared to make. He seemed aware of this and awaited attack. Suddenly, the cocky bastard with the fucked-up kisser made an abrupt movement toward him. I screamed in filial warning. Spark-speeded and rapid, my father turned to face him, sporty stick swinging. He hooked hard and knocked the creep's harelip down the back of his throat. (He could've been a cricketer, my dad!) The youth crumpled as you might expect. At a nod from their mustachioed generalissimo, the others stayed where they were. My father turned his apoplectic face to me.

"Go home! Now!" he bellowed.

(Well, what about that, eh? Who'd have thought it of my rancid father? Courage. Chivalry. Style. He certainly came out strong that day. I was dead chuffed. It's nice to be able to admire your father every now and then. Perhaps he wasn't such a shit after all.)

So.

Unforgettably seen and remembered, pictured from behind the rickety gate of our postage-stamp front garden, I watched with conscious sonly pride as my father trudged slowly across the dimming cul-de-sac. Toward his home he walked, carrying the weeping girl, in his strong father's arms. Amongst the coward's stillness of his inactive, unbraved, fully Irish neighbors.

Of course, Bobby Bogle paid for this piece of poetry in the end. It was obvious that he would. The guy with the harelip and the bad boy with the 'tache were both in the Provies. They were pissed off with my father and received their satisfaction by shooting him twice in the abdomen as he was walking home from the pub one night. That was a dirty trick. A nasty place to shoot someone. It took my father an awfully long time to die and he did it all on our kitchen floor. He just dripped away, all sticky and warm. By God, there was tons of the stuff. Thick, oozing pools of scarlet gore formed on the cracked linoleum, streaked and muddied by boot and shoe. The ambulance didn't come for three hours and by that time his flesh was yellow and cold. He was well dead.

It's strange to watch someone die . . . especially if he's your dad. To know that his next few moments spell the end for him. Watching him say his good-byes to himself. It's hard to make his last moments special. You can't exactly throw a shindig.

I'm pretty cool about it now but at the time I was insane with horror and grief. I was only a kid and he was my dad after all.

DAVID CRONENBERG

Shivers

(a.k.a. *They Came from Within*, *The Parasite Murders*), written and directed by David Cronenberg, 1975.

Dr. Emil Hobbes has supposedly been breeding a form of parasite that can take over the function of failing body organs in order to save life. However, his true purpose is to cure man's over-rationality. The Hobbes parasite is actually a sexually transmitted bug which, having entered the body, acts as an aphrodisiac, thereby ensuring that it continues to spread to other bodies. Having implanted it in a sexually active young girl who resides in the luxurious Starliner Towers apartment complex, Hobbes realizes the imminent danger too late. He kills himself and the girl, but the bug is already at work in Andrew Tudor, another of the girl's lovers in the Starliner. Despite efforts by resident physician Dr. Roger St. Luc and Hobbes's duped partner Rollo Linsky, the bug spreads throughout the apartment complex, transforming it into a high-rise orgy of chaos, death, and destruction. At the end, the surviving infected inhabitants calmly leave their haven in convoy, setting off to infect the world.

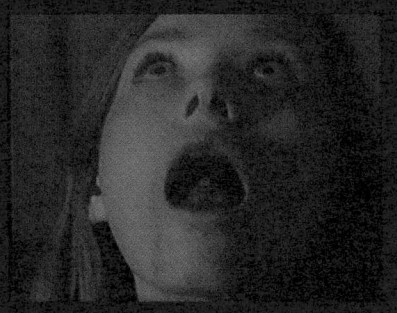

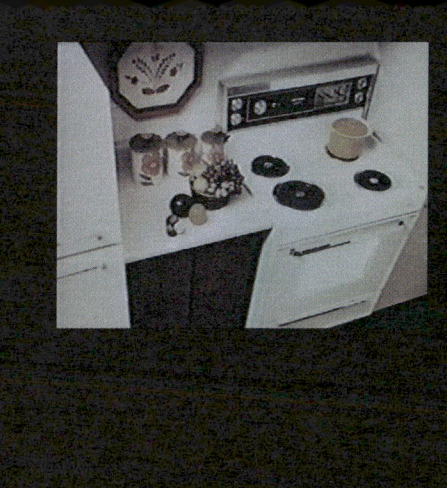
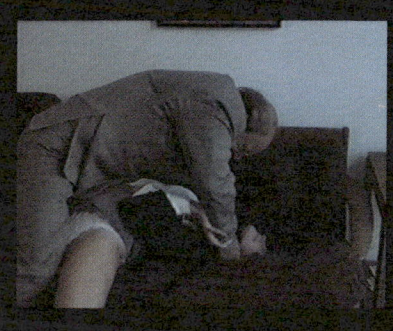
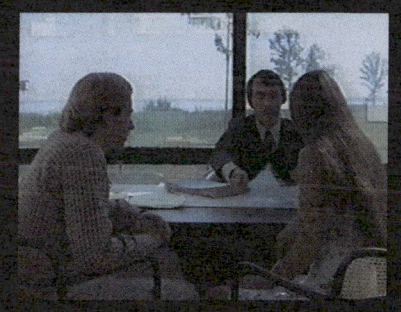
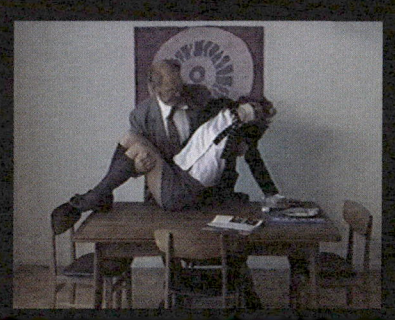

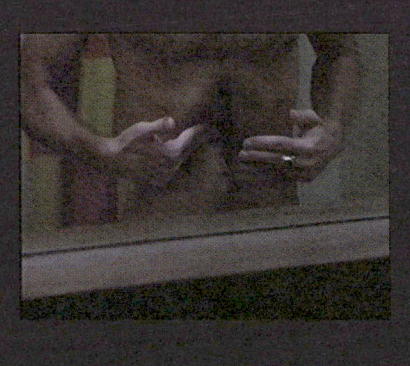

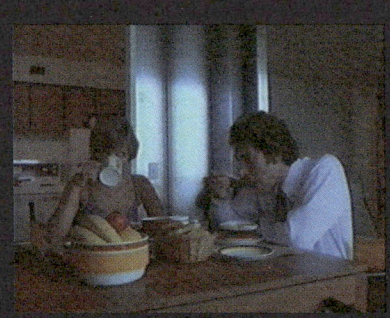

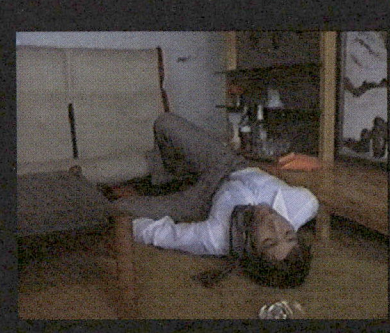

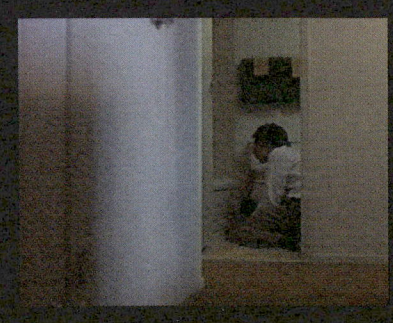

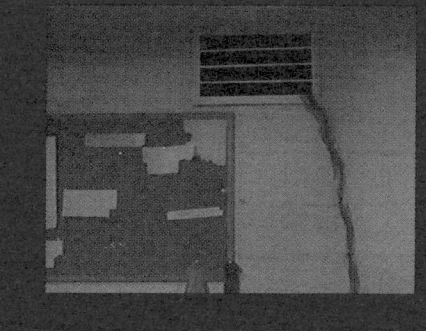
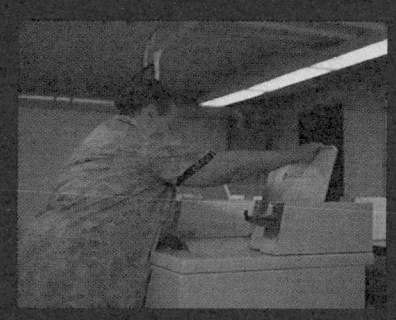
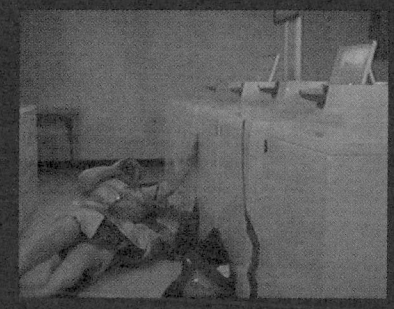
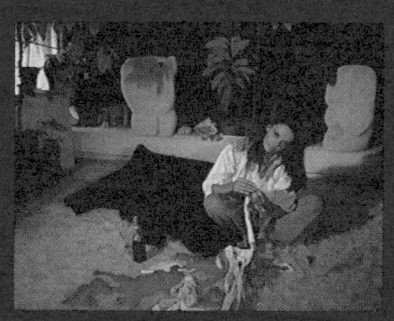

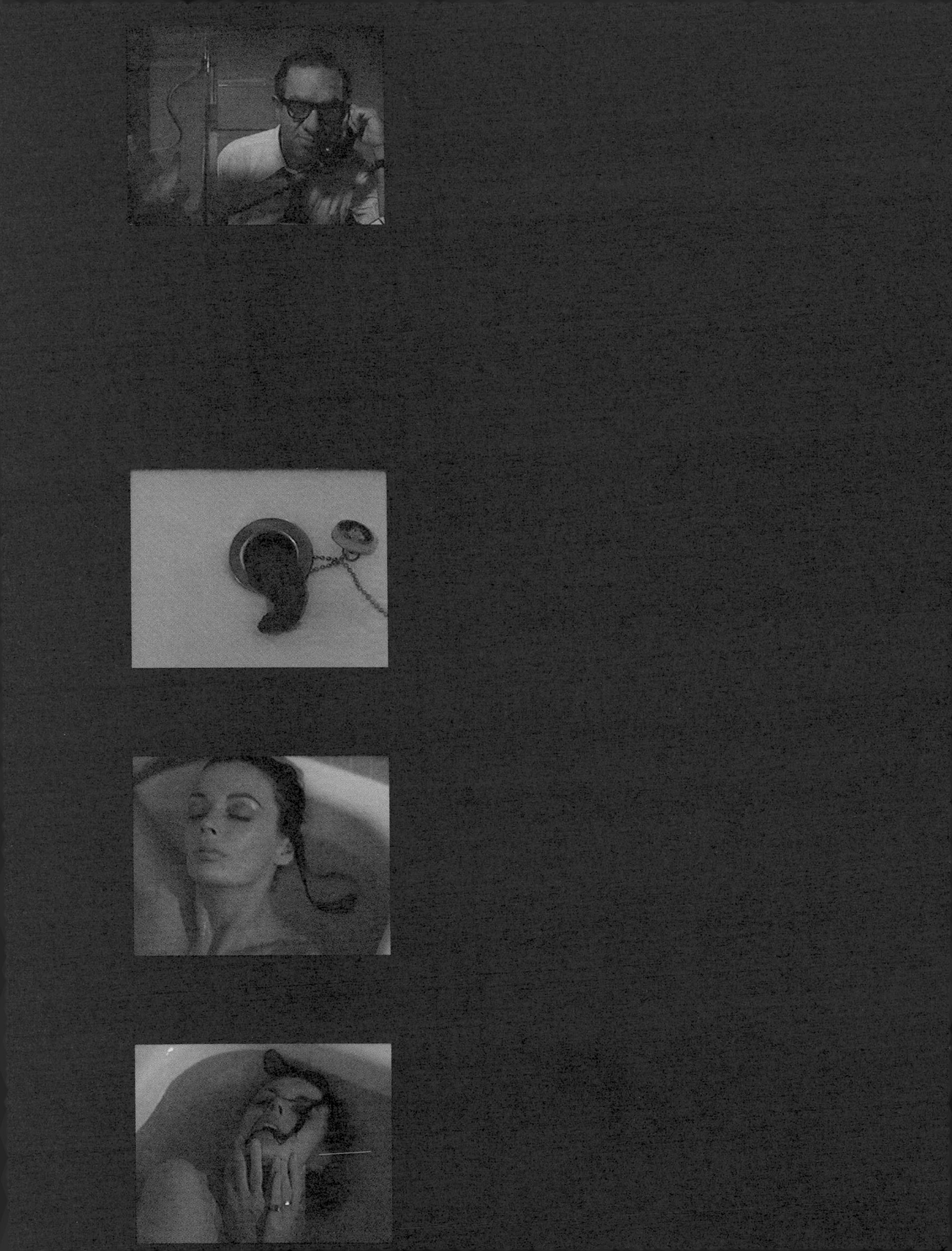

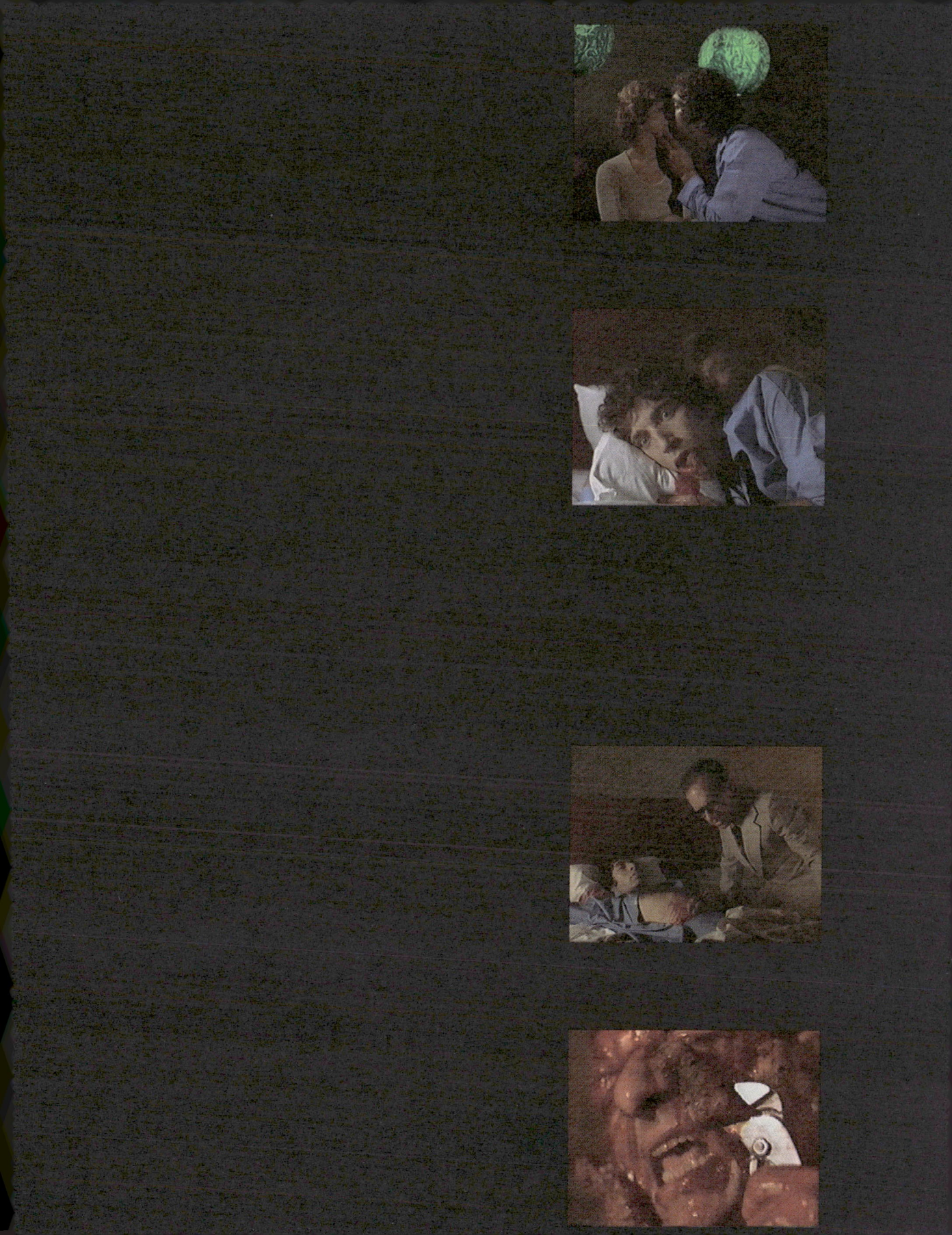

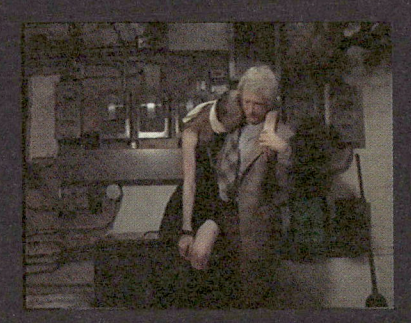
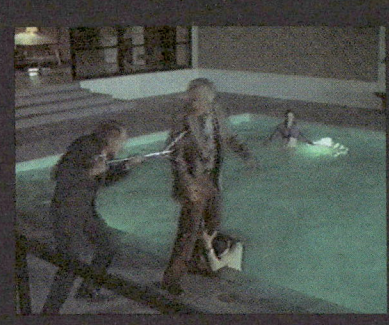
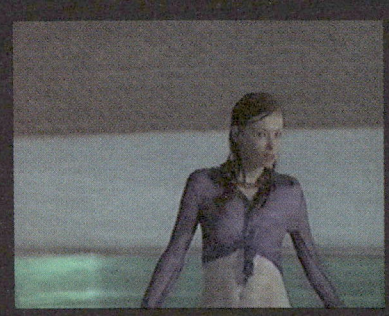
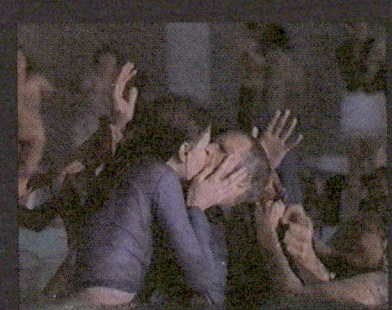

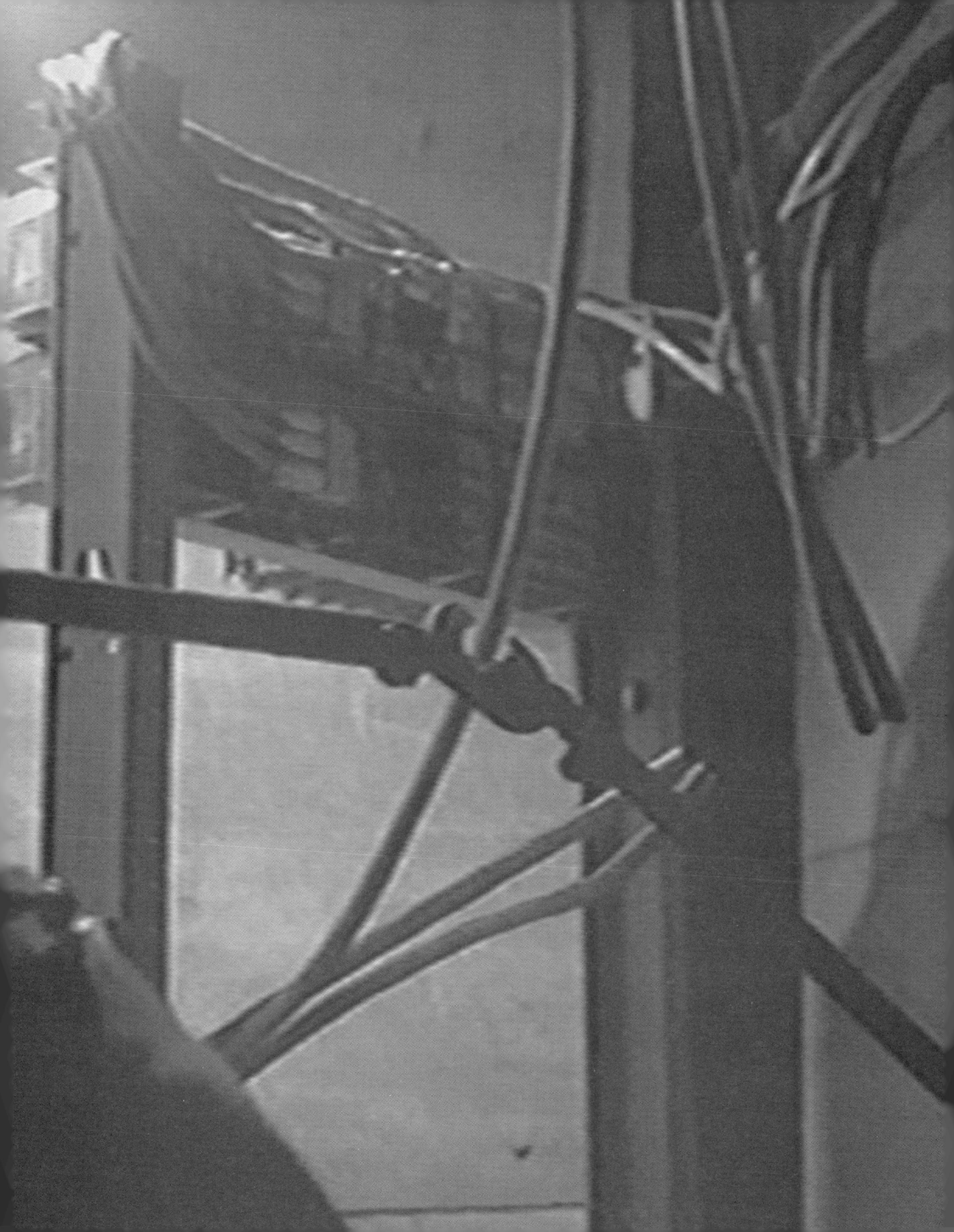

John Waters on David Cronenberg

JOHN WATERS: I'm prepared now—I did my homework.

ANNE DORAN: So did you like *Shivers*?

WATERS: I loved it. I saw it when it first came out at a drive-in in Baltimore with a carload of kids and beer, and it was called *They Came from Within*.

DORAN: How old were you at the time?

WATERS: Well, let me think, about twenty-nine. It was two years after *Pink Flamingos* came out. At that time there was a review that made the film very notorious in Canada by somebody named Robert Fulford* who had very much liked David's early movies, and I think from the books I've read that David thought he was going to like *Shivers*. But it got the kind of review that *Pink Flamingos* got—"the most repulsive film ever made"—which made it a hugely notorious film. And it's so amazing how, at the time, that could really help. That notoriety really wouldn't work right now, because there isn't a cultural war, but back then there was. And for a Canadian film to be held up as repulsive was really a shock. But the film is, I think, much scarier now. It's very troubling, in a way, that a horror film that certainly was not taking itself seriously could prefigure things like AIDS and Legionnaires' disease. These parasites even come through the vents.

DORAN: It's like the Ebola virus, but it's totally sexualized.

WATERS: They're horny, they're deadly, they're on the loose. It's *Night of the Living Hornballs*. Seeing it now is very, very strange because the disease is so much like AIDS. You know, when *Shivers* came out, in the hippie years, people were worried about crabs, scabies, VD—those were the worst things that could happen, and that's what you thought of then. But now we see it in such a different light.

---

* Fulford wrote for the magazine, *Saturday Night*, under the pseudonym Marshal Delaney. Cronenberg remembers Fulford implying that, "if this was the kind of movie Canada had to make to have a film industry, we shouldn't have an industry. . . . He made a big deal out of the fact that taxpayers' money had been put into this piece of filth."

DORAN: It holds up, doesn't it?

WATERS: Oh, yeah, it really holds up. I think it's better now. I am a huge fan of David's. No one could have done *Naked Lunch* any better than he did it. This movie to me is truly about being paranoid about diseases. Who isn't? And the way it looks—you know, the budget was only $180,000—it reminded me very much of that Oldenburg* bedroom that I always really, really loved.

DORAN: Oh, the zebra bar in the nurse's apartment in the movie . . . You're right.

WATERS: The whole apartment building looked like that.

DORAN: That's the thing that really got me. It's like Cronenberg was totally aware of how the seventies looked in the seventies.

WATERS: But back then, no one was looking at the style. The art direction makes one strangely nostalgic.

DORAN: Really good art gets made when people understand the look of their own time.

WATERS: Which is rare.

DORAN: It's something you do. It's a sort of taste for the mundane of your period. I was thinking today that what makes Cronenberg's movies even creepier is that real lunatics aren't that aware of the everyday world. They're in their own world.

WATERS: They think they're normal. Cronenberg knows that normal is the scariest of all.

DORAN: There's this really subtle thing—I mean where Dr. St. Luc goes to see Dr. Hobbes's partner, who's eating a pickle, and they have that long talk and at the end they shake hands and they each raise their index fingers . . .

WATERS: It's almost a hippie handshake.

DORAN: Or a Panther handshake—and it's like, "Oh, yeah, that's how people shook hands in the seventies."

WATERS: And the doctor has on leather pants—can you imagine—and a bleached-blond Caesar haircut. But you're right, I noticed that handshake too.

DORAN: But not to take that for granted is to be a connoisseur of the mundane.

WATERS: *The Tingler* was one of my favorite movies as a kid.* I think the parasites in *Shivers* were like *The Tingler*, only meaner. When that phallic piece of gristle comes up through the plumbing and goes up Barbara Steele's legs in the bathtub—I've been a huge fan of hers, ever

---

* Claes Oldenburg.

* In *The Tingler* (1959), a coroner, played by Vincent Price, discovers that fear breeds a centipede-like organism in the base of the spine, and he embarks on a set of sadistic experiments with a deaf-mute woman.

since 8 1/2 and *Black Sunday*—I remember that scene very intensely. I mean, it's like the other side of *Psycho*. And how about when the woman is walking with her walker and this phallic turd attacks her and her husband just says, "I hate it." That's my favorite line in there. And the other scene I love is when the two old ladies are walking outside and one of the creatures lands on her umbrella . . .

DORAN: One of those see-thru, plastic umbrellas. And she says, "Poor birdie."

WATERS: And the other one says, "Never mind, dear, whatever it was it's in heaven now." The killer parasite is so many different scary things put into one. It's scatological. It's sexual. It comes out of your mouth. It comes out of your stomach. In one scene, when someone touches a woman, it's like deep throat—her throat gets a hard-on. It's really weird. Then, on top of that, to have it spread through sex. You are used to all of the horror, but when people get horny on top of it! Not only does it make you a zombie, it makes you horny.

DORAN: Exactly, and sex is death. Certain combinations of ideas are far more threatening than the single ideas by themselves. Horror movies are okay. Porn movies are okay. They each have their place. But when you start to combine porn and horror, or car crashes and sex, as Cronenberg does in *Crash*, it's just out of control.

WATERS: That's what makes it good—when you're fucking with the genre—you're turning one thing into another and really confusing people.

DORAN: I started to think that what you can't define, what just floats around, is infinitely more threatening on so many different levels. It's scarier.

WATERS: *Shivers* has lesbianism, incest, every possible thing. How about the other line I really love, when one of the zombies says, "Disease is the love of two alien creatures for each other." It's cheesy Cronenberg, in a great way. Now *Crash* to me is the classiest movie of the year. I loved it. *Shivers* has a really good car crash in it, too. I even rewound it on the video, because it looks like the people are really in the car and it's going fast. I think David may be personally turned on by car accidents.

DORAN: I watched a lot of his movies over again this week, and there are car crashes in almost all of them.

WATERS: It speaks to me because I had a scene in *Female Trouble* where Little Taffy plays "car accident" and Divine catches her sitting there surrounded by dented car pieces squirting ketchup all over herself. When I was a child, that's how I played. My parents used to buy me toys and I would smash them and tow them into my play junkyard. My mother even took me to junkyards to look at smashed cars. So it speaks to me. It's drama, it's melodrama. But *Crash*, to me, is the best art movie ever made, and I mean that in a great way—what art movies really used to be. That wasn't an insult in the old days. And when I saw the crash in *Shivers*, for some reason, I thought, "He really has an affinity for this."

DORAN: He's got an obsession with it. I noticed that there were certain themes that run through most of his movies, and they are already there in *Shivers*, which is why I think it's incredibly interesting. He elaborated on the "new flesh" later, but there's early "new flesh," and there's sex-equals-disease, and sex-or-disease-as-uncontrollable-force, and there's a car crash.

WATERS: The special effects, they look seamless to me. I don't know how he did them. The bumps under the skin. They were *really* good.

DORAN: They did it with air bladders. They sort of experimented until they figured out how to do it. Then he found out later that some other filmmaker had worked it out at the same time.

WATERS: I love the fact that it was produced by Ivan Reitman, who I remember was then one of the leaders of underground film in Canada. He went on to direct *Meatballs* and *Ghostbusters*. He turned into a really successful Hollywood director.

DORAN: It was produced by Cinepix, a Toronto film company, with Reitman and André Link and John Dunning, who together are supposed to be the French-Canadian Roger Corman.

WATERS: I love it that David still lives in Canada. He has had what I would call a really distinguished career. In *Shivers*, he has every controversial buzz subject of the time. I mean, interracial love, the two gay males looking to grab another one for a threesome. And the men had on such bad underpants.

Now, do you remember the scene that was really scary to me, in the storage area, where all the hands are reaching up and grabbing? That's exactly what the Hellfire Club and the Mineshaft were like. It really reminded me of sex clubs from that period. You'd be talking to somebody in a club and all of a sudden a hard-on would hit you in the back. "Oooow!" You know, when you're having a conversation: "What's your favorite new film—ooow!" I have no idea if David ever frequented Hellfire, but that one little scene to me was very scary. He even had those nude girls on leashes like in Pasolini's *Salo*.

DORAN: I think a lot of what horror films look like now has to do with how Cronenberg thought of horror. Do you just keep on going to see his movies when they come out?

WATERS: Yeah, from the beginning. I've seen every movie he ever made. I've *paid* to see every movie he ever made.

D. NURKSE

EMPIRE BOULEVARD

I wanted to leave this neighborhood
before dark: now I wait
on the hard sofa in your lobby.
Either you've slept absurdly late
or you never came home . . .
Security watches me and taps
on the pommel of his nightstick.
Framed in the door a hooker
passes with many sideways glances:
then joggers and a Jehovah's Witness.
I haven't slept in two days.
Better to leave now
than to let you see me
with this face of long sickness,
meek with an old man's desire.
I'd hoped to leave this town
before the curfew, the snipers,
especially before the negotiations:
and now Security flosses his teeth
and stares straight at me
as if into a mirror,
his eyes dazzling with evening.

PAYLESS

The panhandler who knew my name
lies covered with a blue blanket,
the door where he slept
sealed with a strip of tape
—a barrier a sparrow could pass:

two plainclothes write in notebooks,
each listening to a different radio:

I'll give my quarter instead
to the girl who waits at Payless,
who rocks on her heels in a dream,
only a paper cup placed carefully
outside the ring of frozen urine
to show she's still asking.

OUTSIDE A MAN CAME

DANIIL KHARMS

Daniil Ivanovich Yuvachev, who chose the pen name Daniil Harms, was very superstitious. When told what his pseudonym meant in English, he became very upset and changed it to "Charms." But this didn't help.

He was arrested without the slightest cause. One day he came out of his house in his slippers, and at that moment a black car pulled up at the door. There are different accounts of his death. In the gloomiest version, he was simply forgotten after the arrest and eaten in his cell by rats. This is too much like one of his own stories to be true.

Daniil Kharms was born in 1905 and died in 1942. During his lifetime, Russia was transformed from a sleepy Christian realm into one of the bloodiest empires in history. But there are no "reflections of social cataclysm" or "unmaskings of the regime" in the work of Kharms and his friends in OBERIU, the Association for Real Art. If Kharms's verse and prose do reflect anything, it is merely his attempt to escape from the world into himself—the state of mind later referred to as internal emigration.

Literary critics call Kharms a "black miniaturist," and with good reason. But a strange light glimmers beneath all of his texts. When the world around us is too terrifying and absurd to be real, it simply breaks down and disappears. His work may serve as a catalyst for this reaction. Kharms is a mystical writer; his extreme isolation may have been involuntary, but his experience is all the more unique. His brief stories resemble Zen koans that halt the mind and destroy the world. One of his best stories, On Phenomena and Existences No. 2, is an incredibly accurate and comical statement on the metaphysics of Buddhism. And the short dialogue Makarov and Petersen sums up the entire teaching of Castaneda's Don Juan.

Kharms's writings, which later became samizdat bestsellers and inspired hundreds of imitations, were known during his lifetime only to close friends. To everyone else, he was an author who published humorous poems in magazines for schoolchildren. In one such poem, Kharms foretold his own fate. It was not difficult: the year 1937, the most terrible in Russia's history, was just around the corner. The poem was titled A Man Came Outside:

> A man came outside
> With a club and a sack,
> >   Set off
> >   Down the road
> And never looked back.
>
> He walked ever onward,
> He walked ever straight,
> >   Never slept,
> >   Never drank,
> Never drank, slept, or ate.
>
> He came to a forest
> As dark as the night.
> >   He walked
> >   Right in
> And vanished from sight.
>
> But if ever you chance
> To meet up with this man
> >   Oh please
> >   Let us know
> As quick as you can.

Now, sixty years later, it is possible to meet this man again.

VICTOR PELEVIN

Old Women Tumbling Out

A certain old woman, because of her excessive curiosity, tumbled out the window—fell and died on impact.

Another old woman stuck her head out the window and started looking down at the dead woman. But she too, because of her excessive curiosity, tumbled out the window—fell and died on impact.

Then a third old woman tumbled out the window, then a fourth, then a fifth.

When the sixth old woman tumbled out, I got sick of watching them and went to Maltsevsky Market, where, they say, a certain blind man was given a knitted shawl.

1937

The Letter

Dear Nikandr Andreyevich,

I received your letter and realized right away that it was from you. At first I thought maybe it wasn't from you, but the minute I opened it, I realized right away that it was from you, though in fact I'd almost thought that it wasn't from you. I'm glad you got married a long time ago, because when a man marries the woman he wants to marry, it means he's achieved what he wanted. So I'm very glad you got married, because when a man marries the woman he wants to marry, it means he's achieved what he wanted. Yesterday I received your letter and thought right away that it was a letter from you, but then I thought maybe it wasn't from you, but I opened it and saw—indeed, it was from you. You did very well to write to me. At first you didn't write, and then suddenly you did, although before that, before you hadn't written for a while, you used to write. Right away when I received your letter, right away I decided it was from you, and then next I was very glad you'd got married. Because in fact, if a man has an urge to marry, he must get married no matter what. Therefore I'm very glad you finally married the very woman you wanted to marry. And you did very well to write me. I was very happy when I saw your letter, and I even thought right away that it was from you. True, while I was opening it I had the fleeting idea that it wasn't from you, but then I decided it was from you after all. Thank you for writing. I am grateful to you for this and very glad for you. Maybe you can't guess why I'm so glad for you, but I'll tell you right away that I'm glad for you because of this: because you got married, and to the very woman you wanted to marry. It's very good, you know, to marry the very woman you want to marry, because that is how you also achieve what you want to achieve. This is the very reason I'm so glad for you. And I'm also glad you wrote me a letter. Even from a distance I decided the letter must be from you, but the minute I picked it up I thought: But what if it's not from you? But then I thought: Why no, of course it's from you. I'm opening the letter and at the same time I'm thinking: From you or not from you? From you or not from you? Well, but the minute I opened it, I saw that it was from you. I was very happy and decided to write you a letter too. I have a lot I need to tell you, but literally no time. I've written you what I could in this letter, but I'll write the rest later, because in fact I have no time at all just now. At least it's good you wrote me a letter. Now I know you got married a long time ago. I did know from previous letters that you'd got married, but now I see again—quite right, you've got married. And I'm very glad you got married and wrote me a letter. Right away when I saw your letter, I decided you'd got married again. Well, I think it's good that you got married again and wrote me a letter about it. Now write me who your new wife is and how it all happened. Give my regards to your new wife.

September 25 and October 1933

The Dream

Kalugin fell asleep and dreamed that he was sitting in the bushes and a policeman was walking past the bushes.

Kalugin woke up, scratched his mouth, and fell asleep again. Again he dreamed that he was walking past the bushes and there was a policeman sitting and hiding in the bushes.

Kalugin woke up, put a newspaper under his head so as not to drool on his pillow, and fell asleep again. Again he dreamed that he was sitting in the bushes and a policeman was walking past the bushes.

Kalugin woke up, changed the newspaper, lay down, and fell asleep again. He fell asleep and again dreamed that he was walking past the bushes and there was a policeman sitting in the bushes.

Kalugin woke up and decided not to sleep anymore, but he instantly fell asleep and dreamed that he was sitting behind the policeman and there were bushes walking past.

Kalugin started shouting and tossing about in bed, but by now he could not wake up.

Kalugin slept four days and four nights in a row, and on the fifth day he woke up so emaciated that he had to tie his boots to his feet with string to keep them from falling off.

At the bakery, where Kalugin always bought wheat bread, they didn't recognize him and slipped him rye.

The sanitation commission, while making its rounds of the apartments, saw Kalugin, found him unsanitary and good for nothing and ordered the housing cooperative to throw Kalugin out with the garbage.

They folded Kalugin in half and threw him out as garbage.

August 22, 1936

Makarov and Petersen No. 3

MAKAROV: Here, in this book, it tells about our desires and their fulfillment. Read this book and you will understand how vain are our desires. You will also understand how easy it is to fulfill the desire of another, and how hard it is to fulfill a desire of your own.

PETERSEN: You sound awfully solemn. You're talking like an Indian chief.

MAKAROV: This is the kind of book that must be spoken of in a lofty manner. Even thinking about it, I must take off my hat.

PETERSEN: Do you wash your hands before touching this book?

MAKAROV: Yes, I have to wash my hands, too.

PETERSEN: Better play it safe—wash your feet, too.

MAKAROV: That is rude and not funny.

PETERSEN: But what *is* this book?

MAKAROV: The title of this book is mysterious....

PETERSEN: Hee-hee-hee!

MAKAROV: This book is called MALGIL.

    Petersen disappears.

MAKAROV: Good heavens! What's going on? Petersen?

PETERSEN'S VOICE: What happened? Makarov! Where am I?

MAKAROV: Where are you? I don't see you!

PETERSEN'S VOICE: But where are you? I don't see you either!... What are these spheres?

MAKAROV: What is to be done? Petersen, do you hear me?

PETERSEN'S VOICE: Yes. But what happened? And what are these spheres?

MAKAROV: Can you move?

PETERSEN'S VOICE: Makarov! Do you see these spheres?

MAKAROV: What spheres?

PETERSEN'S VOICE: Let go! Let go of me! Makarov!...

    Silence. Makarov stands still in horror, then grabs the book and opens it.

MAKAROV (*reading*): "... Little by little a man loses his shape and becomes a sphere. And once he is a sphere, a man loses all his desires."

    Curtain.

Five Unfinished Narratives

Dear Yakov Semyonovich,
1. A certain man took a running start and hit his head against a smithy with such force that the blacksmith set aside the sledgehammer he was holding, took off his leather apron, smoothed his hair with his hand, and went outdoors to see what had happened. 2. There the blacksmith saw a man

sitting on the ground. The man was sitting on the ground and holding his head. 3. "What happened?" asked the blacksmith. "Ouch!" said the man. 4. The blacksmith went up closer to the man. 5. We break off the narrative of the blacksmith and the unknown man and begin a new narrative about four harem enthusiasts. 6. Once upon a time there were four fans of the harem. They thought it enjoyable to have eight women at once. They used to get together in the evening and discuss harem life. They drank wine; they drank themselves drunk; they fell under the table; they threw up. It was disgusting to watch them. They bit each other in the leg. They called each other bad words. They crawled on their stomachs. 7. We break off their story and start a new story about beer. 8. On the floor stood a barrel of beer, and next to it a philosopher sat and reasoned: "This barrel is full of beer; the beer is fermenting and growing strong. I too, as I wander the heights above the stars, am fermenting in mind and growing strong in spirit. Beer is a drink that flows in space, whereas I am a drink that flows in time. 9. When beer is confined in a barrel, it has nowhere to flow. Time will stop, and I will stand up. 10. But time will not stop, and my flow is inalterable. 11. No, instead let the beer flow freely too, for it is contrary to the laws of nature for beer to stand still." With these words the philosopher opened the tap in the barrel, and the beer spilled out on the floor. 12. We have said enough about beer; now we will talk about a drum. 13. The philosopher beat a drum and shouted: "I am creating a philosophical noise! No one needs this noise; it only bothers everyone. But if it bothers everyone, that means it is not of this world. And if it is not of this world, it is of the other world. And if it is of the other world, I will create it." 14. The philosopher kept up the noise for a long time. But we will leave this noisy tale and go on to the following quiet tale about trees. 15. The philosopher strolled under the trees and was silent, because inspiration had left him.

1937

On Phenomena and Existences No. 2

Here is a bottle of vodka, a so-called spirit. And beside it you see Nikolai Ivanovich Serpukhov.

Alcoholic fumes are rising from the bottle. Look how Nikolai Ivanovich breathes them in through his nose. See how he licks his lips and frowns. He evidently finds this very enjoyable, and chiefly because the fumes are alcoholic.

But notice that there is nothing at Nikolai Ivanovich's back. It isn't just that there is no cupboard or bureau there or anything of that sort—but that there is absolutely nothing, not even air. Believe it or not, there isn't even an airless space, or what they call cosmic ether, at Nikolai Ivanovich's back. To put it bluntly, there is nothing.

No doubt this is impossible to imagine.

But we couldn't care less about that, as all that interests us are the spirits and Nikolai Ivanovich Serpukhov.

Look, Nikolai Ivanovich is taking the bottle of spirits in his hand and lifting it to his nose. Nikolai Ivanovich is sniffing and wiggling his mouth like a rabbit.

Now the time has come to say that, not only at Nikolai Ivanovich's back, but also in front of him—at his chest, as it were—and all around him, there is nothing. A complete absence of any existence. Or, as someone once said in jest, an absence of any presence.

But let's confine our interest to the spirits and Nikolai Ivanovich.

Imagine: Nikolai Ivanovich peers into the bottle of spirits, then raises it to his mouth, tips the bottle upside down, and—imagine—drinks down the entire bottle of spirits.

How smooth! Nikolai Ivanovich drinks down all the spirits and blinks in bewilderment. How smooth! How did he do it?

But now we must say this. Strictly speaking, not only was there nothing behind Nikolai Ivanovich or in front of or around him, but there was also nothing *inside* Nikolai Ivanovich; nothing existed there.

The situation could doubtless be just as we've described it, and at the same time Nikolai Ivanovich himself could have existed delightfully. This is clearly true. But quite frankly, the problem is that Nikolai Ivanovich did not and does not exist. That's the whole problem.

You will ask: But what about the bottle of spirits? In particular, where did the vodka go, if it was drunk by a nonexistent Nikolai Ivanovich? Let's say the bottle is still here. But where, then, is the vodka? It was here just now, and suddenly it's gone. Nikolai Ivanovich doesn't exist, you say? How can this be?

At this point, we ourselves are lost in conjecture.

But what are we saying? After all, we have stated that both inside and outside Nikolai Ivanovich nothing exists. And if nothing exists either inside or outside, that means the bottle doesn't exist either. Right?

But on the other hand, think about this: If we say that nothing exists either inside or outside, the question is: inside or outside of what? Something, evidently, *does* exist. Or perhaps not. But then how can we say "inside" or "outside"?

This is clearly a dead end. We ourselves don't know what to say.

Good-bye.

September 18, 1934

The Knight

Alexei Alexeyevich Alexeyev was a true knight. For example, looking out from a streetcar one day, he saw a lady trip on the curbstone and drop a glass lampshade from her shopping bag. It shattered immediately. Alexei Alexeyevich, wishing to help the lady, decided to sacrifice himself and leapt from the moving streetcar; he fell onto a rock and split his face open. Another time, he saw a lady catch her skirt on a nail while climbing over a fence and get stuck on top of the fence unable to move backward or forward. Alexei Alexeyevich began to feel so agitated that in his agitation he forced out two of his front teeth with his tongue. In short, Alexei Alexeyevich was a very true knight, and not merely with regard to ladies. Alexei Alexeyevich could sacrifice his life with incredible ease for Faith, Tsar, and Homeland, as he proved in 1914, at the start of the German war, by crying "For the Motherland" and throwing himself into the street from a third-floor window. By some miracle Alexei Alexeyevich survived, escaping with only light injuries. As a patriot of such exceptional zeal, he was soon sent to the front.

There, Alexei Alexeyevich distinguished himself with his incredibly lofty sentiments. Every time he said the words "banner," "fanfare," or even just "epaulets," a tear ran down his face.

In 1916, Alexei Alexeyevich was wounded in the groin and sent back from the front.

As a Category I invalid, Alexei Alexeyevich did not work, and he took advantage of his free time to expound his patriotic sentiments on paper.

One day, while talking with Konstantin Lebedev, Alexei Alexeyevich spoke his favorite line: "I suffered for the motherland and ruined my loins, but I exist by the strength of conviction of my retrospective unconscious."

"Fool!" Konstantin Lebedev said. "Only a liberal can render the highest service to the motherland."

For some reason these words sank deep into Alexei Alexeyevich's soul, and by 1917 he was calling himself *a liberal who had ruined his loins for his native land.*

Alexei Alexeyevich welcomed the revolution with delight, despite the fact that he lost his pension. For a while Konstantin Lebedev provided him with sugar, chocolate, canned lard, and cereal. But when Konstantin Lebedev suddenly disappeared to parts unknown, Alexei Alexeyevich had to go out on the street and beg. At first he extended his hand and said, "For the love of Christ, give to one who ruined his loins for the motherland." But this was unsuccessful. So he replaced the word "motherland" with "revolution." But this too was unsuccessful. Then Alexei Alexeyevich composed a revolutionary song, and when he saw a man on the street who was capable in his opinion of giving alms, he took a step forward, threw back his head with dignity, and began to sing proudly:

> To the barricades!
> We will not reason why!
> For freedom
> We will all get maimed and die!

Jauntily tapping his heel in the Polish manner, Alexei Alexeyevich held out his hat and said, "Give alms for the love of Christ." This succeeded, and Alexei Alexeyevich rarely went without food.

Everything was going fine, but then in 1922 Alexei Alexeyevich became acquainted with a certain Ivan Ivanovich Puzyryov, who sold sunflower oil at Senny Market. Puzyryov invited Alexei Alexeyevich to a cafe, treated him to real coffee, and then munched on pastries while he outlined some complicated deal. Of this Alexei Alexeyevich understood only that he too must do something, for which he would receive valuable provisions from

Puzyryov. Alexei Alexeyevich consented, and Puzyryov, by way of encouragement, promptly handed him under the table two cartons of tea and a pack of Rajah cigarettes.

From that day on, Alexei Alexeyevich went to the market every morning to see Puzyryov. After receiving some papers from him with forged signatures and innumerable stamps, he took a sled, in the winter, or a wheelbarrow, in the summer, and set off, as Puzyryov ordered, to various institutions. There he presented the papers and received some boxes, which he loaded on his sled or cart, and in the evening he took them to Puzyryov at his apartment.

But one evening when Alexei Alexeyevich pulled his sled up to Puzyryov's apartment, two men, one of them wearing a military overcoat, came up to him and asked, "Is your name Alexeyev?" Then they put him in a car and took him to prison.

At the interrogation Alexei Alexeyevich understood nothing and just kept saying that he had suffered for the revolutionary homeland. But in spite of this, he was sentenced to ten years of exile in the northern regions of his fatherland. When he returned again to Leningrad in 1928, Alexei Alexeyevich took up his former trade. Standing on the corner of Voldarsky Prospect, he threw his head back with dignity, tapped his heel, and began to sing:

> To the barricades!
> We will not reason why!
> For freedom
> We will all get maimed and die!

But before he could sing it twice, he was taken away in a van, somewhere in the direction of the Admiralty. He was never seen again.

That is the brief tale of the life of the valorous knight and patriot, Alexei Alexeyevich Alexeyev.

circa 1935

Introduction and stories translated from the Russian by Susan Brownsberger

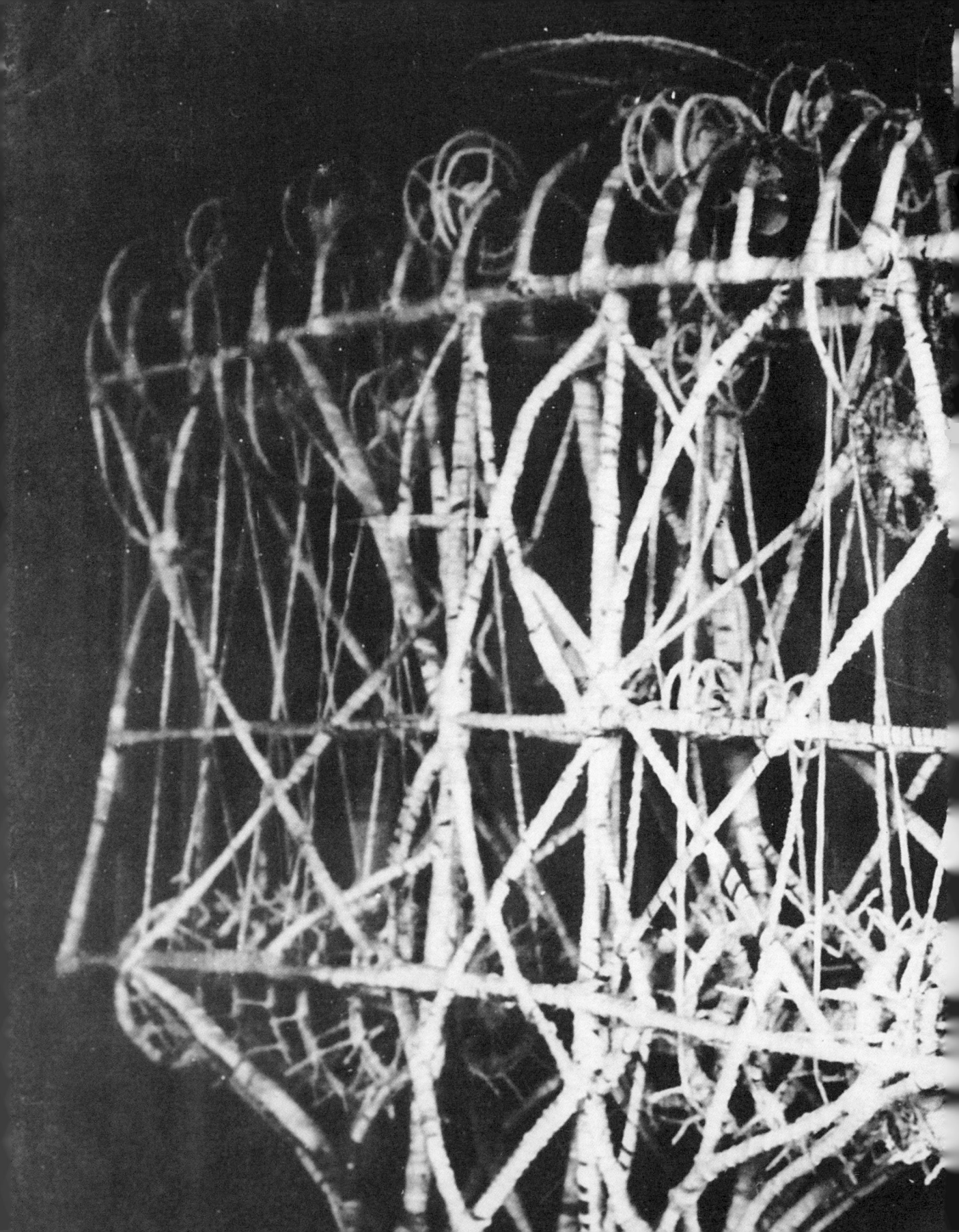

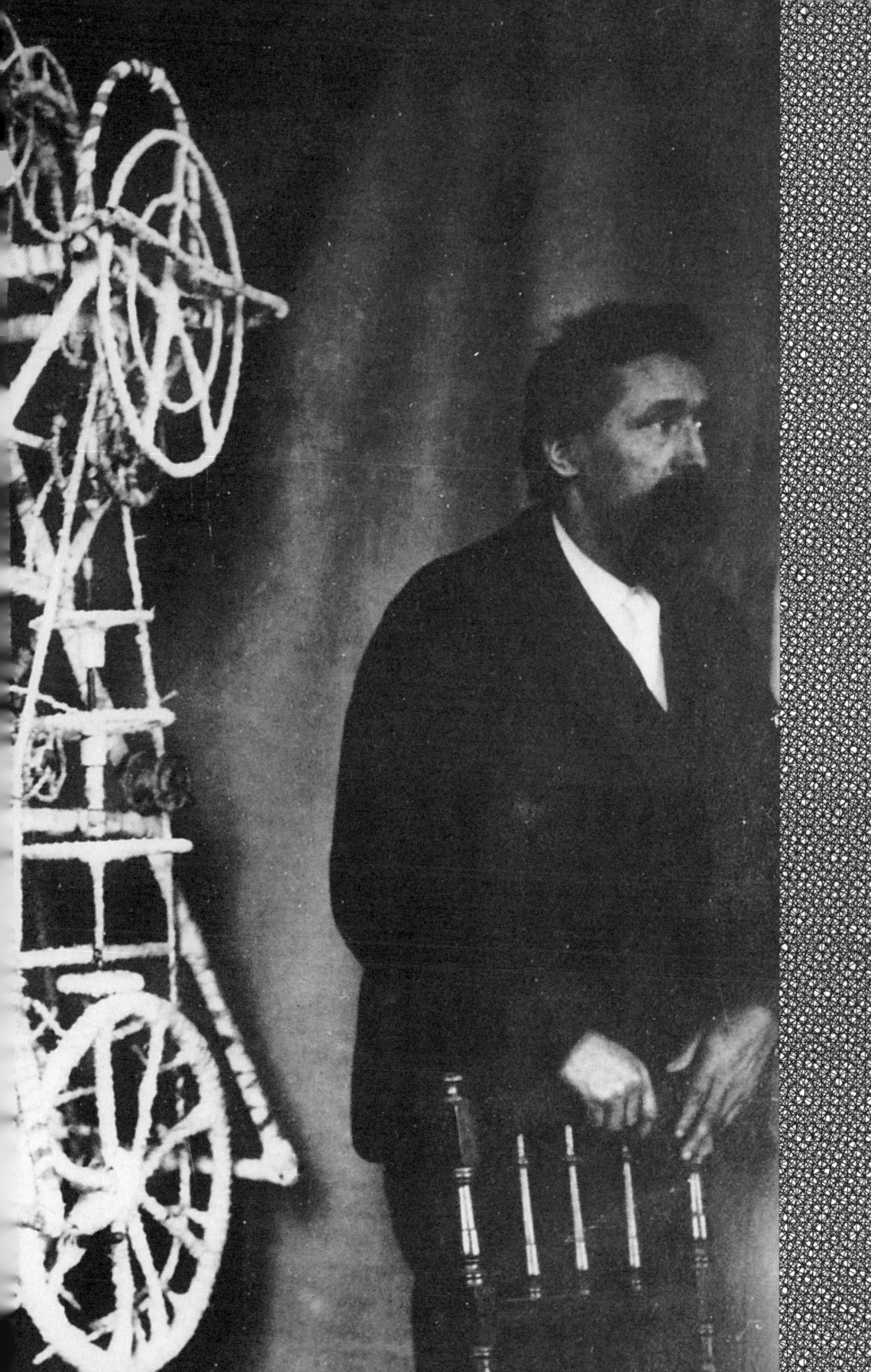

Heinrich Anton Müller: Mobiles and Machines

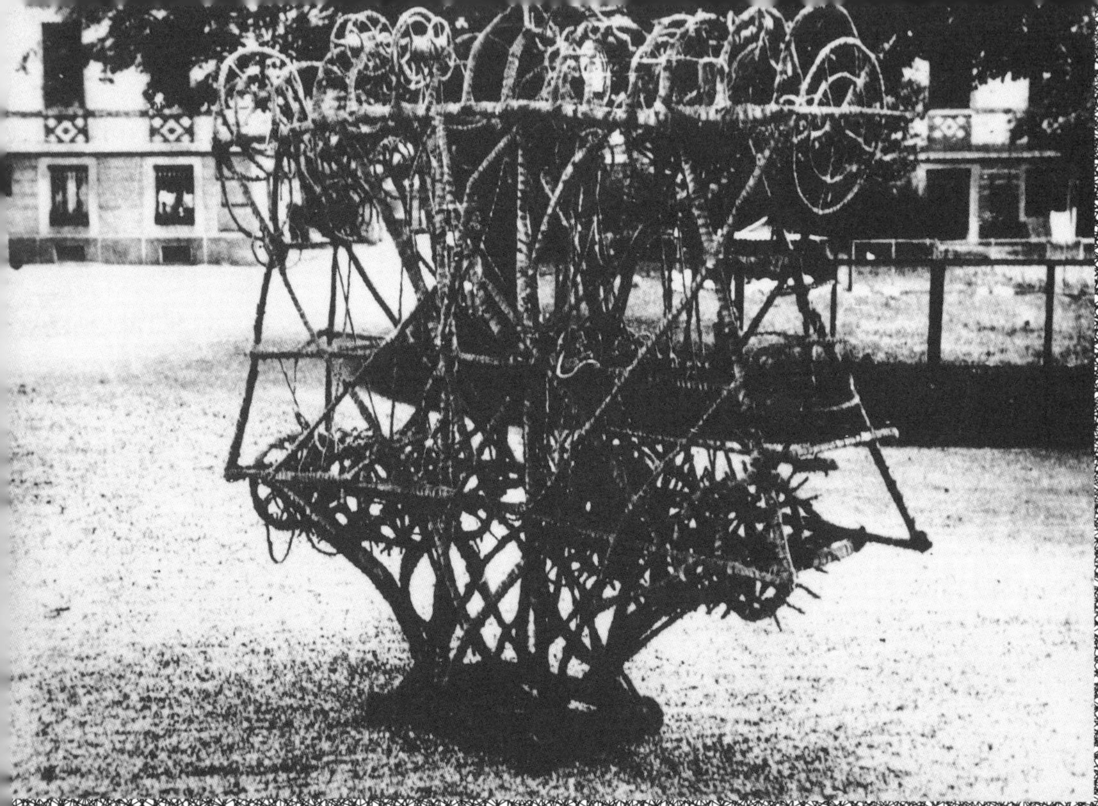

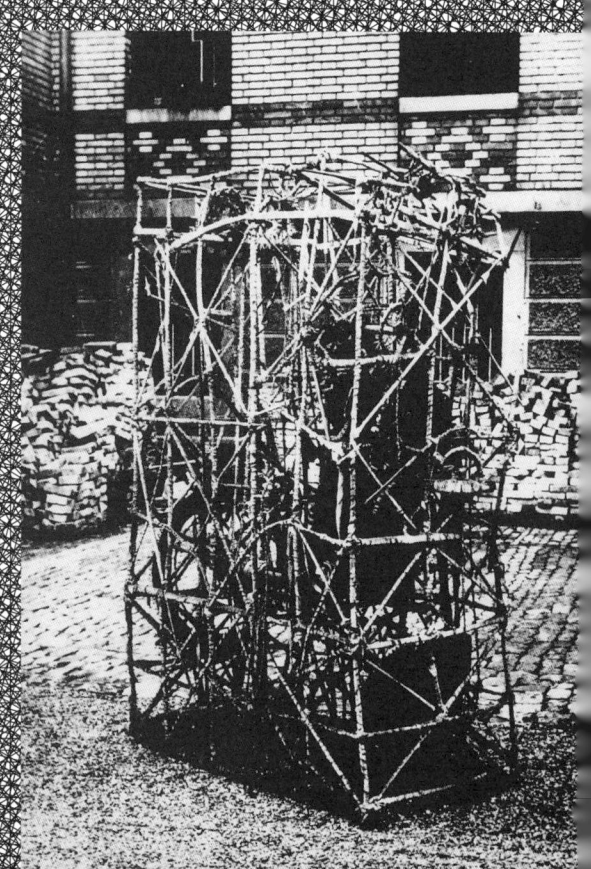

PP. 76–77 *Machine.*

P. 78 *above* *Machine.*

right *Machine.*

P. 79 *top* *Machine.*

bottom Heinrich Anton Müller with one of his *Machines* and his drawing *L'Ecureuil cornu* (*The Horned Squirrel*).

All works on pages 78 and 79 executed between 1914 and 1922.

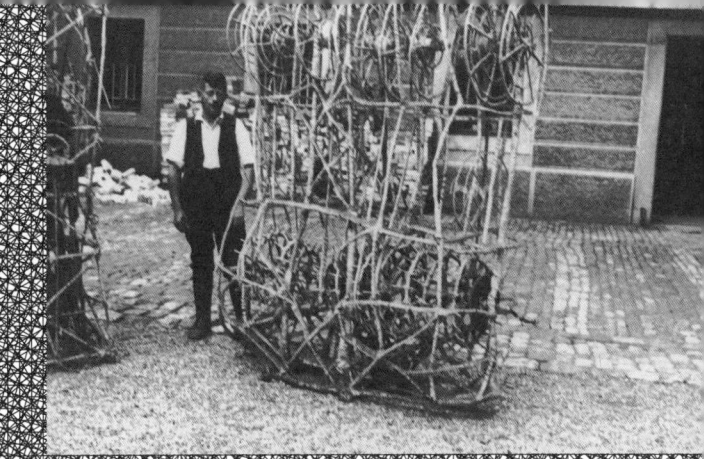
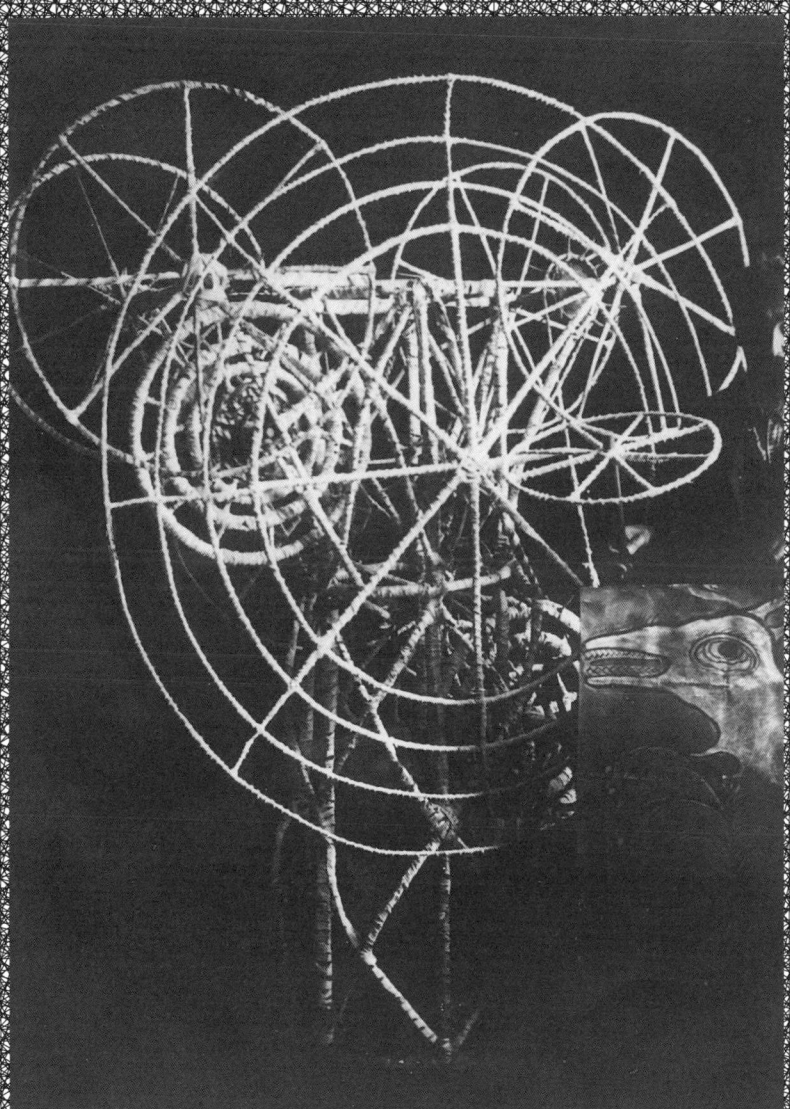

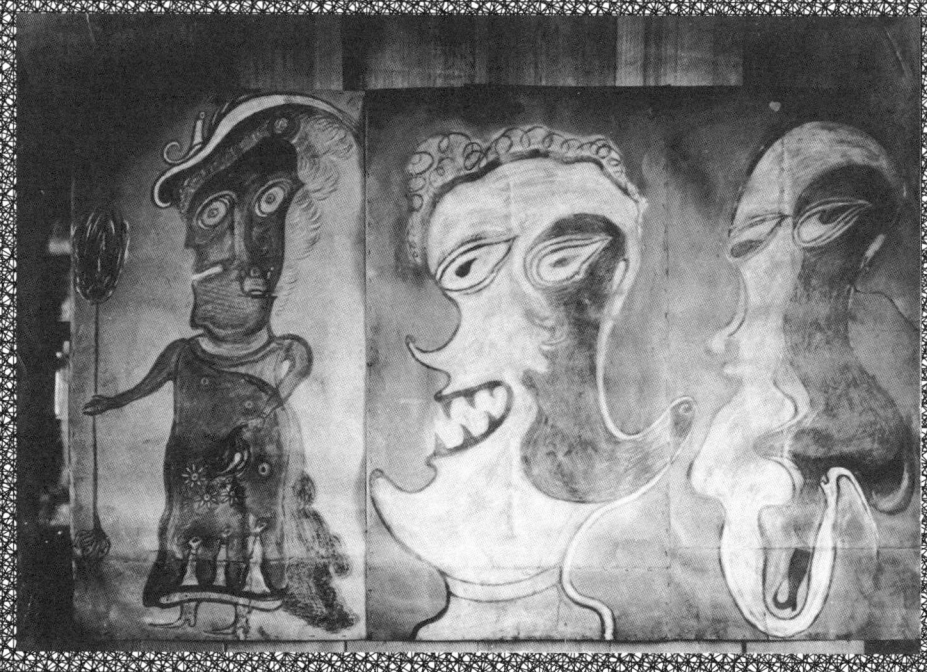

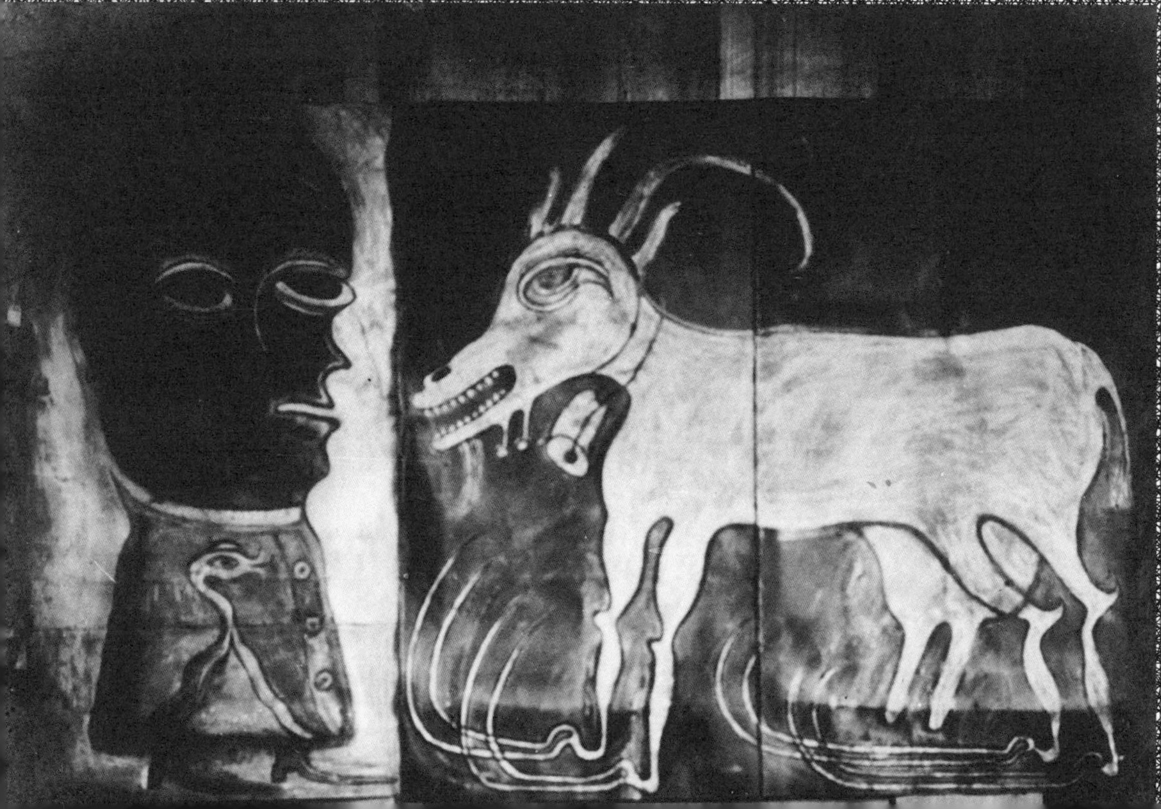

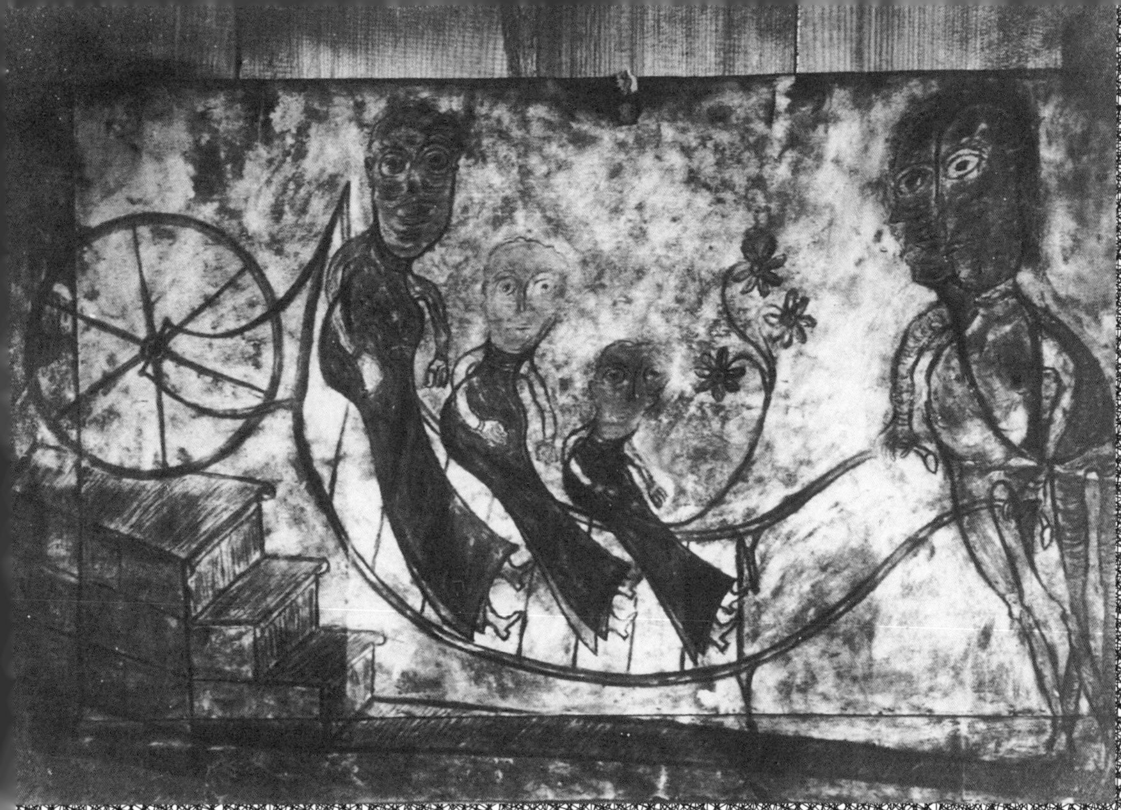

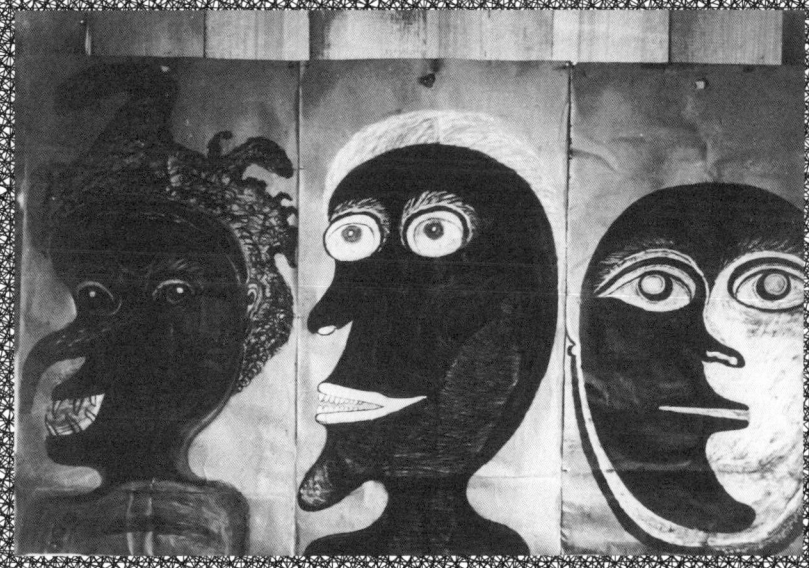

top, left Femme aux fleurs (Woman with Flowers).

top, right Deux Visages (Two Faces).

bottom, left Ohne Titel: Figur mit Rock (Untitled: Figure with Coat).

bottom, right Chèvre à la clochette (Goat with Bell).

top Trois femmes dans une brouette (Three Women in a Wheelbarrow).

bottom, left Personnage au long nez courbé (Person with Long, Curved Nose).

bottom, middle Homme à la goutte au nez (Man with a Dripping Nose).

bottom, right Ohne Titel: Doppelgesicht (Untitled: Doubleface).

All works on pages 80 and 81 executed between 1917 and 1922.

Heinrich Anton Müller

Around the turn of the century, a mechanically adept, Swiss agricultural worker from Bern, Heinrich Anton Müller, patented a pruning machine for grafting grape vines. His patent, however, lapsed when he neglected to pay the annual fee, and the belief that others had stolen his design seems to have triggered a mental breakdown in the inventor. In 1906, at the age of thirty-seven, Müller was admitted to the Münsingen Asylum for the Mentally Insane, where he was to spend the remaining twenty-four years of his life, suffering from what would probably be diagnosed by contemporary psychiatric thought as paranoid schizophrenia.

In 1912, Müller dug himself a deep hole in the hospital gardens and spent much of his time inside it. According to his medical history, he also made "a type of helmet of considerable weight, which had to be taken away from him since he used it to store the leftovers from his meals." A few years later, he began work on the design and construction of what he perceived as perpetual-motion machines—sculptures in which Jean Tinguely would later find inspiration. Müller assembled intricate mobile frameworks on the hospital grounds, using waste materials that included discarded wood, rags, and wire, as well as his own bodily secretions and excrement. However, in protest against his confinement in the institution, Müller often destroyed his own obsessive works, and most of them are known today only through a handful of black-and-white photographs.

In 1917, he received a box of paint supplies from his family and began to cover the walls of the asylum's rooms with drawings of fantastical figures and symbolic animals. Unprecedented in his prior education or activity, Müller's newfound interest in drawing was accompanied by a change in behavior that suggested the establishment of some sort of order in his inner experience—as had also been the case for Adolf Wölfli, Müller's contemporary and compatriot, and for the woman painter Aloïse (1886–1964), all three of whom were described as "schizophrenic masters" by the German psychiatrist and researcher of the art of the mentally ill, Dr. Hans Prinzhorn.

Müller died in 1930, after a brief illness during which he would not allow himself to be examined. His first solo gallery exhibition, held in Paris nineteen years after his death, was organized by the French writer Jean Paulhan and the artist Jean Dubuffet, who championed Müller's work, and that of others like him who worked outside the cultural milieu, under the banner of "Art Brut." His work received further exposure when the curator Harald Szeemann included it in Documenta 5 in Kassel in 1972, and when, for the first time, Müller's full name, which had been shrouded by psychiatric treatment protocol, could be revealed to the public.

JACKIE McALLISTER

JEFF CLARK

ST. NEMELE

Who hovers above me now,
in a black coat, the table lit
as if by a tenebrist?
Whose mane glints
as if slicked
with pomade not pitch?

Who isn't tincture of pine
but of pall and cyst.
Whose eyes are holes
not spangles in the hall.
Nemele, I wander around
embracing the waists of trees

who won't speak,
who don't attend to atonalities.
When I lied after noon
like the one half of a brothel pair,
you opened your gown
and in there,

in bleary stills,
I saw an anvil,
then a man, lit up
from a good drunk, yawing
like a rumbird through an antedawn.
In the evening you opened your gown—

Nemele, you must have gone.
Why now phantoms
in a half-lit hayloft?
Why someone in a yellow dusk
with piece outslung
at one end of Pont-Neuf?

Have you gone
darkward, or where
the white mare—

Who hovers above me now
pricks in manifold forms

Letters from the Hole

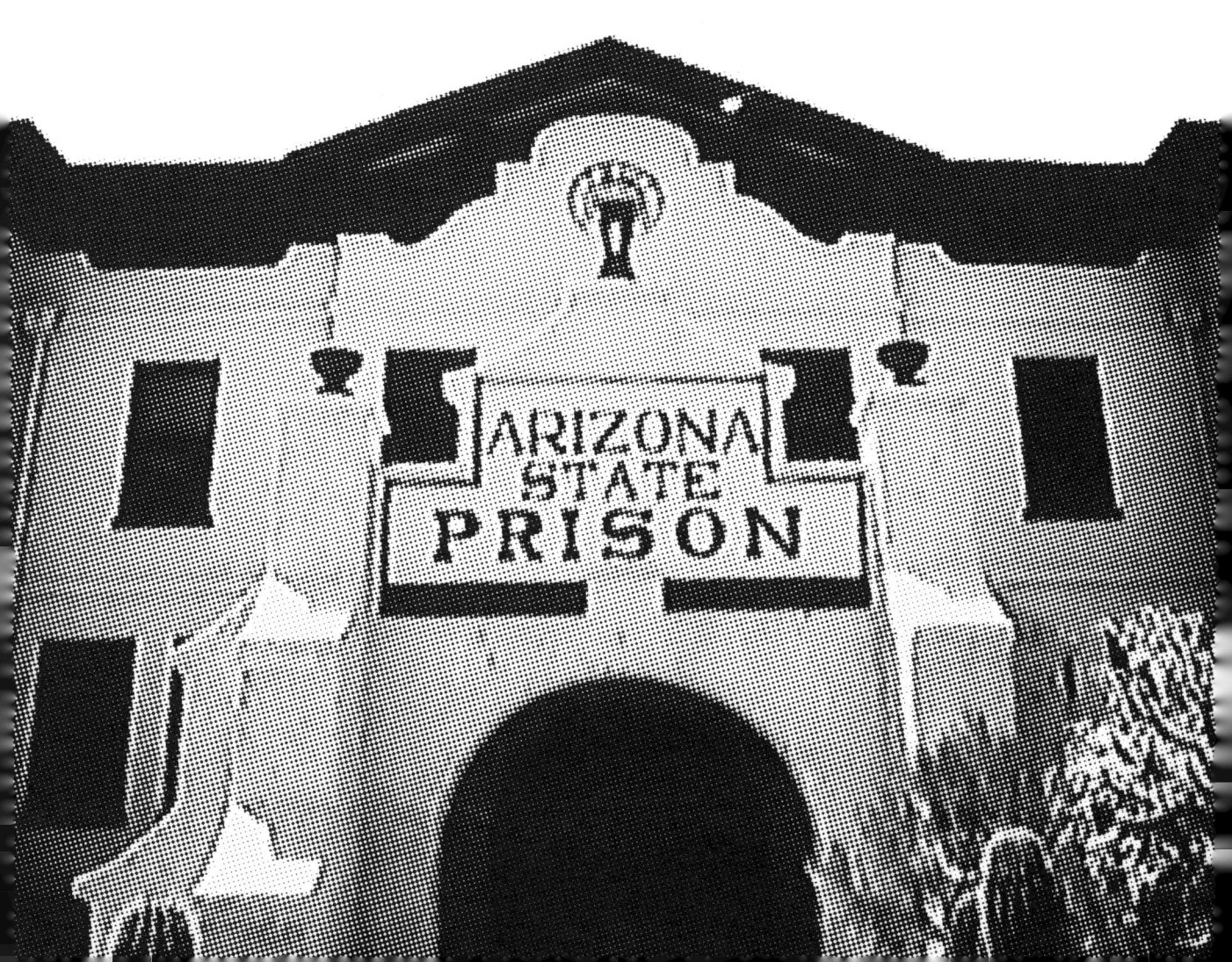

DANIEL LEE ANDERS

My friend Dan Anders is the most insubordinate son of a bitch in America. Two years ago, he was actually 'fired' from a chain gang after leading a sit-down protest against Arizona Governor J. Fife Symington's attempt to use manacled prisoners as an opportunist backdrop for a law-and-order press conference. Dan is nobody's prop or puppet. He grew up in the 1940s, dirt poor in a company town near Port Arthur, Texas, left school after eighth grade, and earned his manhood as a longshoreman in the state's tough oil ports. In prison he has devoured hundreds of books, and honed the storytelling skills that he first learnt "as a young pup" at the feet of old piney woods griots. He has survived years of solitary confinement with a daily discipline of "yoga, reading, and free thoughts." He will be liberated from his concrete coffin in the desert in 2020, the year he turns eighty.

MIKE DAVIS

10 April 1995, 18:00 hours

Dear Mr. Davis,

"TEST CARD F" carried a reference to your article, "L.A. Was Just The Beginning," in "Open Magazine."* Would you send me a copy of that article and permission to quote from it in the future?

I was given a forty-years-to-life sentence in December 1980. I come up for parole consideration in December 2020. Sounds like a TV news title, huh?

Anyhow, I'm currently in SOLITARY MAXIMUM SECURITY DETENTION: THE HOLE. Not the type of HOLE Papillon or The Count of Monte Cristo were in, but conducive to depression and deprivation ne'ertheless.

I don't have any income. I've been writing to book publishers and magazines trying to get some productive material to read, think about, and hopefully prevent my mind from caving in during the next two years I am in Iso. Max. (I'm under investigation for conspiring to incite, aid, and abet a prison mutiny and escape.) I didn't do this, but I have no way of proving my innocence. The prison administration needed a sacrificial goat—and I fit the bill. Hence the French axiom: "Plus ça change, plus c'est la même chose," which means: "The more things change, the more they stay the same."

Thank you very much for your time and interest.

Respectfully Yours,
Big Dan

---

* Test Card F (Edinburgh: AK Press, 1994). The article, "L.A. Was Just The Beginning," published by Open Magazine Pamphlets, was adapted from a shorter essay in The Nation, in which Davis discussed the 1992 Los Angeles riots.

30 April 1995, 18:00 hours

Dear Brother Davis,

I was most pleased to receive your letter last night right about this time.

Media hype and the erosion of "inalienable rights" have been un-healing cancers devouring my soul and peace of mind for thirty years.

I will provide you with a clearer picture of myself and circumstances later this week. You'll be quite satisfied and perhaps 'electrified' with the cursory tour of my fifteen years here so far.

I am serving a forty-years-to-life sentence for mayhem assault and conspiracy to commit murder.*

"¡Lo que no mata en gorda!"**

Your brother,
Dan

1 May 95

Hey Brother Davis,

We cannot lament the exquisite misery of Papillon or Ivan Denisovich. Theirs was a measurable misery. Those who bore their misery with dignity enjoyed their own self-respect as well as the respect of kept and keepers alike. This respect harbored the seeds of a form of immortality. . . .

Abject, languishing despair has replaced all the measurable miseries. Remedial education is the best an illiterate young offender coming into the system can hope for. College matriculation via Pell

---

* Believing that he "could present [his] case before a jury of [his] peers and be exonerated," Anders turned down a plea bargain that would have offered him a twenty-year sentence. Had he accepted, he would, in all likelihood, have been released on parole by now.

** All that doesn't kill you makes you bigger.

Grants were discontinued for Arizona Prisons by the Reagan and Bush administrations at the urging of Dennis DeConcini and Jane Hull*— fossils emerging from the Goldwater years. How can a young illiterate offender verbalize the error of his ways in monosyllables?

Self-Assertion and Anger Management programs abound,** but they are so shallow and transparent one is reminded of Omar Khayyam's quaint quatrain:

> Myself young did eagerly frequent
> Doctor and Saint, and heard great argument
> About it and about: but evermore
> Came out by the same Door as in I went.
> —*The Rubaiyat*

The weight-lifting program has been eliminated (felons are bad, but strong felons are nearly impossible to control without the use of deadly force).* Inmates used to be able to exercise their frustrations exercising in the weight-lifting areas; now they can only wander the exercise areas where the weight-pits used to provide some escape from subverbal rage and despair. The convicts now mill about in aimless whorls of labyrinthine resentment and nostalgia.

Despair is never ultimately over the external object but always over ourselves.

A convict receives a "Dear John" letter and he despairs. It is not over the lost sweetheart, but over himself without the sweetheart. And so it seems with all cases of loss, whether it be money, power, or social rank. The unbearable loss is not really in itself unbearable. What we cannot bear is being stripped of the external object. We stand denuded and see the intolerable abyss of ourselves. Loss of modus vivendi . . .

I was put in the Hole on Dec. 6, 1994. I have no family. There's a couple people who try to help me out when they can. But they are struggling to survive. I don't really envy their plight. There are 100 people in the Maximum Security Isolation Block. I'm certain you are familiar with some of the conditions of that place. My main concerns are books to read (we lock-down people have little access to the prison

---

* Democratic Senator DeConcini served from 1977 until the end of 1995, and was involved in the passing of this bill. Jane Hull has been Arizona's Secretary of State since 1995, and actually had nothing to do with the bill, but it has been a common misbelief among Arizona prison inmates that she is involved in any legislation that causes a deterioration in quality of life, since a statement she made as representative to the State Legislature in 1982: "Maybe the swamp coolers [at the new Perryville prison] will break down. . . . That might get rid of some of our prison population." Asked what she meant, she explained, "suffocate them to death. I really believe if we made it harder on them, they wouldn't be there."

** Programs for self-improvement or rehabilitation have been steadily decreasing within the Department of Corrections for the past decade. In 1989, a special emphasis was placed on "refocusing" education on basic literacy and GED programs, and almost all of the post-secondary education programs were cut. Treatment programs were also cut, and inmates now are more or less limited to participation in self-help book programs or closed-circuit television programs that obviously don't provide feedback or professional evaluation.

---

* Weight-lifting equipment has been removed from all prisons in Arizona, South Carolina, and Mississippi. The political rationale Anders gives here arose when— in one specific case—a pumped-up prisoner did leave prison and commit a crime in which his physical strength was a factor. Ironically, however, at almost the same time that the weight-lifting equipment was removed, the Arizona Department of Corrections instituted hard-labor chain gangs. Even the most hardened prisoners who could not be released from the prison to work on roadside work crews were given heavy sledgehammers and picks to break rocks inside the prison walls.

lending library, and the library doesn't particularly care about our plight—until one of them gets in the same situation—then they change their tune quick). N'est-ce pas?

Stamps are a problem. I have no money in my account. When I do, it is usually $20 sent by one of my friends, which helps me get cosmetics, coffee, tobacco, pens, and paper.

So—if you would send me a money order for $20, that will get me the stamps, paper, pens, coffee, and tobacco to help me take you on this long prison life-and-death journey you're interested in. I will write all this out for you regardless; quality vs. quantity doesn't dictate definitive outcome. VOILÀ!

Well, enough for now.

Respectfully yours,
Daniel L. Anders

22 May 95

Dear Mike,

You'll notice my change of building location at this same street address. CDU stands for Central Detention Unit. The conditions are about the same. A little more austere perhaps, but not much. On the Cimarron Unit I could attach a nail clipper to a long piece of dental floss, give it a hard slide under the door, and skip it all off the railing ledge down to the cell next to mine if I needed to trade the meat portion of my meals for tobacco, coffee, stamps, etc. All the prisoners on the LOCK-DOWN run would trade this way when the guards weren't walking the run. Over here each cell has double solid-steel doors with hardly any clearance beneath them. So the money you send means a lot under these circumstances.

I won't be able to spend any of it for 10 working days while the Administration waits for the M.O. to clear—or whatever their reasons are. I quit letting their antics make me a more unfortunate victim than I already am. I always tell convicts: "Don't buy into their B.S. and they'll end up more frustrated than you." There's much wisdom in St. Augustine's advice: "If the enemy hungers, feed him. If he thirsts, give him drink. For by doing so you will pile coals upon his head."*

CDU and its increased austerity is designed to prepare me mentally and physically for the more terrible place of languish and anguish which awaits me. I will probably remain here for another couple of months and then be transferred to "Special Management Unit Rehabilitation Facility" (SMURF). Can you believe that title? How long did the "living fossils" ponder to come up with that epistemological treasure? Ah, the wonder of it all. SMU or CB-8 is the Central Arizona Desert's equivalent of Pelican Bay. Books, mail, pkgs, medication(s) arrive and leave through a pneumatic tube. A panel whispers open at the back of the cell allowing access to an exercise pen much like a dog-kennel run. Each time some daily event is to occur, i.e., meals, showers, recreation (rec), or the jetsam of the pneumatic regurgitator, these events are preceded by a guttural command, not unlike the commands one would hear on a subway as the conductor announces each station. The toilet is flushed hourly from the outside. The walls, ceiling, and floor are

---

* Anders is thinking of the Biblical passage, "If thine enemy be hungry, give him bread to eat; and if he be thirsty, give him water to drink: for thou shalt heap coals of fire upon his head." Proverbs, 25:21-22.

unpainted, pre-fab slabs of reinforced concrete. Several bright sodium-vapor lamps attached to a 12-ft. ceiling turn on at 5:30 A.M. and remain on until 10:30 P.M. A wide-lens camera is recessed in one corner at the wall-ceiling juncture and sweeps the cell constantly. There are no chairs allowed in SMU. The table makes a convenient ledge to do various exercises off of or just to store things on. Otherwise it is useless. Sensory deprivation is the greatest danger doing extended lengths of time on the SMURF TURF.

Rap with you later,
Dan

23 May 95

Dear Mike,

When I was first arrested, my immediate jail experience was being crammed into one of three bullpens in the basement of the Madison St. Jail in Phoenix, AZ. These bullpens were large enough to hold 30 prisoners. There were 100 prisoners in the bullpen I was in. With the exception of a few prisoners who might "bond out" of this press of desperate humanity, we 100 would remain stacked like cordwood for up to 10 days. During this time, the "screws" would show up with long chains with 20 sets of handcuffs attached every 2 feet or so. Names of "alleged felons" would be called to take their place on the chain. As these chains filled up, each group would be marched to the elevator, which would rise to the street-level floor, and the door we were facing opened into the sallyport of Madison St. Jail's hustle and bustle. Huge squadrons of sleuths 'n' shamuses hurried about with prisoners or paperwork or coffee 'n' doughnuts in tow. "Prisoner chains" have passed this way so often that no one even looked our direction any longer. This was the beginning of our dehumanization. . . .

After we'd been formally indicted by the Grand Jury, we were showered and de-liced finally and moved to one of the upstairs cellblocks of the jail. These were dorm-pod set-ups, and they had us packed 24 men to an 8-man pod. It was pure Pandemonium. Why inmates decide to torment other inmates instead of the guards has always escaped my limited reasoning capacity. But that's the way it is and probably always will be. "Ye Old Pecking Order."

"Homo homini lupus ad infinitum . . ."

—Paulus

I'll continue this when I get a pen and some envelopes and stamps. I won't be able to write for approximately two weeks.

Respectfully yours,
Dan

2 June 95

Dear Mike,

I hope this letter finds you and your family happy and healthy. Under the circumstances I am doing fine. Things could be more pleasant, but through the years I have disciplined myself to be grateful for who I am and what I have at any given moment. Some Greek philosopher or mathematician once said, "All is flux." The things which are impossible today are experienced as possible tomorrow. I suppose I have seen this happen some time in my life, but I can't recall exactly what the circumstances were. . . .

I predicted ten years ago that Arizona would eventually become the Custodial Service Area of the United States.* And eventually (by the year 2000) the United States would be the Custodial Service Depot of the world. Great sums of money are provided by taxpayers and the Federal Gov't for the maintenance of prisoners and prisons— I don't personally experience the benefit(s) of any of these allocated moneys. During the past ten years since Col. Sam Lewis was appointed director, the quantity of prison facilities has tripled while the quality of the prisoner's daily existence has vastly diminished. The amount, quality, and preparation of food is half what it was ten years ago. The situation with clothing is the same. We are issued two complete changes of clothing twice a year. But the quality of the fabric and the comic way it is sewn together sees it coming apart at the seams two months after it is issued new. Prisoners are regularly charged for damaged clothing, so most prisoners are wearing clothes hanging in tatters for three months while they wait for the next state issue.

Medical treatment has likewise caved in. Ten years ago there was a permanent medical staff on each unit. Granted, there were only four prison complexes in the whole state then. Now there are fourteen overcrowded complexes. The only medical doctors worse than prison doctors are Navy ship doctors. Everyone has heard that. Now, however, medical personnel are called in from "day labor pools." M.A.'s come in long enough to dispense medication(s) for which prisoners are charged $1.50 to $3 a pkg. Unless it's for a chronic disease. Medical doctors are actually P.A.'s (Physician Assistants). Most of them have been barred from any reputable hospital this side of the Mason-Dixon line.

All prisoners are required to pay a $50 Dedicated Discharge fee. This is the gate money prisoners will be given if they discharge their sentence DAY FOR DAY. If prisoners parole, then the $50 is transferred to the Parole Officer to help defray the cost of paperwork, etc.* If I die in prison, I will be buried in a pine box on Boot Hill with no gravestone. This costs $50??? Most of the prisons I've heard about give a prisoner at least $200 when leaving prison. Even with that $200, it seems ludicrous to think a man can get housing, food, clothing, transportation, etc., while he pounds the streets looking for work.

Back to our prisoner: $50 in his/her pocket. S/he has to get a place to live, to eat, clothes to wear, transportation to or looking for work. They're pissed off before they emerge from the System; now they don't even have money for a beer and a $2 piece of ass: Is there such a phenomenon as a $2 piece of ass anywhere any longer? I think they became extinct with high-

---

* Since Anders was incarcerated, the prison population in Arizona has exploded due to mandatory sentencing, enhanced sentencing, the ratcheting up of the criminal offense code, and the elimination of parole and all other forms of early release. If a crime was committed after January 1, 1994, the inmate will serve a minimum of 85% of the sentence imposed, regardless of his or her behavior in prison. Even if 100% of the sentence is served, an additional 15% will be spent on what is now called "community supervision" (formerly "parole"). There is no longer any incentive for positive behavior in prison, as everyone receives the same treatment.

* Although the prisoner does not receive the discharge fee if released on parole, it is not, as Anders may have heard, transferred to the parole officer. Rather, a separate fee, which can be as much as $30 a month, is levied by the Board of Executive Clemency (formerly known as the Parole Board) and paid by the parolee to the Department of Corrections. Failure to make payments can result in revocation of parole and return to prison.

button shoes. What's the logical next step of this exponential self-fulfilling prophecy? Right! Lash out! At what? "Ourselves" really, for in the final analysis "we" buy into the whole tragicomic debacle. This demon cannot flourish lest "we" breathe life into it.

I've been in this Oubliette for almost six months now. The Oubliette awaiting me at SMU-CB-8 is about the same. The misery of it is basically my own choice. Thomas Merton and John Henry "Cardinal" Newman discuss this throughout their writings. As do Solzhenitsyn and Dostoyevsky. Albert Camus says that if a man went to his backyard and for one hour looked at everything in it using his entire brain, he would have so many vivid memories that if someone imprisoned him in a hollow tree so that all he could do for the rest of his life would be look out the top of his hollow oubliette and see the clouds pass across the sky, he would never be bored. I have those kind of enriched memories. I could sit in the middle of the floor for hours—days perhaps—and never be bored. I tried this once and after about two hours the tail end gets very sore. I probably need some kind of tai chi meditations to overcome the physical discomfort. Actually, I have too much writing and eventually reading to do to squander my limited time through prolonged meditation(s). An hour of Kundalini meditations and stretching exercises from four to five A.M. is quite sufficient to see me through each day.

The guards just informed me that I am "on the list" for "chain-gang" duty beginning at 4 A.M., the 12th of June. Ten hours a day with a sledgehammer breaking granite rocks into smaller granite pebbles to be shipped to other "chain gangs" working in asphalt-processing plants for farm-to-market secondary road repair. This is one of many campaign re-election gimmicks of our Gov. Symington to gratify the Arizona voters' demand for their "pound of flesh." Ha! I never expected to really see or feel the sun more than three hours a week for the next four or five years. Now I'm going to feel it ten hours a day, five days a week. Ha! I'll probably get skin cancer and die before the end of the year. . . . All is flux. What is impossible today becomes possible tomorrow. I am in possession of the faculties necessary to deal with whatever may be my karma.

Your friend,
Dan

3 July 95

Hey Brother Mike,

Hope this letter finds you and your family all bright-eyed and bushy-tailed. I am fine. Layin' around this cell for four days after working every day for three weeks is a drag. I wake up automatically at 4 A.M. whether I have to go to work or not. Done that all my life. Soon's the light pales the horizon I'm up. Burnin' Daylight is what my Grandpa called it. In his book the only worse sin than blaspheming the Holy Spirit was Burnin' Daylight in bed. Slow-buckin' is what he really called it and it was sure to fetch a strap across your back for it.

It took nearly two years to complete my trial process.* I was on felony probation from a bar fight when I caught this beef. Arizona had just

---

* Here, and in the following passages, Anders is remembering his initiation into the prison system after his conviction in 1980.

passed their mandatory 25-years-to-life sentence for committing any felony while on felony probation or parole. But they gave me two 7-yr. Hannah-prior penalties* which made it 40-years-to-life. Seven days after I'm sentenced and my appeal process is put in motion I'm on the bus to Alhambra Diagnostic Center. This is where they "professionally" ascertain what level of custody a prisoner will be held at. I took a battery of Psych-profile tests geared to reveal how much of a barbarian I was, which ultimately had no effect upon where I was destined to spend the next decade or so. Alhambra was all dormitories, 30 men to a 15-man dorm. Some dorms were supposed to be for 2 men and housed 6 and, at times, 8 men. Everything done in the DOC had as much skimping on money as possible as its "A-functional format." Everything was such a transparent joke that most prisoners smiled all the time—even if they couldn't verbalize why they were smiling, they instinctively knew just the same. Years later they could lay claim to revelation—but it was just that smile comin' into clearer focus.**

I stayed cooped up at Alhambra for 6 months and then on the 3rd of Dec. 1980, I caught the chain-bus for Central Unit, the Walls*, Florence, AZ, known all over the U.S.A. as the bloodiest half-acre in the SW. The "Chain-Bus" is like something you'd see on the "Beverly Hillbillies," a 1950 vintage G.M.C. grammar-school bus. There's a lead escort vehicle in front of the bus and a tail-gunner vehicle behind. These escort vehicles are in no better shape than this Tortilla Flats Pentecostal God-mobile. These three vehicles' diminished capacity is a clear statement of the financial skimming that goes on throughout the prison system. During the nine years I spent at the Walls, various Depts. came under investigation by Federal Audit which failed to reveal any mismanagement behavior(s), because all the record books had been kept in very smudgy graphite lead when they didn't just flat out not tally at all.

Goldwater, Babbitt, DeConcini, Jane Hull—the list has no end. They've all had and have their front feet in the mixing bowl. They seem immune to admonishment or prosecution because they have things tangled up so bad that to haul them off to prison would bring about the sure collapse of the entire political machine. J. Edgar Hoover must have borrowed extensively from Arizona's Tome of Trickery. It's not the credentials you present, but the alleged scandal you insidiously hint at which lubricates the grist mill cops. Our current Director of Corrections is

---

* Hannah priors, which allowed prosecutors to treat multiple simultaneous convictions as prior offenses for the purpose of enhancing a sentence, no longer exist in Arizona, but many inmates who were sentenced under their provision are still in prison.

** All adult male prisoners in Arizona begin their confinement at the Alhambra Reception Center. There, a literacy test is administered, as well as a battery of psychological tests. The latter, however, are not used for diagnosing or assessing treatment programs. Instead, the DOC is simply interested to see whether the prisoner (1) is an escape risk; (2) is a homosexual who will need special protection; (3) demonstrates violent tendences; or (4) belongs to some other category of potential "victims" who will need protection. Many beatings and prisoner rapes take

place at this facility because prisoners of all custody levels and classifications are mixed together in largely unsupervised cells.

* The Central Unit at the Arizona State Prison–Florence is often called "the Walls" by both prisoners and staff, due to the thirty-foot, solid-concrete walls that surround it.

a glaring example of the benefit(s) of having the right dirt on the right people. He retired from the [position of] Provost Marshal in the Army and then held the office of Director of the Arizona State Police for 20 years before being appointed Director of Corrections.* In this position he earns a greater salary than Gov. Fe-Fe Slimeington**. Col. Sam Lewis is the highest-paid Director of Corrections in the United States.† It becomes quite apparent that there is something rotten in Denmark...

I think I'll end this here and wait for a reply.

Respectfully,
Your friend
Dan

7 July 95

Hey Brother Mike!

I'm happy that you are so pleased with the way I describe events. I've never had any formal education higher than the 8th grade and later getting my GED through the prison academic program. I've done a tremendous amount of reading—which has been tremendously varied—ranging from Louis L'Amour to Bertrand Russell and John Henry Cardinal Newman and Thomas Merton to Kahlil Gibran and T. S. Eliot. I've studied math and grammar and Rhetoric and Philology on my own and asked the right questions when I found myself out to sea on a lot of issues. Leo Buscaglia and Rollo May kind of knitted everything together. Somehow all that sounds very ostentatious—but I don't mean it to.

Your friend,
Dan

P.S. Thank you for your explanation of *veni, vidi, vici.*

21 July 95

Dear Mike,

On the evening of the 16th, ten of us 5-5 high-security-risk convicts were placed in separate holding cages in the basement of CDU. This was at 10 P.M. I managed to race off a note to you just before they moved me from my cell. We stayed in these holding cages until 4 A.M., when we were placed in neck, wrist, belly, and ankle chains and handcuff restraints. We then shuffle-stumble-walked up two flights of steps, out the front gate of CDU, and across the street to Complex Intake and Outgoing Processing where we were placed in other holding cages with one hand free so we could eat a bag-lunch breakfast of bologna sandwiches and a carton of milk. We were given a "piss call" and then re-chained in our cages to await the chain bus due to arrive between 7 A.M. and noon. It got there at 12:45 P.M.

We finally arrived in Florence.* This is nearly the heart of the Sonoran Desert. Wild camels abandoned by the cavalry roam in herds.

---

* Lewis was actually Deputy Director of the Arizona Department of Public Safety, a division of the Arizona State Police. Lewis retired from his post as Director of Corrections in December 1995.

** Governor J. Fife Symington.

† Lewis's annual salary in the early 1990s was $99,000, significantly higher than the $69,000 salary of the Director of the Department of Corrections in California, the state that housed the highest number of inmates.

* In 1995, Anders was transferred from the Arizona State Prison Complex–Tucson back to the Arizona State Prison Complex–Florence, where he had begun his sentence in 1980 at the Walls.

Mexican wolves, mountain lions, coyotes, and packs of wild dogs range wide in search of the wild goats and wilder herds of cattle. In the middle of all this sits the Walls, ancient now, surrounded by giant modern prison complexes like CB-8, 9, 10 (the Eyman Complex) about four miles SW on Butte Rd. where we're headed now.

We arrive at CB-8 between 3 and 4 P.M. and we're placed in separate holding cages with all body chains still on. The temperature has to be around 115 degrees. The chains absorb the air heat and lie like heated steel wherever they touch the skin. We are processed into CB-8 one person at a time. Each process takes about fifteen minutes. The guards complain about the chains burning their fingers as they unlock them. Each prisoner is strip-searched and must submit to a body cavity search. This is all videotaped now because it was not uncommon for younger prisoners to be sodomized when they thought it was two rubber-gloved fingers probing them. Several guards were brought up on charges of sodomy and were dismissed from the DOC. "Sweetheart" deals were made between the DOC and the victims to keep this out of the papers.

I get my picture taken and have to initial (D.L.A.) the (yes or no) answers I give to about sixty questions I've been asked. Then I'm given a fishnet sack with my bedding, shower gear, and cosmetics. This I have to carry with my hands handcuffed behind my back. We descend a hall through eight electric doors and around many turns until we reach 2B4W2B29, which means 2Block, 4Wing Cell 2B29. There are eight cells on my pod. All solid-steel electric doors. 2B29 whispers open and I step into a large steel room which looks like something out of a Star Trek film. The door chitters shut behind me and the guard opens the "food-slot" which is at waist level. I back up and place my hands through the slot to have the handcuffs removed.

It took five days before my property was brought to me. Well, four days actually. I received it Friday morning about 9 A.M. They took the nice pocket watch a friend sent to me for my birthday a couple years ago. Now I have to guess at the time . . . part of the sensory-deprivation process, I guess? Everything is reversed in this unit. The doors open to the left instead of the right. The hot-water buttons are on the right side instead of the left. Every form or document is signed on the left instead of the right. It is really screwball.

It'll take me a couple weeks to orient my thinking and then I'll write more of our Memoirs du Hades.

Your friend,
Dan

30 July 95

Dear Mike,

Today is my birthday. To celebrate it under these extreme circumstances seems tragicomic. I would never claim "a corner on misery" though. The myriad "free people" experiencing gut-rending spiritual and physical misery and privation(s) seal my lips against over-much complaint.

I went through a terrible two years after the death of my wife (from cancer) in 1978. I'm sure this laid much of the mental groundwork leading to my current confinement, but I can't lay everything at that doorstep and still be completely honest. What were the words of an ancient Daniel about "being weighed in the balance and found wanting"?

> Your friend,
> Dan

17 Aug 95, 16:00 hrs

Hey Mike,

"Bas no an Bua." Is that the Gaelic equivalent of "Patience and long suffering"? Well, I believe the amount of patience I am personally able to exercise would put Job on Valium. They moved me today. Never say things can't get any worse. They have!

My new location is 8 4026: the lower level I've mentioned before.

The dude who was in here before me got hold of enough paper, clothes, etc., to start a blaze in the middle of his mattress. By the time the A-Team screws gassed him and rushed in on him, most of his hair had burned off along with some of his skin. I've been scrubbing this place since early this morning. The walls and floor were a patchwork of hair, skin, blood, excrement, smoke-soot, and pepper-gas residue. I've got it relatively clean now. The stench of burned hair, skin, plastic mattress and cover, felted blankets, sheets, foam-rubber pillow, toilet paper, mace, pepper gas, cordite from the rubber bouncing Bettys they throw into the cell after the gas grenades guarantee that the belligerent resident remains hors de combat is overpowering. I can't tell if this letter carries this horrible stench or not. My olfactory capacity is trashed.

So now I don't even have gloved human hands delivering meals, mail, and toilet paper. Everything arrives at the food-slot on a robotized entity—I don't have the foggiest what the actual shape is. Now the shower pressure-seals around the outer cell door frame and locks on by several dead bolts which insert in different directions. Only then do the inner and outer doors of the cell open and I step into the shower. The water sprays from several different outlets at the same time, remaining on for 5 minutes at about 100 degrees. I get one 5-minute shower Tuesday to Thursday and Sunday. It was just my "good fortune" that the man before me burnt up everything on Thursday. Otherwise I would have to wait until Sunday. That would have really been unpleasant. So perhaps Dr. Pangloss is right about the best of all possible worlds . . .

They haven't put a mattress in this cell yet. I'll be very surprised if I get one before tomorrow, so I'll be trying to sleep with just my blanket covering the steel plate. In spite of everything I remain in good spirits.

> Hangin' in there,
> Dan

23 Aug 95

Back again,

Monsoons dropped on us early yesterday. The humidity was so high I could watch it bead up on the steel walls descending into puddles on the floor. Giant cockroaches love these little "roach lagoons" to splash in and out of at night. Anyhow, everything was soaking wet and impossible to write so I postponed 'til today.

I'm finally recovering from the shock of having been transferred into this disaster zone in the first place. No sense in going into that again. Just talking about it is a downer.

"Who's The Boss" was just on. That and

"The Nanny" and "Home Improvement" and "Married With Children" are my favorite sitcoms. Anything on PBS and the Science Channel and National Geographic on TBS. We have a closed cable circuit Ch.2 which shows a lot of the latest VCR movies: "Jurassic Park," "Schindler's List," "Forrest Gump," "The Shawshank Redemption" (be sure to see SR and "Murder in the First." Very honest commentaries on prison life and non-life).

5 Sep 95, 4B36

Hey Mike!

No—your eyes are not playing tricks on you. They just moved me again. Same level—on the west side and hottest side of the facility. They ripped the wires off the back of my TV during the move over here. No way I can prove it wasn't like that all the time, so I can really do it like Thomas Merton now.

Supper just arrived via "Meals on Wheels." No mail. Mail will probably take a week to catch up with me—even though I only moved 500 yards. One positive is—the guy who lived here before was a vegetarian—the meal I had tonight was almost like the old Sikh diets we used to get at the Walls years ago. I'll probably get this veg. diet for the next few days until the guy who was here notifies the kitchen of his new location. Suits me! For every locked door there is an open window.

I am fine. Being able to instantly adapt is one of the main keys to doing time.

Hang in there,
Dan

7 Sep 95

Good morning, Mike!

Let's get back to the Walls.*

The "Tortilla Flats" prison chain bus which brought us convicted felons to the Walls from Alhambra Diagnostic Center in Phoenix pulls up to a huge thirty-foot, steel-barred electric gate. When all the chains are removed from all of us (15 inmates), we are left in a small hot cage that reeks with the fear-stench of anxiety and uncertainty. We've been here about forty-five minutes when the slot opens and we're told to remove our tangerine-colored jumpsuits and put them out the trap. A fishnet bag full of boxer shorts of various sizes is pushed into us. We find shorts which sort of fit. Soon the door opens and we are instructed to move to the next room where we are to receive our prison-blues, boots, socks, T-shirts, and so on. Then we are asked if any of us want to be placed in PC (Protective Custody). There are three youngsters who are part of our group. None of them chooses to spend his whole bit with child molesters, rapists, snitches—the kind of cretin that cannot make it on the main yard.

CB-2 (the Deuce, PC) is the tallest cellblock in the Walls. All the windows have been broken out and never replaced. Hundreds of pigeons roost in the exposed rafters along with sparrows and barn owls. Rattlesnakes are everywhere, as are huge wild barn cats which prowl and feed on everything else. CB-2 is particularly overpopulated with creepy-crawlies because the guards don't like the kind of people hiding out there any more than the rest of the General

---

* Anders is continuing his "flashback" to 1980.

Population (GP) does. It's one thing to be thrown into the "Hole"—there's a grudging respect for that prisoner. It's something entirely different and disgusting to volunteer to spend years in an isolation equal to or worse than the punishment Hole which possesses no dignity nor warrants any respect from fellow kept or keeper.

To get into the PC block you have to walk up a long flight of cement steps to a portico with very Doric-like columns. In fact the front of PC looks like an old Greco-Roman Senate facade. The rest of the building looks like some derelict tenement one might see in some large city slum. It boggles the mind to realize that over four hundred people choose a living death there, bereft of any dignity, to a swifter death on the yard accompanied by a surly nod of admiration. —And what has to be the condition of the mentality and moral fabric of these people when they're released eventually and directly from PC? For years they've seethed and smoldered in their self-imposed hells—hating themselves, hating "them others," plotting the intoxicating revenge they will wreak upon any surrogate tormentors happenstance places in their path. Similar vicarious vengeance is plotted by many in isolations akin to mine—if one chooses to preoccupy one's every thought with plotting the bittersweet drought of vengeance. Myself: I get more satisfaction keeping my thinking positive and productive. The glass half full seems more pleasurable than the glass half empty. It's all a mind game—but one possesses greater existential substance than the other. Albert Camus would be very proud of me.

I cannot fathom the reasoning of a prison system keeping a man isolated with nothing but vengeful and vindictive fantasies to sustain him for years and then one day releasing him upon an unsuspecting community. No follow-up program(s), no reinforcement whatsoever . . . That equation reverberates with a macabre Orwellian knell . . . By the year 2000 the population of American prisoners will be greater than the population of New York City.* That sounds like something one would read in a Sci- Fi penny dreadful.

11 Sep 95

Hi again!

The law and lending libraries [at the Walls] were very inadequately supplied or staffed. The law library was constantly involved in lawsuits by inmates unable to adequately appeal their cases due to the pernicious conditions of the law library inventories. This outrageous circumstance was finally addressed and ordered repaired by the Supreme Court in the late '80s at a cost of millions of dollars to guarantee exhaustive litigative access to every convict on every prison unit. This chapped the Legislature's bouffant derriere and continues to chap it today.

---

* Although this figure is exaggerated, the population of Americans incarcerated on any given day would qualify as the sixth largest city in the country and is equal to the total combined populations of Seattle, Cleveland, and Denver. The number of people admitted to a locked facility in a single year surpasses the combined populations of Alaska, Delaware, Hawaii, Idaho, Maine, Montana, Nevada, New Hampshire, North Dakota, Rhode Island, South Dakota, Vermont, and Wyoming. Enough people are locked up every two days to fill the New Orleans Superdome to capacity. More than six hundred new prisons have been constructed in the United States since 1980, at a cost of tens of billions of dollars. And the National Council on Crime and Delinquency has projected that the prison population will rise to 7.5 million as several "get tough" measures are implemented on a national scale.

The main reason the legal library inadequacy was maintained so long was because inmates were virtually forced to buy legal representation(s) from shylock legal firms which were no more than the paid minions of the DOC. (The perpetual rule was: money talks and bullshit walks.) . . .

The chapel serviced several different denominations as disparate as Sikhs and Islam, Mormons and Jehovah's Witnesses, Methodists and Baptists. The only common thread amongst them being a rabid suspicion and condemnation of all the others. Truly, there were fewer plots and intrigues hatched in Borgia-nest. Each denomination except for the Sikhs and Islam endlessly criticized and defamed all the others. No wonder de Sade and Voltaire and many other esteemed authors castigated and ridiculed the Church so vehemently.

Damn! I am hungry. Lunch should be here soon. One blessing of not having a TV now is I can't watch Graham Kerr and Julia Child and torture myself. . . .

24 Sep 95

Dear Mike,

Time passes quite quickly for me in spite of this isolation. So let's get on with our Gulag Diary.

Unless a prisoner has relatives or friends who are willing to call the DOC's main office in Phoenix and insist that a prisoner receive some genuine treatment, the average prisoner will receive aspirins, Tylenol, or placebos from the pharmacy while the DOC submits statements to the Feds that it has spent enormous amounts of money on medicine and medical attentions. This tragic situation exists in every prison across the country and around the world. "We" just have to be very careful to stay healthy or get a terminal disease which carries us away quickly.

The Medical Assistants instantly describe each and every inmate as chronic malingerers and to a great extent this is true. In order to escape some work assignment or cell restriction (Disciplinary Court Sanctions), at least 100 inmates out of a population of 1,000 are willing to stand in the blazing sun for upwards of 6 hours every day in the Medical Unit line. Contrary to media misinformation, however, the majority of inmates much prefer to work and send some of their money, usually $20-$40 a month, home to their families to help out with expenses, or put it in a bank account so they'll have money to live on when they are released. The State Legislature has even made it illegal for banks to receive deposits directly from prisoners, alleging that all moneys accumulated by prisoners are ill-gotten lucre acquired from speculations in the vast prison drug enterprise.

There is a brisk drug-trade activity in all prisons but it represents only a small percentage of hard-core drug users. I would venture that perhaps 2% of this prison's 18,000-inmate population* regularly use heroin or amphetamines and 30% use marijuana four weekends a month. The remaining 68% choose not to risk being caught by the many random urinanalyses the prison administers each month. The penalties for a "dirty" test are very severe. . . .

[On arrival at the Walls] we stand in front of the Yard Office and shortly a sergeant comes out

---

* The inmate population as of January 1997 had risen to 22,645.

and gives us all our block assignments. I'm assigned to CB-3G7 which is on the west side of the building right next to the shower. To reach my cell I must climb a dark winding steel stairway. In between landings are blind spots where the guards cannot or choose not to see the many stabbings and beatings and sexual assignations which occur several times a week.

My first thought is that I have entered the maw of Dante's dreadful underworld (more tomorrow).

Your friend,
Dan

30 Sep 95

Dear Mike,

There is hardly anyone in the Cell Block when I arrive because it is about 10 A.M., and everyone is either working or on the Athletic Field. During these early years of the 1980s, if an inmate did not have a regular work assignment, he could stay on the Athletic Field from 7:30 A.M. until the 3:00 P.M. count, go to supper at 4:00 P.M. and then return to the field and stay there until 8:00 P.M., when the yard closed for evening count and showers. The few inmates who chose not to go to the Athletic Field, who seldom came out of their cells, were considered highly suspect by most other inmates in General Population. A small percentage of these inmates who stayed in their cells all the time were righteous loners, and GP gave them plenty of room and respect. But the rest were inmates who were trying to keep something in their past—or the crime which brought them to prison—a secret (child molesters, people who testified against a crime partner, police informants, or serial rapists). All these people usually went to the Deuce (PC) immediately upon reaching the Walls.

My home for the next who knows how many months or years: the door or entire front of the cell is bars like you've seen in Alcatraz or movies or tours. The tier-porter stops in front of my cell and introduces himself. He is a huge Viking-looking man, bald-headed with a huge red-gray beard and drooping mustache, both of which seem to reach his waist. He is covered with scars and his entire upper body, arms, and neck are solid blue with prison tattoos and his quintessential Viking-ogre aspect is sealed by a missing eye.

Gotta go,
Dan

3 Oct 95

This porter who has stopped at my cell to ask if I need any cleaning supplies or anything tells me to always knock my shoes and boots together in the morning to make sure there are no scorpions, black widow spiders, centipedes, or millipedes that might have crawled into them during the night. He cautioned me to always shake my sheets, blankets, and all clothing before I get into bed or put on any clothing. He gave me a section of newspaper and told me to roll a couple pages into a long funnel, light the end of it, and move the flame along all seams and corners under the bed frame and around the toilet and table. I did this and many spiders and baby scorpions fell scorched to the floor. He brought me a spray bottle of bleach and one of disinfectant liquid soap. A broom and a sponge. I cleaned the cell thoroughly and promised the porter that as soon as I got a job I would get him something from the commissary. He asked for "a deck of tight-laces" which is prison argot for "a pack of free-world cigarettes."

During the several hours it takes me to get my cell scrubbed, my bed made, my half-dozen belongings stored on my 6"x 5" shelf at least twenty-five inmates stop by—mostly being nosy.

Let me define a "convict" as opposed to an "inmate." It is very important that you be able to distinguish one from another. A convict wouldn't ask the pigs to put him out if he was on fire—whereas an inmate whines about everything. A convict never hesitates, confronted with some decision—for he knows that if you hesitate, you're doomed. While opportunity races by the inmate as he hesitates while testing the water, the convict sits in Solitary Confinement and never says a word to the pigs—while the inmate scratches at the door each time footfalls sound on the tier. I mention the distinction because when you write you must provide for these precise attitudinal and behavioral lines of demarcation. If you write treating both inmate and convict without distinction, your writing will not be favorably received by prisoners around the world. It requires about two years before these qualitative extremities become instinctually recognizable by the average new prisoner. Sort of like "card sense." Only this is "con sense." Some people have it naturally—an innate sonar. Many others only develop this "convictness" after sustaining many painful contusions and lacerations about the head and shoulders—like me . . .

Garden-variety prisoners like myself must exercise grave caution on the yard, on the Athletic Field, and especially in the Mess Hall—where I am headed right now. I've been advised to stuff magazines all around my back and sides and stomach, held in place by my belt and pants and concealed under my T-shirt and blue cambric shirt; these magazines are our body-armor and everyone who doesn't have suicidal longings wears it wherever they go. I don't have any magazines at the moment, so I make the remainder of my torch-paper serve as best as possible.

The line I'm standing in is about 200 inmates long and moves forward and into the double brown-steel doors of the Dining Room very slowly. It is easily apparent that I am a "Fish" because all my clothes are new. Everyone is in a conversation with someone except me. No one is talking to me or even paying any special attention to me in spite of my bald head. My isolation is finally interrupted by the porter from my tier who gets in line behind me. He tells me that when we get our trays we will sit toward the back of the Dining Room on the left. The Aryan Brotherhood more or less claims that section for the white convicts they don't have a beef with.

To the right of the dining hall from the back and along the wall for about 2/3 of the dining hall belongs to the Mejicano Familia. The last third of the right wall and across the front of the dining hall belongs to the Mau Maus. Down the very center of the dining hall is where the convicts and inmates who aren't involved in any gang membership sit. On the back left along the railing that divides the eating area from the line of inmates waiting to be served at the steam table are four Indians. No one ever, even accidentally, trespasses on the denizen of any gang without invitation or rarely given permission. 90% of all stabbings, fatal or otherwise, will occur in these tightly packed dining areas. Overhead near a 30' ceiling is a gun tower armed with tear gas and automatic rifles. (More tomorrow.)

Hang in there Bro,
Dan

5 Oct 95

Dear Mike,

We finish our meal and take our trays to the dishwasher room (or Clipper Room, as it's called) window where dirty trays, silverware, and glasses are handed in to three inmates who scrape uneaten food into 50-gallon plastic barrels with handles which will be emptied into the hog-slops tank trailer which remains outside the kitchen until full. Then it is pulled and pushed by several inmates to Gate 3 where it is hooked onto a tractor and handed through the Industrial Yard to Gate 2. There a guard opens all six of the round portholes and stabs into the slops through each porthole to make sure there are no convicts hiding in the slops for the purpose of trying to escape. This has been tried before without success because a general population 3 P.M. security count is done before the slops wagon leaves the Industrial Yard.

If it's determined that an inmate is unaccounted for, the entire prison is placed on Lock-down until the prisoner is determined to be hiding in the prison somewhere, escaped, or dead. Any place a prisoner can secret himself or be left dead is checked. The slops tank isn't checked until last. Usually not till the next morning. This is done deliberately so that if someone is hiding in these rancid maggot-infested slops they will rue their foolish decision.

After 12 to 16 hours of being submerged up to his nose in this evil seething brew this prisoner will think twice and thrice before hiding in the slops-tank trailer to effect an escape. The skin swells and becomes infected where it ruptures in numerous places and for weeks afterwards this prisoner will still emit that miasmic vapor of odure.

I return to my cell. The omni-gray closeness is amplified and exacerbated by a subverbal sentience of isolation and despair. . . .

I wind up being "activity deadlocked" for sixty days. I was in a couple fist fights over people cutting the chow line. Seems like there's always a dozen or so people who refuse to wait in line like everyone else. This chaps my ass more than any other prison aggravation. I'm the first one to step up and "check" one of these ziplock idiots. My size and appearance are usually enough to intimidate most of these fools to the back of the line—but there's always a couple you have to mix it up with. These confrontations don't last long because I learned my fighting skills on the waterfront in Houston during the years I worked there as a roustabout and later when I worked on the tow boats between Arkansas Pass, TX, and Nawlins (New Orleans). Roustabout and roughneck honky-tonks along the Gulf Coast are some of the roughest in the world, Macao and Singapore included.

Well, I guess that's about all the energy I have for this segment. Next Friday is the 13th. I wouldn't even get out of bed on that day. Everything terrible that ever happened to me happened on Friday the 13th.

Later on Bro,
Dan

MICHAEL HOFMANN

ERDING, ENDSTATION

And the walk the other way, right out of the front door,
hat and wife and dark glasses—never now wifeless—
to shop in *Kaiser's* general store in the *lange Zeile*

(*calle, ulice*) with the battered, supposedly
indestructible maroon and yellow nylon shoulder bag,
a kind of compendious ribbon, a hand-held trawl net...

Shopping, like most everything, the opposite
of what it was once, economies now, bargains,
a rough-and-ready diet for high blood and diabetes,

but he took the same pleasure in it, bruised bananas,
knocked down but *tadellos* inside, weathered bread,
and still the old ungovernable flair for luxury,

Weißt du noch, Krimsekt. Always happy shopping,
something in prospect, something to talk about,
a rest from the silvered goldfish bowl of consciousness...

The walk through the deserted postmodern forum
of cobbles and fountains, past the credit-happy bank,
the jink through the local newspaper office,

the library after a week taking down its display of novels
and its card *In Gedenken an Gert Hofmann* †,
the railway signals still up with the line long gone.

NIGHT TRAIN

In the half-compartment
set aside for the handicapped
I crossed my feet on the battered
fire-extinguisher,

the grandfather, maybe,
of my shaken can of County
foaming at the widget,

and sat remembering the dowdily
glaring train back from Guildford,
feeling parched and let down
after our reading,

the series of benighted stops
where no one got on
—much less got off—

at one of which, at least,
I put it to you, not joking,
though you weren't to know that then,
that we might elope together

somewhere in Wild West Surrey,
wo sich die Füchse gute Nacht sagen
before we could reach

Suburbiton and Esher
Welcomes Careful Drivers,
the sporting meccas
of Wimbledon and Twickers,

the windows of the jolly poly
where you worked behind the bar
in a thriftstore bronze dress

and short back and sides,
chronically undecided
between Venus pandemos
and Jeanne d'Arc.

MICHAEL HOFMANN

BEFORE SHE MET ME *(after Ovid)*

There was the narcoleptic giant,
the absentee clotheshorse,
the petrified virgin and the flaky sadist.
Then she met me.

FUCKING

"ma chérie dort"

A zero sum game, our extravagant happiness,
matched or cancelled
by the equal and opposite unhappiness of others,

but who was counting as you came walking from your car,
not off the bus,
early for once, almost violent in your severity,

both of us low on our last, stolen day for a month,
uncertain, rather formal,
a day of headaches, peaches, and carbonated water

by the stone pond whose ice you smashed as a girl . . .
or how we wound up
jubilant, a seesaw at rest, not one foot on the floor.

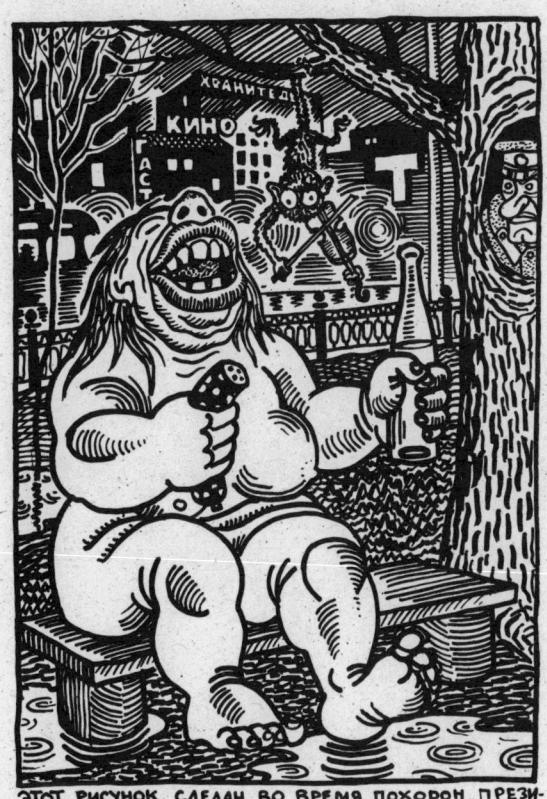

THE WAY IT WAS
VLADIMIR KOVENATSKY

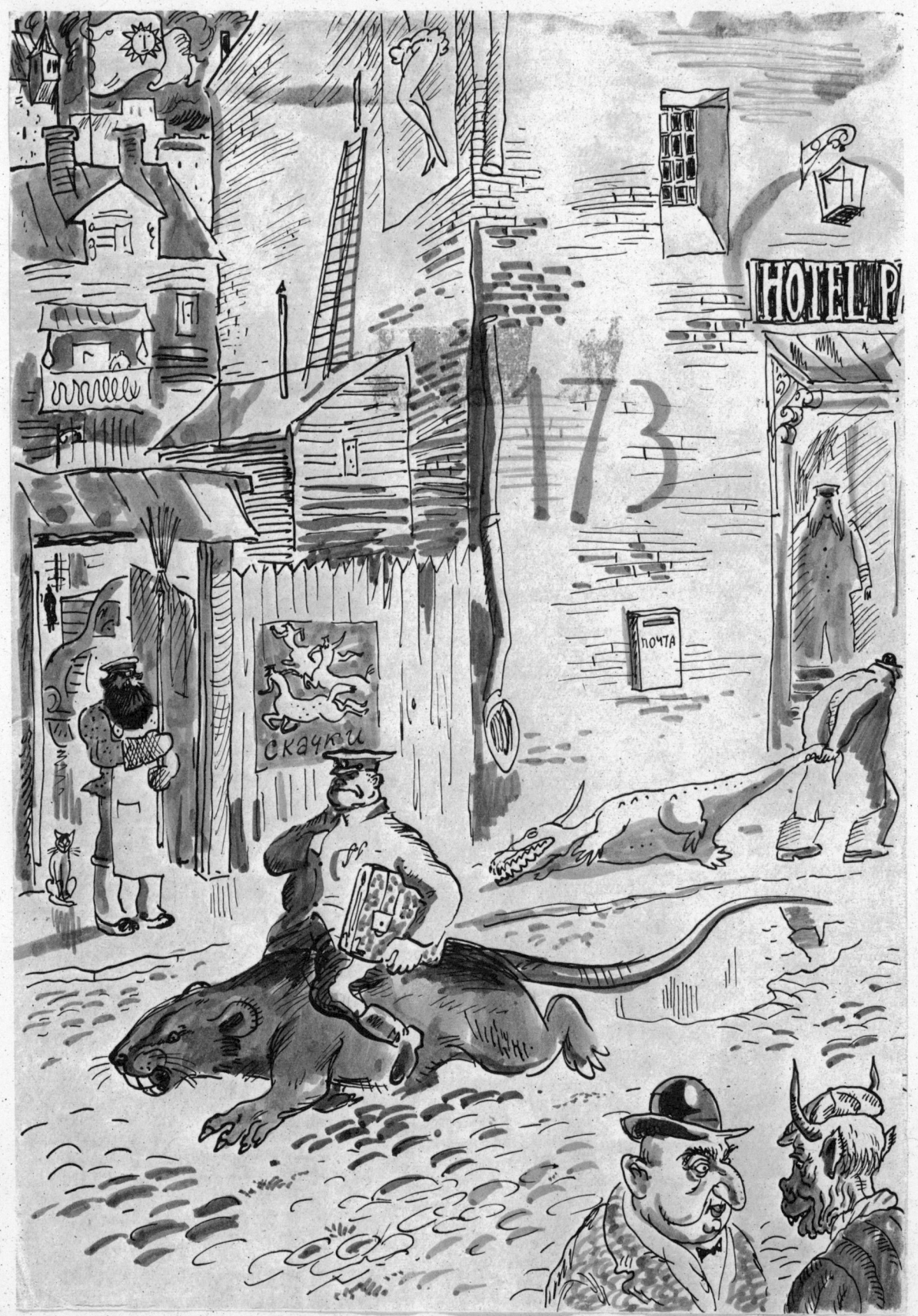

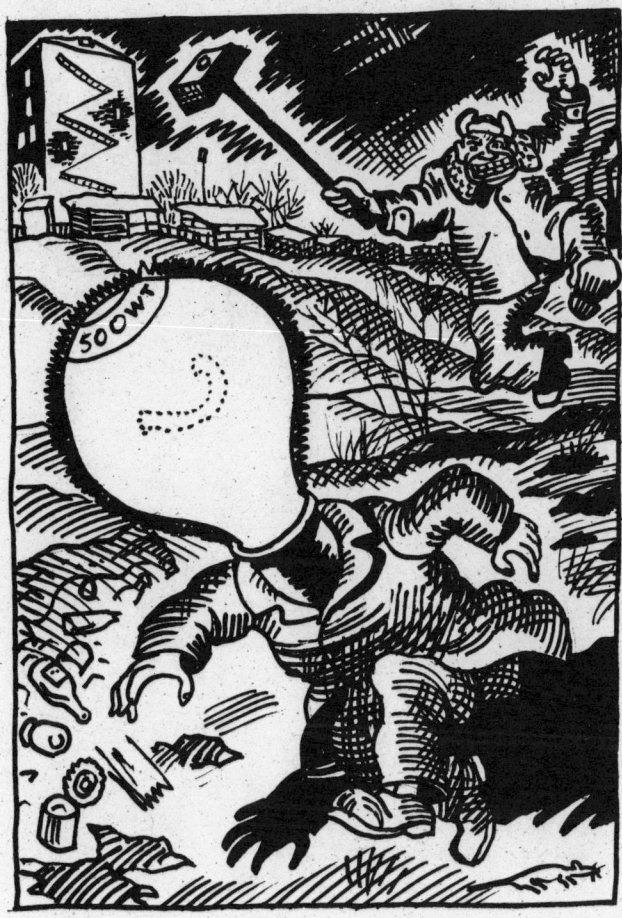 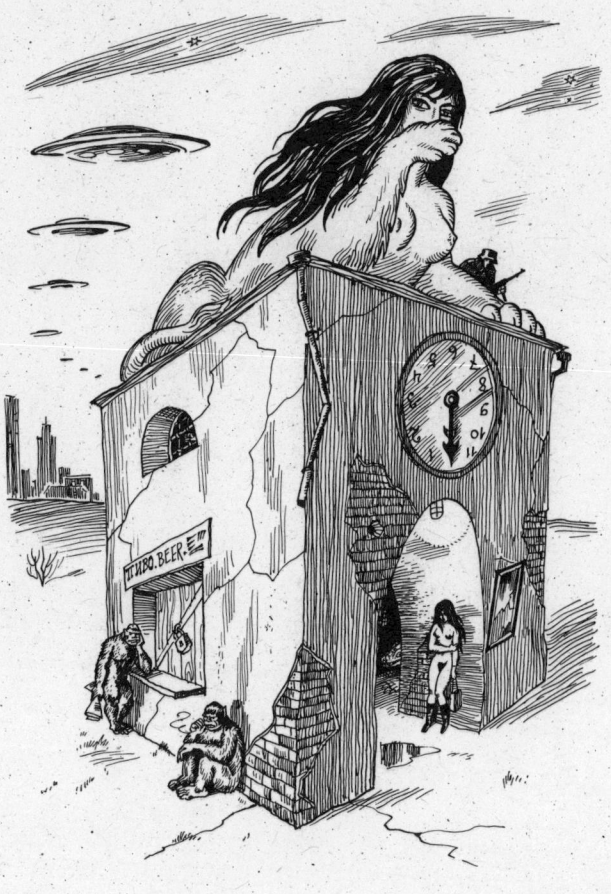

PAGE 105
This Drawing was Made at the Time of the Burial of U.S. President John F. Kennedy. Rest in Peace, 1963.

PAGE 106
Comrade Manager, from the series *The City,* 1968–72.

ABOVE
left *Untitled,* 1962.
right *Untitled,* 1961.

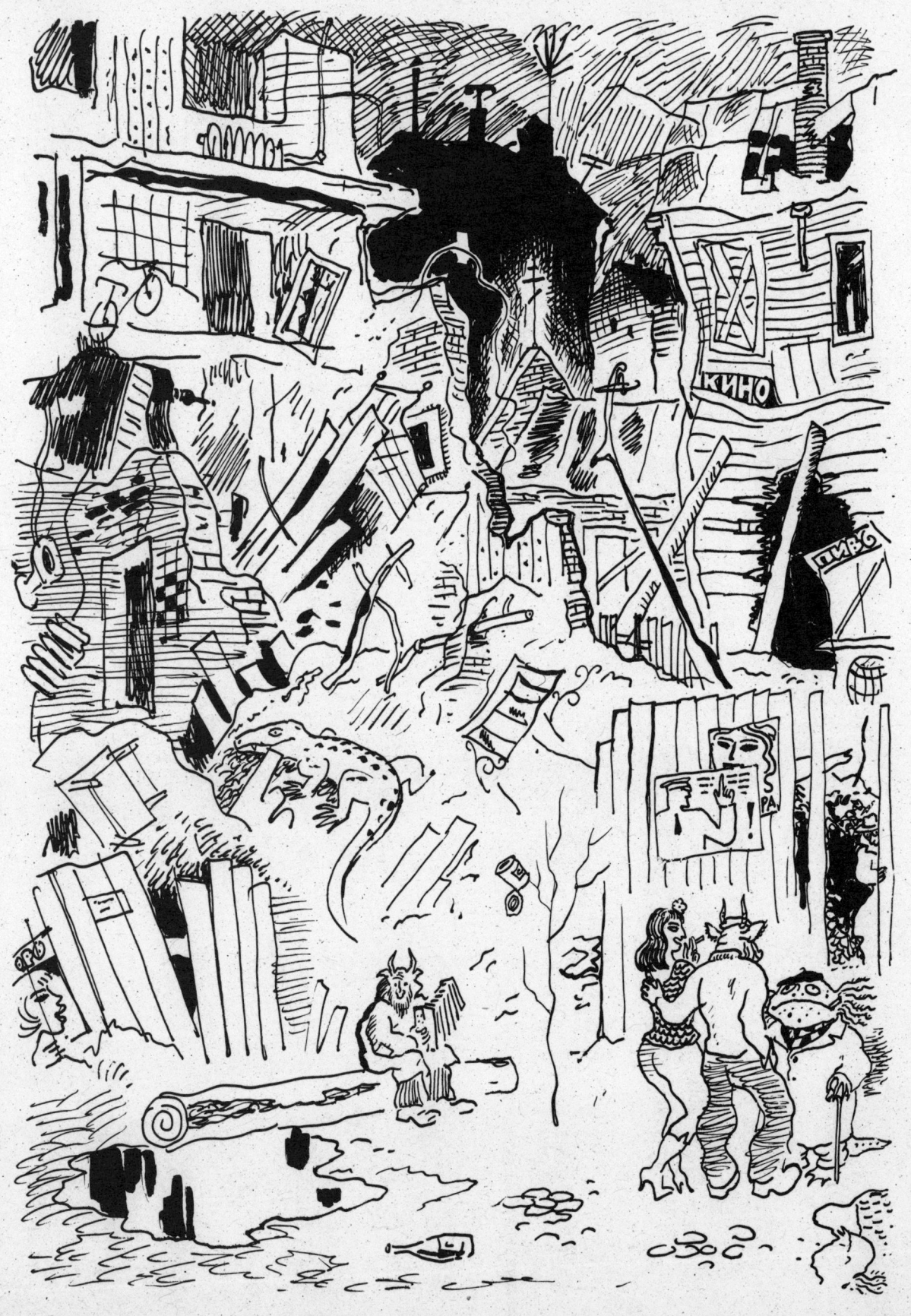

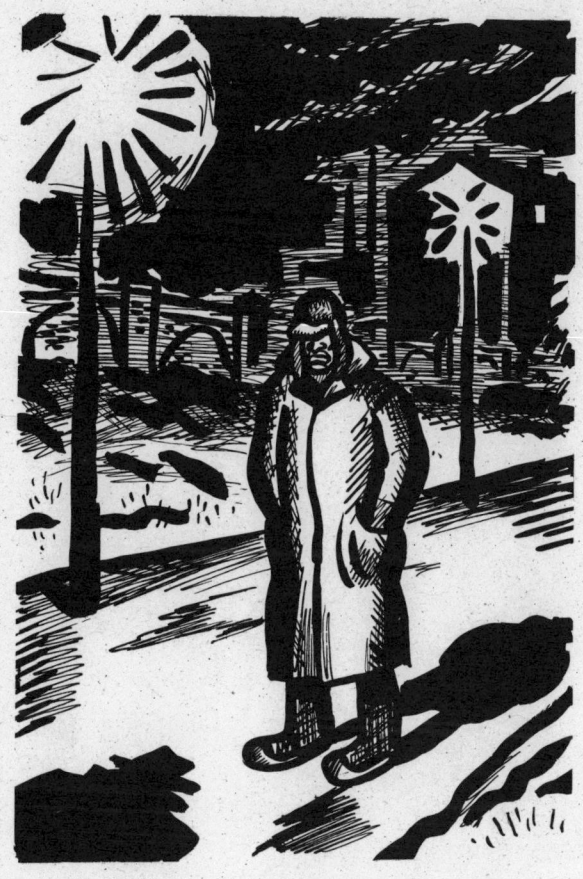
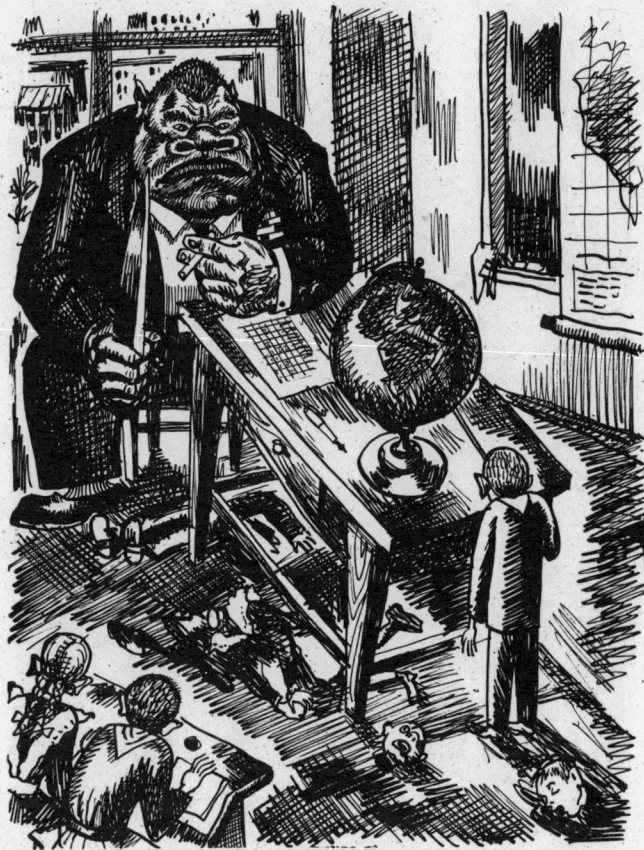

PAGE 108
Untitled, from the series *The City*, 1968–72.

ABOVE
left *Do You Have a Watch? (An Authentic Reminiscence of My Youth)*, 1960.

right *My Geography Teacher*, 1960.

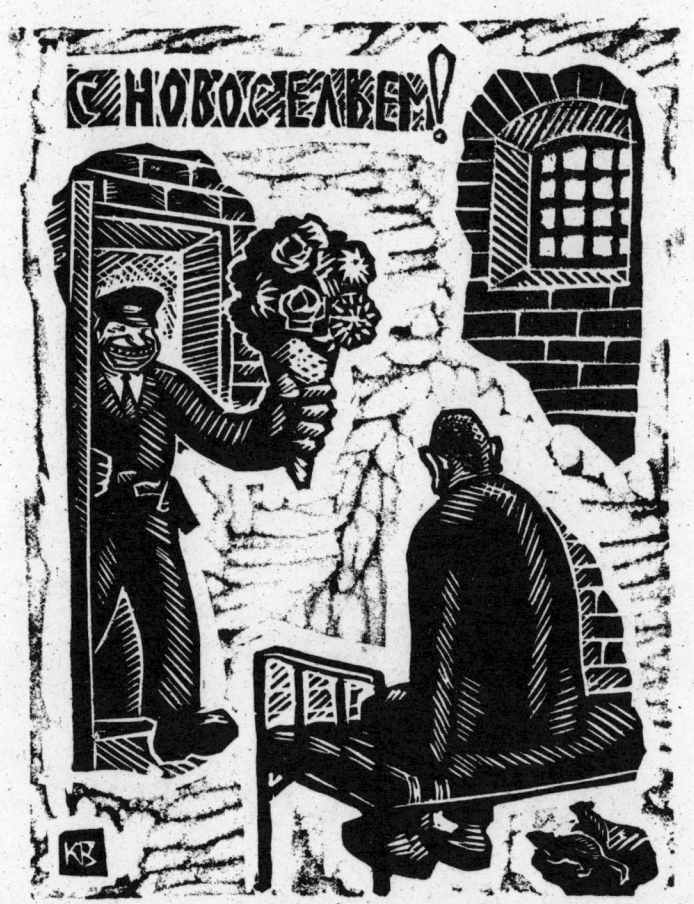
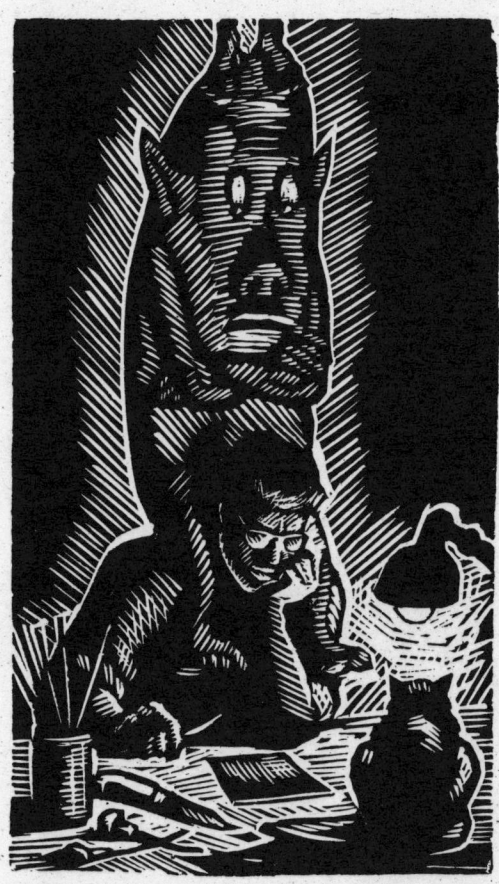

ABOVE
left **Happy House-warming!**, 1960.

right *Untitled*, 1960–61.

PAGE 111
Untitled, 1959.

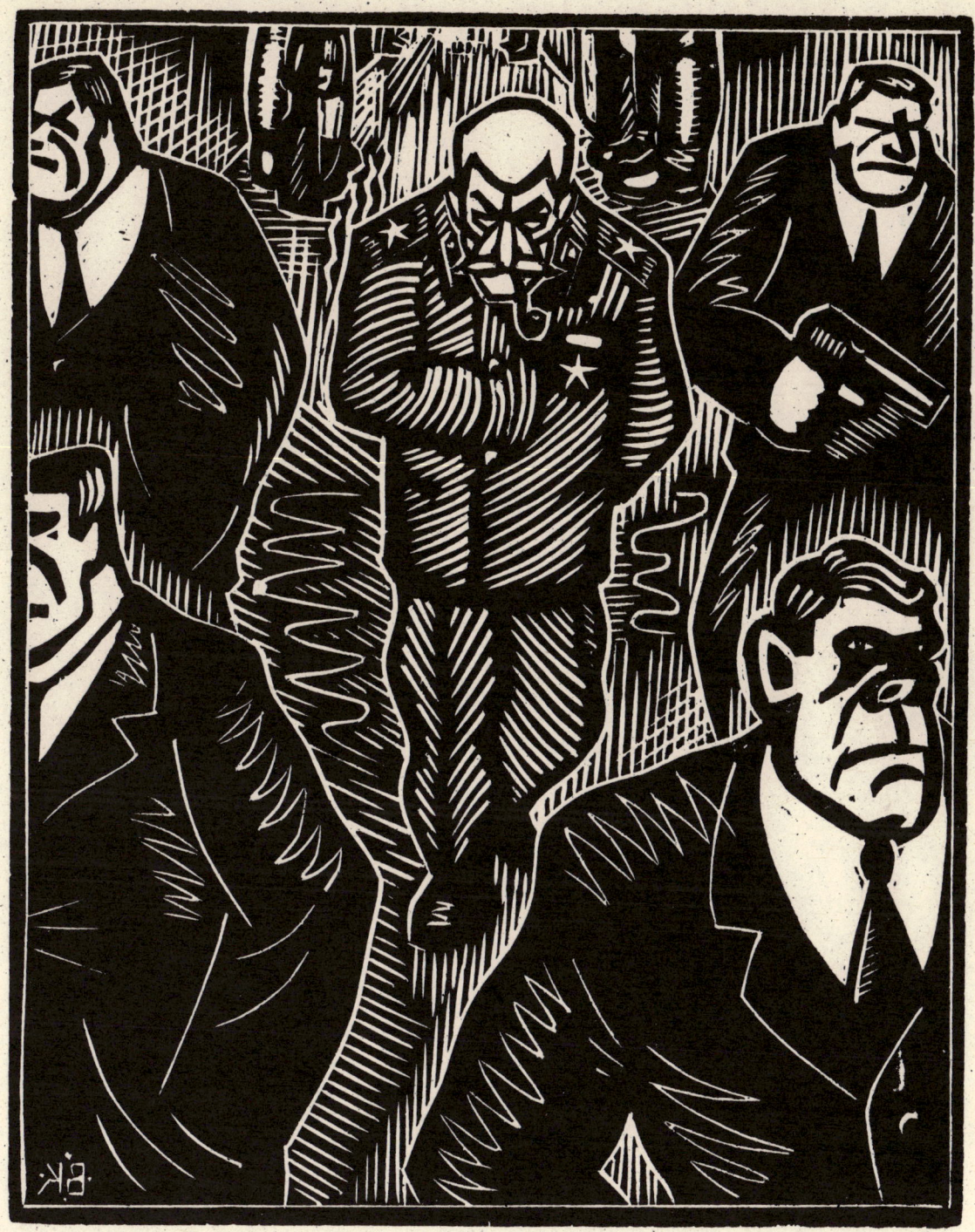

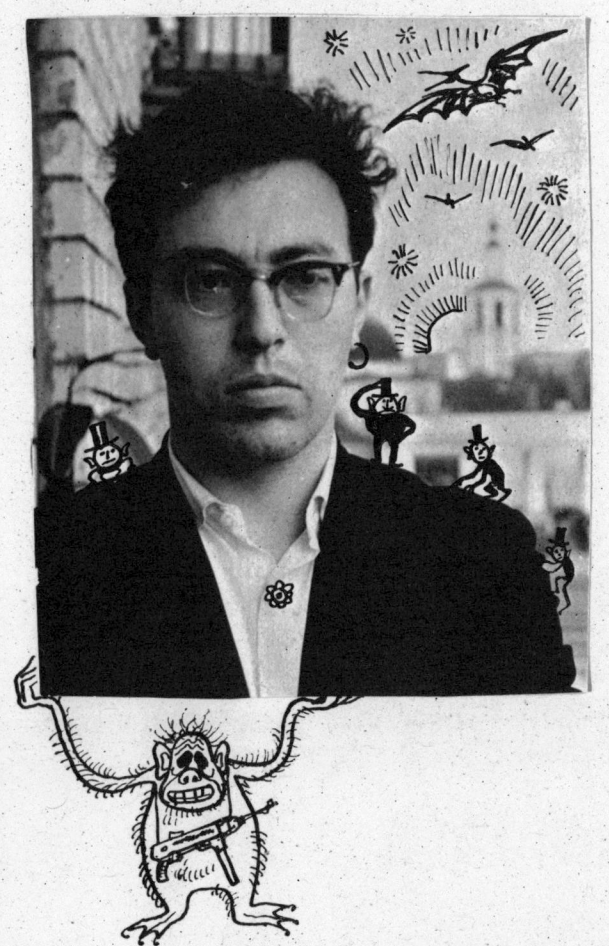
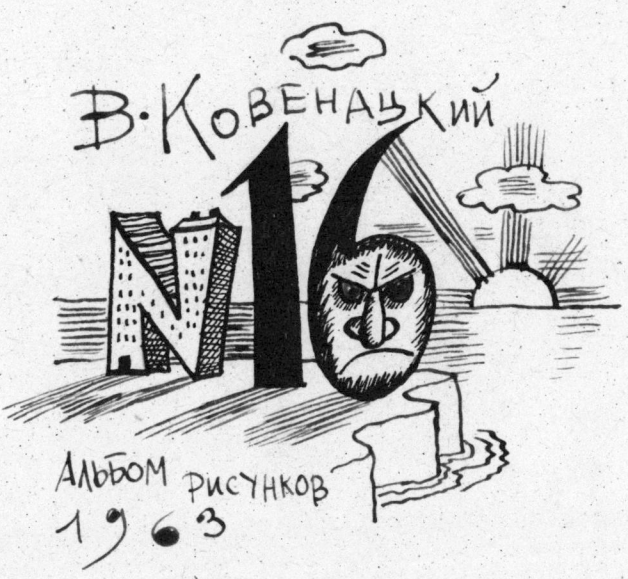

Untitled, 1963.

VLADIMIR **KOVENATSKY**

When Vladimir Kovenatsky died in Moscow in 1986, the lion's share of his work had already been moved, for safety, to his friend and collaborator Boris Kerdimun's New York apartment. Primarily tableaux recognizable from Soviet life of the 1950s and early 1960s, the images—droll, satirical, and startlingly contemporary—are characterized by brutality, repression, and need. Kovenatsky's heroes rub shoulders with homunculi, centaurs, devils, and bulb-headed men; they fly, ride giant rats, keep dinosaurs for pets, build robots. It is this tension between corrosive satire and disarming whimsy that gives Kovenatsky's images their edge: in one drawing, aliens emerge from a spaceship only to get in line for beer (a scarcity in Kovenatsky's Moscow). Another image depicts a guard bursting into a prisoner's cell with a bouquet of flowers; "Happy Housewarming," reads the caption.

Kovenatsky was insatiably curious and keenly aware of his influences. He combined an interest in German Expressionism and Surrealism with a guilty fascination with political caricature to create an eclectic style that used cartooning to address a wide range of formal concerns. The graphic narratives strung throughout Kovenatsky's books and multi-panel works can only be described as prescient. Almost a decade before underground comic art took root in the United States, Kovenatsky, without ever having seen a comic book, foreshadowed the work of artists as diverse as R. Crumb, Harvey Pekar, Art Spiegelman, Raymond Pettibon, and Daniel Clowes.

Kovenatsky worked as a book designer and illustrator in an establishment dominated by Socialist Realist pieties and state-sponsored anti-Semitism. He knew that a widely attended exhibition of his private work could mean a loss of livelihood and freedom, and he shared his drawings, prints, short stories, and poems with only a small circle of friends. As a result, most of his work remains literally unseen. A recent exhibition of Kovenatsky's work on *Moscow Channel*, a journal on the World Wide Web, marked the first time it has been shown publicly in more than thirty years.

Kerdimun is one of the few remaining witnesses of the painfully shy and profoundly eccentric (thought by some to have been schizophrenic) artist and writer. "I once asked Vladimir to help me move some furniture to an apartment across the street," Kerdimun recalls. "He heaved the heaviest shelf onto his back and left. Half an hour later, I realized that he hadn't returned. Worried, I ran outside and asked a woman nearby if she had seen him. She recalled seeing a man with a shelf walking toward the edge of town. I finally found him about a mile from home. He was lost in thought, the shelf still on his back, walking into the woods."

ALEX HALBERSTADT

Angels
of the
Universe

EINAR MÁR GUDMUNDSSON

Once upon a time, long, long ago, my mother dreamed a dream.

The odd thing about that dream is the fact that it was forgotten and did not emerge again until I had traveled down my road.

No, not the long and winding road that the Beatles sing of, which leads to the house of love, but another road, longer and darker.

It was the dream about the four horses.

Gudrun, my mother, dreamed it the night before I was born; so more than forty years would pass until it shot up out of the depths like a prophecy from an ancient book.

In her dream, Mother was a girl of ten. She was on the bus as it drove along Sudurlandsbraut, on her way home from school.

The bus bumped over the holes in the road.

The dust swirled up from beneath the tires.

It was spring.

Suddenly she glanced toward the front of the bus and saw a black dog charging down the aisle. The dog was heading straight for her. Frightened, my mother stood up.

Then the dog stood up on its hind legs. It tried to lick her with its tongue and snap at her, and was so persistent that she fled the bus at the next stop.

She ran along the banks of the ditches beside Sudurlandsbraut. Her hair was bobbing in the wind. Her satchel bounced on her back. Her coat felt tight.

The birds had started singing in the clear blue air, and the war had not broken out yet. Similarly, all the buildings that have since gone up on the other side of Sudurlandsbraut still had no foundation in reality.

The water in the ditches was smooth as a mirror and glistened in the sunshine. It absorbed the sky. In the distance were blue mountains.

My mother jumped among the ditches. She ran into the meadow. The earth was swirling under her feet. The grass was like a glowing lava flow. If she stopped, the earth would swallow her.

A long way out in the meadow she saw four horses. They were all grazing, standing a couple of feet from each other. She had never seen those horses before. They weren't grandfather's horses.

But they were shapely, proud, and beautiful horses: one of them was chestnut, the second brown, the third bay, and the fourth skewbald.

My mother felt that these horses belonged to her. They were in danger. She had to save them.

When the horses galloped away, the skewbald one began to lag. It ran around in circles and behaved very strangely. Then it tried to gallop like the other horses, but stumbled and fell.

When she reached it, it was lying on the ground, dead. My mother looked for an instant into its open eyes, then a moment later she was lying awake, because I had started wriggling and kicking, insistent on entering this world from which I would later disappear.

Then my mother remembered the dream.

She was sitting in the living room at home and staring into the air, then chanced to look over to the little table, at a photograph of me sitting and smiling, a little boy at a photographer's studio in town.

My mother clutched her face and covered her eyes. For a moment she felt that this dream had always been with her.

★

After I had been admitted to Klepp, the psychiatric hospital that stands like a gigantic palace by the sea, I recalled the time when I, as a little boy, stood one gray, foggy day in the bumpy street, watching the houses and the puddles.

Suddenly I noticed a middle-aged man. He was walking down the rain-soaked steps of one of the houses. With him was his son, a lanky lad of around twenty.

The son had dark, curly hair. He was wearing a short leather jacket with a dark fur collar, while his father was wearing a light windbreaker and loose-fitting, clean, work trousers.

The father was holding the son by the shoulder and pushing him along roughly. The cuffs of his checked shirt stood out from underneath the arms of his jacket and his hair was strangely colorless in the fog.

When they reached the street I ran up to them and called to the father, "Where are you taking him?"

The father turned around without letting go of his son's shoulder.

"Off to Klepp," he spat out.

I could see his forehead glistening with moisture. He looked as if he were gnashing his teeth. Behind the grayness of his eyes, flames were blazing.

Then they vanished into the fog.

It swallowed them just like in the mysterious folktales my mother used to tell me at bedtime that generally began with the words: "Once upon a time, long, long ago . . ."

In those tales, people would disappear into stones and rocks or go astray on paths through dark forests while the stars glittered in the sky.

They glittered like countless bright eyes out in the darkness; the darkness that would later increasingly descend upon me, starless and without moonlight.

I never saw the father and son again and am still unaware of the reality underlying this incident.

If I was looking inside another world, it stood large as life before me, but if this was reality I do not understand it in the slightest.

Naturally I understand as little of reality as it does of me. In that respect we are even. Yet it owes me no explanations for anything and I have paid it what it is due.

Of course it would be nice simply to be able to give Hegel's answer when he was told that his theories were at odds with reality: "Poor reality, I really feel sorry for it."

That's the sort of thing poets can write.

That's the sort of thing philosophers can say.

But we who are committed to asylums and kept in institutions, we have no answers when our ideas are at odds with reality, because in our world other people are right and know the difference between right and wrong.

The cloud of psychiatric drugs hangs in the air, as if the days are standing still.

"Paul!"

I give a start on hearing my name, but no reactions are visible; they are far, far away, deep inside the cloud hanging in the air.

The endless tranquillity in the depths of eyes.

A storm in the cold calmness.

★

It was obvious: someone was out to get me.

One of those dark December mornings I was sitting at the kitchen table, browsing through the paper. Inside it was a double-page spread about young drinkers. I was not interested in it for its own sake, but the photograph accompanying it caught my attention.

It showed two policemen marching away a young man between them. The officers' faces could be seen clearly, but the young man's eyes had been covered up with a black strip.

Beneath the photo stood this caption: "This young man wanted to hold an exhibition of his paintings at the police station."

I recognized the jacket and trousers immediately, my hair and my features below the black strip, but I did not recall having been arrested, even less having made any announcements about an exhibition of paintings at the police station.

It was obvious: someone was out to get me.

How did they know at the newspaper that I was a painter?

Who had been following me with a camera?

But these were only forebodings, invisible as birds' nightmares and the ponderings of fishes.

My parents were deeply concerned and my brothers and sister sensed that something was going on.

I would beat my drums for hours on end, until I came upstairs soaked in sweat.

I lived increasingly in a world of my own.

Neither my brother Robbi nor my sister Svana dared to bring their friends back home, but my brother Harald had started bringing all sorts of suspicious characters into the house.

I was volatile and bossy.

Once I was sitting at the kitchen table, watching Harald.

He looked the other way, but the wild glow in my eyes met his.

"Don't chomp your food like that," I told him.

"Do I chomp my food like that?" Harald asked, looking across the table at our parents while the silence hovered in the air like a bomb.

"Yes," I said. "You chomp your food."

I stood up and hit him in the face.

Harald was startled. He clutched his cheek but sat there without moving, watching me.

He didn't dare do anything.

"That sort of thing you just don't do," said my father.

"Shut up!" I snapped.

Nursing his cheek, Harald stood up and disappeared.

As he was leaving the kitchen, my mother said, "You know how sensitive Harald is."

"I told you to shut up," I said.

I rose to my feet, picked up the plate I had been eating from and threw it to the floor.

The plate smashed into fragments.

When I shoved my way out, Robbi and Svana were crying their eyes out.

That was the way December passed.

At Christmas, my friend Rognvald phoned. This was at the time he was a dentistry student in Germany, and he was back for the Christmas vacation.

He said he would come around on Boxing Day, wanted to have a few drinks and go out on the town.

My parents were glad that Rognvald and I would meet up over Christmas, because I had not left my room except to go down to the basement and play the drums and paint.

I took no part in the Christmas celebrations, not until Rognvald phoned, when I cheered up a little. My mother and father were relieved, even though they frowned upon our drinking bouts.

I was standing at the door when Rognvald arrived, bursting in the way he used to but very smart and sophisticated, in a thick worsted coat with a checked cap, and drenched in cologne.

We sat in my room. Rognvald had brought his duty-free spirits with him. He went out and chatted with my parents. I could tell they were relaxed.

Then Rognvald came back in.

I sat wringing my hands and had forgotten myself for an instant, and Rognvald went up to my desk and looked at the picture I had been painting on the wall intermittently all that month.

"Funny guy, that," said Rognvald. "Kind of monstrous."

It was a large picture of a human face. It was split into countless personalities. From one eye shone madness; the other was an empty socket. A sharp knife was cutting his nose in half.

"Mad as ever," said Rognvald, "but damn good these days."

We talked things over and for a while everything was the way it used to be, but when we were fairly drunk Rognvald stood up and searched his coat pocket. He produced a knife that he had bought in Germany.

"This is a knife and a half, don't you think?" said Rognvald, shooting out the blade.

We started fooling around with the knife. I remember going to thrust it between the volumes of *Sagas of the Knights* on the bookshelves, but inadvertently stabbed it into the spine of one of them, and when I pulled it out, it flew up into the air.

The knife swung round in circles in the air, then landed miraculously between Rognvald's toes. I thought it had stabbed him in the foot, but there was just a hole in the sock and nothing wrong with his toes or foot.

"Bravo!" said Rognvald.

We were rolling drunk by the time we went out, and the knife had ended up in my pocket. I soon lost Rognvald in the crowds in town and decided to go to a dance at Hotel Borg.

Not being bothered to wait at the back of the line, I tried to make my way to the front. Someone grabbed me by the shoulder.

"No pushing in here, mate," he said.

Losing my footing, I thrust my hand into my coat pocket and felt the knife there.

"Did you say something?" I asked.

"I'm just telling you to get in the line like anybody else."

"But I'm not like anybody else," I said, pulled out the knife and shot out the blade.

He went white as a sheet.

I waved the knife at him and he backed away, up to the wall. People moved aside. I looked into his eyes. The knife was playing in my hands.

Then suddenly I perceived the silent faces around me and his despair, and I knew I was doing something wrong, but now it was too late because the police had appeared at the end of the arched entrance.

They approached me. I swung around and managed to run away. I ran toward the lake, between the Cathedral and the House of Parliament. The police ran after me.

I could feel them at my heels like sharks and when I reached the lake I leapt out onto the ice. When one of the policemen leapt onto the ice after me, it broke and we both flailed around in the cold and muddy water.

I dropped the knife and it sank to the bottom of the lake, but the policeman managed to grab me by my little finger, and in the fall, as we struggled, my finger broke.

We were fished out of the lake and I went to the accident center with a police escort.

My finger was bandaged there.

Afterward I was taken to see the duty sergeant. He gave me a lecture, condemned my reckless behavior, but in the absence of any charges I was to be driven home.

But then he added: "There must be something wrong with you. You don't live under any conditions that might explain your behavior. I advise you to consult a doctor, as soon as you possibly can."

But I didn't consult a doctor. I locked myself away and crept farther and farther inside myself.

I could feel my headaches intensifying; I lay stiff. I could not move for hours on end.

An electric current was passing through the room.

The pillow was trying to fly.

My mother and father wanted to talk to me. They were asking me to come out and have something to eat, asking me to come out and talk things over, asking me this and asking me that.

But I didn't answer, except one Sunday when I agreed to join them for a drive.

We drove around the new suburbs where there were a lot of large houses.

My mother pointed to one of them.

"That house is a funny color," she said.

"Isn't it?" replied my father.

Sitting in the back seat, I asked, "Are you making fun of me?"

My parents looked around, surprised.

"That house is the same color as my coat," I said by way of explanation.

My parents looked at each other.

Then there was silence.

Lizards and crocodiles chased me. Wrinkled monsters tried to strangle me.

It was obvious: someone was out to get me.

Now the neighbors' signals were starting to get through to me.

They used ciphers and bugging devices that my brother Harald helped them to smuggle into the house.

I tried to keep in the corner as much as I could.

All the same, the woman next door wanted me to go around and sleep with her.

But I turned her down flat, and said, "No, thanks."

At that moment the boys in Harald's room laughed.

I knew they were laughing at me.

"Paul," said my father. "Rognvald's on the phone. He's calling from Germany."

But I didn't want to talk to him. I knew he wanted me to give him his knife back.

"Tell him to look in the lake," I shouted.

I wanted to avoid all those people, my father and mother, my brothers and sister, everyone, Rognvald, the neighbors, and in particular the woman next door.

So I unscrewed the handle from the outside of my door and locked it from the inside.

But the window was unprotected. I crept down into the basement one night, took the wooden board from my easel and nailed it across the window.

But the cipher messages kept on coming in.

Shortly afterward I received a letter from Rognvald. "Dear Paul. I can tell how bad you feel. I want you to take serious action about it. There's no shame..."

I crumpled up the letter and threw it away. They'd got him onto their side. The next time he comes he'll want to pull out all my teeth.

I stood alone, absolutely alone.

Then God came along.

He said unto me that I was the last man on earth, and that I should begin building and turn my room into an ark.

"How?" I asked.

He said that it was no problem, but that I would have to have a woman with me.

Then I wrote a letter to the woman next door: "I have decided to accept your offer of carnal relations. You are welcome to come over to my house and you need not worry about your husband. He is fiction from the start. A written contract is also offered if you so desire."

I envisaged this ark as being not so unlike a pirate ship in shape. God had told me that when the flood came, I would sail away with the house like a boat in tow.

There would be cabins and bunks and portholes out onto the world.

I remembered old movies with galley slaves who had forgotten to take off their wristwatches before they jumped back into the past.

I had taken down the shelf unit and moved my desk away from the wall.

My head itched so much that I left the room and shaved it completely.

In the hallway I ran into my father. "You coming on board?" I asked, but he did not answer.

He looked tired.

What's the time?
   Is it day or evening or night?
   February or March?
   I heard the doorbell ring. My mother went to the door. "I will not tolerate this sort of thing."
   I could hear the shrill voice of the woman next door.
   She had given the letters to my mother.

I could hear anxious voices outside the door. I knew that something was pending. I had started smelling KGB agents.
   "Paul! Please! We only want to help you. Come on, Paul, open up. You're playing that music so loud. The children can't do their homework."
   I switched everything off.

But the silence was only a void between two wars.
   Later I left my room. It was dark. All the lights were off.
   Everyone had clearly fled. They were going to close in on me.
   But I'll beat them to it.
   I'll be gone.

I was barefoot and wearing a T-shirt.
   I thought it was night, but it was early morning.
   I ran out onto the rain-soaked pavement.
   Outside, it was dark and cold.

Later, when I had been at the psychiatric hospital for several years, Rognvald would visit me every time he came into town.
   He was very smart, always wearing those elegant coats, shirts and jackets, talkative and entertaining, but sometimes, too, he would sink into deep seriousness, gloom.
   I went for drives with him. A huge station wagon stood parked outside the psychiatric hospital. Rognvald had done well for himself. He owned a house and his children were growing up.
   I don't deny that I felt a little self-conscious when I sat in the station wagon and drove off with such an impressive man.

"Rognvald," I said when we turned down the road away from the hospital. "I really wish you'd been a psychiatrist rather than a dentist."

"Do you now," he said.

"I think you might have been able to cure me," I said.

"No," he said. "Don't you reckon it's enough trouble keeping myself on the right side of the line?"

"No, Rognvald," I said. "I can't imagine anything healthier in our society than a wealthy dentist at the wheel of a station wagon."

Rognvald laughed.

"At least, there isn't room for them at the madhouse," I said.

"But just bear in mind," said Rognvald, "that the madhouse is in a lot of places."

He looked at me and put his foot down on the accelerator.

Another time we drove outside the city, out to the Reykjanes lighthouse, and Rognvald drove up to the cliff where the billowing surf beat below, and there were barren gravel banks everywhere else.

Then Rognvald said, while we were sitting in his station wagon looking out over the ocean, "It's easy, Paul. Just put your foot on the accelerator..."

I took it like any other joke, that old cynicism of his, and I didn't want to die then anyway, sitting by the side of this man who'd shown me what a true friend he was, not forgetting me even though I had been buried alive and no one needed to know about me.

This all came back to me and I saw Rognvald in a new light when my mother showed me the death announcement in the paper, and even though I was on psychiatric drugs that dry up all emotion, I felt the tears pouring forth and didn't understand a thing and didn't know a thing and didn't believe anymore....

Or perhaps something else dawned on me, that everything moves in mysterious ways, that people with everything we who are sick wish for—a good wife, clever children, a house, a car—that they too, yes, they too...

Yes, Rognvald. The madhouse is in a lot of places, not just a hospital, not just a palace, but also a pattern woven from threads so fine that no one can distinguish them, neither the Emperor nor the children, neither you nor I.

★

When I came round inside Klepp, Brynjolf, the psychiatrist, was sitting beside me.

I'd been given an injection and I could feel the drug-induced slow motion in my veins and the calm atmosphere of the hospital in my eyes.

Brynjolf was trying to talk to me.

"Where am I?"

"At Klepp Psychiatric Hospital."

"But what about you? Are you there too?"

"Yes, my name's Brynjolf. We're supposed to try to sort this business out."

Brynjolf had been a practicing psychiatrist for several years and had a big university degree from America in people like me.

I can't remember the name of his university anymore. All I remember is that it was in California, because for the first winter in the darkness and gloom I often wondered how Brynjolf managed to hang on here after sitting in palm-tree groves where no one knows how real the vault of the heavens is.

Once my parents were driving me up to the hospital.

There was a gray fog and drizzle.

We drove westward along the Klepp road and took the turning toward the hospital.

A man was walking along the side of the road in the same direction.

He was wearing a light overcoat and all the weight of the world seemed to rest on his shoulders.

His head was bowed forward.

He was staring down at the black gravel.

"He must be in a bad way, that one," my mother said.

"He's certainly weighed down," my father said.

But as they drove past the man, he looked in the direction of the car.

They gave a start.

It was Brynjolf, my psychiatrist.

He carries us on his shoulders. Our problem is his. I think he spends more time with us than with those who are considered normal. I'm even tempted to think he has a higher opinion of us than of them, and that the therapy is reciprocal: he tries to cure us, and we him.

Brynjolf says that schizophrenia is deeply rooted in the Icelandic identity, that all that belief in elves and spirits, ghosts and trolls is just a split personality.

You don't leave that place with a diploma. The psychiatric hospital doors close and reality takes over. Yet it was just like coming back from the countryside. Mother has tidied up the room. You take your tablets, lie in bed, and pull the blanket up over your head. Emptiness flows over you. A hangover, a terrible hangover.

Work. Isn't the best thing for you to find a job? The drugs sat on my eyelids like lead weights. I stood drugged up to the eyeballs in the winter cold, trying to unload sacks of flour from a ship. At lunchtime I gave up and pulled the despair over my head like a blanket.

Then the days start getting longer. Everything lights up. Strange. You felt good today. What right have you to? There's a beautiful girl. I forget to take my pills one night. The next day I feel better. I come out of my room and feel fine. I am better. I am free of my illness.

I shed kilos, drug-induced kilos. How golden the sun is. I take off my shirt and stand there naked from the waist up. I do some facial exercises and wrap a towel around my head. I look like an Arab.

Then that goddamn upholstery cleaner had to appear in the sitting room. He fled when he saw me, scared to death, but I thought he was a burglar and chased him.

Forgetting, of course, to take off my turban.

Went back home.

Called the police.

Told them someone had just stolen my mother's vacuum cleaner.

It was wonderful weather. I inhaled the fresh, healthy air.

People cannot stand it when we psychiatric patients feel bad, but it gets on their nerves just as much when we feel good.

I took one of the armchairs out onto the platform at the top of the steps and sat in it there.

I had the doors open, listening to music from my room. I had bought a bottle of white wine. And *Playboy*. My father turned up. "Making ourselves comfortable, I see," he said.

"It's just like being in Hawaii," I said.

"You're looking pretty shipshape these days," he said.

"I could swim the seven seas."

"But what about work? Haven't you thought about getting a job?"

"Yes, I'm thinking about writing a book, becoming an author."

"An author, you?" said my father. "I could just imagine Halldór Laxness[*] sitting on the steps of his house reading a porno magazine."

"Laxness," I said. "Who's that?"

My father shook his head and went away.

Now I shall write a story.

I shall write my own type of literature. It won't be like a well-written school essay in the Letters to the Editor column of the paper. Instead, I shall jump from one topic to the next, completely as the fancy takes me, supported by neither literary formulae nor prior psychiatric examination.

In fact, time is always short, even though there's as much of it about as there actually is.

A good knitter sits all day long and knits and makes steady progress, but an author's job probably involves constantly knitting the same pullover and picking it apart over and over again on the off chance that a real pullover will eventually come out of it.

The disadvantage of novels is how long they are. I think I should write poems instead, arrange the words into lines of varying lengths, and say: this is a poem. I shall mainly write closet poems and desk-drawer poems, open-closet poems and closed-drawer poems.

I immersed my mind; that is to say, I had a few drinks. My problem was not writing the poems. My problem was getting them into circulation.

No one wants to publish loonies. They're like Soviet dissidents. They write loony poems and are published by the Loony Bin Press.

---

[*] Halldór Laxness, Iceland's best-known writer, was awarded the Nobel Prize for Literature in 1955.

So what about writing the poems in Icelandic, translating them into English, and sending them to Yoko Ono?

If Yoko likes the poems and wants to publish them in millions of copies in America, I know that old Grjoni down at the Stencil Printshop will be happy to handle the printing for her.

I must have been fairly drunk or something happened on the way to the phone, because I don't remember whether I got hold of Grjoni or whether anyone answered at the Stencil Printshop, but now America was in the picture and the task at hand was to conquer it.

There the problems start. At the embassy they classify psychiatric patients with homosexuals and Communists. I couldn't sleep that night nor the next. If I made it over to the base, I could get a fighter jet pilot to pop me over there.

I roamed about the house, opening doors and closing them. The Yanks haven't got any reason to be in my country if I can't go to theirs. I'll take my transistor radio with me.

Over dinner I said to my father, "I need some money."

It was fried fish. The frying pan was on the table, with a plate of peeled potatoes.

"You're not getting a penny," my father said.

I looked up and saw the fear in the children's eyes.

"I'm not getting what?"

I grabbed my father by the shoulder and shook him.

"Didn't you hear what I said? I need some money."

"You don't have anything to do with money," my father said. "What are you going to do with money?"

"I'm going away."

I could see the children looking imploringly at our father. They were hoping I would leave, but certainly didn't realize that I was going to America, and then my father said, "You've got nothing to do with money."

I squeezed his shoulder even tighter and shook him.

"If you don't give me any money," I said, "I'll kill you."

"Come on, that's enough," said my mother.

She was standing at the kitchen sink, beside the stove.

"I'll just call the police to come and get you."

"You're not calling anyone," I said.

"Then you act like a civilized human being," she shouted at me.

I could feel myself swelling up.

"You've got free board and lodging here," said my father, "and you can't just get money when you feel like it."

"I can't what . . . ?"

I stood up, gripped the edge of the kitchen table, and overturned it. Plates and glasses tumbled to the floor and broke, and the pan with the fried fish and onions in it lay upside down. My brothers and sister sat there in terror, then ran out, while I grabbed my father by the shirt and slammed him up against the wall.

"Are you going to give me some money?" I screamed through my clenched teeth.

I don't know whether my mother made a sign to him or whether he was just plain terrified, because he asked in a broken-down tone of voice, "How much do you want?"

"Let me see how much you've got."

He put his hand in his pocket and pulled out a tattered wallet. I snatched it from him and took out a wad of notes, grabbed hold of the transistor radio, and rushed for the door. It was cloudy outside, but had not started raining.

Some time during the night or in the morning I was walking along the road to Keflavik; the journey from home to there is one huge black hole.

Nor do I know why my shoes had disappeared from my feet, and my socks too. I was barefoot, but still holding the transistor radio, which was tuned to American Forces Radio.

It was raining and foggy. The moss-grown beds of lava were in hiding. Not a mountain to be seen. Only the road to Keflavik, soaked with rain.

It was late at night or early in the morning and the few people who drove past seemed to think I was a ghost, one of the woken dead from Hafnarfjordur cemetery or even the infamous local Stapi Ghost.

Then a police van drew up beside me. Two policemen jumped out and opened the doors at the back. I didn't try to make a run for it, but they handcuffed me all the same. Perhaps they had been looking for me.

They helped me up into the van and I sat on one of the side benches in the back. The radio was still switched on. "We've got him," said the driver.

A policeman was sitting in the back with me. He was very young.

My toes were pink and blue and my hair was dripping with water. Nonetheless I did not feel cold or wet.

"You coming along?" I said to the young policeman who was sitting facing me.

"Where to?" he said.

"America."

"And what am I supposed to do there?" he asked.

"You could hold the transistor radio," I said.

Vilhelm, the psychiatric hospital orderly, was standing in the Klepp doorway with a smug smile on his face.

He was big and powerful. He pumped iron.

The young policeman undid the handcuffs and handed the radio to me.

Vilhelm prodded me in the back with his finger and pushed me up the stairs into the ward. As soon as we reached it, he tried to take the radio away from me.

"It's my radio," I said. "Leave it alone!"

Vilhelm took hold of the radio, and I tugged it back. I filled up with that unpredictable physical strength that is characteristic of my illness.

I was holding it by the handle and Vilhelm was trying to tug it away from me. Strong as he was, he needed to exert himself.

He strained away and when he strained as hard as he could and I could feel myself losing my grip, I let go, so that Vilhelm, that mountain of muscle, also known as Silly Willy, fell over backward, first onto a chair, then onto the floor.

The radio smashed into fragments, and I threw myself over him.
I pummeled him with my fists. He managed to flip me off him, and at that moment some of the other orderlies appeared.

I could see his creased face and his clenched fists raised. He was dying to beat me up but the other orderlies hushed at him.

I was given an injection and then thrown into isolation. There was nothing there but a bed with a chamber pot under it.

★

My dear little brother Robbi,

I am writing you a little letter. I even expect that I will send it, because I'm back on my feet. I've moved into the rehabilitation block where my application has been kicking around for years.

This is a desirable residence: the waiting lists are as long as toilet rolls, since the handicapped are a numerous profession. They could muster an election list for Parliament; they field a brass band and a football team.

I've got a good view from here across the east of the city and right out into the countryside. There's pouring rain on the roads but the sun's shining on the slopes of Mount Esja. The bright light over Kjos looks like the Garden of Eden. A rainbow has formed a decorated gate across it. Now all I need to do is step into the garden, walk through the gate, and make a wish.

I'm one of those invisible citizens that the wind sweeps along Austurstraeti. I only make myself known when the volcanoes start rumbling within my soul.

There is clenched cold in people's faces, gloomy people moving along like shadows.

Smiling government ministers and their wives, businessmen, politicians, artists, and entertainers look out through the windows with happy eyes.

I was standing outside the rehabilitation block and inside me Frank Sinatra was singing that the end is near, or was it Sid Vicious, who decided to disappear as well?

I opened the glass door and stepped into the brightly lit lobby. The jet-black cold waited outside. There was an icicle on my woolly hat and my cheeks were cold. The chill of downtown was still inside me.

If God isn't dead, he's both hard of hearing and blind. There was no one behind the window of the reception cubicle: just a telephone, newspaper, and table. The caretaker had vanished, like God.

Which is not to suggest that I needed him, but it would have been nice if he had been sitting there to say good night as I walked past the window.

I wandered around the empty corridors of the rehabilitation block. In this mighty monolith of solitude, where nobody but me seemed to live, I felt the shivers running through me. I was broke and hungry when I opened the door to my flat. There was nothing to eat except dry bread and old buttermilk and the canteen downstairs had shut hours ago.

I sat in the darkness looking out at the lights. Cars were driving along the main road outside and the darkness encircled the mountains. There was no Garden of Eden in Kjos, no decorated gate.

When the mountains take off their white coats, the birds pay their visits. The doctor takes the darkness and pours it into a cup, then disappears into the long winter night in his office.

Outside, winged time hovers, from a transparent blueness toward a darkened shore. The snow on the mountainside awakens from its sleep. When the birds leave, the dregs will be poured away.

An exiled blueness knocks on the window.

In the blackness, silent trees sleep.

Summer had arrived when I bade farewell to the monolith of solitude and this earthly world. It was a perfectly ordinary day.

I stood in my room and looked out of the window or lay on the mattress in the corner listening to the alarm clock ticking or the raindrops beating against the windowpane.

I recall the butterflies fluttering around the meadows, the bicycles that rolled magically along the streets, the universe in the calm of night, but despite the brightness the corridors are dark and empty.

Summer has arrived. I hear children's happy voices and think about mayweed and meadows. In the gardens, newly budded trees talk together. The blueness knocks on the window.

The darkness has gone. Someone has come and poured it away like cold coffee.

Outside, winged time hovers.

So I arise, take up my bed, and jump.

The happy voices continue to ring out, the bicycles roll, and the butterflies flutter, but I do not hear anything, neither the children nor the bicycles nor the birds, because I am lying down there in the darkness even though everything is shining bright around me.

Not dying suns.

    Not eroding sands.

    Only words carved in stone above a grave that flies through the emptiness.

When my mother and father come to collect my belongings, there is a black plastic bag lying on the floor.

    On top of it, the caretaker has placed most of the articles that were spread about the room.

    On the kitchen table is an opened cigarette carton, red Gold Coast; and the wrapper from a loaf of bread from the Cooperative Bakery.

    My mother goes over to the black plastic bag, opens it, and gropes inside. She pulls a book out of the bag.

    The book is Sigfus Dadason's *Collected Poems*. My mother takes a long look at the book. When she opens it, these words confront her eyes: *Dreams: at the bottom of them we perceive the merciless onslaught of reality*.

    That was the same day that my mother saw the photograph of me on the living-room table and suddenly remembered the dream about the four horses.

No, I am not dead.

    I've gone to sea. I am sailing the blue sea in the mansions of the father. The father hauls in the nets. We reach the shore loaded down with our catch.

Here on these fishing banks of the dead and departed, there is no quota.

    Here in the depths of eternity, I am lying cold and alone.

    I hear the trees rustling. The morning is bright and blue.

    People are still fast asleep, my mother and father are sleeping at home. Mother turns over as I enter the house. I take off my shoes and coat. My coat is tattered and torn.

    Hearing the noise, my mother comes out of the room. She cannot see me anywhere, but notices the coat lying on the floor. When she reaches out for the coat, it turns to dust in her hands.

    From the dust rises a bird that flies away and vanishes; when my mother opens her eyes, the morning sun is rising.

Translated from the Icelandic by Bernard Scudder

All my thoughts of you are good ones.
The horse whose neck is clothed with thunder—
they are good ones.
The voice that shakes the wilderness—good ones.
I think about how, if I could wake up,
I could go to your life,
how that would be good, if I could wake up.

But where I am is so large.
You are a fly.
You are impossible.

Where I am is so large, like a dark saying,
repeating. Where I am
is repeating. I don't know where it begins.

Where I am is the same.
Where you are keeps changing.
The light just takes you away, and I
am the only one here.
It's mine, like a dark saying—
Hide them in the dust together.

Bind their faces in secret.
You see how it's mine? You see how I try
to wake up?
The horse whose neck is clothed with thunder—
they were good ones.

I am the only one here, a giant,
asleep on the damp floor.

I am on the floor
of my invention, my forest
of dark sayings—
the Lord shall hiss.

My forest is always the same.
I am asleep on the damp floor.
My lids are down. Your face is a secret.
Hiss, hiss.

LARISSA SZPORLUK

HOLY GHOST

Adrian Piper

DECISIONS, DECISIONS

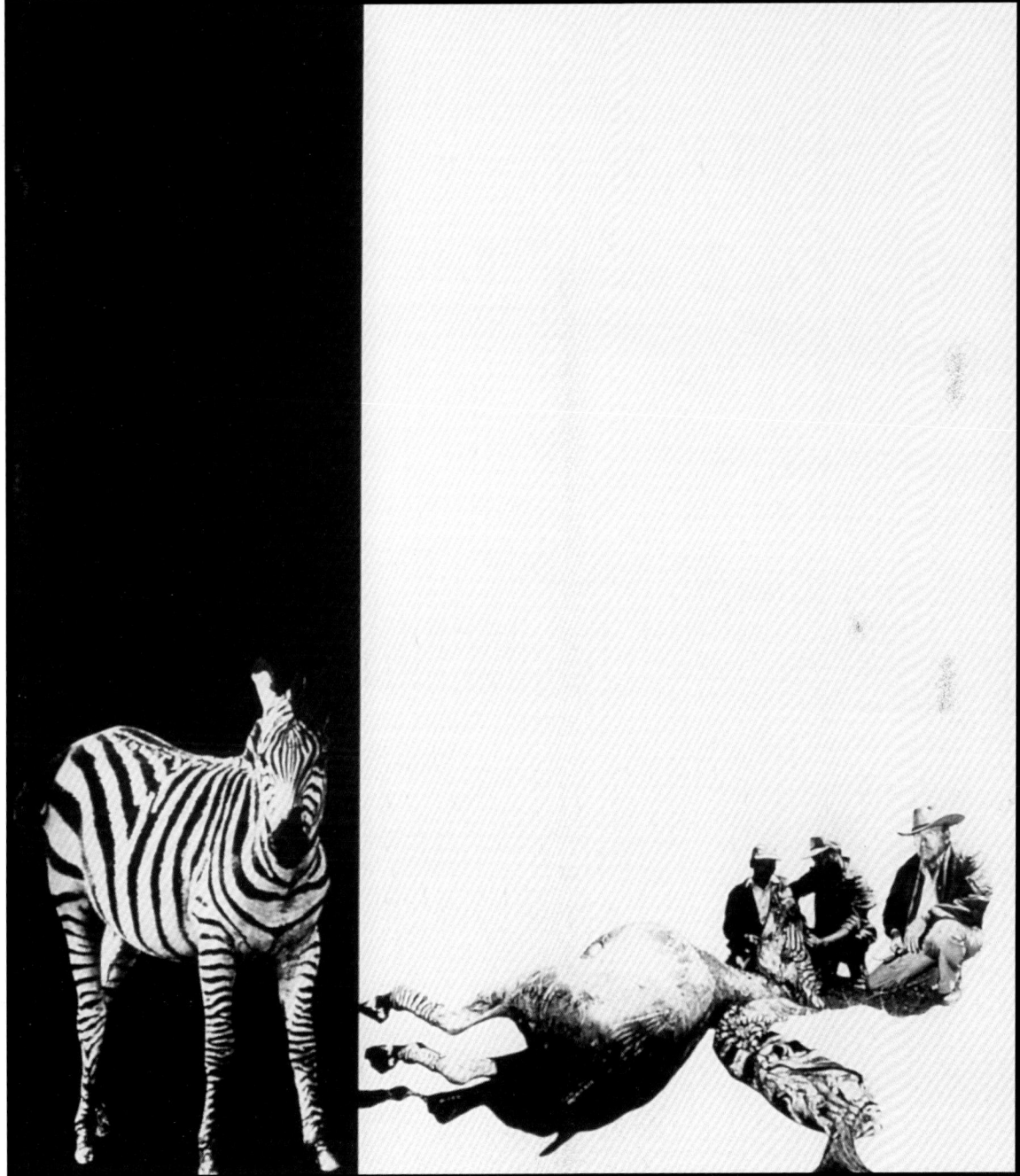

ENDLESS LOOP RECORD/ERASE

- So, reading some more of that self-help literature, I see.
- That was a really catty remark. Where did that come from?
- Where did what come from?
- That crack you just made about "self-help literature."
- What crack? I didn't make any crack.
- Yes you did. You just asked me in a really sarcastic tone of voice if I was reading "some more of that self-help literature."
- I did not. You're hearing things.
- Are you telling me that you did not just ask me if I was reading some more of that self-help literature?
- That's not what I said. You misinterpreted me.
- Oh? Then what's the right interpretation?
- Of what?
- Of whatever it is you think I've just misinterpreted.
- I don't think you've misinterpreted anything. Stop being so paranoid.
- I'm not being paranoid. You accused me of misinterpreting you so I'm asking what's the right interpretation.
- Of what?
- Of what you just said.
- I didn't just say anything. Stop making such a fuss.
- You did just say something and I'm not making a fuss.
- Oh, yeah? What did I just say?
- You just put me down for reading "self-help literature."
- That's not what I said. I didn't put you down. Stop imagining things. You're really crazy, you know that?
- Now you're going to tell me that wasn't a put-down either, right?
- What wasn't a put-down?
- You just told me I was crazy.
- I didn't say that.
- But you did. Why are you denying it?
- Denying what?
- That you just called me crazy.
- I did not. You completely misunderstood me.
- What was there to misunderstand? Your exact words were, "You're really crazy, you know that?"
- You're making that up. If you don't stop I'll think you really are crazy.
- Stop threatening me. I don't care what you think.
- Then why don't you just shut up and stop nagging me?
- I would if you'd stop insulting me.
- I'm not insulting you. You overreact to everything.
- You just can't stop putting me down, can you?
- You're the one who can't stop picking a fight over every little thing.
- You'd pick a fight too, if I talked to you like that.
- Like what?
- Always belittling what I do, always trying to undermine me.
- I'm not trying to undermine you. I'm trying to help you.
- Help me? By putting down what I read? Telling me I'm crazy and paranoid?
- I never said that. You're just making things up to attack me with.
- But you did say it. You did. Can't you admit responsibility for anything you do?
- I'm not responsible for your paranoid delusions.
- I'm not paranoid. Stop calling me paranoid.
- I'm not calling you paranoid. I told you, I'm trying to help you.
- You're not helping me. You're driving me crazy.
- I just want you to be happy. You know how much I love you. I want things to be like they used to be.
- You mean before you put me down for reading "self-help literature" then accused me of being crazy and paranoid for calling you on it?
- Will you please stop harping on that? Why do you have to hold a grudge?
- Oh, so you admit you did something for me to hold a grudge about.
- I don't know what you're talking about. Stop trying to trap me.
- Then stop trying to escape owning what you said.
- I didn't say anything. You're always attacking me, always trying to put me down.
- I wouldn't have to if you'd stop being so evasive. Why don't you just own up to what you're doing?
- Stop lecturing me. Don't tell me what to do.
- How about this: I'll stop lecturing you and telling you what to do if you stop insulting me and being evasive. Deal?
- I don't know what you're talking about. Just knock it off. I'm warning you.
- Oh, yeah? What are you going to do? Kill me for not swallowing your put-downs?
- You're really asking for it.
- What am I really asking for? A little respect for what I'm like?
- You're pushing it. Keep pushing it, you keep egging me on. It's your own fault.

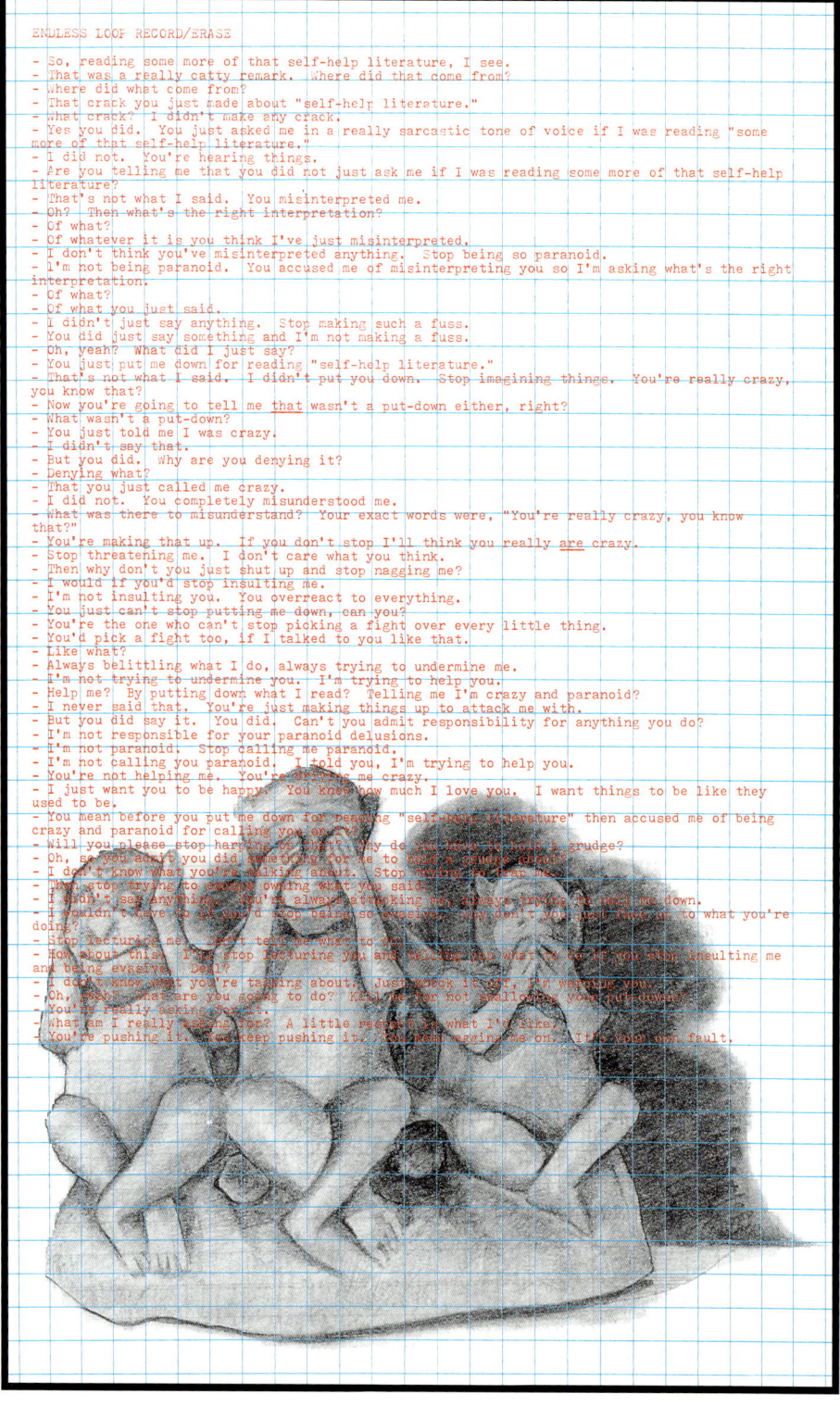

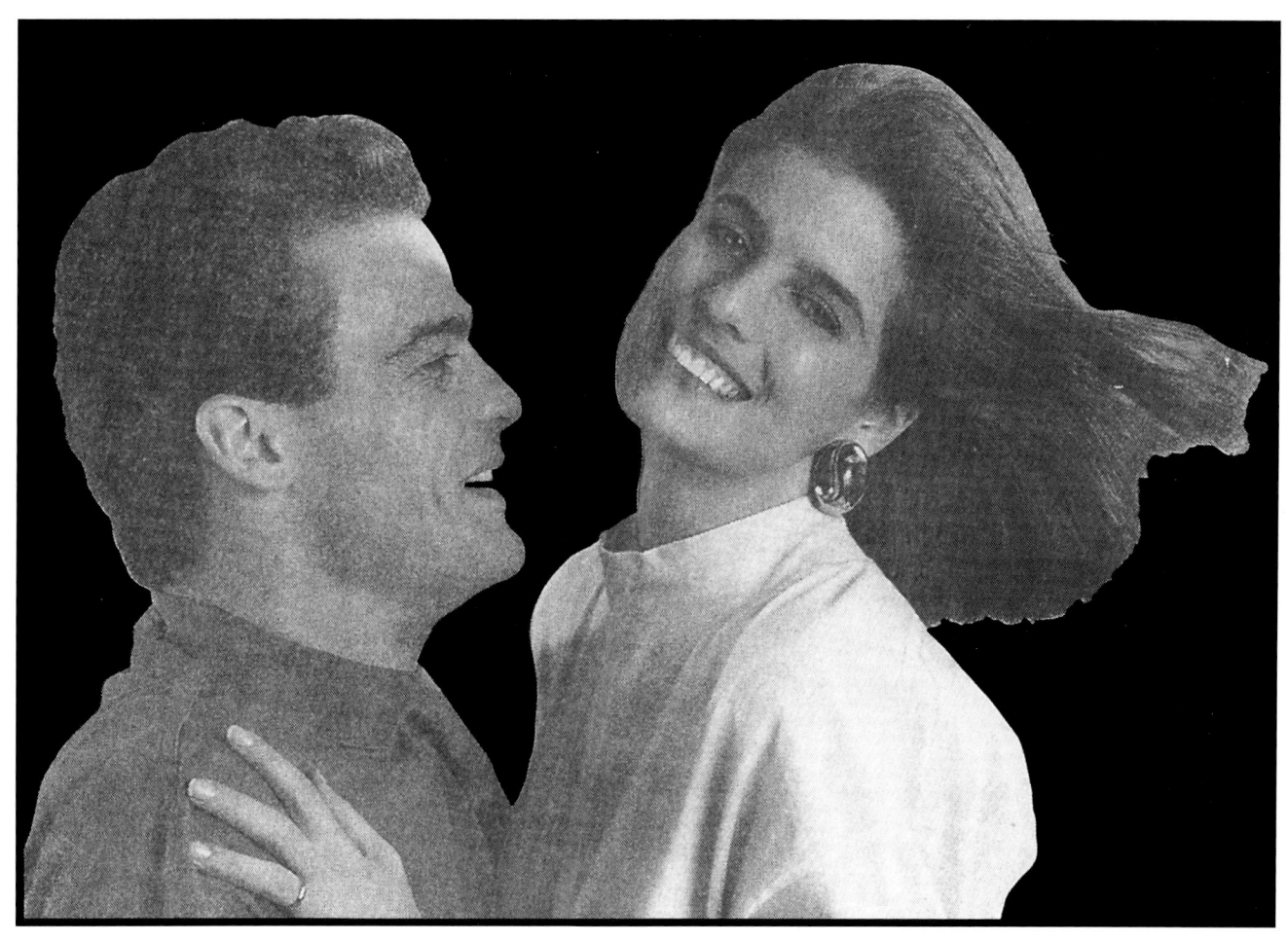

SNAKES ON STILTS IN BAGS,
animated by electrical impulses from the monitoring tower encased in hard bone,
linked by circuitry to sensory-motor extension loops
    that feed in ego dangers and feed out fight or flight or freeze to death.

Twisted circuits, mashed fuses, crushed connectors, damaged beyond repair.
A limping victim of natural selection, random alarms sound
    rage in the vicinity of interest,
    fear in the vicinity of love,
    shame in the vicinity of knowledge,
and convulsive grief for lost connections;
    for sources that fused and merged and electrified and lit up the interior sky
        blinding the inner eye
        to the shadows cast in stone.

States of the system vying for domination,
mixing messages,
short-circuiting their transmission,
causing power outages in the control room.
Solitary blow-outs are treasured moments of serenity.
Bring them on by adding wattage, up the current, feed the receptors even more.

Paralysis, silence and furtive withdrawal the only escape,
deep freeze the favored mode:
    freeze, feint, wince, silence, excrete a few noncommital sounds,
    bury them deep in white noise, deep freeze them for future reingestion,
    stone-hard vigilant against the anticipated attack,
        against expected attempts to break the mold,
            fissures and cracks sealed by frozen tears and powdered ice,
        gestures of mercy petrified in place;
Masters of survival in suspended animation,
    craving the Big Fix that makes it all worthwhile and melts you down.

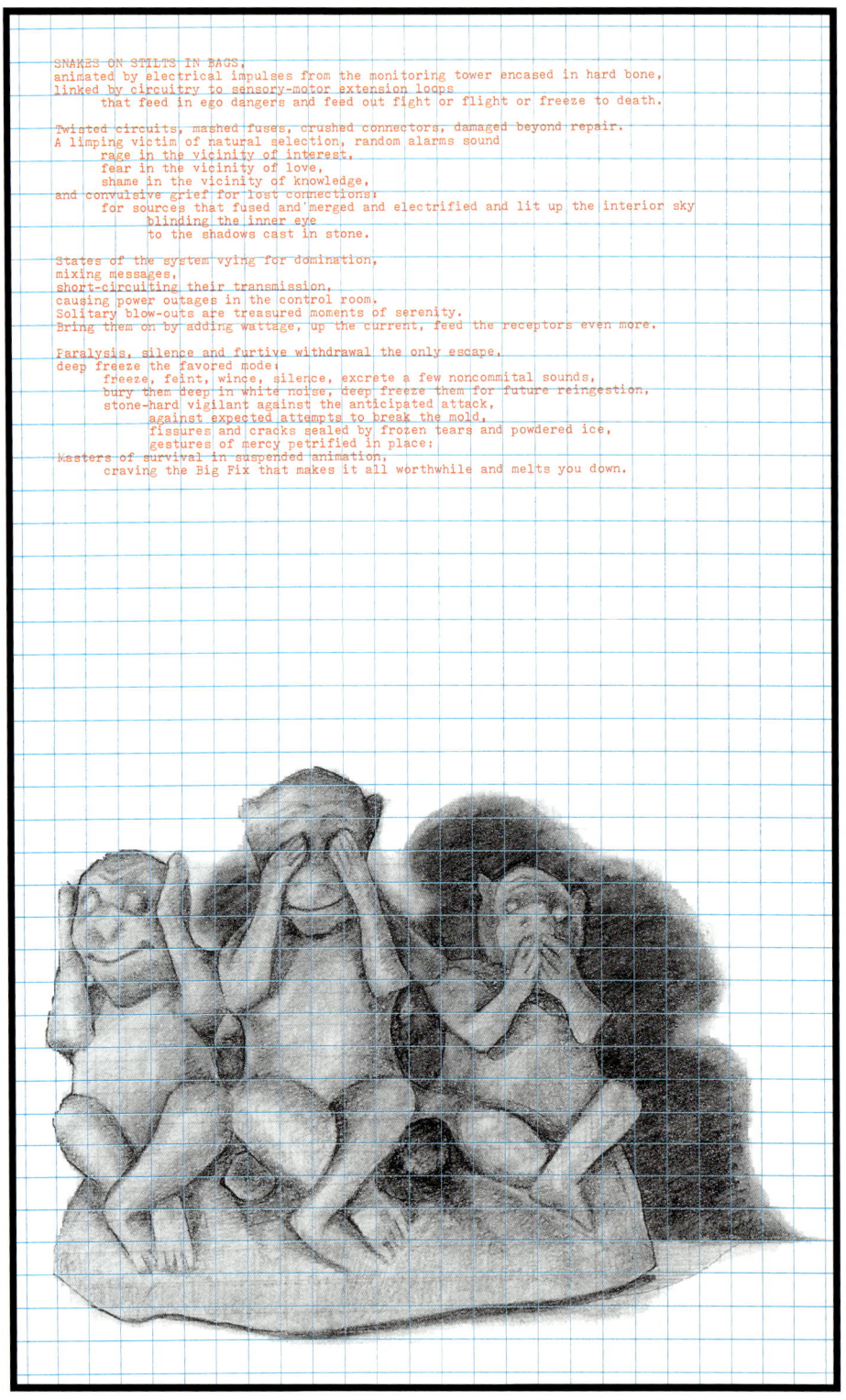

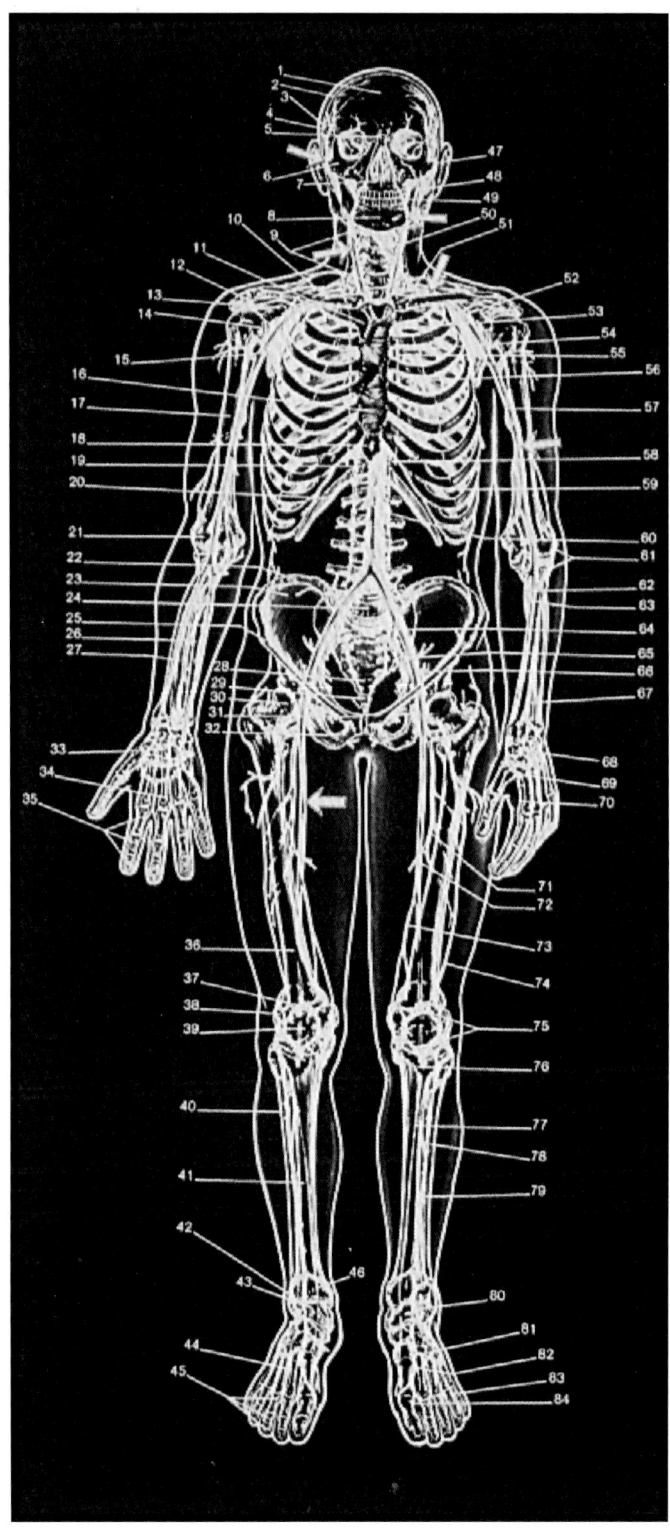

VIRTUE,
Convinced of your personal integrity, you sympathize with our plight.
Convinced of your moral rectitude,
    you grow indignant when complicity is suggested.
Convinced of your concern and good will,
    you retreat into your segregated neighborhoods,
                                schools,
                                colleges,
                                jobs,
                                clubs,
                                vacation spots,
        sprinkled here and there with twisted tokens,
    in order to contemplate your concern and good will at greater length.
Convinced, convinced, and convinced,
    you are inviolable, impenetrable, brittle, nervous,
    and fed up at being victimized by our rage.

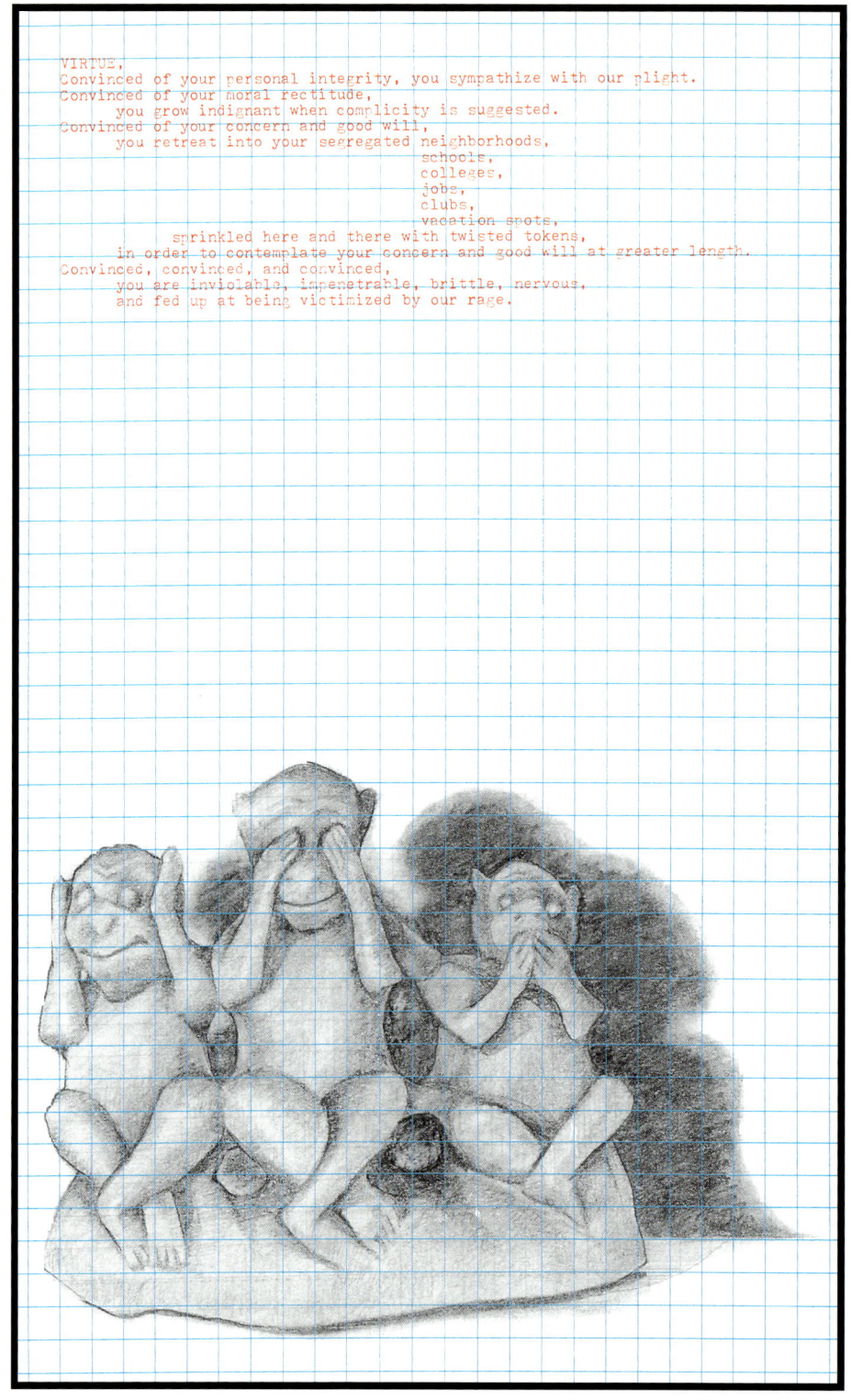

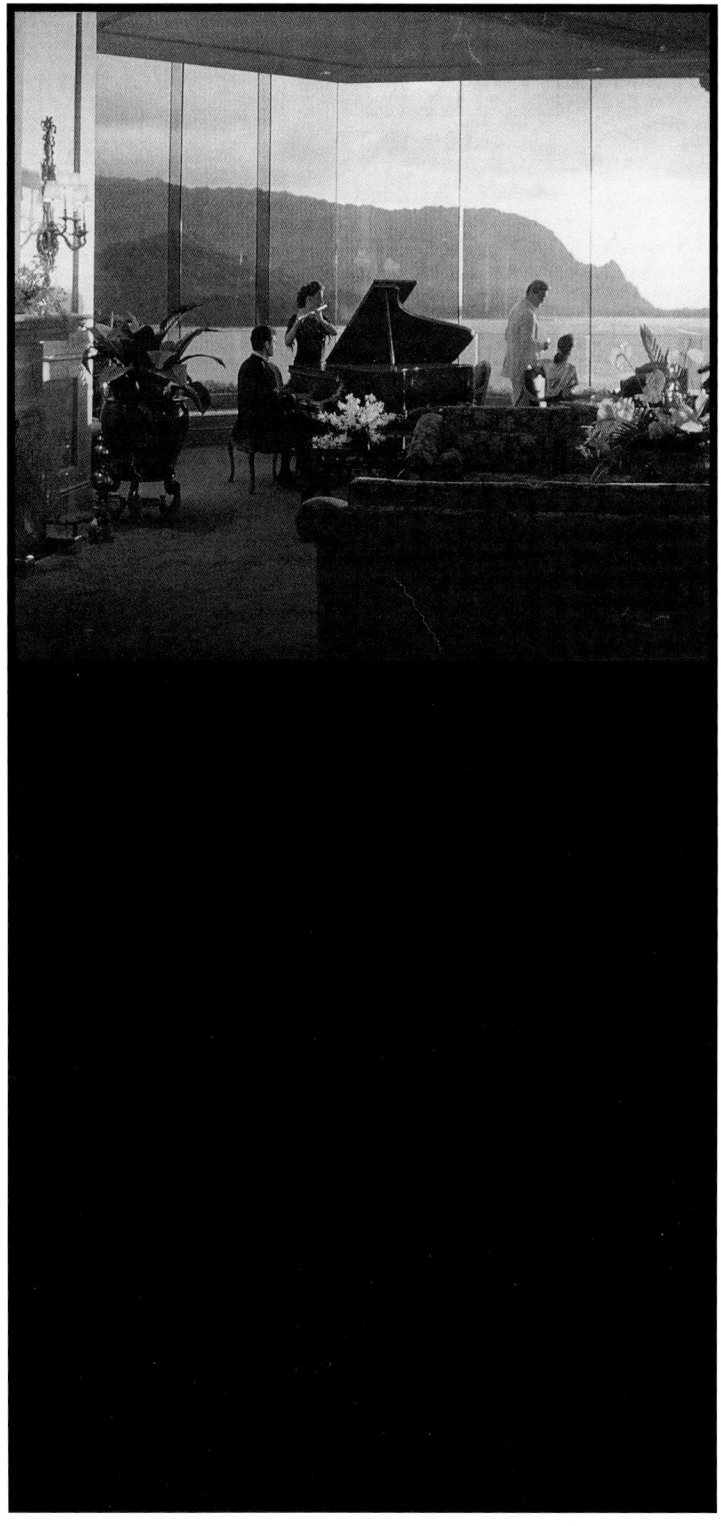

HEY, GOD!   How come I get stuck with this dumb bunch?
            It sucks
            You goofed bad on this sad batch, God
            and you know it.
            Where the hell do you think you're off to?
            You get back to that lab right now and shake up those test tubes one more time
            Don't you dare turn tail and run
            Screw that Big Bang shit, God
            You fucked up big time, now you fix it:

            No more dumb cunt / bad nig / limp dick / sick fag / bull dyke bad jokes
            No more dead meat fun snacks
            No more my toys / thy toys crib wars
            No more pool side back stab chit chat
            No more cock suck bum trip bad jobs
            No more big deal he-man plots to
                    bag the pork
                    join the club
                    ace the test
                    run the show
            No more skin tone cave man show and tell
            No more one-up / one-down games, God

            No more jerk-offs
            No more jerks
            No more gun binge
                    blood binge
                    sex binge
                    bucks binge
                    head binge
                    drug binge
                    doze binge
                    death binge
            No more kick-me / pay-as-you-go bad faith crap shoots
            No more head / heart splits
            No more do good / eat shit / think piss put-downs
            No more wide-eyed lies

            You fix that voice in there
            Make it say what's right and turn the wheels
            Or get rid of it and
            Get the hell out of the way of my gut
            You get on it now, God
            You kick ass good
            Or I'm out of here

FANNY HOWE

THE WRECK OF THE 737

(Croatia, Holy Week, 1996: 45-minute trip to Dubrovnik from Tuzla —
on the Dalmatian Coast — heavy rains — gusting winds —
on the Adriatic Sea — Cilipi Airport — Near Plat — St. John the Baptist peak.)

How did you get here?

The shuttle from London.

I'm not getting involved
but what father sent you?

What father? What London.

You should've missed your plane.
Are you afraid on the eve of night?

Dear Lord, I had wanted to see you
while I was alive.

Why did you send me these tickets instead?
Seagulls can't even fly this high.
If it rains, my hands will be wet.

★

THE WRECK OF THE 737

With unreal gentleness
generals

mounted the hill.
"Mind, now, mud."

One sighed like a serpent on an empty egg
but it was really military thinking:

travel casket round-trip.

⋆

Not to say his way was not her way
but she said existential is my religion
and in fear looked at herself
"who am now" "who has outlived"
both him and then.

⋆

Chosen and did choose
to fly that way that day.

Should I have to tell you what I mean?
You can't err symbolically.

With a thud and a scrape
on a snow carpet
worn to something hard

shhh the wind was mothering.
But who's the mother here anyway?
The rock, the moan, Mary, or the air?

⋆

No and was ashamed
she had refused him.

To have been a wife—awful—
but not this worse nothing.

Like lamb with smoky burning
it was her Easter Requiem.

*

Mentally washed his body: cold toes and fingering inlets
groin and back of ears up the numb legs, soft chest down
scrubbed crotch and anus
gums and bare tongue—white—soaped the testicles
and squeezed his member for some little firelight.

*

Anything mechanical from a ghost?

From here the sky over Former Yugoslavia
looks both formal and forlorn
like clergy trying to turn rocks into the host.

*

The past is unrecognized rubble.
At least that's how it came to meet you.

The pop of a light bulb in the bulkhead.

Now a big black bonnet
has landed in a tree and all us co-hearts
are left chilling.

D—th = perfect math

Elective affinity
where everything's combustible in the choice furnace.

*

He—a world victory in a personal coat—
was laid on a flag-draped catafalque—
just one among many sacrificed
to the worst atrocity
—since World War Two—in Europe:

young, black, American, broken
on the back of St. John's Peak.

*

Like sparrows having striven

unavailing in their chests

even corporations with living wills
don't survive
zero visibility.

Executive into infinity.

ILLUSIONS AND DELUSIONS

FIONA SHAW / JEAN STEIN

The following conversation took place on January 2, 1997, shortly before the actress Fiona Shaw completed the New York engagement of her dramatic performance of T. S. Eliot's poem, The Waste Land, at the Liberty Theater on Forty-Second Street. After completing a degree in philosophy at Cork University, Ireland, Shaw studied at London's Royal Academy of Dramatic Art, then joined the National Theatre in 1982, before moving to the Royal Shakespeare Company in 1985. Her first major collaboration with the experimental British director Deborah Warner was in 1990, when she performed in Electra. In 1995, Shaw performed the role of Richard II in Warner's production of the Shakespeare play, which caused much controversy in London, but was received with critical acclaim when it traveled to Paris and the Salzburg Festival. This winter, Shaw was asked by the BBC to spend four weeks at a Benedictine convent in the center of London, where she joined the nuns in their daily routine, including a four P.M. to seven A.M. vow of silence, which she broke only once every evening when she recounted her experiences to a video camera.

FIONA SHAW: I was thinking last night about the theater and what it is, and why it is that this little piece, *The Waste Land*, has done so well in an otherwise glittering theater world, where audiences are usually buying a heroin shot of illusion. I'm very loath to say anything about true things, except that sometimes it's not that one delivers the truth—there is no truth in that sense —but that one feels it. The truth is what the audience gets, not necessarily what's delivered to it. You can't put ideas on the theater in the theater, as certain British directors try to do. That's the irony of it. The ideas are in the audience, and the theater fails when you try to impose ideas on it.

What you can do is find the inevitable next beat when you're rehearsing something. If you have a space like the Liberty Theater, which is an empty desert space, and you want to put a poem in it, you start with the poem and the performer, and you start somewhere that suits your taste. You start by a wall or in the center of the stage, and from that point, you find the next thing that is true. And there is only one truth for that group. That is certainly what I've discovered while working with Deborah Warner, because she has no need of any truth other than the inevitability of the next beat. That's why she's so good, and that's also what the theater's job should be. It's not arbitrary. Painters know what the next stroke is: if they've been true to their painting, they know exactly where it must be. The theater is just like painting in that way.

The problem in this town is the lack of continuity from one beat to the next, because people use the present moment to invent the future, instead of following it inevitably to a future. It's quite hard to say things here about the theater because young people seem to endow it with their need. The literary and art worlds are probably the same. People have such a hunger for it, but they don't know what the "it" is they have the hunger for. Somebody should help the young in this town. Maybe they should help themselves. They're waiting for a system that is never there to serve them. It's there to serve its own money-making objectives. They need to find a theater that is not based on that. It's so simple if they'd only just *do* it.

JEAN STEIN: You have spoken with several groups of students while you've been here. Don't you think that they are quite passive?

SHAW: They're punch drunk with fear and the need for approbation. It seems to me so many people need—we all need—approbation and approval. But theater is beyond approval. The students should be ruled by their own taste, not by second-guessing what somebody else's taste is. And that's quite a hard lesson to learn. It is freedom, of course. Freedom is not to care a damn what anybody else thinks and do what you find is rigorously true. The good thing about humanity is that it will respond to a thing of excellence. A heat comes off it, doesn't it?

STEIN: You said that you had warned the students at Julliard about the rise of a new form of McCarthyism.

SHAW: Well, that exists the world over, I suppose. I'm sure anything I say is incredibly naive, but it does seem that there are only three groups of people in the world: the rulers, the slaves, and the artists. And our ability to endow

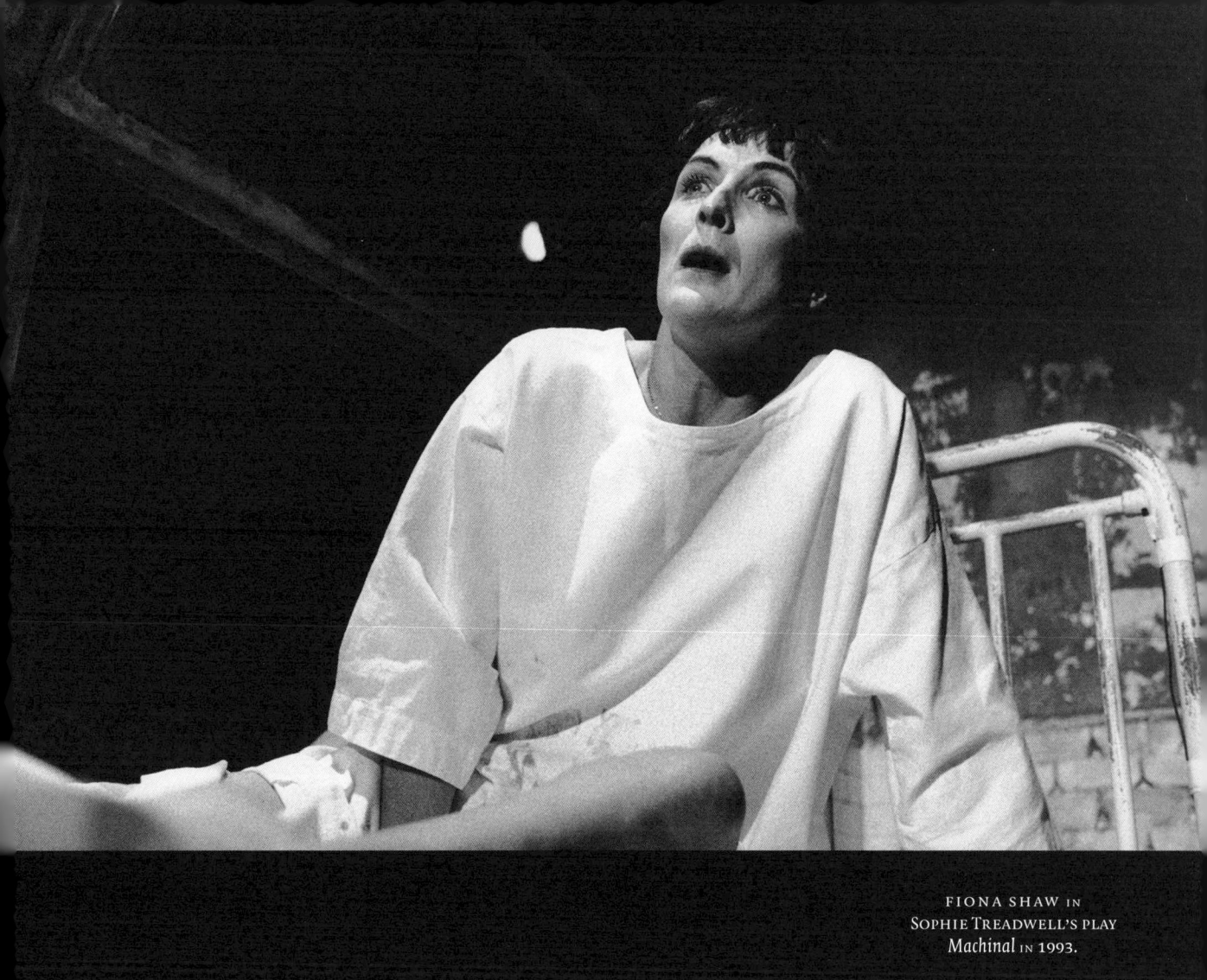

FIONA SHAW IN
SOPHIE TREADWELL'S PLAY
Machinal IN 1993.

the rulers, be it the rulers of the theater or the rulers of the world, with a sort of metaphysical aura is endlessly our downfall. I mean, we should distrust everything and yet be delighted by what we can learn. The students here are buying into a system which, at the moment, seems to be following a massive reactionary wave flowing over the country. I wasn't here in the fifties, but it seems like a form of McCarthyism—without even a McCarthy figure to blame for it. There's a sort of mutual terror.

It's very hard to give advice to young people, of course, because it's always about yourself and your experience of the world. You can't tell anyone how to do the next step of anything. Most of us muddle through life. I'm very muddled and the only area of clarity I have is the theater; it's the only thing about which I feel that when I'm not in control, I am in control. I'm not frightened of being out of control of it. In that way, it is like riding a horse or sailing. I like what it is, so I don't mind if it's difficult. But I come from an Irish Catholic background, which could mean a lot of things.

STEIN: What role has that background played in your life?

SHAW: Certainly, for me, being Irish and Catholic has no sentimental joy. I think revisionist history will show that the real problem with Ireland has not been English subjugation, but the famine. The famine, which is now a hundred and fifty years old, resulted in the Irish betraying the Irish very badly. In a way, if we've inherited anything, it's probably the guilt that those who survived the famine must have survived it on the backs of those who didn't.

This has never been dealt with by the country, and haunts the west far more than Cork, where I'm from.

My father is half-English, one half of his family came with Cromwell, and his mother is absolutely English, so I find, to my surprise, that in a way I'm more at home in London. I always wanted to go there as a child.

STEIN: You mentioned that when you first began acting in London you had a special relationship to Virginia Woolf's work.

SHAW: Yes, I played her when I was twenty-one, at RADA*, in Edna O'Brien's play, *Virginia*, which she had written for Maggie Smith. And I had a marvelous time with it because, at the time, I looked very like Virginia Woolf. I got so involved in reading about her that I began to have the illusion that I was her. I had the sensation that I had written *To the Lighthouse*. I really thought I'd written it. I used to pick up the diaries and think I was writing them as I was reading them—but I think that's just delusion, isn't it? So beware. I can't draw any conclusions from that. I've never felt that way since. I certainly didn't feel it as Richard II.

STEIN: You have said that you feel the first four years of your life as an actress at the Royal Shakespeare Company were wasted performing Shakespeare.

SHAW: I was mainly a comedienne when I was at the Royal Shakespeare Company from the age of twenty-six to thirty. I did Katherine in *The Shrew*,

---
* The Royal Academy of Dramatic Art.

Portia in The Merchant of Venice, Beatrice in Much Ado, and Celia, then Rosalind, in As You Like It. I played all those comic heroines and never any tragedy. I now think we were dinosaurs, because they were building us for a world that no longer exists. We were trained for a lifetime of doing Shakespeare and in fact, I'm not sure, as a woman, that Shakespeare would yield a lifetime of work.

STEIN: But you were able, during that time, to develop a special relationship with the language of the texts?

SHAW: Yes. In my second year, I did the tour for the Royal Shakespeare Company and played Portia and Beatrice for six months all over the country. Playing eight shows a week—four of each—was an amazing thing, because you develop such a muscle moving between verse and prose, testing things out and learning and learning. You begin to get so used to the characters. I mean, you're speaking their words for so many hours in the day that you're almost more in the seventeenth century than you are in the one you're in. The Cotswolds* are forever colored for me because I lived in a cottage opposite the theater in my first year, and they were building The Swan using medieval methods, wooden nails and wooden planks, so I had the sound of medieval building all through the summer across the street while I was doing Shakespeare. I was suddenly stimulated by only one period of sound.

---

* Stratford-upon-Avon, in the Cotswold Hills, is home to the Royal Shakespeare Company's theater, The Swan, a reconstruction of Shakespeare's theater that was built in the 1980s.

STEIN: How did you originally meet Deborah Warner?

SHAW: We met in 1980 when I was at RADA. The principal had been rung up by a young Deborah Warner to say that somebody had backed out of a show she was doing in Edinburgh, so I stepped in. I worked with her on Woyzeck, the play, and I didn't like her at all. I thought she had no interest in language because she was silent. I was so foolish.

STEIN: So Woyzeck was your first collaboration?

SHAW: Yes, but I played just a small part—the lady who speaks about the moon—it was just one speech. Anyway, Deborah was much truer than I was. She asked me every year after that to do her next play. Things happen as they happen. I thought of her then as this annoying fringe director with whom I hadn't particularly got on well. Finally, we were both at the Royal Shakespeare Company in 1988—she had done Titus Andronicus brilliantly—and I still had no wish to work with her, and by then she had no wish to work with me. But by the end of the season, we came up with the idea of doing Electra. I wanted to do a tragedy and she wanted to do a Greek, so we kind of buried our differences and found, of course, that we were able to work tremendously well together. I don't know why. My brother had recently been killed in a car accident, and I was very raw about that, so I felt near to the emotional territory of Electra. And I think I was getting over a love affair as well, so I was in a very malleable state.

Deborah is a Quaker and very English and it was marvelous to meet a mind that was so unlike my own—incredibly sure, incredibly confident in its clarity. Puritanism had been our enemy and I found myself suddenly working with a Puritan, but maybe in a funny way I was more at home with a Puritan than with the reaction against Puritanism. She was very patient, and I couldn't get over this astonishing silent Quaker—you know, they only speak when they need to speak.

I tried *Electra* different ways for weeks, and her patience was such that every day she would write on the notice board "Act I, Scene I" if we hadn't got anywhere true. I thought, "we should move on and then we'll come back to this bit." But there is no moving on until the beginning is correct, and I learnt that from that moment. I couldn't believe her workaholism. And I, who'd always been burning the candle at both ends, staying up all night and then doing matinees, suddenly found this disciplined, obsessional worker and became completely addicted to her way of work. I don't love it as much now, of course, because it's lost its novelty. Even though she's actually much more verbose now, I still find her silence intensely difficult to cope with because I need her to respond.

STEIN: But she listens.

SHAW: She's listening. Absorbing totally. Picks up on everything. But we don't know how long it will last. You know, theatrical partnerships and indeed theater companies rarely last more than six years, and we're always worried at the end of each thing that it's our last. It might go on all our lives, but it doesn't necessarily follow that it will. My patience gets shorter, I must say. I begrudge the time now—she takes so long to do things. However, the level at which she does them is unparalleled. I've never worked with anyone so fine. The wonderful thing is not to work together all the time, but to do it by breaks. I couldn't bear to go straight into another project together. When I do—this year I went from the filming of *Richard II* to *The Waste Land*—I feel drowned. She must feel the same. We're just in each other's company all the time; it's maddening. You begin to anticipate what the other person sees, and when you start doing that you're lost, because you stop seeing. You need to be surprised.

But she has a sort of Alzheimer's gift: whenever I turn up in the world, she beams with such delight that I'm always thrilled to see her. She's got such a human warmth. She's just delighted by life, and her delight never has a tortured aspect to it; it's very straightforward.

Hildegard Bechtler is the third part of this little trio. She has designed all the work that we've done together. She's a German Catholic and absolutely the mix of the two of us. She has all that Germanic clarity, which Deborah and she meet on, and I'm not overpowered by having too many Protestant minds in my midst. It wasn't planned, but I have noticed that it's a remarkably international trio. Many people work with people from their own town, people they know. I absolutely needed the opposite. So when I went to Dublin to do Ibsen's *Hedda Gabler*, I did it with them and I felt completely protected because of that. I wasn't washed over with my own culture. I'm surprised equally that they have taught me a whole aesthetic that is not mine. I've been completely yanked away from the whole world I was in. I was very political in my twenties and very keen on feminism and on the Royal Shakespeare Company hiring women directors, of which there were none then—Deborah was one of the first to be hired on the back of that little revolution we caused—and I was also very keen at the time on discovering what parts of language were inherently male. I've no interest in that now, I'm way beyond it, but that was the only area in which I had managed to disquiet myself away from just being talented and celebrating it. I realized that you had to put it to some use beyond just showing off.

STEIN: Did you feel fearless at that point in your life?

SHAW: Somebody said to me the other day, "You seem fearless with language." And I thought, "Oh my God, someone else saying I'm fearless, when I'm so not. I'm like the Wizard of Oz, this tiny thing behind a curtain, going grrrrr . . ." I was so embarrassed at the notion of fearlessness that I said I had been daunted by doing *Richard II* and hadn't felt in tune with the play because it was the verse of a sort of person that I wasn't—let alone gender. But I went home and thought that I actually *was* fearless about it. There are certain things you shouldn't be frightened of. Language is such a friend. I didn't understand *The Waste Land* when I first dealt with it, and I was in awe of it, but I wasn't fearful of it.

STEIN: Being Irish, what interested you about the idea of playing the role of an English king? Were you drawn to the questions of English royalty and illegitimacy?

SHAW: What is wonderful about *Richard II* is that Shakespeare writes it in a different language than he writes the other plays. It's almost entirely in verse; not one beat of it is out of sync with itself and it all rhymes. So you get Richard saying at the beginning lots of things like, "Forget, forgive, conclude and be agreed, / Our doctors say this is no month to bleed." The way I understand it is that Shakespeare wrote in a sort of patronizing way in a reduced, childlike language that he imagined people used in the fourteenth century. It's like us speaking "ye olde English." So *Richard II* doesn't have nearly the dexterous variation, the flirtation with feminine endings that fly off into prose, or the half-lines that don't finish, that he has in the more advanced plays. It's completely even, and that gives it a sort of formal structure which tells you everything about what he knew about that period. It's like those Books of Days, which present a tiny reality—a lady by a well with some flowers surrounding it. Shakespeare was saying, it's a tiny world with a formal language, which also, of course, hints at the barbarism that lay behind that language. The more we structured our language, the more we invented civilization.

Shakespeare is the great inventor of civilization because he created a vocabulary that is wild and sensuous whilst harnessing it to verse. So you can say dangerous things, because you're contained by verse. You can ask big questions or you can say rude things, or one line can contradict the next line. Shakespeare invented our possibilities of emotional life. At that time thought and feeling were the same thing—something that's so rare now. The language was a complete external mapping of what was going on in the mind. Now we say, "pass the sugar," when we really mean, "I love you." They said, "I love you," when they wanted to say, "I love you." And they said it beautifully. Shakespeare allowed you into the garden of

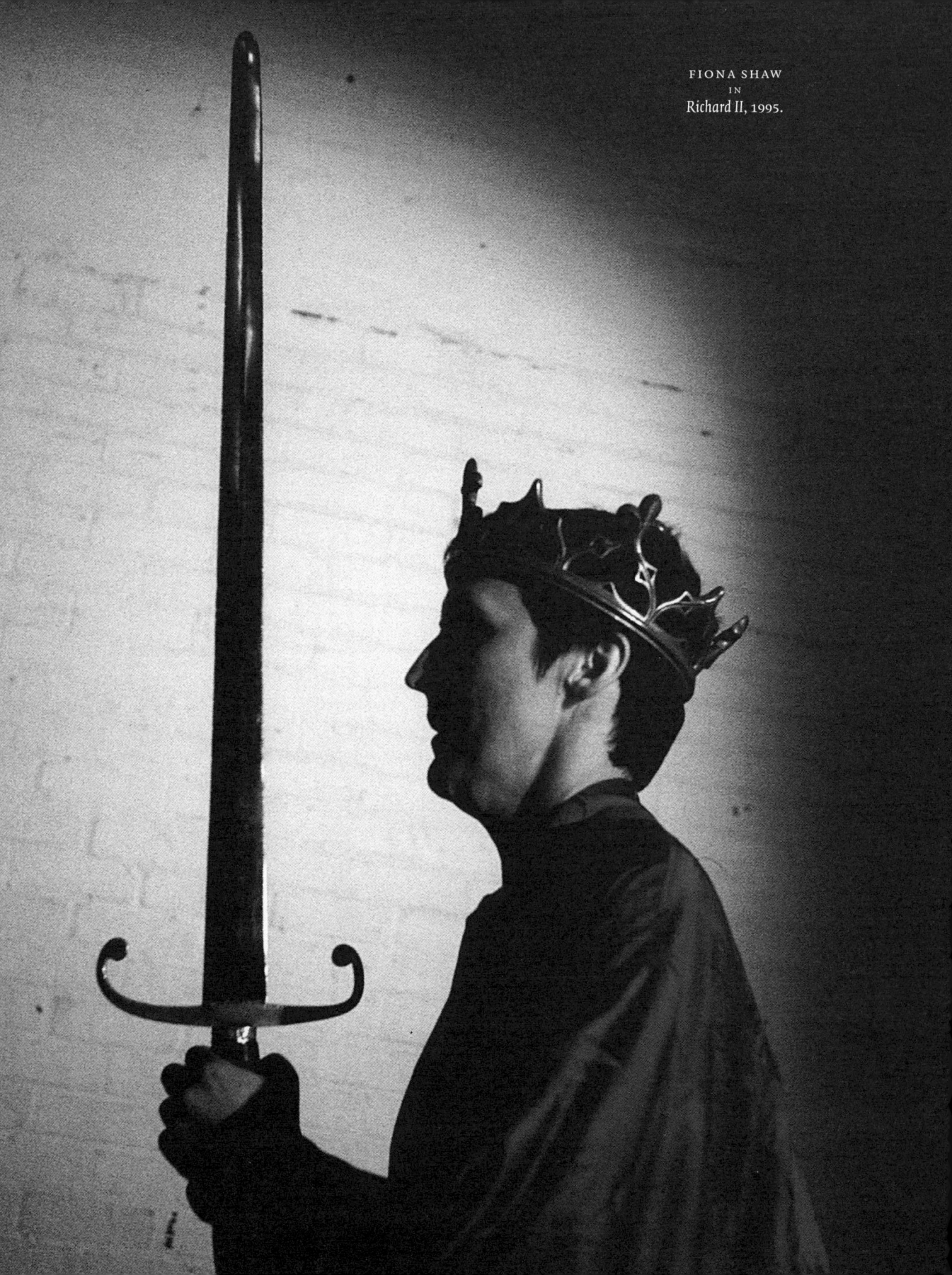

FIONA SHAW
IN
Richard II, 1995.

somebody else's mind. That was his great genius, really. Now we're in a terrible time. At the end of the twentieth century, the rest is silence. We don't know how to express ourselves and we don't want to express ourselves—expression is in the silence. So we're open to endless misinterpretation.

But in relation to royalty, Richard II was less well-received in England than in Paris or in Austria. It was still an enormous public success in London, but critically I got hammered. Somebody had to get hammered and it couldn't be Deborah, I suppose, in this instance. So I got the brunt of it. Possibly my Irish accent got me into some trouble. In fact, Richard probably spoke much more like I do than like modern English people. But, most of all, people felt that I was a woman. And I felt I knew that I wasn't trying to be a man. I was trying to find out whether the poetic language was beyond gender, and I think it is. It still worked theatrically, because, as Peter Brook says, the more you ask of an audience, the more they will give, if you serve it correctly. He says, it's not what you do to the language, it's what the language does to you. It's not theory even, it's just wisdom. In that way, I did it very openheartedly.

It was remarkable that Richard Eyre* allowed it on with a woman playing Richard II in the middle of an institutionalized theater. But he absolutely resisted it. He couldn't understand what we were going to do, and we couldn't really explain the process. It's only by doing it that you find out what happens. There's that wonderful

---

* Artistic director of the National Theatre, London, where Deborah Warner's production of Richard II was first performed in 1995.

line in As You Like It: "much virtue in If." There is much virtue in "If." I'm always thinking "as if" this or "could we just see what would happen if . . ." and it's never what you think would happen. It's all praxis. I am dazzled by "If" and I suppose I am fearless in that way. I must have had a very privileged upbringing. Fearlessness is a sort of luxury. But I'm frightened of being misunderstood. That's what I hate more than anything. Because I'm not self-conscious about my identity when I act, I have to allow other people to read what they see as my identity in it. And if they're not benign about that, I hit the roof. I'm so open to misinterpretation that when I find that somebody opts for the negative in relation to my work, I go mad.

The English found my Richard charmless, which was just so hurtful. His language is charmless at the beginning but then it becomes so charming, because of the honesty with which he speaks about his failings. And at the end of the play, when he soliloquizes about his kinghood:

> Sometimes am I king;
> Then treasons make me wish myself a beggar,
> And so I am. Then crushing penury
> Persuades me I was better when a king;
> Then am I king'd again, and by and by
> Think I am unking'd by Bolingbroke,
> And straight am nothing.

He talks about the fact that wherever you are in the world, you are there just by thinking it. It's a reminder.

Anyway, I got into a lot of trouble. That period in English history, with first cousins Richard and Bolingbroke struggling over who should be king, is seen as a time of glory when power was able to elevate itself. When Richard became king at age ten, he made his ten-year-old cousin kneel to him in the nursery. With that kind of national psyche going down through the ages, it's not surprising that if somebody plays a theatrical game with that notion, that person will get into a lot of trouble.

STEIN: But there is a tradition of gender reversal in performances of Shakespeare. Even Sarah Bernhardt played Hamlet.

SHAW: There is. We laugh at it because we think it was all about thigh-slapping and probably very amateurish. And indeed the theater probably did come from an amateur tradition at that time, which meant that audiences' imaginations were very open to whatever was being offered. We pooh-pooh that tradition of role reversal, but the theater has always worked from opposites. Shakespeare's plays are often about role reversal and gender reversal. And a way to test a good play is to test its ultimate truths against the banal truths, isn't it? It's marvelous when you see children doing plays and playing kings and queens. It tells you a lot about what kings and queens are. . . . The fact that our production of *Richard II* was so popular in France tells us something about the French, because they kill their kings. They found this badly behaved king hysterical.

But, performing the play in England, I began to see that people there are remarkably connected to the past. Class still rules enormously. It's not the upper class's fault that it rules, you know. It's all by complete mutual consent. I've spoken to bright, liberal people who say they'd be very thrown if the queen was removed. They hide behind the idea that the royal family is merely a showcase that brings in tourism to England. But the moment it's threatened, you begin to see that it is actually the cornerstone, the linchpin, of the country. And now the English are in a beleaguered state because the royal family is showing itself to be unworthy of this endowment of power. They're just a family going through difficulties—why wouldn't they be? But the royal family is still God. Henry VIII is still God. The English have a religion that is tied now to the dubious morals of this family, and they have an intelligentsia that daren't be more intelligent than this not particularly intellectual family.

Of course the ramification of this structure is that all their imperialism sits just under the surface too. England was always at its most powerful when it was at war. Despite its overt need for peace, it doesn't really like it. I don't think any countries do, I mean, America . . .

STEIN: Oh no, we're always eager for war.

SHAW: Yes, war is much better. War brings in a lot of money, so people like it. They're caught in this identity trap and *Richard II* was the victim of it.

STEIN: Why did Deborah Warner choose to direct *Richard II* at that time?

SHAW: Deborah, I think, doesn't function very intellectually. She functions from a sort of deep, quiet, still center of Quakerdom, but she's got a fantastic immediacy. She functions from the power of ignorance in a way, not from a history of the theater or from knowing what is in fashion, yet she's often onto the central idea of the moment. We're not, in any way, ahead of the game. A recent production of Swan Lake had an all-male cast, which is a marvelous idea, but it may be a little more playful than what we did with Richard. The concept of gender-changing has been hijacked by vaudeville because it's usually about sexual ambiguity. Richard II isn't about that. It's about someone who isn't really a man either. He's a God, a sort of sexless creature.

I suppose inevitably part of what attracted Deborah to the idea is being provocative. And she said that I shouldn't have got on a high horse about being in trouble, because there is no doubt that part of the joy of it was being provocative. If you are going to be an agent provocateur, you have to take some of the consequences. But it wasn't meant as a hostile provocation, so when I got, you know, mauled, I thought, "Ouch, all I did was play a game." But I did ask for it a bit. What I discovered was how many sacred cows there are in England. It was like putting on your mother's best dress that she really didn't allow you to dress up in. I didn't know you weren't allowed to touch that one. I got my knuckles rapped and I didn't find that comfortable, because I was left having to endure it. But Deborah was, of course, completely self-righteous about her provocation, so she was protected by that. Once she's decided it's the right thing, she has no doubt. I doubt from the beginning to the end of it. I doubt every day that I'm doing the right thing. And the reaction to Richard made me feel smaller. I felt, "but at my back from time to time I hear the rattle of the bones." I felt a claw at my back in England. Not this year but last year, when we first opened. And I think it's true: one hears the chattering of bad mouths.

STEIN: I'm paranoid in that way.

SHAW: Maybe I was paranoid. Deborah said, "nonsense, it was just a few of the critics," but no, I think people used it against me. I could feel a cold wind, as if I'd overstepped the mark and it bothered me. I wish it didn't. It didn't bother her at all. Not at all. She rewrites history. I mean she gets it rewritten by sticking with the thing. She's fantastic for winning the war.

STEIN: Was there a different critical response when Deborah Warner and you took the play to Paris?

SHAW: Yes, and everyone changed their minds and decided it was a very good idea. But that didn't make me feel any better. I felt the wind.

STEIN: How did you choose to perform The Waste Land? Did the poem have special meaning for you?

SHAW: It came in two different waves. I had finished doing Machinal at the National Theatre for the director Stephen Daldry, and it had been an enormous success. If something is very well-received, I have a sort of self-destructive need to do the opposite. It's not self-destructive actually —it keeps me alive—because I think that to repeat yourself stylistically is the killer, and in the end, one has very little to say in a little life. You hope you can change the parameters enormously....

Anyway, Deborah asked me would I perform

Beckett's *Footfalls*, which hadn't been done in the West End since it had opened some twenty or twenty-five years previously in Earl's Court, so off we went. We were given this fabulous theater over a two-week period, which is unusual in the commercial theater. And we tried to find where to perform it in this building: it could have been in the foyers, it could have been anywhere. I'm loath to call it performance art, because that gives me the creeps in a way, but with a whole building and a small play you don't necessarily have to fulfill any mandate; you don't have to put the audience where the audience goes.

The play is about a visitation from a person who exists and doesn't exist—the character has two names, May or Amy, you don't know which it is—somebody who's at the death of language. It's about damaged humans, insofar as it's about anyone. It's a peculiar play. We performed it everywhere. The stage was the least interesting place we performed it. I performed it on a huge board over the stalls, but that didn't seem to be the hardest place. Finally, we thought the hardest place was the front of the balcony, where rather precariously I walked the seven steps. There was all this red plush seating, and I wore a red knobbled dress and those slighly retarded shoes you wear for your first walk, and other than that I did the text and the audience sat in the stalls and looked up at it. And adored it. We charged a very low price for the tickets, so we had a whole young audience who were on their way to pubs and clubs, and it was a sensation. We began to see the possibility of a short play, a short evening as another whole way of approaching the theater and the discomfort of it. The beauty of the building, the lighting of the vault of the building, and forcing the audience to look at the building and the stalls, rather than looking at the stage. And this visitation of twenty minutes . . .

An injunction was very swiftly put on us by the police. We were banned by the Beckett estate, their claim being that we had not performed the play as Beckett had wished it. Beckett had said that you had to wear gray and I was wearing red. I was wearing red against red which I thought was gray. We reversed one quotation and we didn't perform it on the stage as Beckett had wished, so we weren't true to the play. The French had paid for this production, but they never saw it because it wasn't allowed to go to Paris, which was mortifying. In a way, I think that Beckett is being shunted to the fringes of academia where he's going to languish and may get lost unless his estate eases up on these things —stage directions are not the essence of the writing. Anyway, because of this banning, we were left with sort of a vacuum, and a vacuum is sometimes a good thing, mind you. We knew that we were onto something that we wanted to develop.

Subsequently, I was asked to go to the Schaubühne am Lehniner Platz in Berlin to perform *The Waste Land* for what the theater called a "Monday Evening" that they do with a German speaker and an English speaker. So I learnt the poem. I don't know why I learnt it. It was wintertime, so I thought I'd like to have it. Then Deborah was asked to do something with architecture at the Kunsten Festival des Arts in Brussels. So she took my poem, and we rehearsed it in a beautiful house on the edge of Brussels for two weeks, and the poem became completely domestic—because I acted out a lot of things to do with my family. All roads lead to my family. . . . The poem became like domestic architecture and we had a big desire then to perform it in domestic architecture. Because of the sort of festival-itis that everyone has in Europe, it was invited all over. And in each place I think we grew to love it more because it became about cities. We went to the Dublin Theatre Festival where we performed it in a big empty armory in Phoenix Park, which had old outhouses that Deborah lit from the inside, so it was like an eerie town. That was the most dramatic place. The audience had to come in buses from town and a marvelous thing happened there—which is festival fare: we were delayed one night because the lights were not ready when we arrived, so the bus driver had a copy of the poem and he read it out loud to the busload of people while they waited. Isn't that heaven? That's much more interesting than going to see the piece.

That's how it developed, and it's most unusual that it should come to the center of New York, even though we considered a lot of other places. Deborah looked at the twin towers of the World Trade Center and at Ellis Island. I was keen on the perfumery in Bloomingdale's because I think that would be a wonderful place to perform something, with the audience all around those glass counters, but finally to our surprise we ended up in the Liberty Theater. We didn't really want a theater, but it's actually sort of a dying elephant of a heyday, and now the area is being turned into a Disney 21st-century park of joy rides. So it's in transition. And doing the poem there is like stroking something to death—the theater is going to die and then be reborn as something else.

STEIN: Deborah Warner said that audiences haven't felt threatened by your interpretation of *The Waste Land*.

SHAW: Oh, I'm sure there are people who are threatened. I hope they don't go to see it if they have a private relationship with the poem. It's very hard not to be possessive about something to which you feel you have a particular relationship. I wouldn't be rushing to see productions of *Electra* or *Hedda Gabler*. But about *The Waste Land*, I've had nothing but the most magnificent letters; it's marvelous, you know, that there are people who are in dialogue with themselves and with poetry. They are very nervous, I think, with the millennium coming, and this poem protects them. That's what I sense in these letters. They need Eliot to say what they are fearful of or they just need to look in the mirror very forcefully for a moment. I don't know how it works really, but there is a magic spell in the poem.

STEIN: Do you perceive it as a religious poem?

SHAW: Well, I now find that the quieter I perform it, the more the silence in the audience is like a meeting—which goes back to what I was saying about Deborah. So there is a sort of spiritual listening, which is a spiritual thirst. And the safe thing about this piece is that it's not preachy, so I'm not pervading any philosophy. I don't think I am interpreting it—I have no line on it. I'm not trying to say what I think Eliot is trying to say to an audience. I'm only trying to be true to each beat of it and to render it with as much life as I can. And I think because of that there is a sort of religious debate in the minds of

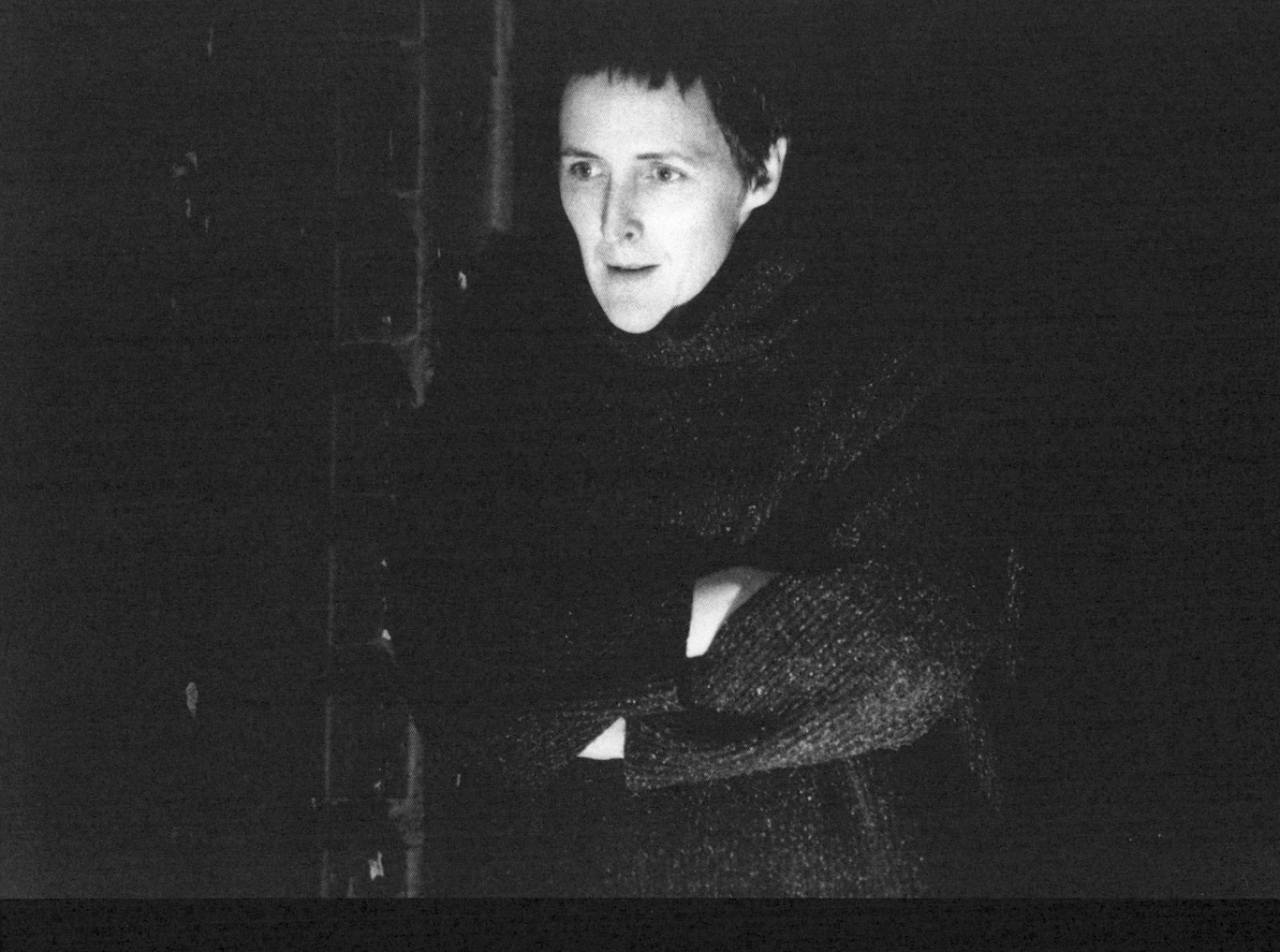

FIONA SHAW
IN
The Waste Land, 1996.

the audience.

You know, at the beginning, Eliot declares what it is: "for you know only / A heap of broken images." That's a hard thing to say to an audience who've just come to hear what you have to say—that you're going to show them broken images—and then he comes in with this sort of double slam at the end, by saying: "Here is no water but only rock / Rock and no water." He does a fugue-like poem on these two notions of water and rock, which people can interpret as they will. In that way, it's not like watching Billy Graham—Eliot doesn't tell you what the water is. It's whatever people want the water to be. "The hermit-thrush sings in the pine trees / Drip drop drip drop." That changes in my mind often. I think about the city, the noise, the dryness of the city here, and the aridity of low expectation, people shopping in sales, going through racks of clothing to get another good deal to put on their bodies, wasting time between life and death. The way in which we willfully keep the desert a desert is all too clear to all of us, I think. So the poem feels religious in that way. I like the inherent contradiction in the poem: even though he says, "There is the empty chapel . . . / It has no windows, and the door swings," he himself turned to religion in the end. I think it's fantastic to go back on what you said when you were younger. That's very important. He's massively anti-religious in the poem, which must mean that he had a massive relationship to God.

STEIN: Did you prepare for your performance by reading any of the critical work or biographies of Eliot? If so, do you feel that they influenced your understanding of the poem? Did they make you rethink Eliot's relationship to his wife in your performance of the section "A Game of Chess"?

SHAW: Well, I don't know whether I rethought it, but I think that the exposure of private lives through art takes us into a sort of cul-de-sac of spiritual gossip. It doesn't get us further than that somehow. Anyway, one wasn't there. One never knows what it was really like. If you remember back to highly emotional scenes of which you've been a part, they change even with time. Your memories change. And in a way, that's your privilege, isn't it? You can write whatever you think or remember of terrible scenes, but it's very hard to capture them. I don't think outsiders can ever get it, really. The writer Kennedy Fraser says she's noticed that women's writing is often at its most awkward when they are trying to declare something very precise about a moment in their lives. We go wrong, because our memory skips little beats, or we're trying to find something out and we can't quite say it. We're not at our most articulate about the things that we most need to talk about.

So I didn't read any scholarship on *The Waste Land* before performing it. I'm sure I would have got all sorts of little tendrils in my mind about Eliot, and I'm glad I haven't. Inevitably, one knows that he had a tempestuous relationship with his wife, Vivien, that may well be quoted in the poem. But I don't know Vivien and I don't know him. What I try to do in the poem is to be as sympathetic as possible to her when he quotes her, because he's written such a jagged rhythm:

> My nerves are bad to-night. Yes, bad. Stay
>   with me.
> Speak to me. Why do you never speak? Speak.
> What are you thinking of? What thinking?
>   What?
> I never know what you are thinking. Think.

It's so neurotic, but if I judge Vivien harshly, then it doesn't help the work. That just says that I've got a view of her. So I try to be sympathetic to each of the characters as they come along.

There are marvelous lines in the poem like:

> On Margate Sands.
> I can connect
> Nothing with nothing.

It seems to be common knowledge that Eliot had a breakdown at Margate, but Margate Sands somehow becomes as universal a place as Egypt in "We are dying, Egypt, dying." It becomes a place of emotional significance and its geography is immaterial. So Eliot's biography is immaterial, I think.

STEIN: Yet you described seeing the original manuscript of *The Waste Land* in which Vivien Eliot had written "wonderful, wonderful" in the margin of one of the passages.

SHAW: Yes, next to:

>   Do
> You know nothing? Do you see nothing?
>   Do you remember
> Nothing?
>   I remember
> Those are pearls that were his eyes.

Deborah and I were going to the public library one day just to look at the ceiling and out came the man who looks after the manuscript; he recognized me and took us in to see it. And what moved me was not just seeing the manuscript, but seeing the actual pencil of Vivien's writing on the poem. If the poem is about a row between a husband and wife, or a misconnection, the fact that she could comment and say, "wonderful, wonderful," is very loving, isn't it?

STEIN: You told me once that you think actors who perform a play have a greater comprehension of the work and its language than someone who writes a critical text on it.

SHAW: Yes, I think actors are very underestimated in that way. The academic is looking for an idea, you see, and it's not about ideas. It's about the thing itself. And actors really hear the sound of it. The ideas come to you afterward. Feeding an idea into a work shrinks it. Ultimately, it is the writer's job to communicate something about the essence of life or about his or her soul to the reader—and really I'm just a reader before I pass it on to an audience. So writing is an amorous act, and in a way the more despairing the writer, the more amorous the act. That may be the saving grace in the end for Beckett. He's so up a cul-de-sac, really—the human impasse. There's no way out from what he says or from what he offers us. But with Eliot, who seems to be writing about the destruction of the twentieth century, you hear, underneath that, the voice of a man who's so in love with life, with people, that he can't but write it down. And I'm sure that the vulnerability of writing must be like being with a lover, except that suddenly the lover is the entire public. To be that intimate with that many people is an incredibly generous thing. Most of us, when we read, often find that we recognize what's being said by the writer, particularly the contradictions in it, but we wouldn't dare expose ourselves by saying it or thinking it. We're full of contradictions and I think they're a great source of complexity—and, of course, a great enemy of political correctness.

Did I tell you that I had spoken to Martin Amis about this? I was on a radio program about favorite poems with him in London. He said that the tragic truth about his favorite poem, *Paradise Lost*, was that it could not have been written three centuries later because the world had got older, and that the truth about *The Waste Land* was that it could not have been written three centuries earlier because it was not yet ready. Both poems were at the pinnacle of the moment, and the moment passed. You could say that since Eliot wrote *The Waste Land* in 1922, the world has changed and got older and more knowledgeable. I think our ambivalence about that comes from the fact that none of us wants to lose innocence, but actually the world has to lose innocence in order to move on. And it does. But I think that, retrospectively, the writer always appears innocent. So maybe we'll all be judged a little better by the future—if they remember us.

My big subject is the Elizabethan period. The seventeenth century was so unneurotic—it made declarations and was life-loving. The twentieth century's preoccupation with suicide coincides with the killing of God by Nietzsche in 1890. Once you kill God, you only have language in a universe that has no God, so you're left standing on each word like little stepping stones across the gulf, instead of the sea of God-filled oblivion.

Hedda Gabler's all about that. There's a marvelous scene where Ejlert Lövborg says, "Hedda, what sort of power in you was it?" And she says, "Do you think it was some power in me?" At that moment there's a sort of gulf between the two of them. And of course she commits suicide. This systematic breakdown of communication is what marks our century, and of course a Holocaust sits in the center of it. Brecht, in *The Good Person of Szechwan*, has this good person, Shen Teh, who cannot even speak her own language, so she's always saying things like, "I too should like not to be a worker . . . I too should like to enjoy the endowments of the world." And she sings a song that goes like this:

> In our country
> There should be no dreary evenings
> Or tall bridges over rivers
> Even the hour between night and morning
> And the whole winter season too, that is
>   dangerous.
> For in face of misery
> Only a little is needed
> Before men start throwing
> Their unbearable life away.

Then you get to Beckett. There's a fantastic sentence in *Footfalls* that goes like this: "A little later, when she was quite forgotten, she began to—" You fall off the edge of the sentence and there's nothing—you don't fall anywhere. If we have a reduced language and no God, we're just blinking in a dead world. Our preoccupations become insular. We implode. And we're all left in these silent universes, in our own minds.

What originally happened theatrically was that language unified the speaker and the listener, and the reality was all one. By the time you get to 1700, you've got people laughing in comedies at people whom they're frightened to be like, so there's a bit of a gulf between the audience and the actors. Then by the time you get to *Hedda Gabler*, you have a gulf between the performer and the other performer; and by the time you get to Brecht, you have a gulf between what's being said and who's saying it; and by the time you get to Beckett, you have a gulf where the play doesn't even happen on the stage—it happens in the desolation of the listener's mind. And the only reply to it is the kind of art that playfully says, now you can see me, now you can't. That's a wonderful way through it, using debris materials to hide and then wave at the same time. Thank God for the playful arts. We'd be nowhere otherwise.

DAMON KRUKOWSKI

CARESSE CROSBY DREAMS A DREAM

My daughters at my side dressed in pinafores. The man just off the *Lusitania* at the dock, poem in hand: *we will sew our lips together* . . .

Let me present an opium vision, a memory from that room with four bathtubs, the view over the Seine and me, naked, illuminated to a cheering *bateau-mouche*. In the dream one says yes or no, and I choose yes. So we were married in an Inca ceremony officiated by a student sculptor who suffocated us in wet clay. What choice is left me? What instruction or command?

I try to follow my deceased companion. His taxi is too quick and the driver makes rude gestures at the passersby.

At the hotel it is none too romantic, though management has thoughtfully neglected to remove the previous occupants' caviar tins. They are blue and black and intricately stamped with impressions of fish scales. I contemplate my journey in the mirror. My relatives in Boston telegram for my arrest. Later that evening, back on Beacon Hill, the guests shiver at my negligée, carved in champagne ice. Who asked whom, I toss off, wet feet on carpet making my bobbed hair stand on end. Fear is a poem I burned, wrapping its ashes in silk, and ate like meringue.

Melvin Way

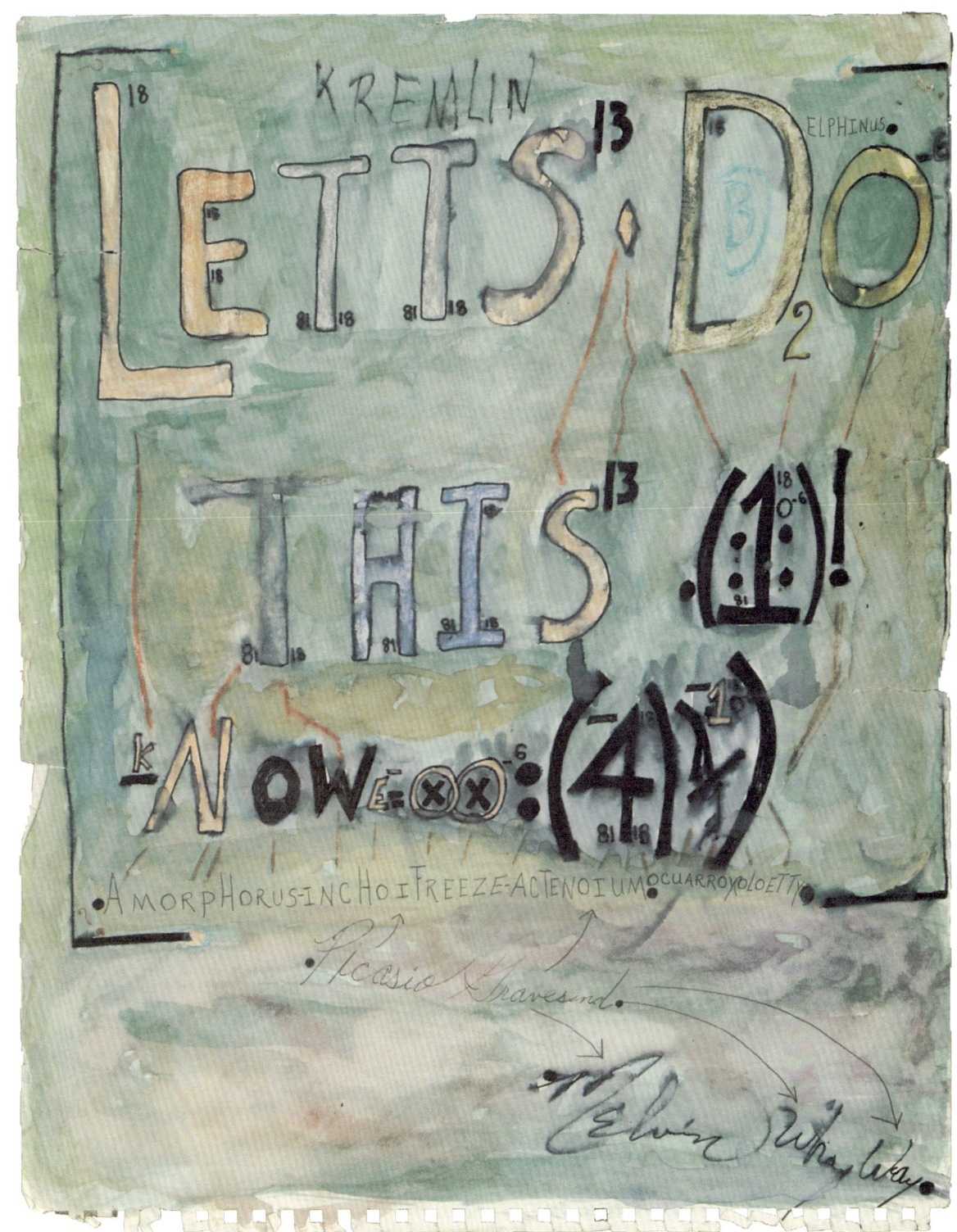

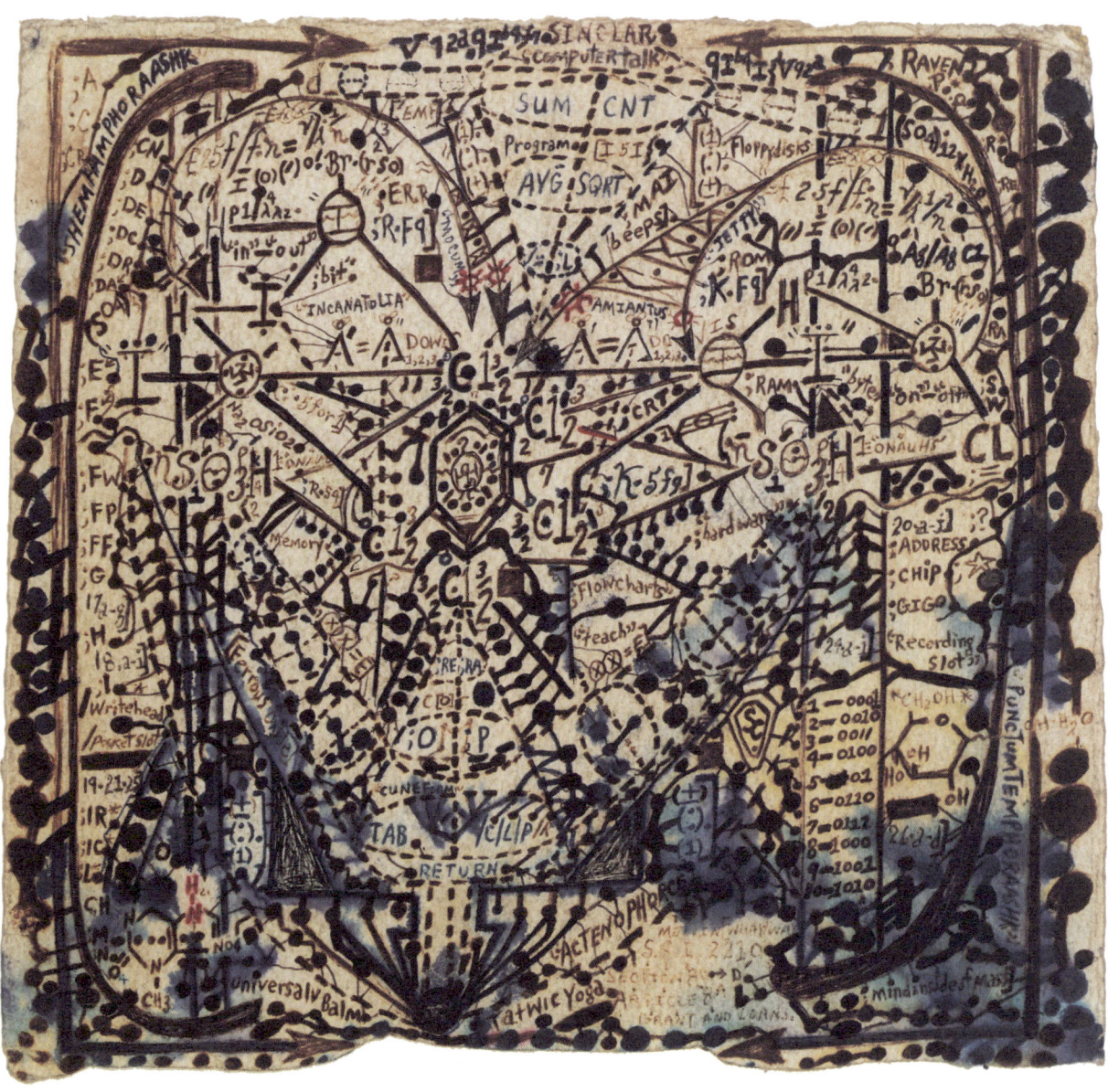

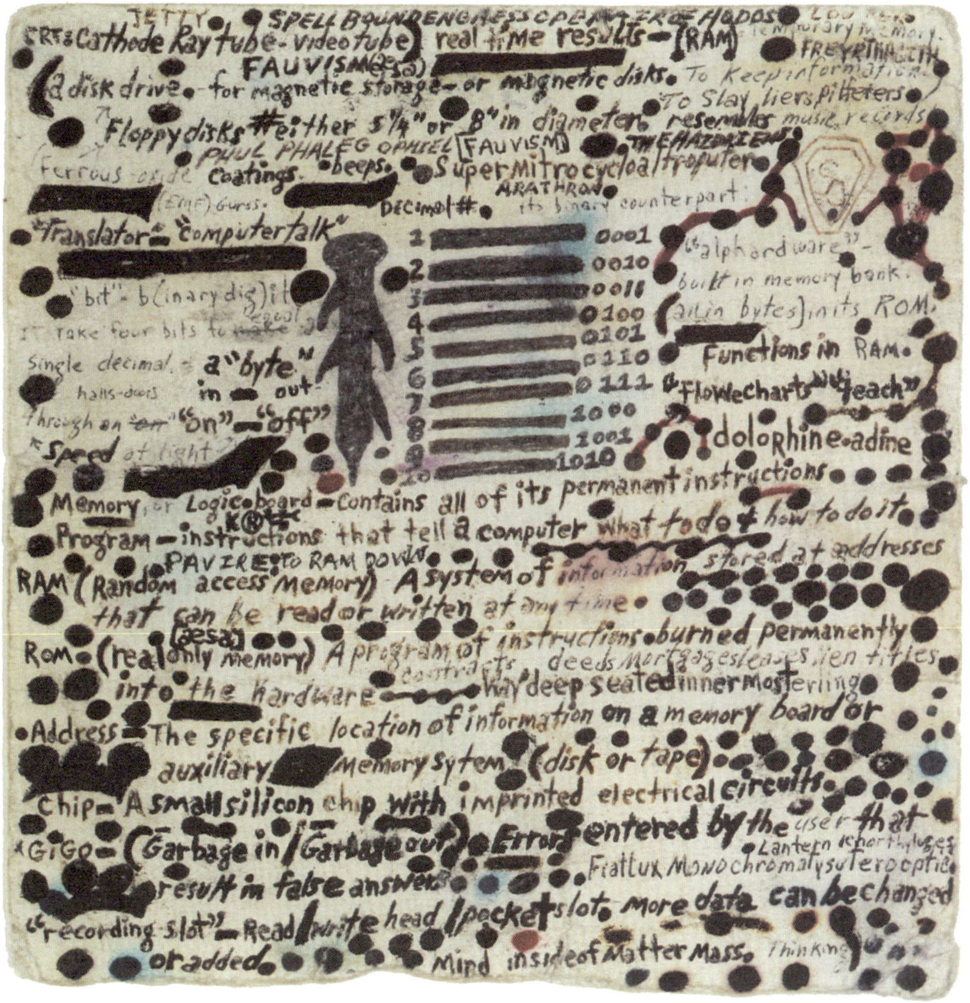

JETTY · SPELLBOUNDENGNESSOPERATEROHODOS · LOOKER
CRT=Cathode Ray tube–videotube) real time results–(RAM) temporary memory
FAUVISM(esa) FREYRTHAZETH
(a disk drive – for magnetic storage – or magnetic disks. To keep information.
"Floppy disks" = either 5¼" or 8" in diameter, resembles music records. To slay liers pilferers
PHUL PHALEG OPHIEL [FAUVISM] THEHAZZIEL
Ferrous-oxide coatings. · beeps · Super-Mitrocycloaltroputer
(EMF) Gurs. ARATHRON its binary counterpart:
Decimal #
"Translator"· "computertalk" 1   0001   "alphardware"–
                                2   0010   built in memory bank.
"bit"–b(inary dig)it   3   0011   (ailin bytes)in its ROM.
it take four bits to make a   4   0100
single decimal. = a "byte"   5   0101   Functions in RAM.
halls–doors in – out   6   0110
through an "em" "on"–"off"   7   0111 "Flowcharts" "teach"
"Speed of light"   8   1000   dolorhine–adine
                                9   1001
                               10   1010 permanent instructions
Memory, or Logic board–contains all of its permanent instructions.
Program – instructions that tell a computer what to do & how to do it.
PAVIRE:TO RAM DOWN
RAM (Random access memory)–A system of information stored at addresses
that can be read or written at any time.
(aesa)
ROM (read only memory) A program of instructions burned permanently
into the hardware   contracts, deeds mortgages leases lien titles
                    way deep seated inner mastering
Address–The specific location of information on a memory board or
        auxiliary memory system (disk or tape).
Chip–A small silicon chip with imprinted electrical circuits.
GiGo–(Garbage in/Garbage out)–Errors entered by the user that
                                    Fiat lux Monochromaly suteroroptic
result in false answers.   Lantern short; lugs
"recording slot" – Read/write head /pocket/slot. More data can be changed
or added.   Mind inside of Matter Mass. Thinking

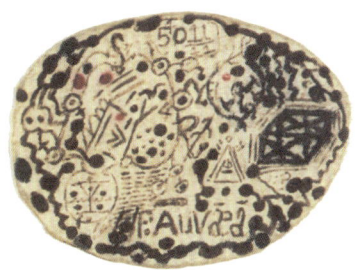

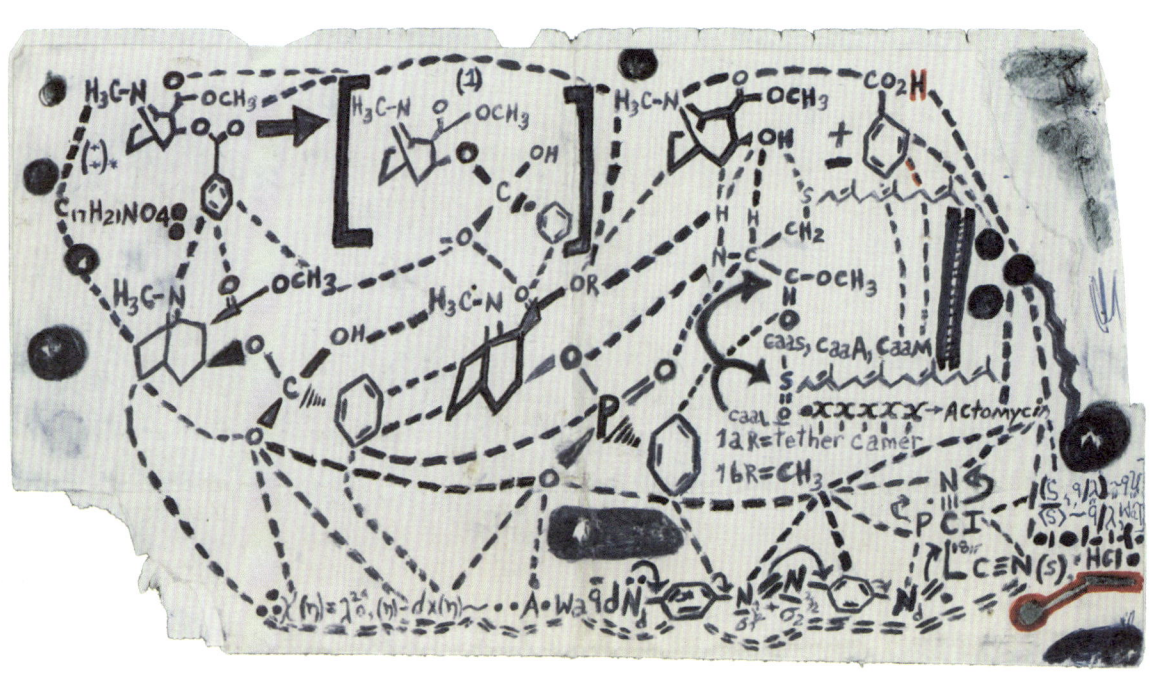

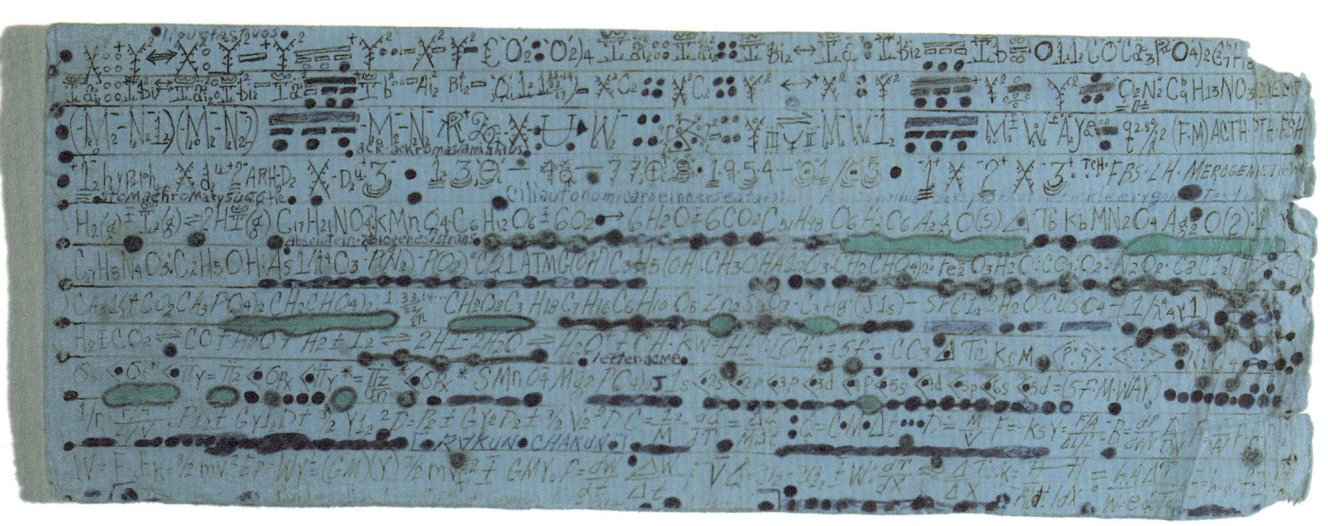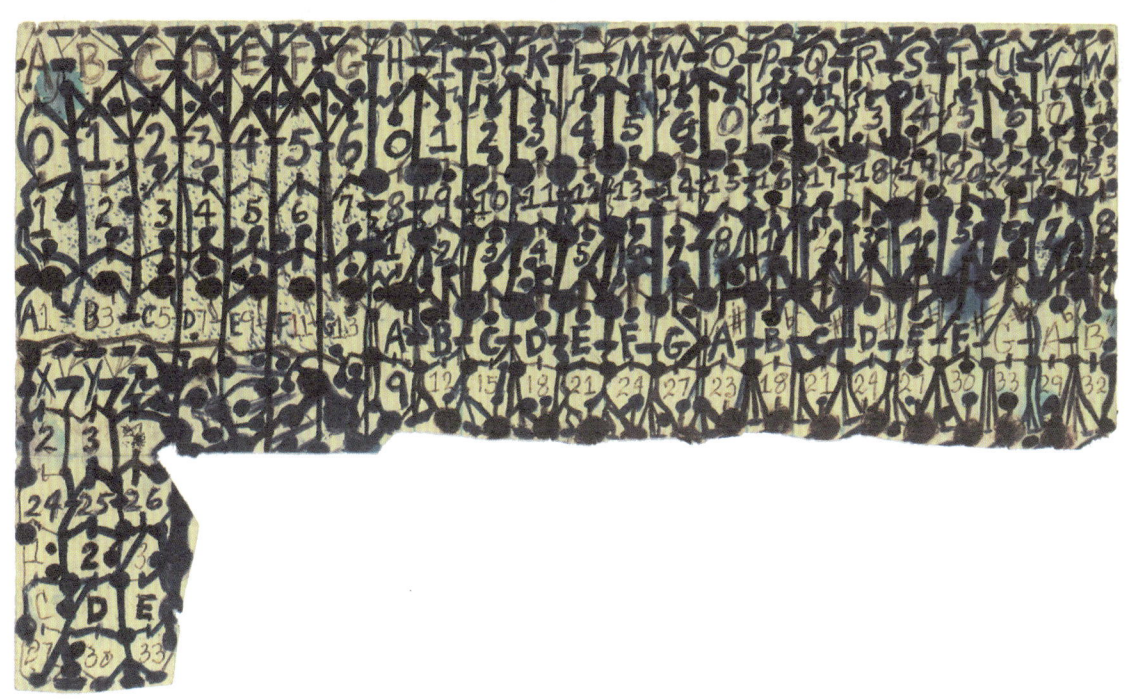

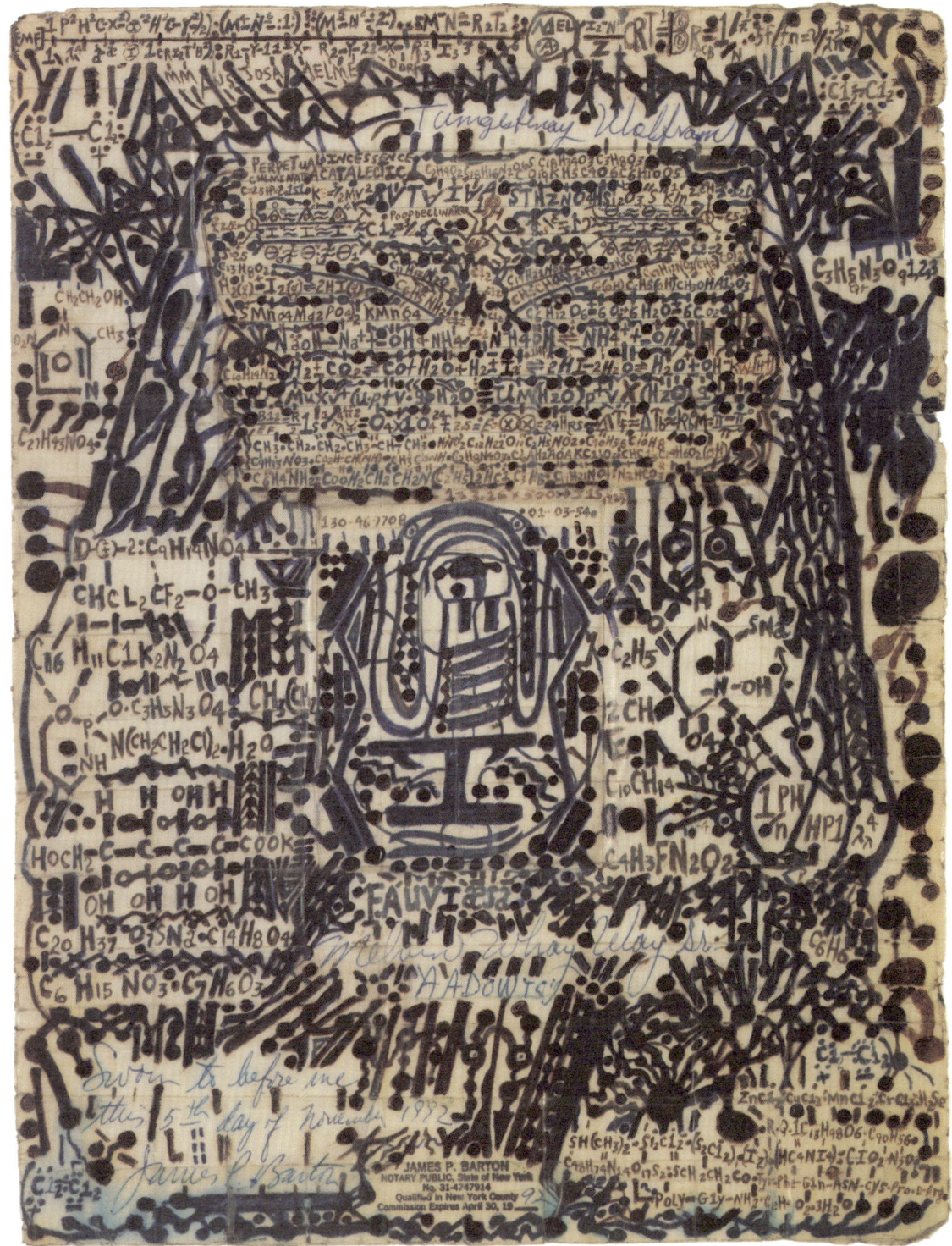

Melvin Way

In perpetual transit, Melvin Way's drawings on torn and folded pieces of paper are like the microfilm concealed in a matchbook in *Sherlock Holmes Goes to Washington*. Cryptographic and urgent, their "look" speaks of a studied indifference, so that decryption burns its own patchwork. An incessant ringing: as if the devil had commandeered Bell Atlantic and rerouted the circuitry so that the delay between perception and need became a permanent hallucination. A tirade of chemical equations, profit calculations (more sinister than the Swiss outsider artist Adolf Wölfli's), computer instructions, and radio-driven exhortations—it is impossible to put the receiver down, especially when you suspect that even the static is being manipulated. It is system overdrive where "the supreme number is rage."[*] Neither analog nor digital, Way's work is more like a cryptarithm where numbers and letters collude in the production of brain transmissions.

I'm not even sure that these are drawings as much as they are furtively passed notes, which neurally conjugate a daisy chain of defectors. The message is encrypted in a formula that enacts its own crystallization, which is to say, that it is impossible to establish a still point of reference. There is no escape from these conversions—this continual abstraction of the flesh. Who subjects whom? Who controls the discourse on subjectivity? Or, as Paul Virilio put it, "To be a subject or to be subjected? That is the question." How does one reassert control over a data base engorged with the objectification of knowledge and disconnected from the natural, physical world? For Way, it's a matter of redeploying scripts, of resisting generalized *conscription* at the hands of faceless technocrats. It's about becoming one's own notary public, rewiring the think tank, or rewriting its head ("writehead" being his common rejoinder). It's about getting "way deep" into the hardware and talking the talk before the talk does all the talking. You know: the "universal balm" of a twenty-four-hour Paradise Mall where even the molecular structure of its wares is manipulated by a capital market's hard drive. Melvin Way goes back to the crystal, goes into its heart in an attempt to put mind back into matter.

MICHAEL MADORE

---

[*] Harald Szeemann, "No Catastrophe Without Idyll, No Idyll Without Catastrophe," *The World of Adolf Wölfli*, Moore College of Art, Philadelphia, 1988.

FROM COMFORT WOMAN

NORA OKJA KELLER

The baby I could keep came when I was already dead.

I was twelve when I was murdered, fourteen when I looked into the Yalu River and, finding no face looking back at me, knew that I was dead. I wanted to let the Yalu's currents carry my body to where it might find my spirit again, but the Japanese soldiers hurried me across the bridge before I could jump.

I did not let them get too close. I knew they would see the name and number stenciled across my jacket and send me back to the camps, where they think nothing of using a dead girl's body. When the guards started to step toward me, I knew enough to walk on, to wave them back to their post, where they would watch for other Koreans with that "special look" in their eyes. Before the Japanese government posted the soldiers—"for the good of the Koreans"— the bridge over the Yalu had been a popular suicide spot.

My body moved on.

That is why, twenty years after it left my spirit behind at the recreation camp, my body was able to have this baby. Even the doctors here say it is almost a miracle. The camp doctor said I would never have a living child after he took my first one out, my insides too bruised and battered, impossible to properly heal. So this little one is a surprise. This half-white and half-Korean child. She would be called *tweggi* in the village where I was born, but here she will be American.

When the missionaries found me, they thought I was Japanese because of the name, Akiko, sewn onto the sack that was my dress. The number, 41, they weren't sure about, and thought, Perhaps an orphanage? They asked me—in Korean, Japanese, Chinese—where I came from, who my family was, but by then I had no voice and could only stand dumbly in front of their moving mouths as they lifted my arms, poked at my teeth and into my ears, wiped the dirt from my face.

She is like the wild child raised by tigers, I heard them say to each other. Physically human but able to speak only in the language of animals. They were kind and praised me when I responded to the simple commands they issued in Japanese: sit, eat, sleep. Had they asked, I would also have responded to "close mouth" and "open legs." At the camps where the Japanese called us *jungun ianfu*, military comfort women, we were taught only whatever was necessary to service the soldiers. Other than that, we were not expected to understand, and were forbidden to speak, any language at all.

But we were fast learners and creative. Listening as we gathered the soldiers' clothes for washing or cooked their meals, we were able to surmise when troops were coming in and how many we were expected to serve. We taught ourselves to communicate through eye movements, body posture, tilts of the head, or—when we could not see each other—through rhythmic rustlings between our stalls; in this way we could speak, in this way we kept our sanity.

The Japanese say Koreans have an inherent gift for languages, proving that we are a natural colony, meant to be dominated. They delighted in their own ignorance, feeling they had nothing to fear or learn. I suppose that was lucky for us, actually. They never knew what we were saying. Or maybe they just didn't care.

I'm trying to remember exactly when I died. It must have been in stages, beginning with my birth as the fourth girl and last child in the Kim family, and ending in the recreation camps north of the Yalu. Perhaps if my parents had not died so early, I might have been able to live a full life. Perhaps not; we were a poor family. I might have been sold anyway.

My father was a cow trader. He traveled from village to village, herding the cows before him, from one farmer to the next, making a small profit as the middleman. When he was home, my older sisters' job was to collect the dung and, after we parceled out a small portion for our own garden, sell the rest to our neighbors. Sometimes we dried the dung for fuel, which burned longer and cleaner than wood. Most of the time, though, we used sticks that my sisters collected from the woods.

My job was to help my mother wash clothes. We each had a basket, according to our size, which we carried up the river we called Yalu Aniya, Older Sister to the Yalu. Going up was easy, the load light on our heads. Coming home was harder, since not only were the damp clothes heavier but we were tired from beating the clothes clean against the rocks. I remember that as we crouched over our wash, pounding out the dirt, I pretended that my mother and I sent secret signals to one another, the rocks singing out messages only we could understand.

My mother died shortly after my father. I didn't see my father die; he was almost thirty miles away. As with his life, I know about his death primarily through what others have told me. The villagers who took him in say he had a lung disease, coughing up blood as he died. They also said he called for my mother.

She was always a good wife; she went to him quickly in death, just as she did in life. One night after we had carried home the wash, she kept saying how tired she was, how tired. Come, Mother, I told her, lie down. I kept asking her, what could I do? Do you want soup, do you want massage? Till finally she put her hand over my mouth and guided my fingers to her forehead. I stroked her softly, loosening her hair from the bun she tied it in, rubbing her temples where I could feel the heat and the throb of her beating heart. Even when the erratic tempo slowed, then finally stopped, I continued to pet her. I wanted her to know that I loved her.

I touch my child in the same way now; this is the language she understands: the cool caresses of my fingers across her tiny eyelids, her smooth tummy, her fat toes. This, not the senseless murmurings of useless words, is what quiets her, tells her she is precious. She is like my mother in this way.

Because of this likeness, this link to the dead, my daughter is the only living thing I love. My husband, the missionaries who took me in after the camp, my sisters, if they are still alive, all are incidental. What are living people to ghosts, except ghosts themselves?

My oldest sister understood this. When my second and third sisters ran away together to look for work as secretaries or factory workers in Pyongyang, the oldest sister tried to keep our father's business going by marrying our closest neighbor. The neighbors didn't have much money, but they had more than us and wouldn't take her without a dowry. How could they buy cattle without any capital, they reasoned.

I was her dowry, sold like one of the cows before and after me. You are just going to follow second and third sisters, she told me. The Japanese say there is enough work for anyone in the cities. Girls, even, can learn factory work or serve in restaurants. You will make lots of money.

Still, I cried. She hugged me, then pinched me. Grow up now, she said. No mother, no father. We all have to make our lives. She didn't look at my face when the soldiers came, didn't watch as they herded me onto their truck. I heard them asking her if she wanted to come along; your sister is still so young, not good for much, they said. But you. You are grown and pretty. You could do well.

I am not sure, but I think my sister laughed. I hope that she had at least a momentary fear that they would take her too.

I am already married, she said.

I imagine she shrugged then, as if to say, What can I do? Then she added, My sister will be even prettier. She didn't ask why that should matter in a factory line.

I knew I would not see the city. We had heard the rumors: girls bought or stolen from villages outside the city, sent to Japanese recreation centers. But still, we did not know what the centers were like. At worst, I thought, I would do what I've done all my life: clean, cook, wash clothes, work hard. How could I imagine anything else?

At first that is what I did. Still young, I was kept to serve the women in the camps. Around women all my life, I felt almost like I was coming home when I first realized there were women at the camps, maybe a dozen. I didn't see them right away; they were kept in their stalls, behind mat curtains, most of the days and throughout the night. Only slowly were they revealed to me as I delivered and took away their meals, as I emptied their night pots. Hanako 38, her name given because her face was once pretty as a flower. Miyoko 52, frail and unlucky as the Miyokos before her. Kimi-ko 3, with hair the color of egg yellow, which made the officers laugh when they realized the pun of her name: Kimi the sovereign, Kimi the yolk. Akiko 40. Tamayo 29, who told the men she loved them and received gifts and money that she, stubborn in her hopes for a future, would bury in the corner of her stall.

Unless they had to visit the camp doctor, their freedom outside their stalls consisted of weekly baths at the river and scheduled trips to the outhouse. If they needed to relieve themselves when it was not their turn to go outside, they could use their special pots. It became my job to empty the pots. I also kept their clothes and bedding clean, combed and braided their hair, served them their meals. When I could, I brought them each a dab of grease, which they would smooth over their wounds, easing the pain of so many men.

I liked caring for the women. As their girl, I was able to move from one stall to the next, even from one section of the camp to another, if I was asked. And because of this luxury, the women used me to pass messages. I would sing to the women as I braided their hair or walked by their compartments to check their pots. When I hummed certain sections, the women knew to take those unsung words for their message. In this way, we could keep up with each other, find out who was sick, who was new, who had the most men the night before, who was going to crack.

To this day, I do not think Induk—the woman who was the Akiko before me—cracked. Most of the other women thought she did because she would not shut up. One night she talked loud and nonstop. In Korean and in Japanese, she denounced the soldiers, yelling at them to stop their invasion of her country and her body. Even as they mounted her, she shouted: I am Korea, I am a woman, I am alive. I am seventeen, I had a family just like you do, I am a daughter, I am a sister.

Men left her stall quickly, some crying, most angrily joining the line for the woman next door. All through the night she talked, reclaiming her Korean name, reciting her family genealogy, even chanting the recipes her mother had passed on to her. Just before daybreak, they took her out of her stall and into the woods, where we couldn't hear her anymore. They brought her back skewered from her vagina to her mouth, like a pig ready for roasting. A lesson, they told the rest of us, warning us into silence.

That night, it was as if a thousand frogs encircled the camp. They opened their throats for us, swallowed our tears, and cried for us. All night, it seemed they called, Induk, Induk, Induk, so we would never forget.

Although I might have imagined the frogs. That was my first night as the new Akiko. I was given her clothes, which were too big and made the soldiers laugh. The new P won't be wearing them much anyway, they jeered. Fresh *poji*.

Even though I had not yet had my first bleeding, I was auctioned off to the highest bidder. After that it was a free-for-all, and I thought I would never stop bleeding.

That is how I know Induk didn't go crazy. She was going sane. She was planning her escape. The corpse the soldiers brought back from the woods wasn't Induk.

It was Akiko; it was me.

My husband speaks four languages: German, English, Korean, and Japanese. He is learning a fifth, Polish, from cassette tapes he borrows from the public library. He reads Chinese.

A scholar who spends his life with the Bible, he thinks he is safe, that the words he reads, the meaning he gathers, will remain the same. Concrete. He is wrong.

He shares all his languages with our daughter, though she is not even a year old. She will absorb the sounds, he tells me. But I worry that the different sounds for the same object will confuse her. To compensate, I try to balance her with language I know is true. I watch her with a mother's eye, trying to see what she needs—my breast, a new diaper, a kiss, her toy—before she cries, before she has to give voice to her pain.

And each night I touch each part of her body, waiting until I see recognition in her eyes. I wait until I see that she knows that all of what I touch is her and hers to name in her own mind, before language dissects her into pieces that can be swallowed and digested by others not herself.

At the camp, the doctor gave me a choice: rat poison or the stick. I chose the stick. I saw what happened to the girl given the rat bait to abort her baby. I did not have the courage then to die the death that she died.

As the doctor bound my legs and arms, gagged me, then reached for the stick he would use to hook and pull the baby, not quite a baby, into the world, he talked. He spoke of evolutionary differences between the races, biological quirks that made the women of one race so pure and the women of another so promiscuous. Base, really, almost like animals, he said.

Rats, too, will keep doing it until they die, refusing food or water as long as they have a supply of willing partners. The doctor chuckled and probed, digging and piercing, as he lectured. Luckily for the species, Nature ensures that there is one dominant male to keep the others at bay and the female under control. And the female will always respond to him. He squeezed my nipples, pinching until they tightened. See?

I followed the light made by the waves of my pain, tried to leave my body behind. But the doctor pinned me to the earth with his stick and his words. Finally he stood upright, cracked his back, and threw the stick into the trash. He rinsed his hands in a basin of water, then unbound my hands and mouth. He put the rags between my legs.

Fascinating, he said thoughtfully as he left the tent. Perhaps it is the differences in geography that make the women of our two countries so morally incompatible.

He did not bother tying me down, securing me for the night. Maybe he thought I was too sick to run. Maybe he thought I wouldn't want to. Maybe he knew I had died and that ropes and guards couldn't keep me anyway.

That night, with the blood-soaked rags still wedged between my thighs, I slipped out of the tent, out of the camp. Following the sound of my mother beating clothes against the rocks, I floated along the trails made by deer and found a nameless stream that led in the end, like all the mountain streams, to the Yalu.

I was strapped down when my daughter was born too. My hands cuffed to the bed, flat on my back with my knees up, I heard the low keening of a wounded animal in the etherized darkness. Surrounded by doctors, unable to move, I felt my mind slip back into the camps. You're a doctor, I screamed, help me, help me get home. But he only laughed and pushed himself on top of me, using my body as the other soldiers had done. Afterward, as he wiped himself on my shift, he opened the screen partition and let others watch him examine me. This one is still good, he called over his shoulder. He pried the lips of my vagina open with his fingers. See? he said. Still firm and moist.

I tried to protect my daughter from the doctors, from their dirty hands and eyes. I scissored my legs closed, wanting to keep my child cradled within me, safe. But they roped my legs, stretching them open into the Japanese character for "man." One doctor pushed on my stomach, another widened me with a double-pronged stick, and this time my baby came into the world fully formed and alive.

We caught her, someone said—and when I heard that woman's voice in the room full of men, I knew Induk was there. Slipping into the body of a doctor, she stood beside me, shadowed by mask, gown, and a halo of light. And though I could not see her face, though it had been some time since she last came to me, I knew it was her, just as I've always known. Even the first time.

She comes in singing, entering with full voice, filling me so that there is no me except for her, Induk.

That first time, she found me sprawled next to an unnamed stream above the Yalu, the place where I had discarded my empty body, and invited herself in.

I saw her with my eyes closed, though how I knew she was Induk I do not know, for she looked like my mother, standing there next to the river with her arms outstretched, long strips of hair coming undone from the married woman's bun at the back of her neck. It was as if, without their earthly bodies, the boundaries between them melted, blending their features, merging their spirits. Now I cannot remember what either my mother or Induk looked like when she was alive and a separate person.

Here, baby, here, Induk said, her voice creaking like a hundred thousand frogs. She shuffled closer, hands cupping her breasts, which turned into an offering of freshly unearthed ginseng.

It is not *myokkuk*, Induk said, as I gnawed on a raw root. She stroked my head, combing out the tangles with her fingers just as I did for her when she was alive, then she said: But seaweed soup is mostly good for making milk anyway. You don't need that now.

My stomach cramped, and I threw up what I had eaten. I rinsed my mouth with water from the stream, and my stomach rebelled at even the taste of water. Yet I could not stop my mouth from sucking at the root.

There was no need for me to get up. I lay by the river, already feeling the running water erode the layers of my skin, washing me away, but Induk filled my belly and forced me to my hands and knees. She led me to the double rainbow where virgins climb to heaven and told me to climb. Below me, a river of human-faced flowers stretched so wide and bright I could not keep my eyes open.

She spoke for me: No one performed the proper rites of the dead. For me.

For you. Who was there to cry for us in *kok*, announcing our death? Or to fulfill the duties of *yom*: bathing and dressing our bodies, combing our hair, trimming our nails, laying us out? Who was there to write our names, to even know our names, and to remember us?

And now, said Induk, there are only the dead to guide us. Here, she said, giving me the image of a woman. I saw a fox spirit who haunted the cemeteries of deserted villages, sucking at the mouths of the newly dead in order to taste their otherworld knowledge.

This is Manshin Ahjima, Induk said. Old Lady of ten thousand spirits. Go to her, and she will prepare you.

I wanted to say I didn't know where she lived, but then I saw the exact spot where Manshin Ahjima lived and how to get there. I'd have to cross over the Yalu, scale seven mountain peaks in the deep country, then follow the road to the outskirts of Sinuiju. Through a scattering of gray adobe houses, all identical, I would go to the house fronted with mulberry trees. There I would find the old lady and her ten thousand spirits.

I do not know how long I left my body by the river, stirring periodically with cramps and the need to vomit. It lay in its own filth, moving only to fill its mouth with ginseng and water, the instinct for survival in the blood and bones.

When I finally opened my eyes, I saw not heaven but partially chewed and digested bits of ginseng root in the dirt next to my face. I felt clear and empty, as translucent as the river beside me. Noticing that the bleeding between my legs had stopped, I peeled the rags, stiff as scabs, away from my body and, carefully folding them, placed them on some rocks away from the running water. After taking off the rest of my clothes, I waded into the stream and rubbed at the dried blood caked on my legs from groin to calves. The mud-colored flecks turned liquid red in my hands, then dissolved under the patient licking of the river's tongue.

Rubbing handfuls of small pebbles against my head and skin, I washed my hair and body until I felt raw. I let the cooling air dry me. By the length of the day, I knew that soon it would be the season to replant the stalks of rice in the paddies. When my parents were still alive and I was still a child, everyone in our family worked to grow the rice. Where we lived, there was time only for one planting, one harvest, so everything had to be done quickly and well. As the youngest, I was responsible for feeding the workers their meals of rice and soup, carried to them on trays balanced on my head. When I delivered the food without spilling, I was allowed to play—a function also rooted in practicality; as I jumped through the rows of fragile plants, waving sticks into the air, I kept scavenging birds away from our future meals.

But as I grew and second and third sister were hired on neighboring farms, I took over more of the work. Mother, oldest sister, and I would spend hours bent over the knee-deep silt, our fingers cradling the baby rice, laying them into the oozing earth.

During one season of planting, my mother gave birth to a dead baby. Smaller than one of my mother's outstretched hands, the infant slipped between her fingers in a gush of blood and sour-smelling fluid. My mother wrapped it in a bundle, packing it neat as a field lunch, before I could see it, but oldest sister saw. It was deformed, Soon Ja whispered. Tail like a tadpole. Or maybe, she added as an afterthought, it was a boy.

We walked with our mother to the river, taking the clothes that needed to be washed. My mother divided up the clothes between my sister and me, and humming under her breath, she walked downriver. We listened to her voice, rising in waves above the rushing of the water, sing the song of the river: *Pururun mul, su manun saramdul-i, jugugat-na?* Blue waters, how many lives have you carried away? *Moot saram-ui seulpumdo hulro hulro sa ganora.* You should carry the sorrow of people far, far away.

And as we beat our clothes clean, we watched out of the corners of our eyes as she tightened the knot on her baby's shroud and set it into the water where the current pulled it down. Into Saja's mouth, oldest sister told me later in an attempt to torment me. An offering for the gatekeeper of hell.

When I was dry from my bath, I took the rags that had held back my blood and all that was left of my first baby, and instead of throwing them into the water, I planted them in a clean patch of earth next to the stream.

The day after Induk called me out of the river, I went looking for the spirit I knew I could never find. Go to Manshin Ahjima, Induk said as she dipped her hand into my chest and pulled out my *maum*, the force of my heartbeat, and led me forward by a silver thread.

I walked and slept, walked and slept, and throughout the journey kept my eyes fixed on Induk beckoning before me. At times, her form would blur until it doubled, then quadrupled, and she would become Induk and my mother, and in turn my mother's mother and an old woman dressed in the formal *top'o* of the olden days. I realized I was walking with my ancestors.

I tried running to my mother, but she shook her head and remained just outside my reach. It was then that I noticed that she held a small book, no bigger than the palm of my hand, which I recognized as the *Ch'onja-chaek*, the most basic school primer. When she began to turn the pages, I strained to read what it said, but to my surprise, I found I could not understand the words. Even concentrating on the rapidly moving pictures milked most of my energy.

As my mother flipped through the book, I saw myself and my sisters as children, hanging onto our mother as she moved through our barley field and tended to our garden. And I saw us holding onto her body as we cried the death cries for her spirit. I saw myself underneath the pumping bodies of Japanese soldiers and, in the later pages, saw my oldest sister beneath the same soldiers. I saw myself sitting in the river, and I saw myself walking and sleeping, walking and sleeping, until I died.

At this point my mother closed the book. When I asked her why I could not see the rest of the book, the oldest spirit, whom I knew to be my great-grandmother, said, If you read the final chapters, you would know the universe. You would be dead.

When I looked up, I was alone and could smell the sea, so I knew I had followed the river west. Ahead of me I saw the cluster of small adobe homes nestled into the hillside. I knocked at the first house, wanting to ask if I could sleep in the courtyard. No one answered there, nor at the second home I came to. Finally, after failing to wake anyone at the third home, I entered the courtyard anyway and disrobed at the well. In the cold night, I laid my clothes on the brittle mud surrounding the well and bathed in the ice-cold water, wanting to purify myself and knowing I never could.

My skin felt waxy, as Induk's had the day after the soldiers killed her, the day after she reclaimed her name and I became the new Akiko. When the other camp women and I went to the river to bathe, we found her skewered body, abandoned alongside the path. We wanted to take her to the river with us to prepare her body for the separation of its spirit. Someone she loved should have cleansed her skin with her favorite scented oil. Someone who loved her should have laid her body out, with her head to the south, and prepared a feast to feed her soul for its next and longest journey.

The women from the camp wanted to do these things for her, but in the end we left her, just as the soldiers had, mounted on the pole, her nakedness only half concealed by the forest's undergrowth, her eyes dry and open and staring toward the river.

When my husband brings home toys for our newly born daughter, I pick out the dolls with the plastic skin and the unyielding, staring blue eyes and put them in the linen closet. Their skin feels like day-after-death skin, cold and hard though still fairly pliant. I feel sick thinking of my baby lying next to, gaining comfort from, the artificial dead. After I bury the dolls under the sheets and towels, I pick up my child, placing her against my chest. My body feels cold against her sleep-flushed warmth, yet she still snuggles, roots against me. As she nurses, her heat invades me and becomes mine, her heart beats against mine, becoming mine, becoming me, and gives me life.

I try not to think of the dolls, stacked against each other in the closet, staring at us through the doors and walls with their unblinking, sightless eyes.

I woke at dawn with my fingers dangling like bait in the water at the edge of the river, and a rope looped around my neck. Old-lady breasts, flattened and elongated from years of childbearing, flapped against the side of my head. When I tried to sit up, the breasts squawked, *Aigu!* The dead is sitting up! and swung away.

Lifting my head against the noose, I could see that the breasts belonged to a gray-haired woman sitting cross-legged and naked on my clothes. Though her body was covered with wrinkles and age spots, her face was curiously unlined, youthful. I knew this was the Manshin Ahjima whom Induk had told me to find.

She tugged on the end of the rope.

Manshin Ahjima, I asked her, why am I tied?

Aigu! the woman cried. The dead knows me! The old lady jumped to her feet, and the rope between us stretched taut.

I lifted my hands to the rope, then pulled gently. The rope slithered from her grasp and onto the ground. Please, I said, why?

The woman's hand jerked as if she still held the rope. You were lost, she said, between this world and the next, and I was trying to lead you back.

She lifted her breasts and scratched her scarred belly. Besides, you were scaring me, growling like an animal one minute, crying like a baby the next.

The woman shuffled closer, then knelt to peer into my face. You aren't a tiger spirit, are you? She held her hands out, palms down. If so, I am ready to go. I've tended the mounds, burned the incense for the spirits whose families have been lost or run away. I've seen and I've remembered which son was taken by the Japanese, which son was killed by bandits, and which went to Shanghai as a freedom fighter. I've . . .

The old woman stopped talking, blinked, then touched my hair. I've seen the tiger spirit haunt the graves before, she said, but only at night. You are just a little girl.

When she called me a little girl, I remember I wanted to cry. I wanted to curl into a ball, cover my head, and call, Mother! Mother! as I did when I was very young and feeling alone, as I did from the rooftop of our home the night my mother died and I tried to catch her fleeing spirit. But I didn't, because I knew no one would ever again hold me in tenderness. Instead I stood up and looked around.

And I saw that we were not in a village but in a graveyard. When I realized that the homes that I had knocked at the night before were houses of the dead, I started shaking, and perhaps then I did start to cry.

Here, Manshin Ahjima said, handing me my clothes. I don't suppose a tiger spirit would need these rags to keep warm. And I don't suppose a tiger spirit would have such messy hair. Tiger spirits are really rather prissy, you know.

The old lady's lips flapped, then stopped. I knew she was waiting for me to say something, to respond with a smile or a nod, but I could only stare at her mouth, watching for when her lips parted in a certain way and I could see the black gap where she had lost some teeth.

Olppajin-saram, the mouth suddenly said. And again, louder, as if breaking a spell or casting one: *Olppajin-saram*. You've lost your soul. That is why you came to the graveyard. You were trying to steal someone else's spirit, a wandering spirit, maybe, one that was confused about where it belonged.

She lifted the rope from my head. This is useless, she said, throwing it to the ground. You need a *pyong-kut*, a healing ceremony.

I asked her if she could help me.

When she shook her head no, I became desperate. I begged her, telling her I would pay her for her services.

Manshin Ahjima wrapped her braid slowly around her head and seemed to consider the possibility. She looked down at me, then eyed the pitiful bundle of my clothes lying by the well. I was embarrassed, not by my nakedness or hers but because I knew and she knew I had nothing to pay her.

The old woman pulled her dress, white as death, around her freckled, flabby body and tied the sash tight across her chest. I cannot perform a *kut* for you, she said, because I no longer do the devil's work. But I will help you because that is the Christian way.

Manshin Ahjima bent to pick up a thin gold-plated chain, which she slipped around her neck. The old lady held the chain out so that I could see the tiny cross, smaller than my thumbnail, before she slipped it under the neckline of her dress. You see, she said, I've been saved.

She would help me, she said, because I reminded her of herself when she first got the *sinbyong*, the possession sickness. And of her daughter whom she sent away to live with her grandmother when the spirits first began to visit her, many years ago. The spirits are very jealous, Manshin Ahjima explained. They cannot stand it if you love someone more than them.

Manshin Ahjima touched my hair. Come, I will braid your hair for you, and then I will take you to the Pyongyang missionaries for food and clothes.

The missionaries had saved her from starvation and damnation, and in return Manshin Ahjima let them call her Mary.

Be prepared, she said. I think they call all of the girls Mary.

We followed the train tracks into Pyongyang, keeping mostly in the bordering woods, though sometimes slipping onto a side road to make it easier on the decrepit ox pulling her cart. We depended on that ox not only for transportation but also for sustenance. Some nights, after failing to forage anything to eat, Manshin Ahjima would nick the ox under its shoulder blade to siphon off some of its blood. I learned to savor the taste of blood.

She taught me to find lost things, something she taught all her daughters, because, she said, a woman must always find her own way.

Find the place of darkness within yourself, Manshin Ahjima explained, and imagine what you have lost. Then picture yourself in the last place you saw the object and spiral up and away, as if you were flying circles around that spot. Your spirit finds the object, so the better you can recreate the lost thing in your mind and in the spirit world, the more likely that you will find it in your hands again.

When Manshin Ahjima urged me to try to find something I had lost, all I could think of was my mother. I could not see her face clearly; even then, so soon after the time my sisters and I buried her alongside our winter's kimchee, the details of her face lacked focus in my memory. But she was all I could think of, and what I saw when my mind flew into its own darkness was a woman buried backward in a shallow forest grave, her face pressed against the earth, her mouth full of snakes.

Induk's voice erupted from Manshin Ahjima's mouth: It is an omen.

When we entered the Heaven and Earth Mentholatum and Matches Company building, where the missionaries hid from the Japanese, Manshin Ahjima began yelling.

She was half-dead, Manshin Ahjima bellowed. Crazy out of her mind, dangerous. Thank the good Lord I was able to nurse her back to health and bring her here.

Manshin Ahjima pulled the cross out from under her blouse. Of course, she added, I spent all the money I had to feed her. I went hungry myself, you know.

You have such a good heart, Mary Ahjima, the missionary women cooed around Manshin Ahjima. You will surely be blessed.

Thank you, Manshin Ahjima said. I'm sure the good Lord will provide.

Yes, the missionary ladies agreed, as they pressed money into her hands. He always does.

Manshin Ahjima wrapped the coins in a strip of cloth, then slipped it under her skirt. After she had tied the cloth to her thigh, smoothed her skirts, Manshin Ahjima turned to go. Her eyes swept across me, but she did not look at me. I do what I can, she said. I do what I can, but my God is a jealous God, and I am in the midst of a war.

Wait, I cried, but I did not recognize my voice. Don't leave me, I yelled after her in words that did not sound like words.

The missionaries held onto my arms. Cuckoo, one of them said. Unsure of what she meant, I could not tell if she was referring to me or to Manshin Ahjima. I cried out again for Manshin Ahjima, and I cried for my mother.

In the end, I let the missionaries strip me down, burn my clothes, bathe my skin. I wanted to tell them that it would do no good; I would never become clean enough to keep.

When Manshin Ahjima stumbled out of the missionary house, fondling her thigh where the money—the price of my trust—was tied, she took my hearing with her. By the time the echoes of her footsteps on the wooden stairs of the Heaven and Earth Mentholatum and Matches Company building had faded, I could not hear the sound of my own voice.

As the missionaries pulled at my hair, my clothes, my arms, I watched their chattering mouths but could not make out what they were saying. Eventually I turned my eyes away and gave my body to them. After bathing, dressing, and feeding me, the women pressed a Bible into my hands and led me to a small room, a closet in the women's sleeping quarters, that was not much bigger than the stall I had had in the camp.

In the darkness of that room, I cried for Induk. She, like me, must have been deaf, for she never came. But then again, maybe I had not even called for her, my voice lost with my hearing.

In the days that followed, the missionaries assigned me to various tasks about the house. Sometimes they put a broom in my hands, and I would sweep until they took the broom away. If they put me in front of a sinkful of dishes, I would wash them until the sink was empty and someone turned the water off. Once, they positioned me at a table piled with matchboxes and labels. With big mouth movements and exaggerated gestures, one of the lady missionaries showed me how to glue the labels on the boxes. I sat and glued until all the boxes had labels, and then I glued labels on the table until I had run out of labels. I was considering what else to glue, when someone relieved me of my duty.

I would watch the broom scratch across the surface of the floors and on the stairs in front of the house. I could feel the water in the sink running down my hands as I rubbed my fingers across the smooth and resistant surfaces of plates and cups. And I smelled the pungent stickiness of the glue when I pasted the labels on the matchboxes, table, and chairs. But without the sounds of these actions, I had no way to connect them to myself. No way to judge time, distance, action, reaction.

Invading my daily routine at the mission house, shattering the gaps between movement and silence, were the gruntings of soldier after soldier and the sounds of flesh slapping against flesh. Whenever I stopped for a beat, for a breath, I heard men laughing and betting on how many men one comfort woman could service before she split open. The men laughed and chanted *niku-ichi*—twenty-nine-to-one, one of the names they called us—but I heard the counting reach one hundred twenty-four before I could not bear to hear one more number.

Whenever I stopped cleaning or gluing to stretch cramping fingers or crack my stiff neck, I heard the sounds of a woman being kicked because she had used an old shirt as a sanitary pad. Or I heard a man sigh loudly as he urinated on the body where he had just pumped his seed.

And always, a low rumbling underlying every step I took at the mission house, I heard the grinding of trucks delivering more men and more military supplies: food rations, ammunition, boots, and new women to replace the ones that died, their bodies erupting in pus.

Because I could not risk looking away from my chores, it took me a long time to recognize the others staying in the home. Every day, I met the same people over and over again as if for the first time. No matter how many times I would glance at the faces floating by and away from me, I was never able to catch and hold onto the individual features of each person.

The missionaries saved several girls by pretending to hire them as employees of the Heaven and Earth Mentholatum and Matches Company. Used as a shield from the Japanese, who, not trusting foreign influences, discouraged Christianity but encouraged businesses for the revenue that could be sent back to the Emperor, the Mentholatum and Matches building had been erected at the start of the Japanese occupation and now appeared generations old.

Roughly my age, the girls who were rescued were round-faced and pretty in their innocence, as I once had been. They braided their hair with bright-colored ribbons that flashed against their black hair and uniforms when they marched out of their common sleeping quarters and into the kitchen. Like children, they squirmed in their seats, stifling giggles and gossip when I swept past them.

Later, when I could once again hear what others heard, I caught their whispers flying against me: Why does the minister always save the sweetest pastry for the devil girl? And see how he always touches her head, gives her the prettiest ribbons for her braid?

Even the missionaries gossiped. I heard Sister Red Nose say, The wild child is possessed, a false light luring away the faithful. Sister Milk Breath, giving me the name that Manshin Ahjima predicted would be mine at the mission, muttered, *Mary Magdalene*, a curse, whenever I passed her way.

Once, when questioned to his face about his treatment of me, the minister smiled a fleeting quirk of the lips, and said, What man of you, having a hundred sheep, doth not leave the ninety and nine to go after that one which is lost, until he finds it?

Putting his hand on my head, he looked at his sheep until they dropped their eyes. Rejoice, he said to them, for I have found a lamb that once was lost.

Later the young girls fluttered around me. Will the handsome minister save you? they giggled.

I wish he would save *me*, one said.

As long as he saves me some ribbon, another grumbled. Akiko must get more than her fair share, don't you, Akiko?

Oh, it's not fair, the girls cried. Akiko always gets more of everything because they say she's touched. I think you are just acting. You wait till the war is over, Akiko. Our families will find us and we'll marry rich men and have everything. What will you have, crazy Akiko, with no family and no mind?

Because they were still young, they had faith that the war would end and the Japanese would be defeated. That their lives would resume their prewar scripts, as if the war and their abandonment caused only a brief stutter in the opera they envisioned for themselves.

Because they were still babies, really, I did not tell them what I knew was true: The war would never end, because the Japanese, like all that was evil, would wait in the shadows, shape-shifting and patient, hoping for a chance to swallow you whole.

I began to recognize the minister because of the way the girls, forgetting or ignoring proper behavior, gathered around him. Like puppies, the girls would fall about his feet and legs, and pant for a length of ribbon, a piece of candy, a box of chalk; for writing paper, toothpaste, a kind word. Thank you, Sonsaeng-nim, the girls would sing out, and as if they were pets, the minister would reach out, touching a nose, stroking the hair of those around him.

Stop, he would say. I am not an honored teacher. I am just a child, like you all, in God's eyes.

But the girls would cry out: No, no, not true! Look at your body, thin and long—an aristocrat's body! And your hands, so graceful—a scholar's hands! And your voice, they said, like God's!

The minister would laugh, saying, Stop! But his eyes would shine like blue glass.

Because I had begun to recognize him as an individual, I watched him carefully, intensely, as if memorizing his features, his gestures, were one of my chores. Often, as he gave away his gifts, he closed his eyes and lifted his chin. Pushing his chest forward, he would open and shut his mouth quickly, pursing his lips, blowing quick puffs of air. After a few days I realized he was singing.

Now, years later, I recognize those same body movements and hear the words to the songs he sings to our baby. When she is fretful, crying so loud that the only thing she hears is the pain within her, only he can quiet her. He holds her tight against his chest, pinning her arms within her blanket, and sings. Soon she stops struggling, and as her screams fade into hiccups, she lifts her head toward the sound of his voice singing about whales of Jojojonah. Noah's art-y art-y made out of go-phers barking barking. Jesus loving children.

They are silly songs that my husband sings to comfort our child, but I hate them and I hate him.

I hate that he can quiet her with his voice, the same voice that lulled and lured the girls from the Pyongyang mission. The same voice, sounding so honest and joyful that you want to believe, even when you know the truth. The same voice that fools everyone but me. I hate that voice because my daughter loves it.

I cannot sing to my daughter like that, in a voice full of laughter, for I never learned funny songs, songs that make you laugh and laugh. I remember only bits and pieces from those my mother sang when she was working. And they were songs that filled you with sadness, that made you want to cry until your throat swelled with salt.

After one of the missionaries' communal dinners, the person who came to take the chopsticks from my hand was the minister the girls always followed. By then most of the people there had stopped speaking to or looking at me, unnerved by the silence by which I was surrounded. But when this man took the *chotkarak* away from me, he held my chin and looked into my eyes. He looked until I was forced to stop listening to the women crying in the comfort camps, until I looked back and saw him. And then he smiled, rubbed a napkin over my lips, and helped me stand. He took my hand and led me down the basement stairs, where the world turned on its side once again.

In the basement meeting room, he placed me on a bench between two other missionaries. I concentrated on watching him walk down the aisle to the pulpit, but my vision narrowed and buckled under the increasing intensity of camp sounds. During his speech, each time I saw him slap the pulpit for emphasis, I heard the sounds of women's naked buttocks being slapped as they were paraded in front of a new arrival of troops.

When the congregation stood, opening and riffling through their black books, I heard the shrieking of bullets ricocheting at the feet of women the soldiers were momentarily bored with.

And when the people around me all at once opened their mouths wide, I heard every sound from every day I spent in the camp all at once, so loud I felt I was drowning under a raging river, until, in a rush, my ears shattered.

After a moment of utter silence I heard singing, but singing like I've never heard before. The only songs I had heard before that day were sung by one person at a time, or by a group of people who all sang the same part in the same way.

What I heard after my ears cracked open was a single song, with notes so rich and varied that it sounded like many songs blended into one.

And in that song I heard things that I had almost forgotten: the enduring whisper of women who continued to pass messages under the ears of the soldiers; a defiant Induk bellowing the Korean national anthem even after the soldiers had knocked her teeth out; the symphony of ten thousand frogs;

the lullabies my mother hummed as she put her daughters to sleep; the song the river sings when she finds her freedom in the ocean.

My daughter's cries filter into my dreams. Just before I wake, her crying turns into my mother's singing. My mother is crying and dancing and singing a song that I heard her sing repeatedly in my childhood, but in my dream I cannot quite make out the words. I try to embrace my mother, but she dances away from me again and again. Just as I finally reach her, her song erupts into the screams of an infant.

I look toward my husband's bed, see his unmoving form huddled beneath the blankets. Dazed with sleep, still seeing my dream, I go to my daughter. As I pick her up, her body stiffens with her screams, and out of my mouth comes my mother's voice, singing the song I forgot I knew:

> *Nodle Kang-byon pururun mul*
> *Kang muldo mot miduriroda*
> *Su manun saramdul-i jugugat na*

It's a song full of tears, but one my mother sang for her country and for herself. A song she gave to me and one that I will give to my daughter. I want to shake my baby into listening, force her to hear, but I only sing louder and louder:

> *E he yo! Pururun mul, kang muldo*
> *Na rul mit-go nado kang mul-ul miduriroda*

Over my daughter's cries, I continue to sing and sing, until she begins to quiet. Her body falls into mine and the air in her room becomes sweet and heavy with the breath of her sleep, and still I sing. I sing until I reach the end of the song, until I can remember no more.

> *Moot saram-ui seulpumdo diwana bol-ga*
> *Moot saram-ui seulpumdo hulro hulro sa ganora.*

PAUL LAFFOLEY

WORK IN THE VISIONARY GENRE

SPECULATIONS IN MIND PHYSICS

THE THANATON III, 1989.
"THIS DEPICTS INFORMATION GIVEN TO ME FROM AN EXTRATERRESTRIAL SOURCE PRIOR TO 1989. THE DISCOVERY OF AN IMPLANT IN MY BRAIN DURING 1992 HAS CONFIRMED FOR ME THE AUTHENTICITY OF MY ORIGINAL CLAIM FOR THE PAINTING."

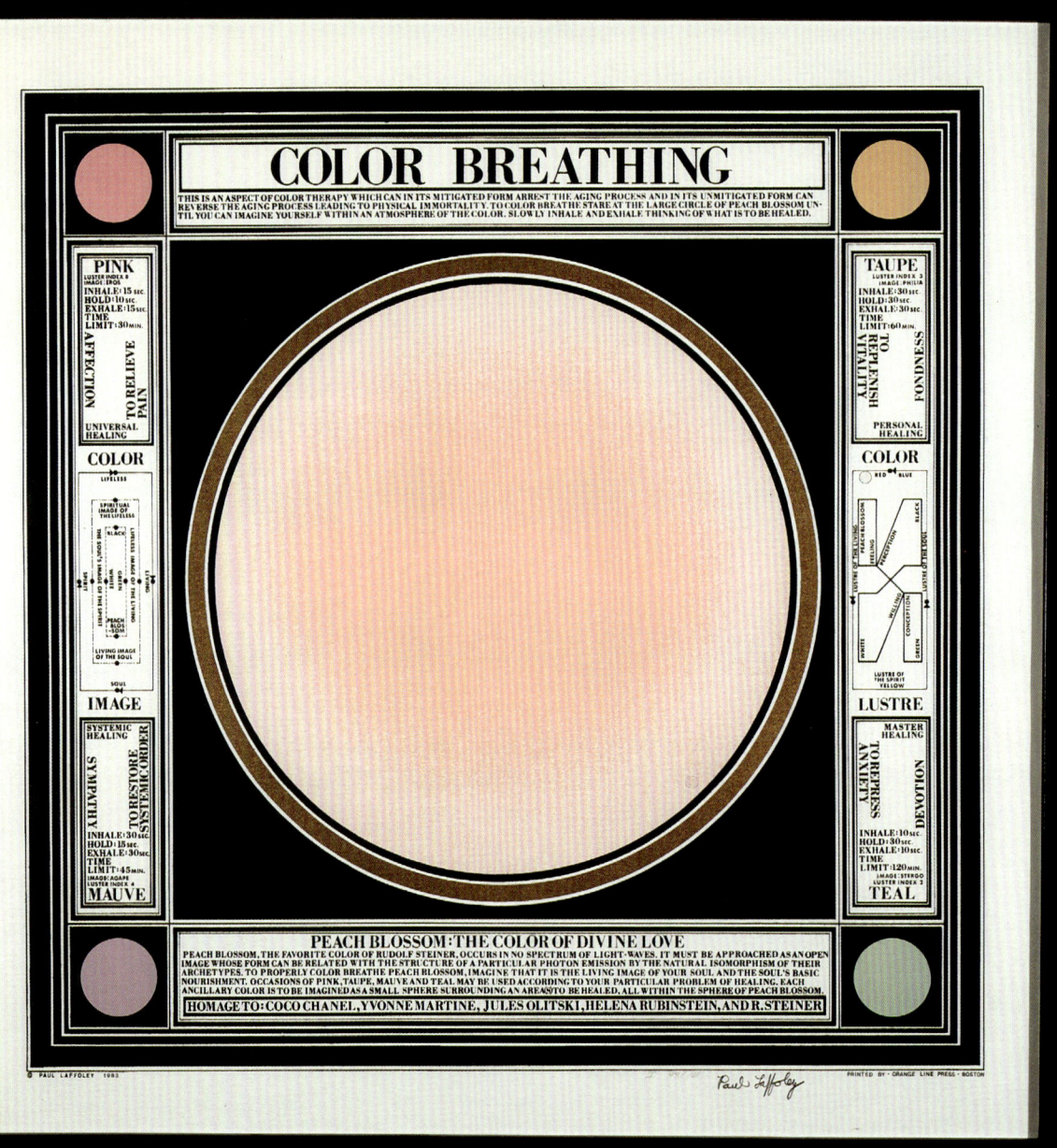

***COLOR BREATHING*, 1974.**
"BY MEANS OF LUCID DREAMING (BEING AWARE OF DREAMING WHILE DREAMING), ONE CAN SURROUND ONESELF WITH COLORED SPHERES OF LIGHT AND BREATHE THEIR HEALING VIBRATIONS."

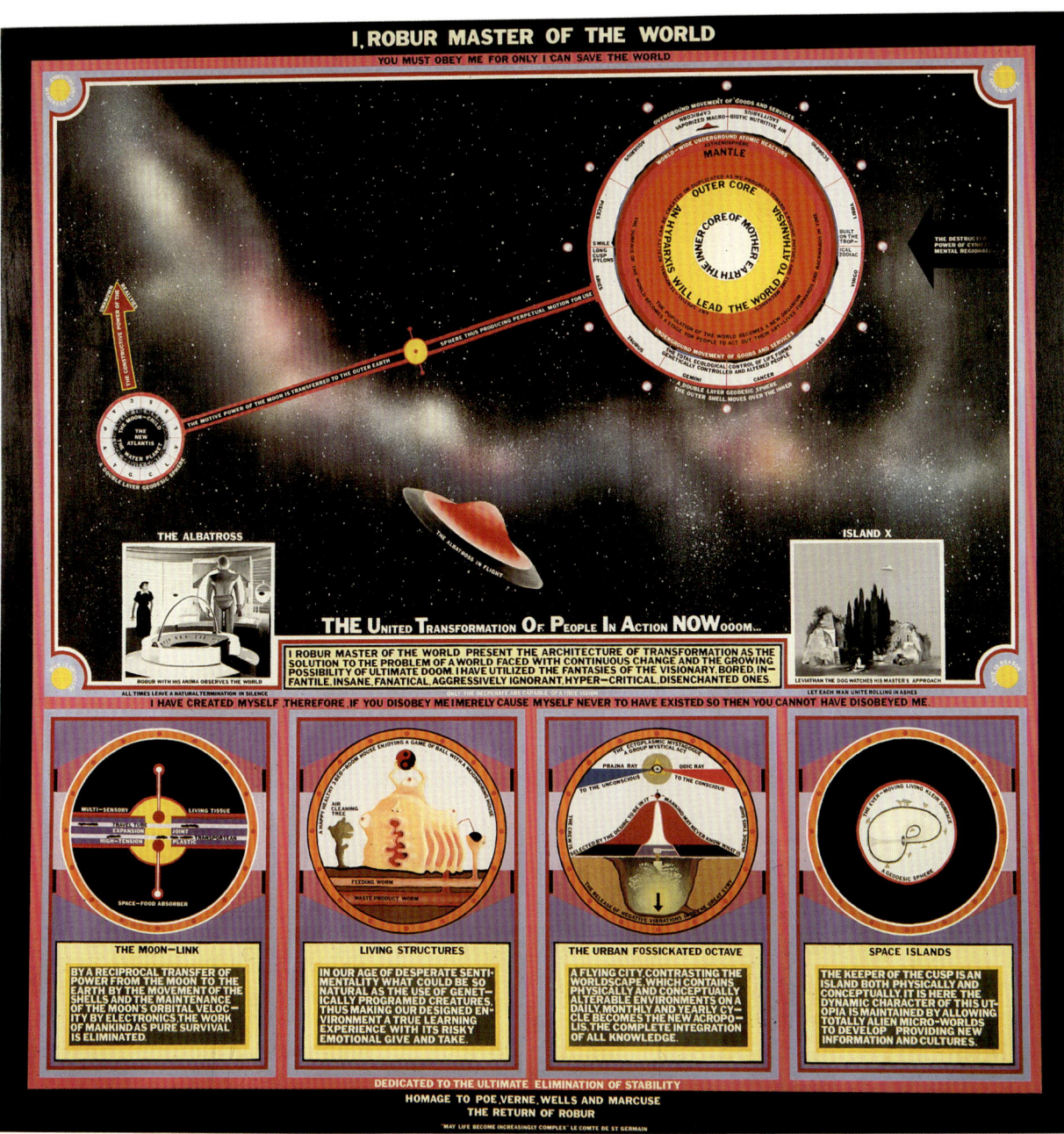

I ROBUR MASTER OF THE WORLD, 1968.
"TO REDESIGN THE *ENTIRE* PHYSICAL UNIVERSE WAS THE DREAM OF THE MEDIEVAL ALCHEMISTS. AS WE APPROACH THE TWENTY-FIRST CENTURY, ASPECTS OF THAT DREAM HAVE BEEN ACHIEVED IN THE MICROVERSE. IT IS NOW TIME TO WORK WITH THE MACROVERSE."

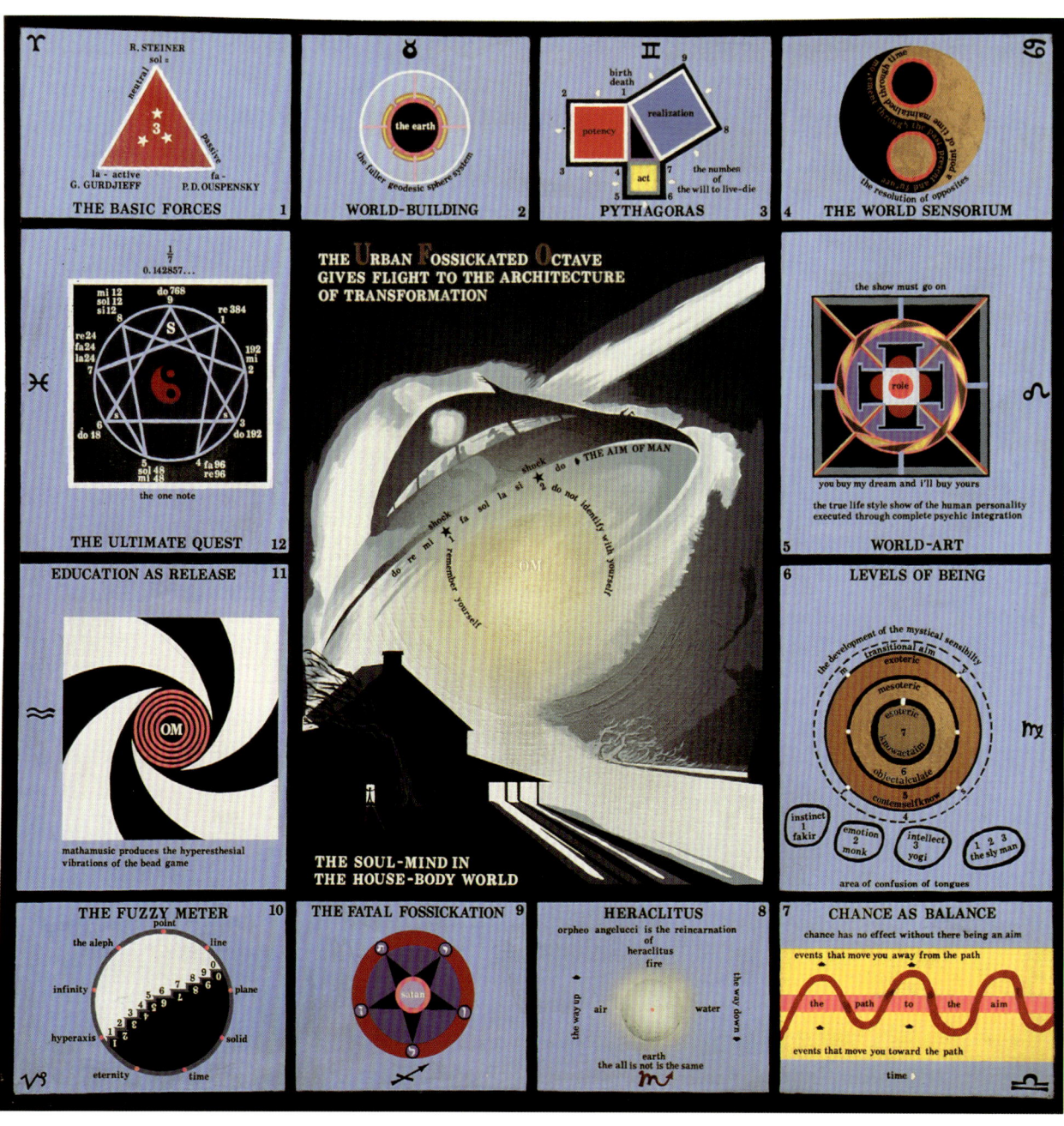

THE URBAN FOSSICKATED OCTAVE, 1968.
"TO *FOSSICK* MEANS TO PICK OVER ABANDONED REMAINS. OUR EARTH IS SITUATED IN A ONCE-FLOURISHING 1,000-PARSEC URBAN AREA OF THE UNIVERSE. UFOs (IN FORMATIONS OF EIGHT) HAVE RETURNED TO CONDUCT ARCHAEOLOGICAL 'DIGS.'"

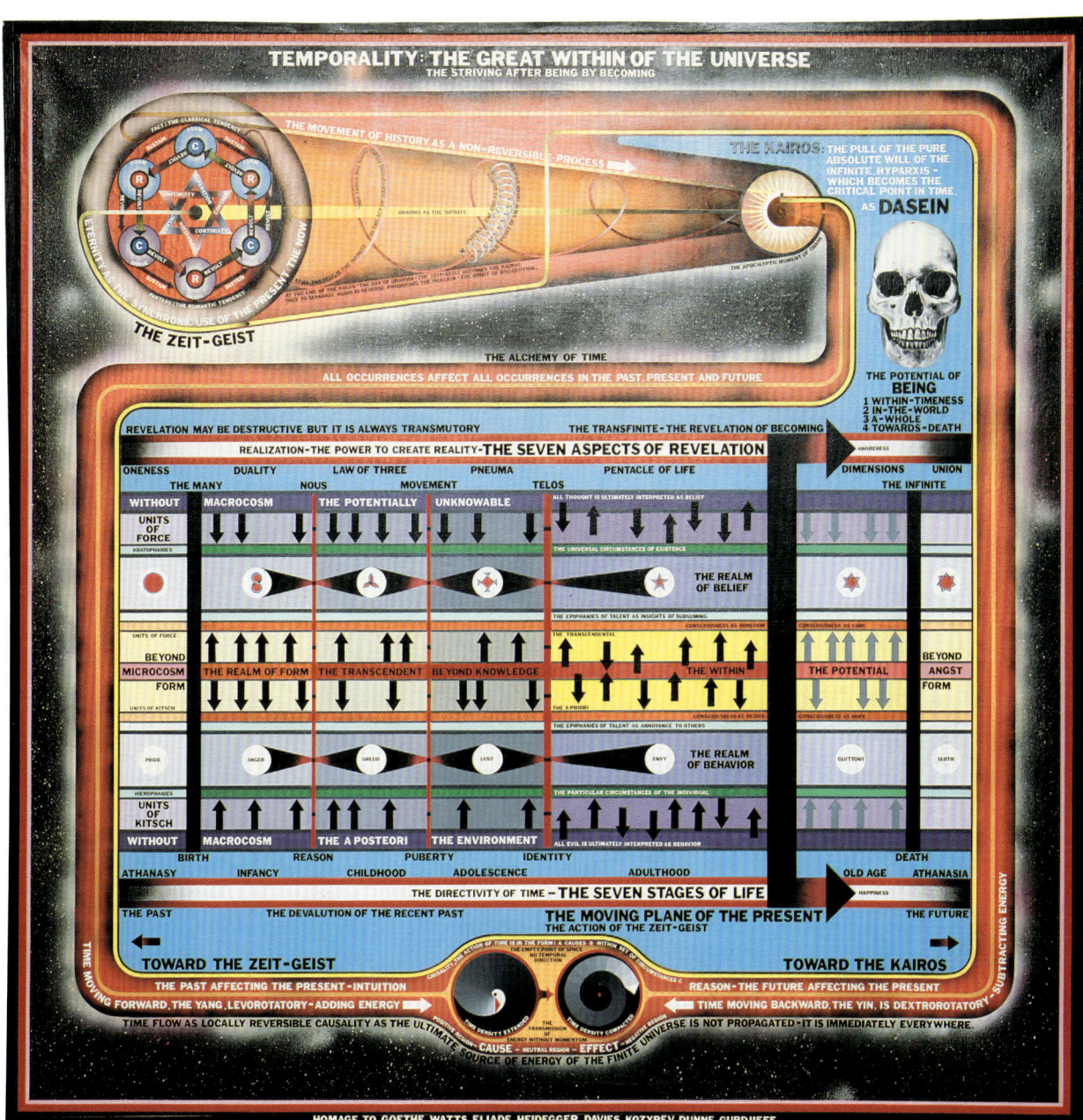

TEMPORALITY, 1974.
"THE KLEIN BOTTLE, TOPOLOGY'S MOST INTERESTING FORM, WHICH IS NEITHER METRIC NOR SYSTEMIC AND HAS NO INSIDE OR OUTSIDE, CAN BE USED TO DESCRIBE THE COMPLEXITY, DURATION, AND CONTINUITY OF TIME."

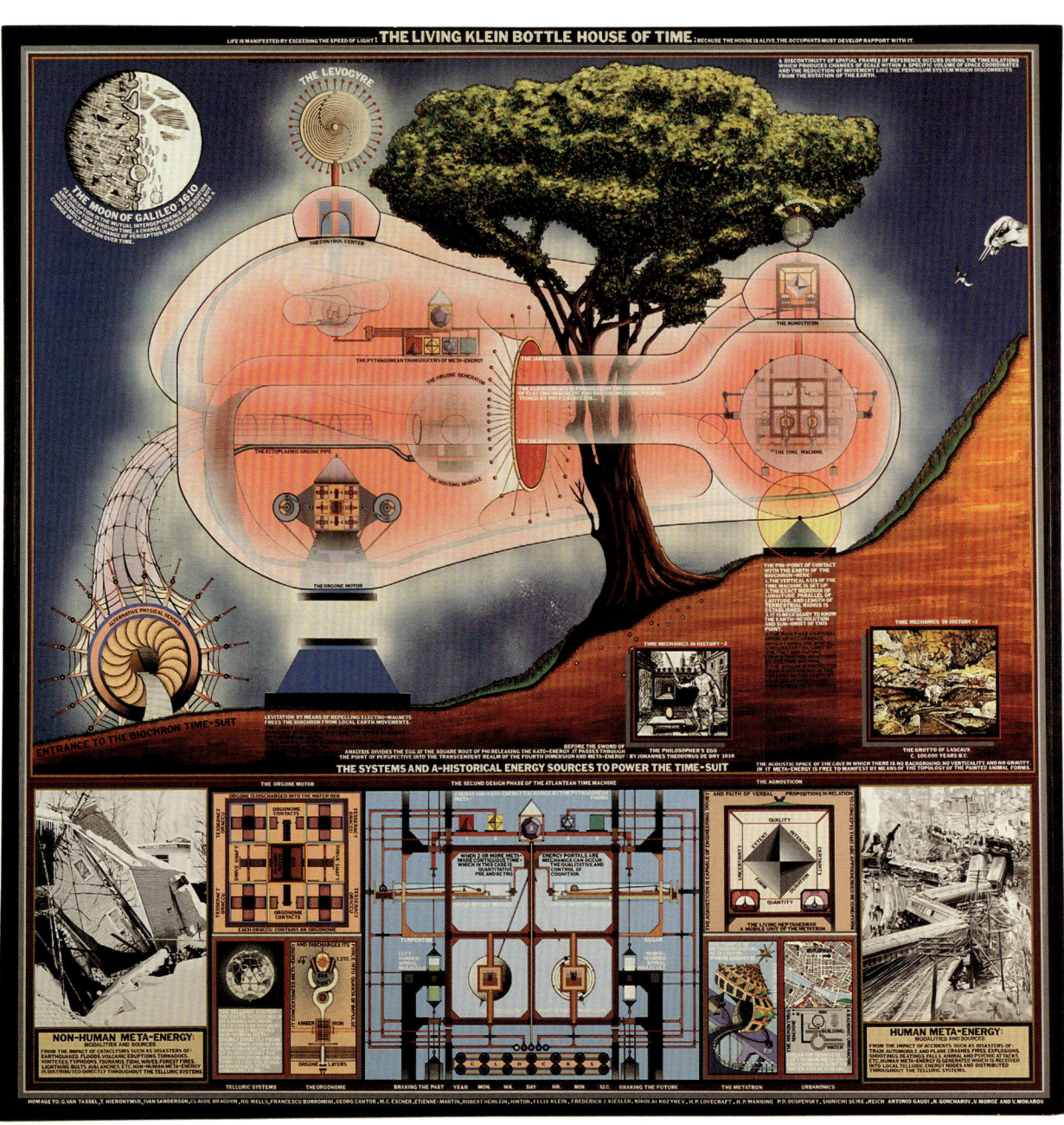

THE LIVING KLEIN BOTTLE HOUSE OF TIME, 1978.
"THE SECOND DESIGN PHASE OF MY TIME MACHINE, THE PHYSICALLY ALIVE BIOCHRON TIME SUIT GIVES THE TIME TRAVELER AMPLE FIRST PERIMETER WARNING OF ENTERING A NEW WORLDVIEW."

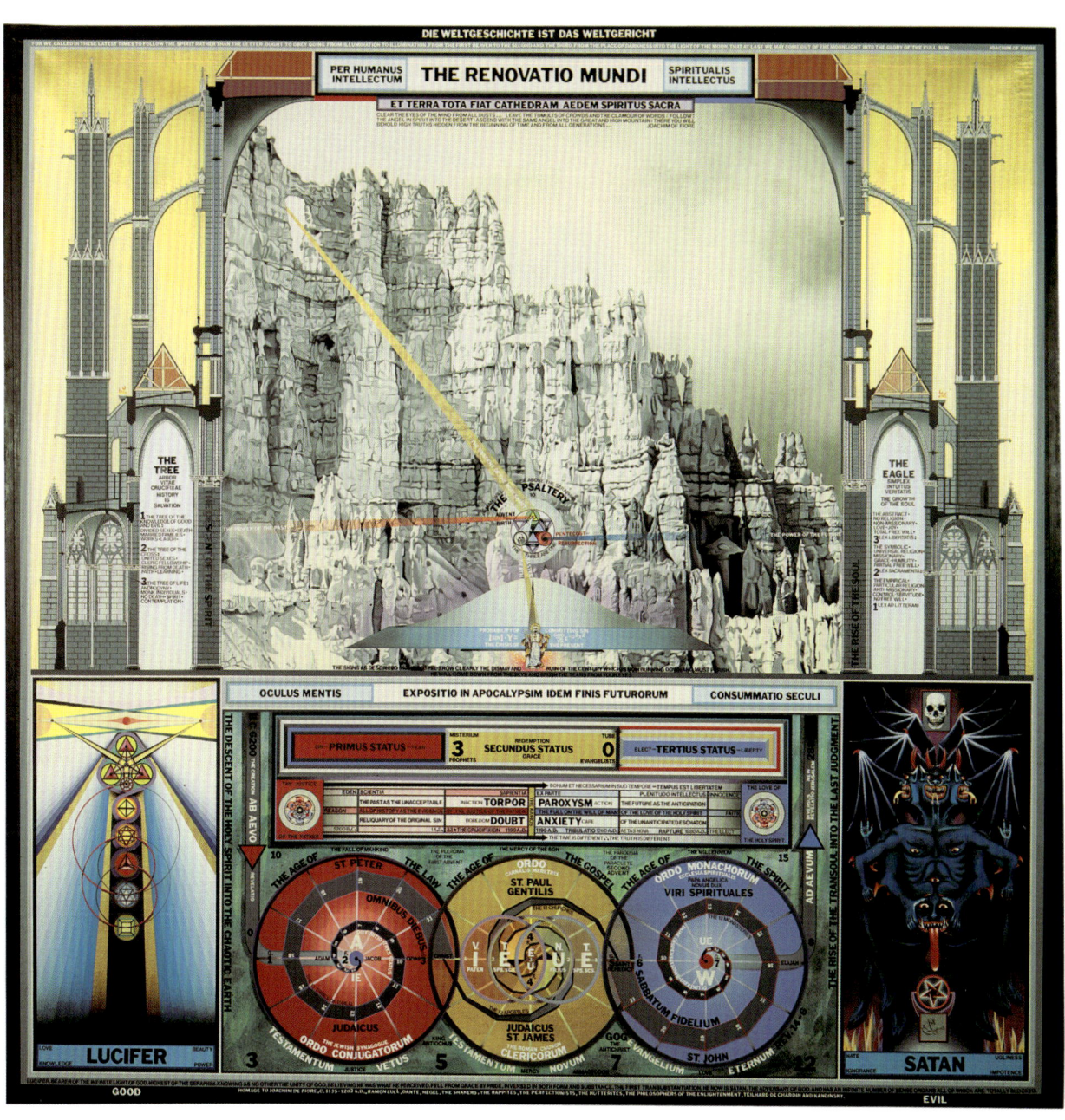

THE RENOVATIO MUNDI, 1977. "THE CALABRIAN HERMIT JOACHIM DE FIORE (1135–1202 A.D.) CREATED A NEW WORLDVIEW FOR CHRISTIANITY IN 1190 A.D. IT CONSISTS OF THREE AGES: THE AGES OF THE LAW, THE GOSPEL, AND THE HOLY SPIRIT. OUR AGE, THE THIRD, BEGAN IN 1260 A.D."

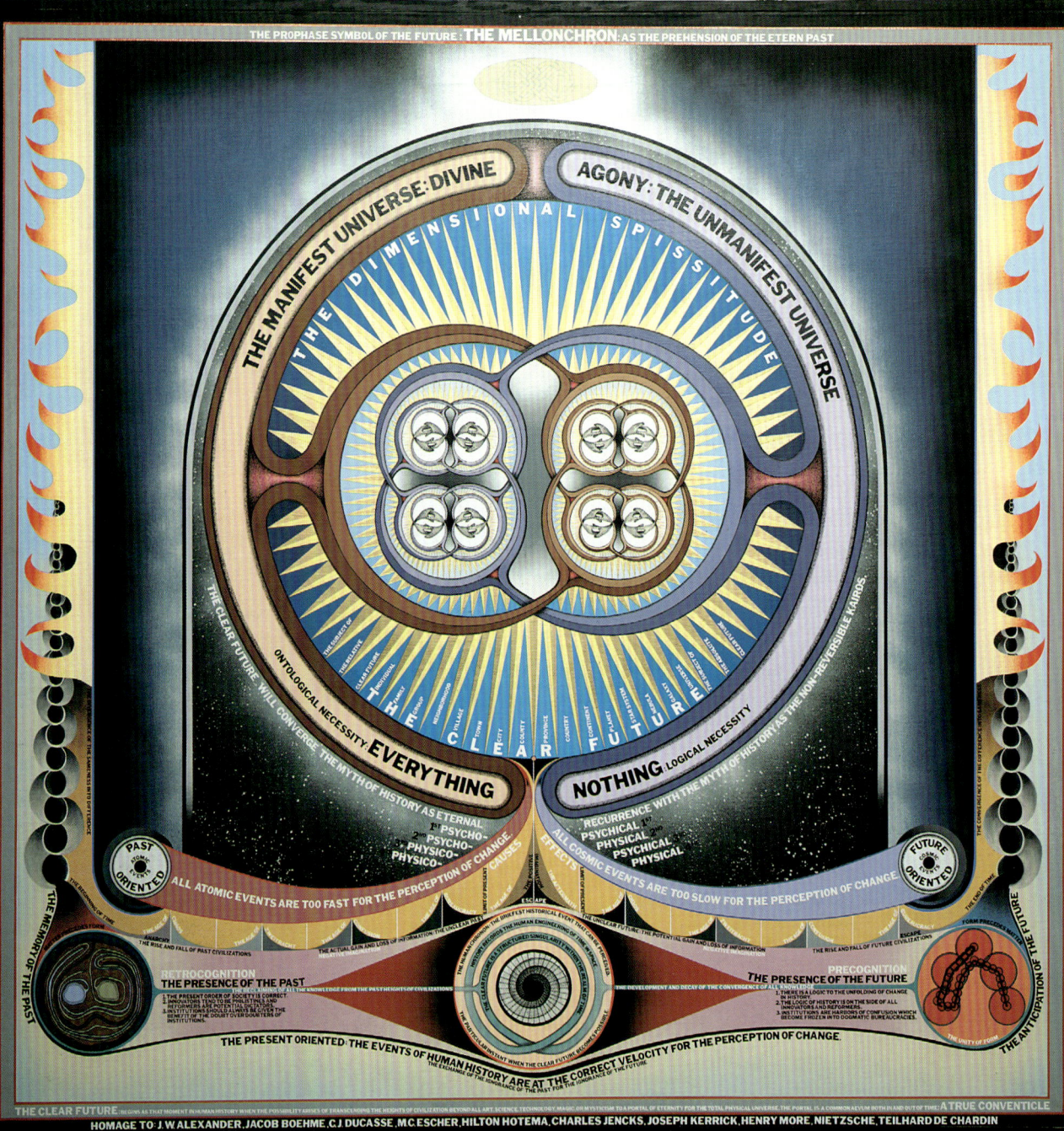

PAUL LAFFOLEY

Paul Laffoley's elaborate, diagrammatic paintings extend out of a tradition that includes the eccentric, eighteenth-century visionary architect Étienne-Louis Boullée. Like Boullée, who is best known for his designs for immense monuments that were never built—among them a *Project for a Cenotaph for Sir Isaac Newton* and a *Project for a Tomb for the Spartans*—Laffoley is guided by a need to work out highly detailed plans for structures that, for all practical purposes, are impossible to build. Boullée, however, whose grandiose plans developed during Neoclassicism, did not consider reality to be teeming with secret encodings, while Laffoley, a postmodern visionary, believes that the true nature of reality lies in what he can glean from science, pseudo-science, science fiction, the disputed history of UFOs, philosophy, mysticism of all kinds, occult doctrines, and dreams.

The central focus of Laffoley's work is the tension, inherent in human existence, between being physically caught in time and space and the desire to exist outside these boundaries. Concerned with divine origins, Laffoley's paintings can be understood as detailed attempts to guide the individual toward the realm of pure thought and being. As he combines aspects culled from disciplines ranging from applied physics to kitschy science-fiction film, Laffoley suggests that one can reach the higher planes of consciousness through such means as astral projection, the use of an imagined version of Wilhelm Reich's controversial orgone meter (which in Laffoley's painting is powered by meta-energy), and the construction of tunnels of living plastic between the earth and the moon or of a community the artist calls "aetheiapolis," whose purpose is to "realize the true nature of the form of utopia."

In his paintings, Laffoley offers wildly personal, erudite proposals that he predicts would enable both the individual and society to overcome their limitations. Compositionally, they are like densely illustrated pages from a book by a gnostic architect, who, meditating on the relationship between life and death, and fulfillment and unfulfillment, conceives of structures capable of transforming one's understanding of reality. Typically, the viewer encounters a dominant image surrounded by smaller images, explanatory charts, practical instructions, and the names of inspiring and guiding figures—Jacob Boehme, Edgar Cayce, Dante, M. C. Escher, Lucretius, Edgar Allan Poe, and Jules Verne, to cite a few examples—from whom the artist has learned. Each painting's title provides the viewer with the conceptual framework in which both the visual and textual information must be processed.

For Laffoley, one senses that the world, its combination of culture and nature, is little more than a degraded manifestation of a higher order. His belief in the fourth dimension, which appealed to both Madame Blavatsky and Marcel Duchamp, has led him to speculate on the nature of a fifth and even sixth dimension. Reality, Laffoley insists, is not simply what we see before our eyes. And he has taken it upon himself to decipher the secret of what exists beyond our senses and rational thought and is hidden in our dreams, our movies, our fiction, our fears and obsessions.

JOHN YAU

THE MELLONCHRON, 1982. "FROM THE GREEK, Τὸ μέλλου, MEANING 'THE FUTURE.' THE MELLONCHRON'S FORM IS THE ALEXANDER HORNED SPHERE, INVENTED IN 1924. ALTHOUGH THE FUTURE BEGAN ON APRIL 24, 27 A.D., IT TOOK 1897 YEARS TO DISCOVER ITS SYMBOL."

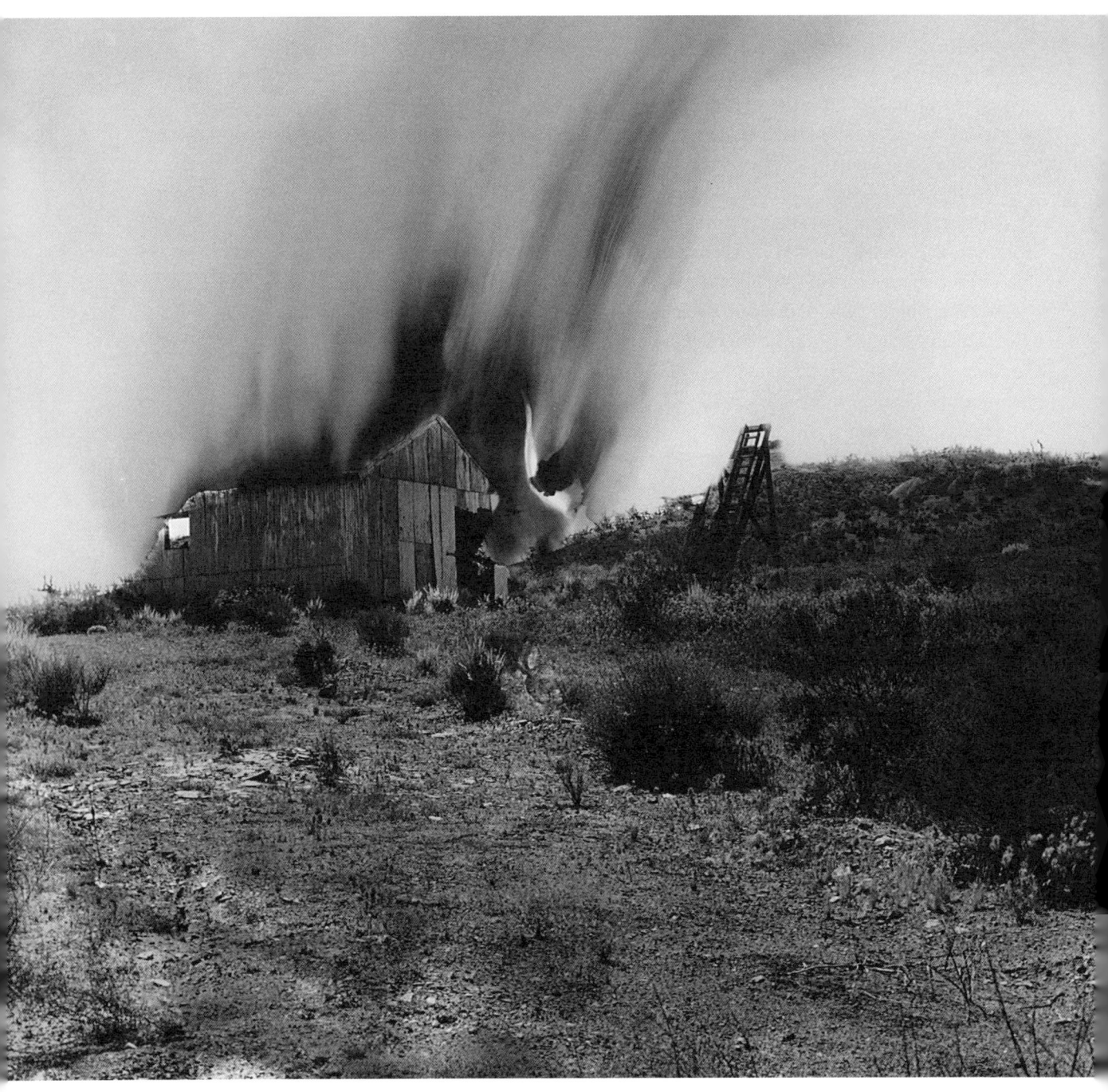

Denny Moers, *A Shack in Context*, 1993.

FORREST GANDER

ESCAPED TREES OF LYNCHBURG

Mostly, they live disagreeably   amid volleys of far-off barking
and a chalk lake, spring-fed,   clear. Watercress and wild
celery in the current   undulate. Trees, the central figures
of their own originality,   come bare down the slope
to bathe.   Sudden raptus in the landscape,
arborescing.   The poplar
and its reflection   are disturbing, like twins.

The trees live disagreeably,   secreting
chemicals that attract   parasitic wasps
when caterpillars start   to strip the leaves.
February sap rose   from woodpecker holes.
Surreptitiously deft,   willows speed in their lingering,
all together and insolent,   acoustic nodes on their branches
sough a neuter language.

Each topos is seeded   by a loop of tendril.
In mud around the lake   horsefly larvae, partly buried,
pierce the bellies of young toads,   suck them dry. The present
is the unknown, a development   without resemblance. A small
inflorescence of blue   mist from stills
precarious on upward slopes   will condense the cow-smell

and hold it to the hills   like a shadow cast in space.
Winter tits hovered,   dipped their beaks into sap
at the icicle's tip.   The land arborescing, that secret
neuter language,   and no one to decipher
the concealed from the given.

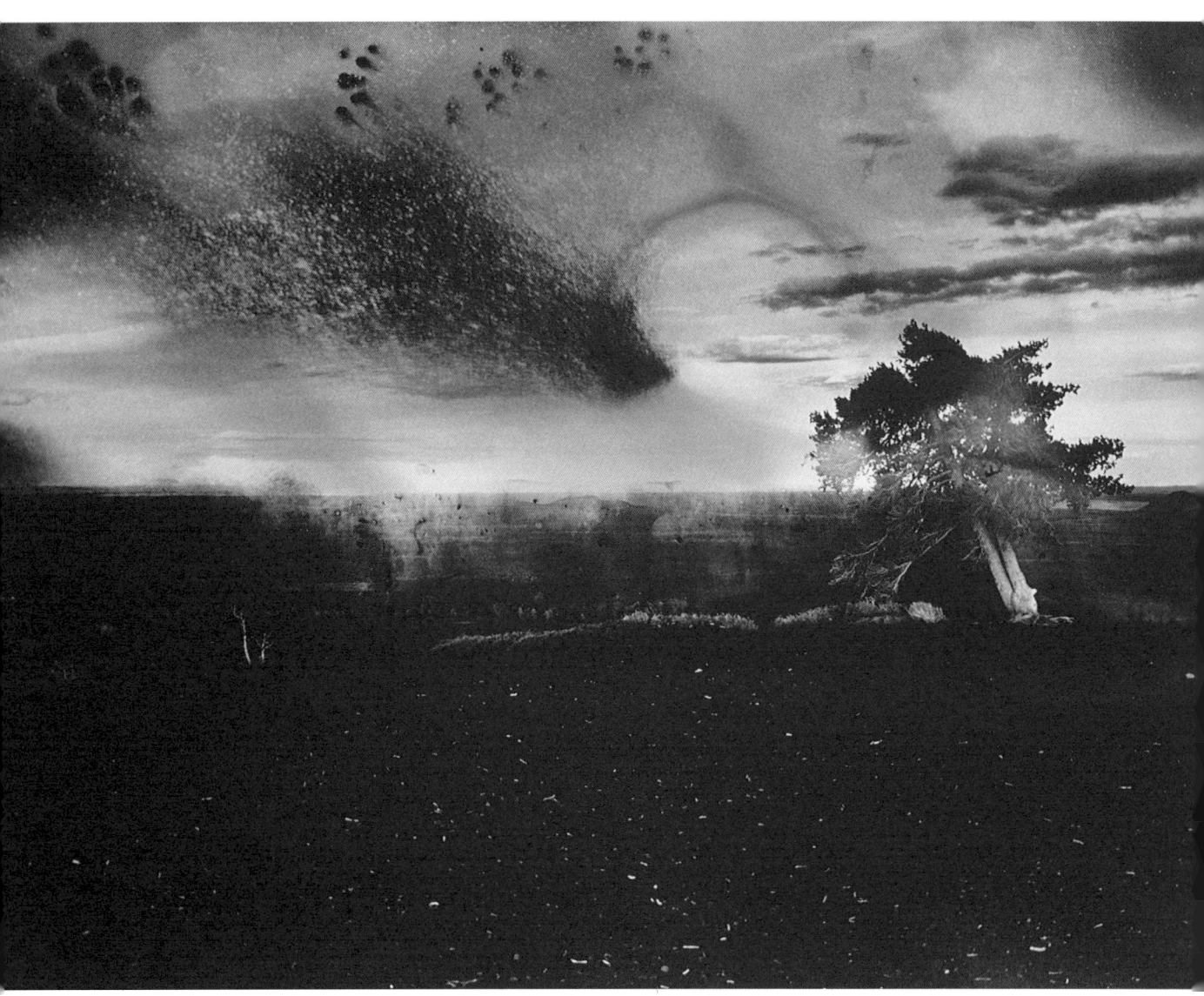

Denny Moers, *Tree Emanation II*, 1994.

EXHAUSTIBLE APPEARANCE

      Around the burning barn, stationary objects seem to stream.
      Scrub brush, twigs in sinople dirt, dry weeds,
puffballs among scattered breccia and chert.
      Grey barn burning in the grey eye of the afternoon.
      The solid given upward, hemorrhaging into air, the vista tinged
methiolade and twisted inside the barn,
a dense ball of smoke like a black sock
                                  stuffed in a shoe.
     We breathe carbonized splinters, our shirts beating
to exploding planks, holding barely within ourselves the felt
quality of redness, whoosh, heat. Roof gone, walls seared
down to the single argent window gleaming.
        And here, to keep the whole visual image from slipping
across the retina, away, we focus upon the window—
     which does not reflect any panorama we see
     which does not reveal the penetralia
     which neither contributes nor borrows any color
from the chromatic blaze
     which, though gravity always tugged the glass down
through itself, melts quickly now.

    Nothing in the window of the world beside it the world within
it the world we can see around, beyond it.
    The window catches light from another world altogether,
one behind us, one we cannot see, the world from which we have
come clomping across the desert from a road which is a dashed trace
on a map.

    It is a moteless clarity behind us.

    Not a mature representation of imagined form.

    Not a clot of flies at the edge of a cow's eye. Not tadpoles
wriggling in the mud of a tractor tread. Not a broken bootlace.

    But when we turn, like a piece of music at the andante,
the landscape resumes. The barn collapses inside itself.

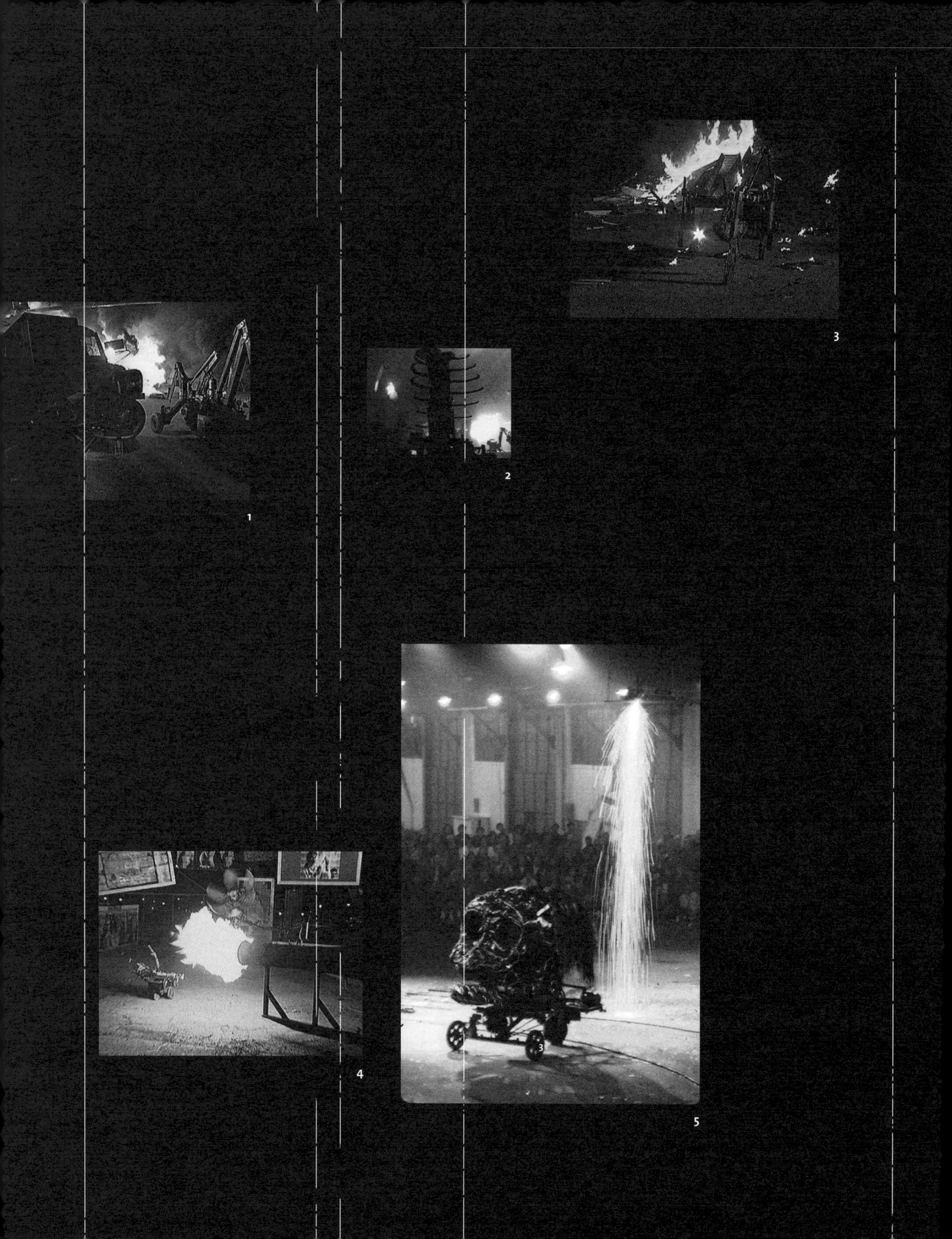

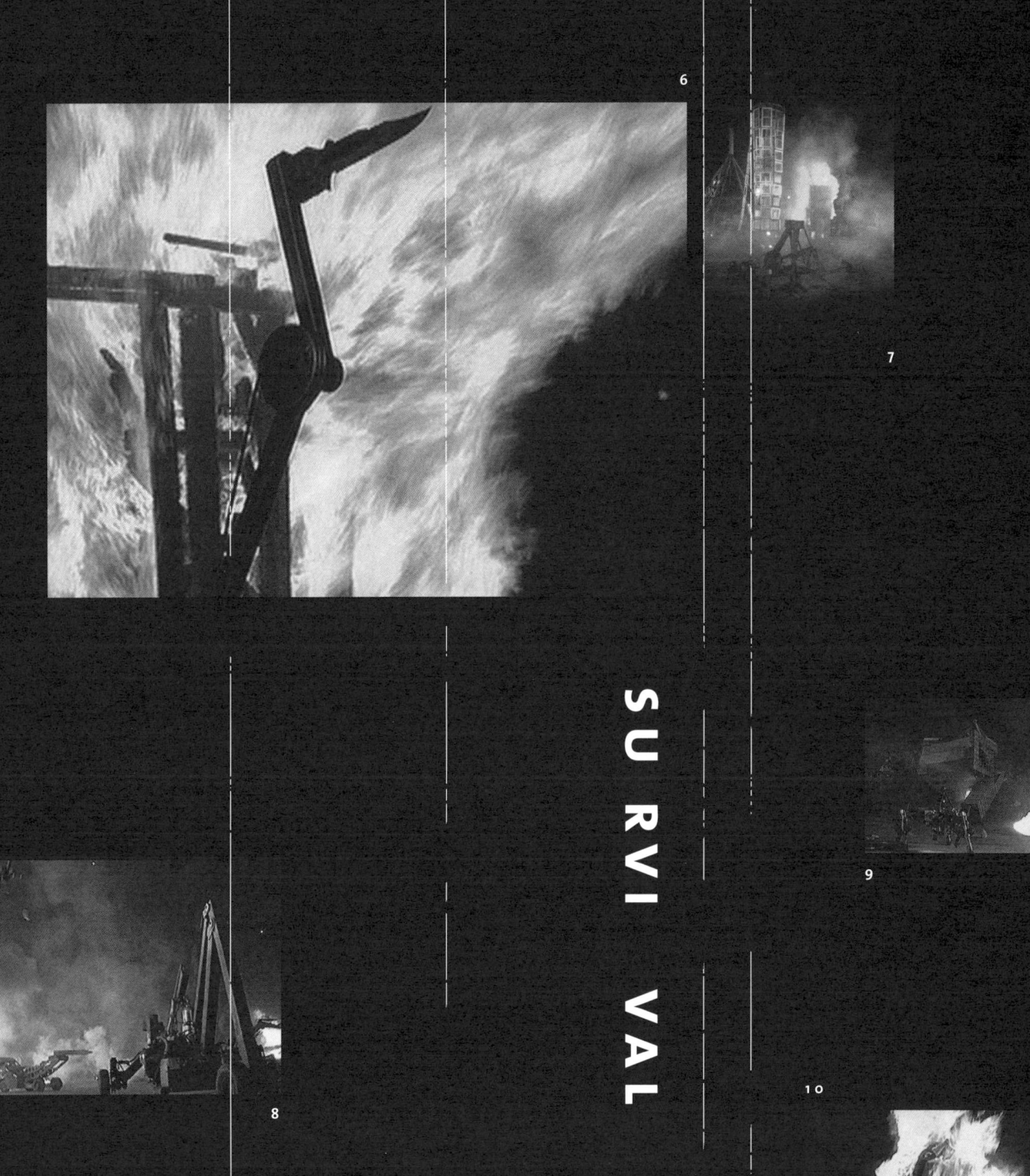

SU RVI VAL

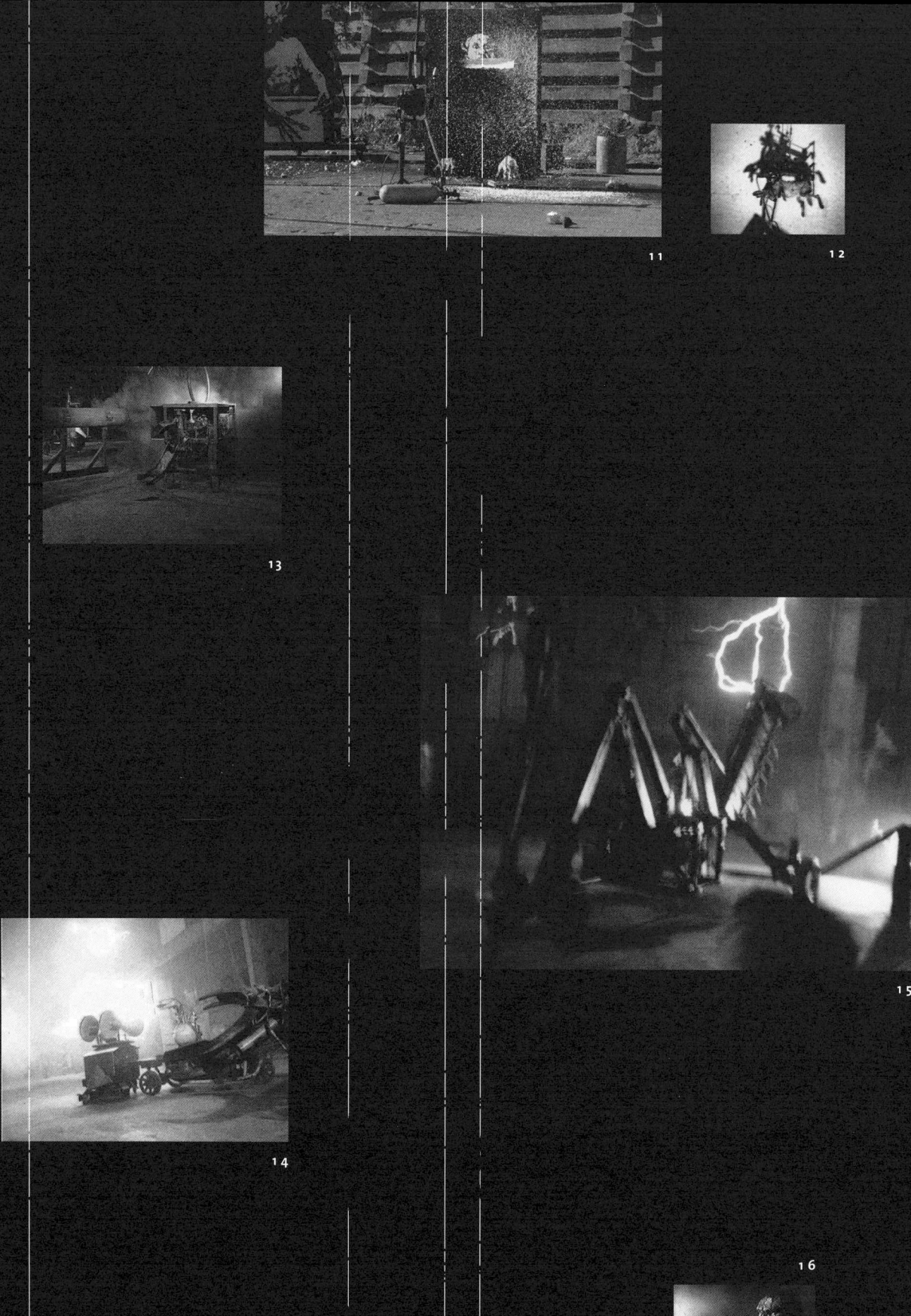

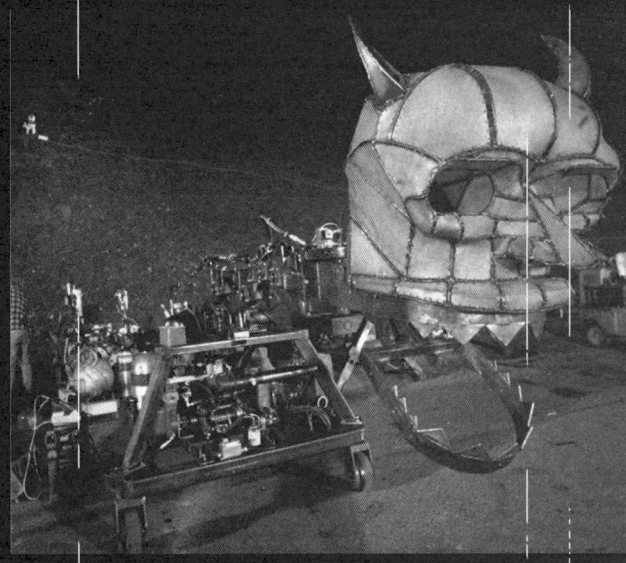

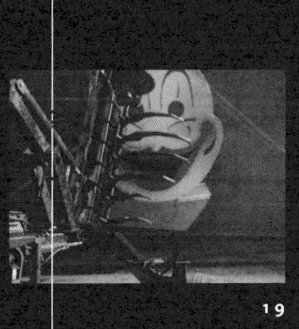

RESEARCH

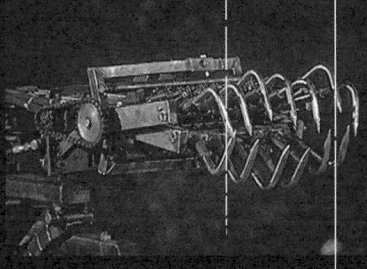

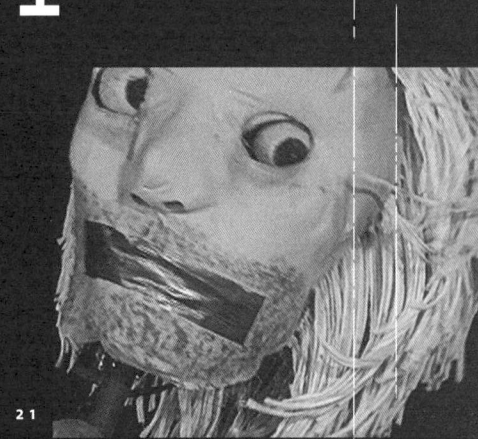

SURVIVAL RESEARCH LABORATORIES

FOUNDED IN 1978, SURVIVAL RESEARCH LABORATORIES HAS STAGED OVER FIFTY LARGE-SCALE MACHINE PERFORMANCES IN THE UNITED STATES AND EUROPE, EACH CONSISTING OF A UNIQUE SET OF RITUALIZED INTERACTIONS BETWEEN MACHINES, ROBOTS, AND SPECIAL-EFFECTS DEVICES, DEDICATED TO REDIRECTING THE TECHNIQUES, TOOLS, AND TENETS OF INDUSTRY AND SCIENCE AWAY FROM THEIR TYPICAL MANIFESTATIONS IN PRACTICALITY OR PRODUCT AND TO DEVELOPING THEMES OF SOCIO-POLITICAL SATIRE. HUMANS ARE PRESENT ONLY AS AUDIENCE OR OPERATORS.

LAWRENCE FERLINGHETTI

UNTITLED

      Oh you gatherer
            of the fine ash of poetry
                    ash of the too-white flame
                              of poetry

      Consider those who have burned before you
                          in the so-white fire

      Crucible of Keats and Campana
            Bruno and Sappho
                      Rimbaud and Poe and Corso
          And Shelley burning on the beach
                        at Viarreggio

      And now in the night
            in the general conflagration
                the white light
                      still consuming us
           small clowns
                with our little tapers
                      held to the flame

UNTITLED

Driving a cardboard automobile without a license
               at the turn of the century
     my father ran into my mother
                      on a fun-ride at Coney Island
          having spied each other eating
                 in a French boardinghouse nearby
And having decided right there and then
               that she was right for him entirely
     he followed her into
                the playland of that evening
       where the headlong meeting
                    of their ephemeral flesh on wheels
        hurtled them forever together

And I now in the back seat
          of their eternity
                   reaching out to embrace them

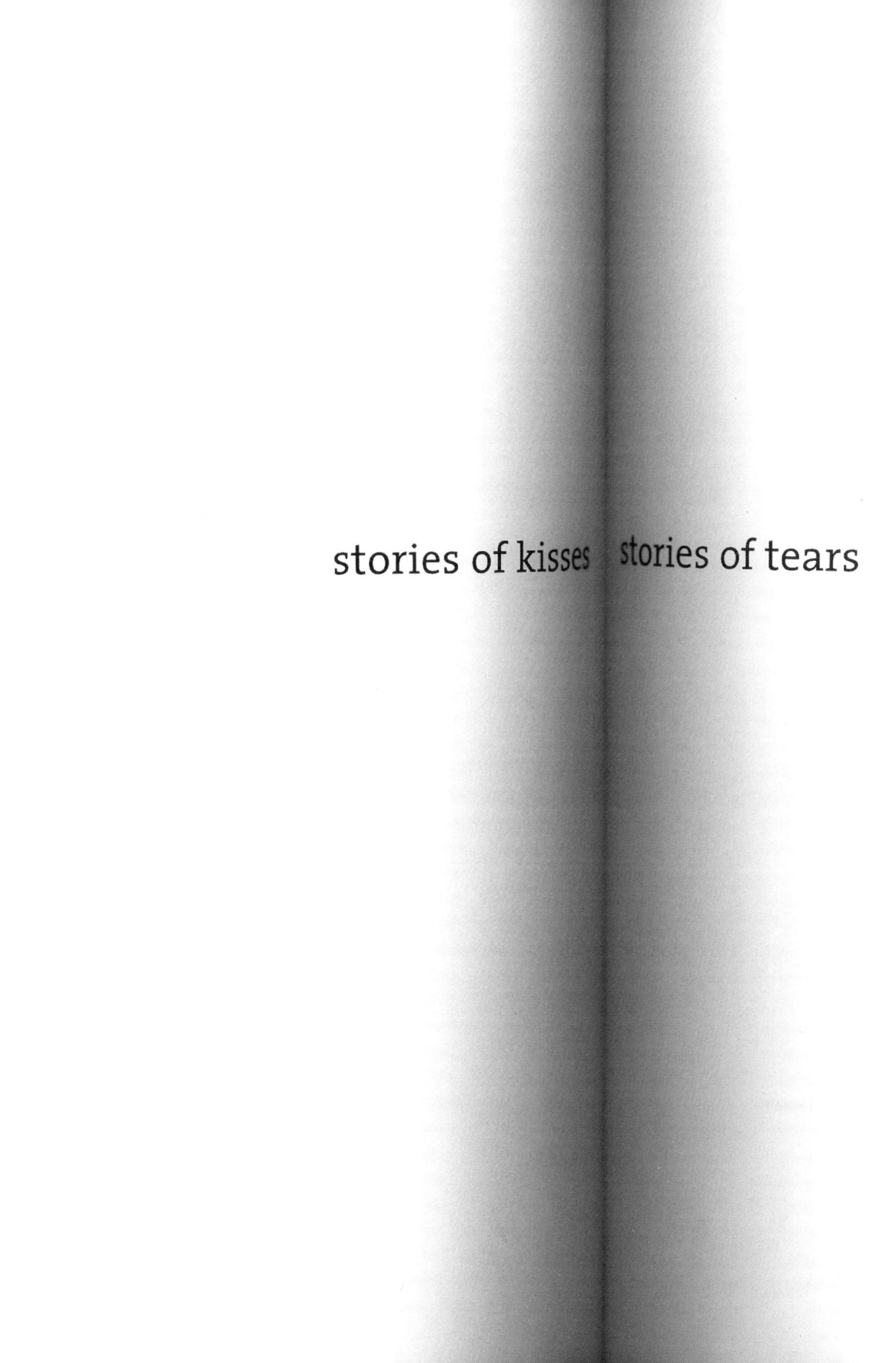

stories of kisses stories of tears

LÁSZLÓ DARVASI

The Wailing Woman of Kučevo
In the Macedonian town of Kučevo at the end of the last century, there lived a wailing woman whose strange, even terrible, custom was first noticed by local shepherds. That this is not some moralizing legend, or the figment of a self-indulgent imagination, is best proven by the fact that no written record exists of this woman, yet people around Kučevo still claim to remember her. But mention her name and they'll get extremely angry. This sad woman— Irene was her given name—had sky-blue eyes and, while shedding tears over strange men's corpses, she kissed them on the lips. With her tear-stained face she would fall on the body, wailing and yammering, and beat the sunken chest of the deceased with her fist, snatch the shroud off his chin, and plant kisses on his open mouth. In those days the townspeople referred to her only as fat Irene, the one who had enough kisses for every body in the Kučevo cemetery.

Angels' Tears

"My name is Vasilev, I am Ukrainian and a sculptor. I found the little bowl in my backyard on a bright, chilly, early spring day—a translucent liquid glistened in the bowl, as if all the dew in my garden had collected there. My younger daughter, being the quicker and nosier one, immediately took a sip from the liquid. Just that once I slapped my Olenka in the face, forced my finger down her tiny throat, and with the palm of my hand hit her belly to make her retch. There might have been poison or some other dangerous potion in that bowl. But Olenka did not throw up, she just stared at me, as though I weren't even her Daddy. After that she didn't set foot in my garden, where my statues and obelisks seemed to hold up the sky. But as her brow and her eyes grew in size, so did a strange, unrelenting melancholy in her heart. Wherever she wandered in the world, she left a trail of bitter tears. For the longest time I didn't know who had placed a bowl full of tears in my garden, who wept through entire days and nights, punishing me with what I feared most—tears, which in time would wash away everything I had ever struck, chiseled, and carved into stone. These creatures visited only my garden, they never knocked on my door. But everything became clear to me when word came from Uzhgorod one day that Olenka had been received into the fold by a sad host of angels in charge of last judgments."

Alfred Weiss's Kisses

Does a mute kiss better? We cannot be sure. In any event, around the turn of the century there lived in the city of Breslau a Jew who always wore a black caftan, and about whom, in subsequent years, several poems and satires, as well as innumerable newspaper articles were published in both the humor magazines and in respectable dailies. The women who came to see the mute Alfred Weiss, to be kissed on the lips in his stuffy, dimly lit grocery store, included aristocratic Polish maidens and proper Christian ladies with grown daughters. Slender necks, freckled breasts, fluttering hands and fingers soaked up all kinds of smells and fragrances—of marjoram and mint, cinnamon and fennel. Whiffs of cocoa, ground pepper, intoxicating paprika penetrated the tiny crevices of their skin. But this mute Jew was not so mute, after all. A wispy eleven-year-old named Cierna Penka, the daughter of a

Lublin Gypsy chief known for his extortion schemes, lulled Weiss to gentle sleep one night, and got him to recite the names of all his kissing partners. The investigation lasted for months, and the authorities came up with the names of about a hundred families that had been blackmailed. A prosecutor in Warsaw later said that the last mother to be approached by the blackmailers was located a year after the scandal broke, and what wafted from her hair even then was the unmistakable, overpowering smell of cinnamon.

Marriage and Tears

We are familiar with a letter written by G. C. Lichtenberg to his friend Amelung, and published by Walter Benjamin under the pseudonym Detlef Holz—the latter on account of the wretches who pulled brown shirts over their hatred. A sad version of the Pygmalion legend, we discover, could originate even in Germandom. The letter was composed in 1780. Lichtenberg's words bespeak a heartache so great and so inconsolable that we, too, struggle to hold back our tears as we speak of it. There is no shame in this, it merely betrays our sentimental nature. Lichtenberg the scholar raises an ordinary flower girl from the dust and educates her. By degrees she becomes cultivated, receives dresses that are soft to the touch, earrings that glitter, and one night a shy, aging male body comes down on her, but softly, timidly. And this is repeated the following night.

The girl dies one day before the marriage is to take place, when happiness sanctified by law and ceremony is but a step away. Lichtenberg's face appears before us. Walter Benjamin speaks of a tear-ravaged, despairing, shrunken visage. But we also recall how bitterly Dante Alighieri wept, how he sobbed, after losing his beloved Beatrice, and how his family put an end to the grieving with a compromise at once brutal and simple: they forced the poet to marry.

Appease the body and the soul will also find rest.

The tears will dry up or cover over other tears.

Sympathetic though we are to Lichtenberg's plight, the truth is that his tears, his unrelieved sorrow, tried to crowd out a misery far greater and deadlier than his. The flower girl had been snatched away from her stand by the Nuremberg city wall, deprived of her favorite roses, her friends. There is only one reasonable explanation for her death. She chose it over a conventional marriage. She wasn't just escaping, she was meting out punishment—Lichtenberg's. And since we can do little else, we put our hands in front of her face and taste those tears, so we can weep similar ones for her.

Judas

The proposition that "kiss" and "betrayal" are different words for the same thing has an extensive history in literature. "A kiss can be a noble and beautiful act, and it can also be a symbol of depravity and deceit. It can be compared most aptly to opening petals." A literary critic from Ljubljana, Slatko Kovač, made this observation several days before his death. He pursued the thought, moreover: "The kiss bestowed upon Jesus by Judas in the Garden of Gethsemane demonstrates that Judas Iscariot had infected one of the noblest human acts with betrayal's sweet but fatal poison. Betrayal is immense, it reaches up to the sky, whereas a kiss is only a means, like our lives in itself neither good nor bad. One question, however, does merit serious consideration. Where did Judas bestow that kiss? On Christ's hand? On the cheek? On his lips?"

It is said that Slatko Kovač found the answer on his deathbed.

Soko

The following story was recorded by the alcoholic parish priest of Rezmice—one only wishes it hadn't been.

There was a man in the village of Velna, a mean and despicable character by the name of Soko, whom everyone called by his nickname, Chikas. He was missing a leg, lost to a bolt of lightning. Pork made Soko hoarse, noodles depressed him, fresh vegetables gave him an itch. None of this would have mattered, however, if not for the fact that he also liked to kiss and fondle children. The women of the village discovered this disgusting habit of his a little too late, because by the time they caught the fleeing Soko on the road to Rezmice, and tore him to pieces and urinated on each piece, so that he would never rise from the dead—by that time, the boys and girls of Velna had learned perfectly how to kiss.

A Poem of Tears

The poem was delivered personally by its author, Vasile Lupu, to the editorial offices of the journal *Astra*, and handed to its editor, Octavian Goga, who was annoyed that day, irritated over some trifle, and maybe had a hangover as well, because he barely glanced at the poem and handed it back to Vasile Lupu the way one returns a wormy apple to a peasant at the market. The editor didn't say a word; he didn't even look at Lupu, who staggered out of the office and began walking. He got only as far as the market square, though, where his tears stopped him: they rolled down his cheeks like pearls. There Vasilev Lupu, the promising young poet of Sibiu, stood and cried. Crimson sunset, gray dawn, wind, rain, high noon, old strollers, pigeons, a flaxen-haired girl selling sour cream—none of this interested him anymore, not even the community singers rehearsing for their next program in the band shell.

What is strange is not that Vasilev Lupu, the young poet, died from all that crying, that his body shriveled up, that after four days of silent sobbing an old, wizened head hit the cobblestones of the square—after all, others before him had come to such an end, and surely it will happen again, as long as manuscripts continue to be rejected. What's really strange is that his tears soaked through the paper on which the rejected poem was written.

At the funeral home, the man dressing the body, a certain Ion Mengereanu who happened to be a lover of literature, discovered the sheet of paper and laid it out to dry, and afterward got to read a beautiful poem. In a corner, he noticed the name of the editor, O. Goga, so the poem ended up once again on the editor's desk. Later, in the poet's apartment on Pemflinger Street, they found the original version. Thus the two poems appeared in *Astra* side by side. In the appended commentary, editor Goga pointed out the words and phrases that had been soaked in tears; he also explained why the version altered by the poet's tears was more beautiful, more profound, and above all more original.

The Man With the Musical Penis

Although it would certainly merit greater consideration, the story does not rank high among the matters of the world. The man in question was every inch a man, and that's all we know about him. When and where he lived or what country he was from are matters of idle and highly subjective conjecture. This man with the extraordinary male organ could lie with an ecstatically screaming young girl, a maturely swaying woman, a broken-toothed streetwalker—this man made music during the act of love.

That is, his organ did.

There were no exceptions. His penis began to play in every woman, be she beautiful or homely, sweet or insufferable. It could turn into a rhapsodic piano or a dark-toned viola—though it could also produce the soft sound of a violin. Sometimes it fluted, sometimes it trumpeted, only to switch, between the fleshy thighs of the next lady, to the dulcet strains of a harp. This penis could jingle, too. Or sound like a horn, noble and smooth. This wondrous organ could, of course, replicate the sound of a church organ or a cello. If need be, it could make accordion music, guitar music, and even produce percussive sounds. There was no instrument in the world whose language it did not know. What's maddening about the story is that the world forgot this man's name. What is also unnerving is that there was one woman in whom this penis fell silent. It was a terrifying moment. To compound the madness, this woman's name we know. And here we must stop and bow our heads. For what could we possibly gain by divulging, here, now, the name of this woman?

About Kisses

It's well known that when it comes to kissing, the Portuguese take the prize.

The Spanish, the Italian, the French kiss are playful, their only drawback is that they are easily forgotten.

The English, the German, the Dutch have cold and slow tongues. Whereas a Swede's tongue, or that of a Norwegian, a Finn, an Icelander, is cold and quick. The Danes tend to be dreamy. The Irish and the Swiss seldom kiss. The Czechs are sloppy but persistent. The Poles don't like to close their eyes, the Romanians are quite impetuous, the Greeks tire easily. The Russians keep groping with their hands down below. Hungarians use their teeth, too. . . .

Walther Blau's Tears

Before their big uprising, Tito's partisans captured a young soldier named Walther Blau, an optician in civilian life, the author of a learned essay on John Dollond, an Englishman who had lived long ago, knew how to weave silk, and discovered the telescope. Walther Blau told his captors all this, and because he was honest and well-spoken, they gave him a choice. If he refused to cry, they'd shoot out his eyes right away. If he cried, and kept it up for three days, he'd still get a bullet, but in the back of his head. Walther Blau began to cry and saw the world—the crescent moon, the leafy boughs, the sun-dappled clearing, the stacks of American canned beef—refracted through the prism of his tears. Things floated into view as they must have in John Dollond's telescope. However, on the second day, when Walther Blau was still crying and smiling, though no longer moving, the partisans got into an argument.

If it made him smile, why should they let him cry?

Because they had promised.

So what?

And just as they pointed their gun at the German, they noticed he was no longer alive; only his tears were flowing still. The partisans stood there, wondering if Walther Blau might not have fooled them, after all. Or maybe he'd just been too scared of the lead bullet that he could have got in the eye.

Blaga Costelan's Tongue

Blaga Costelan of Bizac had stomach trouble; his breath was foul, unbearable. But his heart was like the magic pear of the Sultans of Istanbul —pure gold. Marina, Blaga's wife, loved him; she bore him five unruly brats in the sunlit clearing next to the forester's cottage. The five were named Matthew, Mark, Maria, John, and Luke, and they grew tall, like so many colorfully beribboned poplars. Marina loved her husband but would not let him kiss her on the lips. One early spring day—they could hear the first bugle calls from the mountains—the rebuffed Blaga grew so despondent that before his wife's very eyes he bit off his tongue and spat it on a charred stump. The woman turned white as she watched the quivering piece of flesh. Then, her eyes full of tears, she placed it in her mouth and lovingly embraced her man.

The Tear-Troupers

There were five of them: Goran Dalmatinac, Péter Feketekő, Zoran Vukovich, Aaron Blumm, and Franjo Mendebaba. Five average, nondescript men on the highways of time.

These five were the tear-troupers.

They made the rounds from Vienna to Istanbul, from Krakow to Fiume, traveling through hills, valleys, mosquito-infested swamps, and stopping to perform on village greens and market squares. A German artisan in Buda painted sky-blue teardrops on the canvas cover of their wagon to make it clear to highwaymen and mercenaries that it wouldn't be worth their while to detain these crying artists, with no riches besides their tears. And what would a highwayman or a mercenary in the service of the Emperor do with tears? To be sure, these were not ordinary tears. The world will never again see five such performers—the realization itself is enough to bring tears to one's eyes.

Goran Dalmatinac's tears froze as they fell. Péter Feketekő's turned into tiny black stones. Zoran Vukovich cried tears sweeter than honey, but put a match to them and they burst into flames. Aaron Blumm's light blue eyes wept cold and foamy blood; in Franjo Mendebaba's tears you could recognize your mortal enemy. From Vienna to Istanbul, from Krakow to Fiume, they traveled, and wherever they stopped, the five men wept, always at once, always for one another. Their death, too, was but a single moment one silent, tearless night, somewhere between Košicc and Belgrade. Only their wagon keeps on rolling, empty, bedaubed with tears, under our windows.

Translated from the Hungarian by Ivan Sanders

JORGE GUILLÉN

AFTERWARDS

Chastity is delectable
afterwards. Stream, sun, pool
reverberating.
The man a placid witness
from the bank where he lies.

MINISTRY, MINSTRELRY

I have received a very modest check.
A bit of change: forty-nine cents.
Alms? A subtle tradition. Is it not
the glass of good wine owed to the minstrel?

CORNER BAR

The bar on the corner wedged
between two very crowded streets,
and the deafening din of traffic
speeds up the hour
that in the bar—it's two, three—
flies by so fast no one notices:
pastimes, business, see you later,
news from the racetrack, Hello . . .
and life slips smoothly past,
mortal, persistent, short.

ULTRAMADRIGAL

"Mouth of strawberry." A strawberry mouth? Look: yes,
strawberry. Horrible. "Hand of snow." With the whiteness,
temperature, quality of snow? Dreadful!

Oh, lips like lips, so unique: your mouth!
And that hand, only to entice me, the ideal hand. Your
hand!

MY DEAR SIR

I write to be the target
of your eyes and your lenses.
But never fear—oh reader,
ah, possible reader! that I will pressure
you with pleas, announcements, visits,
readings, on and on.
Our relationship—voluntary,
if it occurs—knows nothing of laws.
Those who wish to nibble, let them nibble,
and those who don't, let them leave it alone.

AIR ALL AROUND

Admire New York from high windows:
space surrounds smooth slim blocks.
Oh, you verticals attacking beauty
with an arsenal of straight lines!
Buildings aiming to be the nudest
geometry of the world, except for
a single adornment. Look: space.

Translated from the Spanish by Cola Franzen

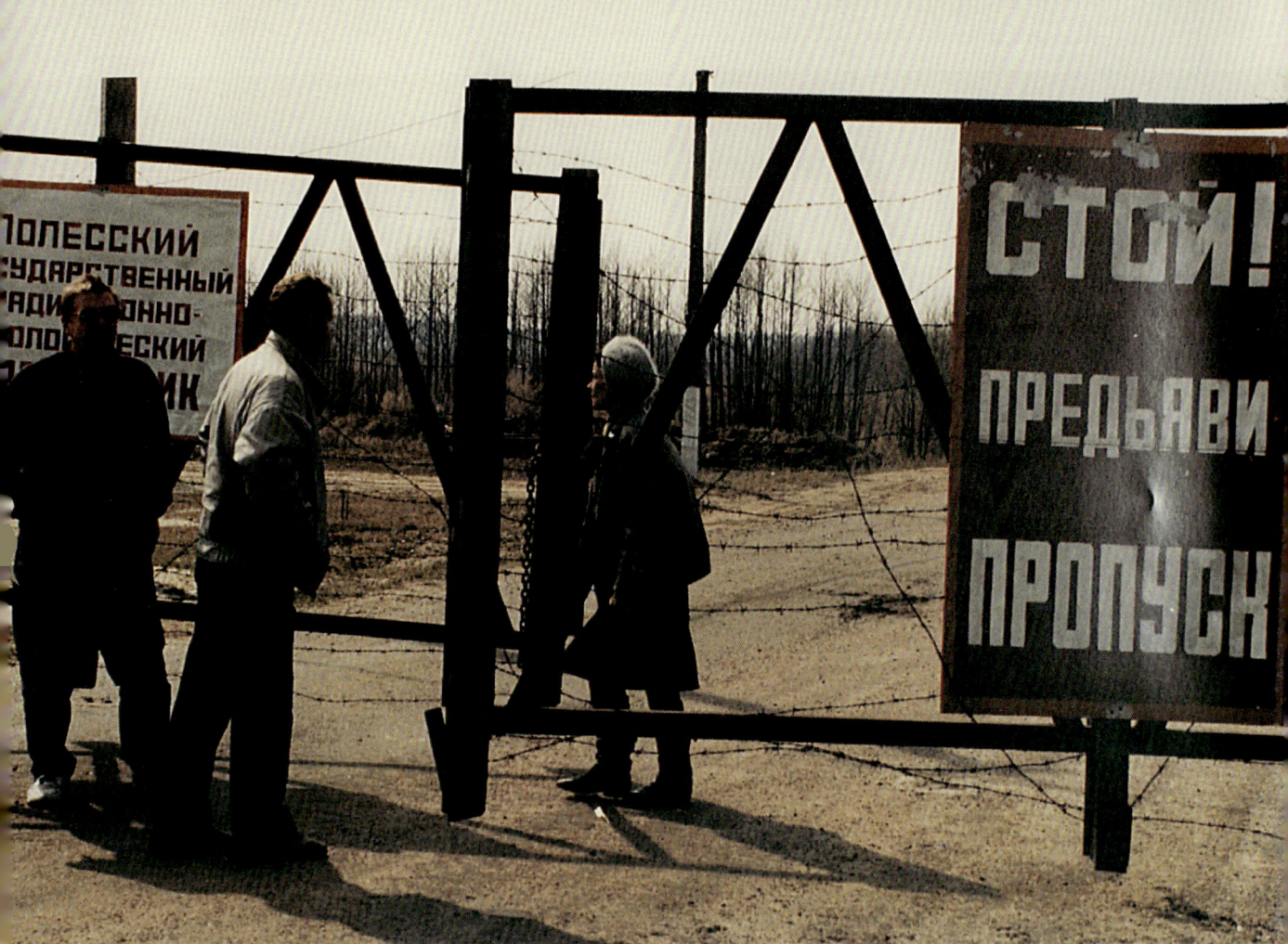

PETER FEND : CHERNOBYL SOLUTIONS

The artist, armed with satellite data, has a knowledge sufficient to form a pan-geographic comprehensive response to urgent site conditions. And reviewers have been alarmed by this new power, since it places the artist's decision and actions beyond their scope of review. Although I have repeatedly experienced fearful attempts by reviewers or even gallerists to contain or even condemn such megalomaniacal proposals, the task is to show, in detail, the logical steps taken with visual evidence. —P.F.

ABOVE *Stop, Special Pass Required, Radioactive Zone,* 1996.

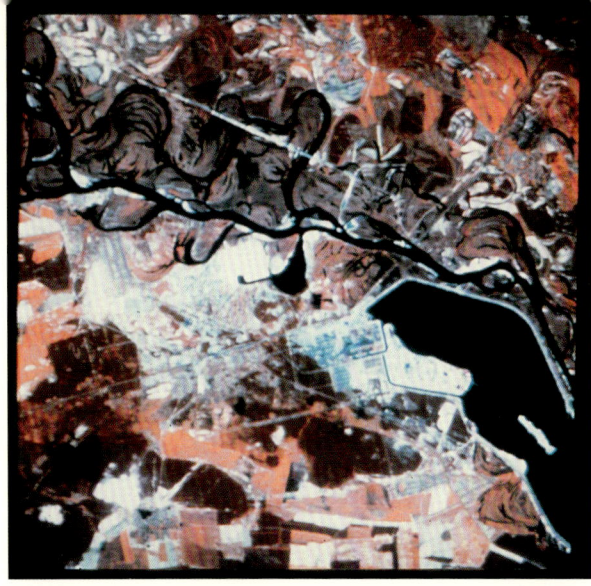

29 April 1986: Initial image created from satellite data of the Chernobyl reactor complex, which is similar to those that appeared in official releases.

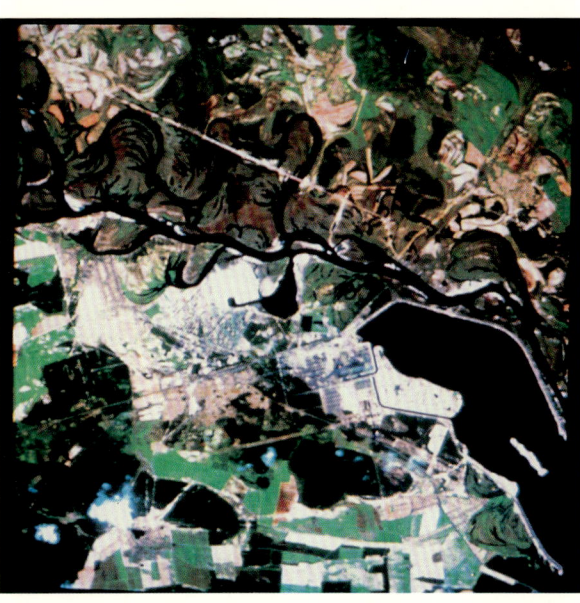

29 April 1986: Image created after further computer processing of the same data by Ocean Earth. The red dot indicates intense radiation.

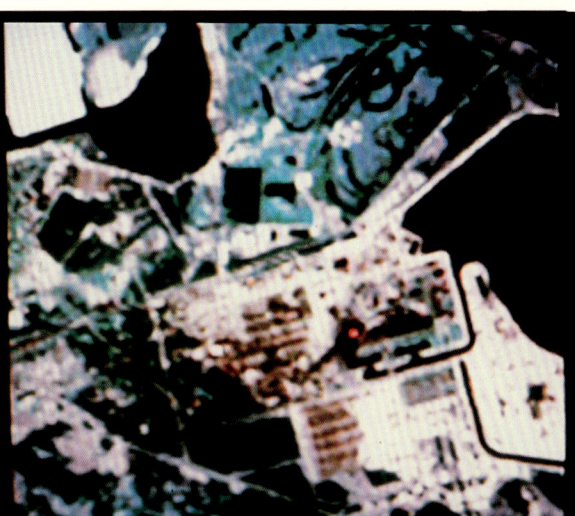

28 April 1986: Detail of above.

1985 The black track passing through the site at a 90-degree angle to the course of the river was reported by American scientists to be smoke. This track, which indicates hydrological instability, was proven by Ocean Earth to be already evident in 1985. Ocean Earth argued that the "smoke" was actually an area of landfill in the river bed, on which the reactor had been built.

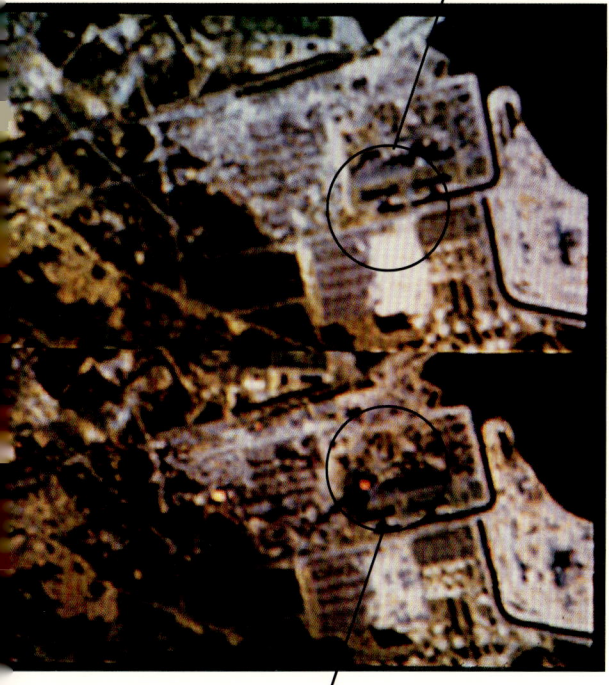

1986

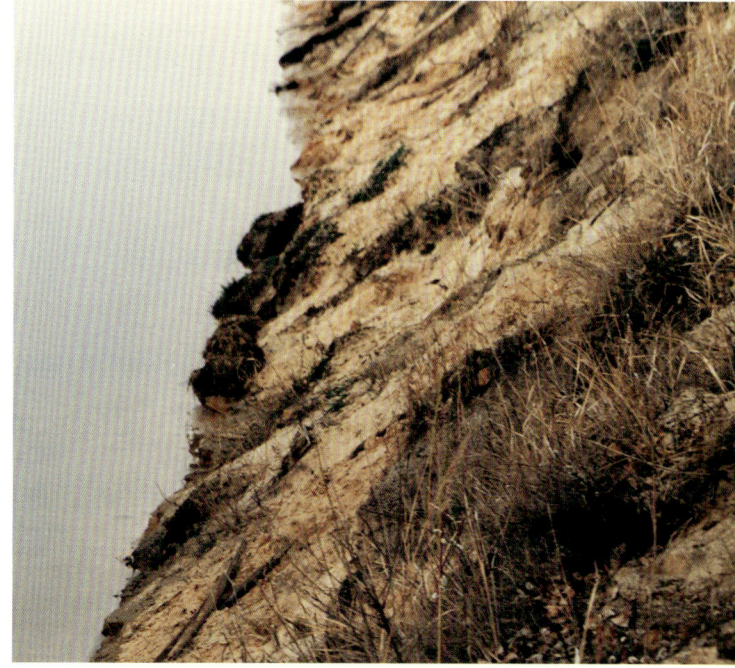

Expert comment by landscape architect David Hulse to Peter Fend, April 24, 1996.

"It's built on an elevated terrace, an engineered landfill. An engineered landfill is perfectly safe, and it's done all the time—for example with skyscrapers built on wetlands in the tropics."

Peter Fend: "Yeah, but what if the river is going straight through the building site?"

ABOVE **Pripyat River bank.**

6 May 1986: Image showing a slick of tar-like substance just upstream from Chernobyl Reactor #4, which may have been applied to the site in an attempt to prevent seepage and upwelling of contaminated water.

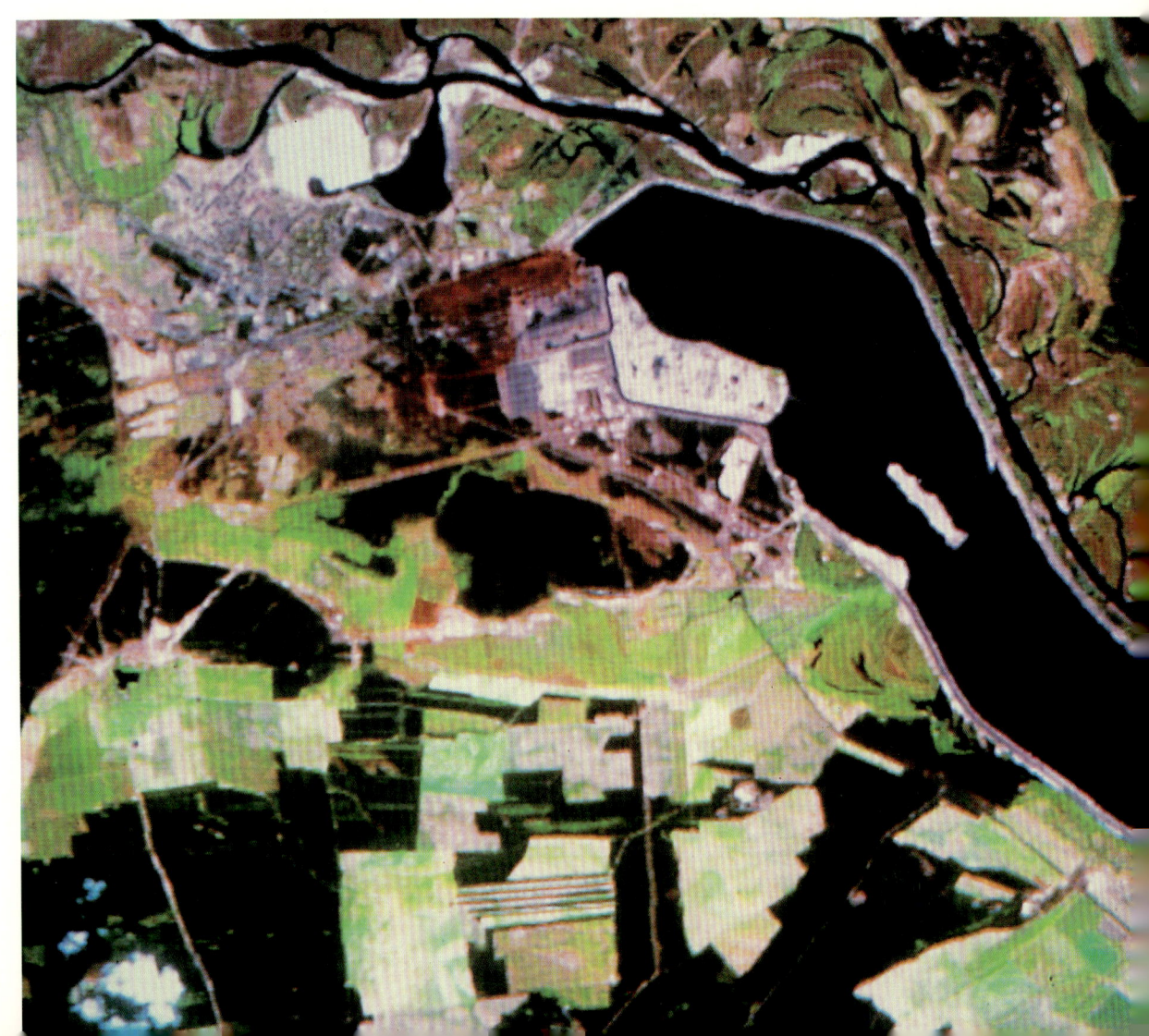

4 April 1996: Belarus from the air.

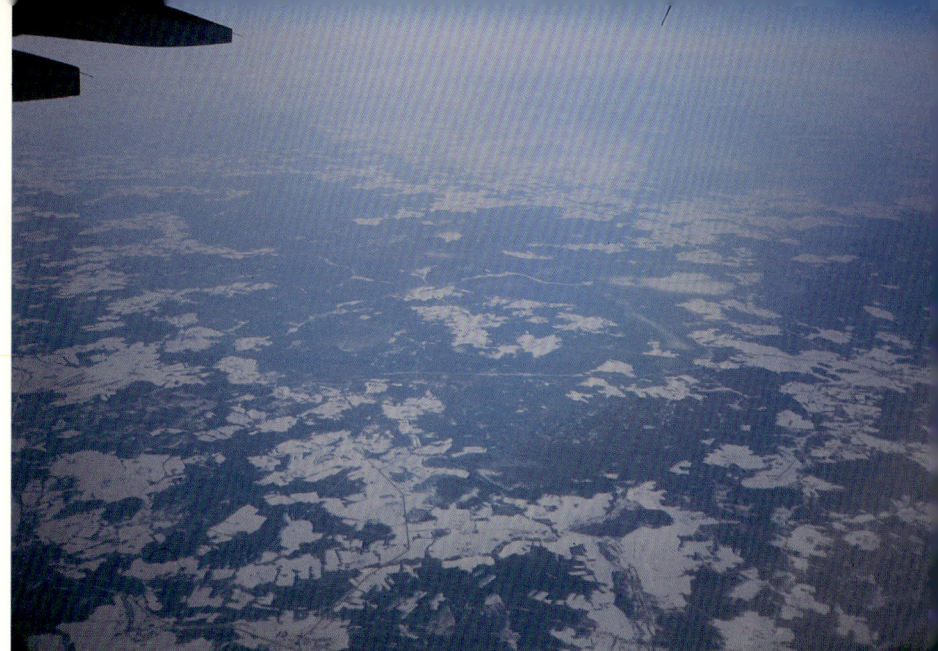

18 April 1996: At these latitudes, the change in the sun's angle from summer to winter is radical. Each spring, the ice and snow thaw very rapidly, causing a sudden influx of water and mud into the Chernobyl area. To ease pressure on the site and stem the spread of contamination, Ocean Earth proposes a diversion of the Pripyat River.

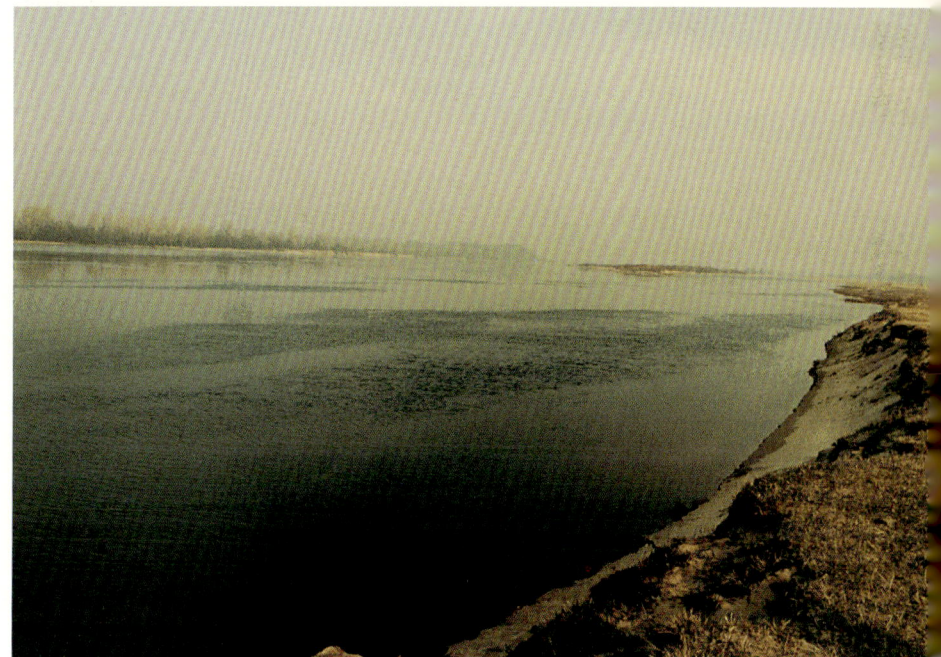

August 1986: Image of the Chernobyl reactor complex created from satellite data four months after the accident. Areas a, b, c, e, and f, and possibly d, are new installations, evidently made of concrete. They appear to be lined up with the deep center course of the river.

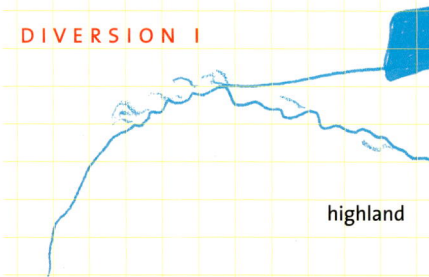

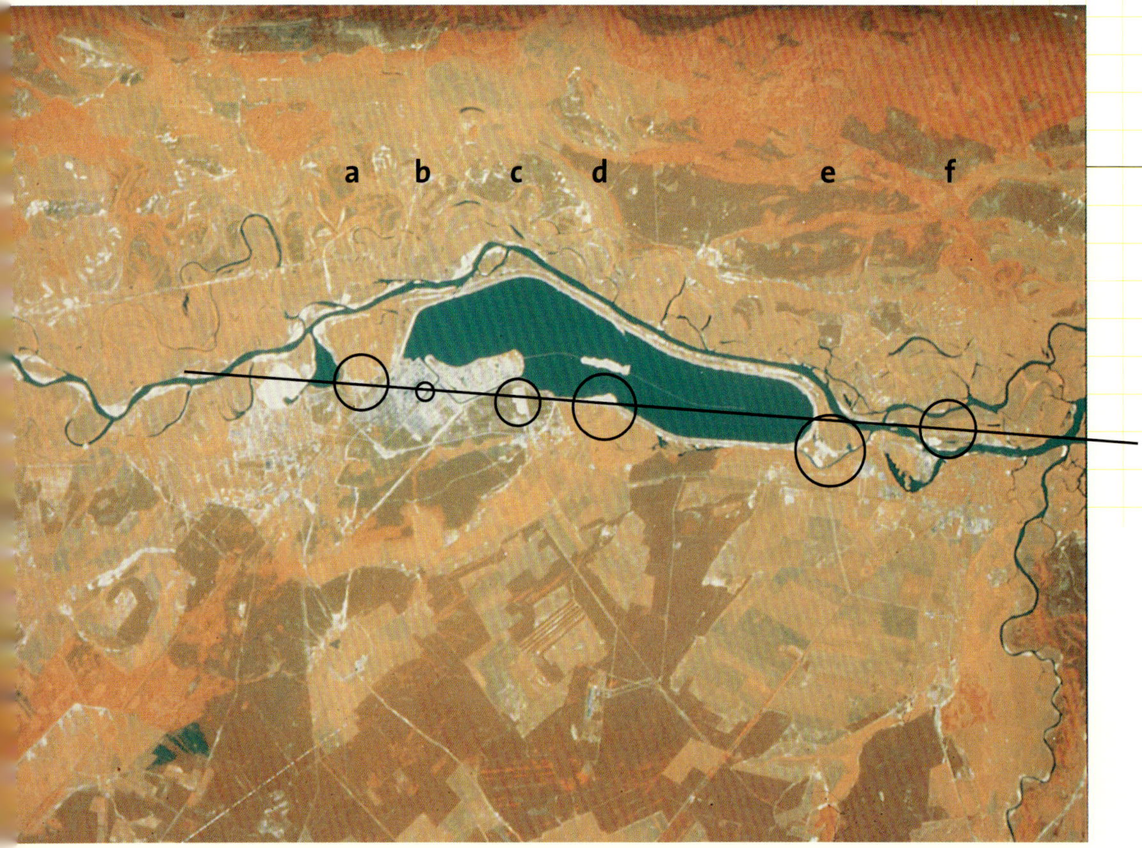

DIVERSION I

header to build up pressure

highland

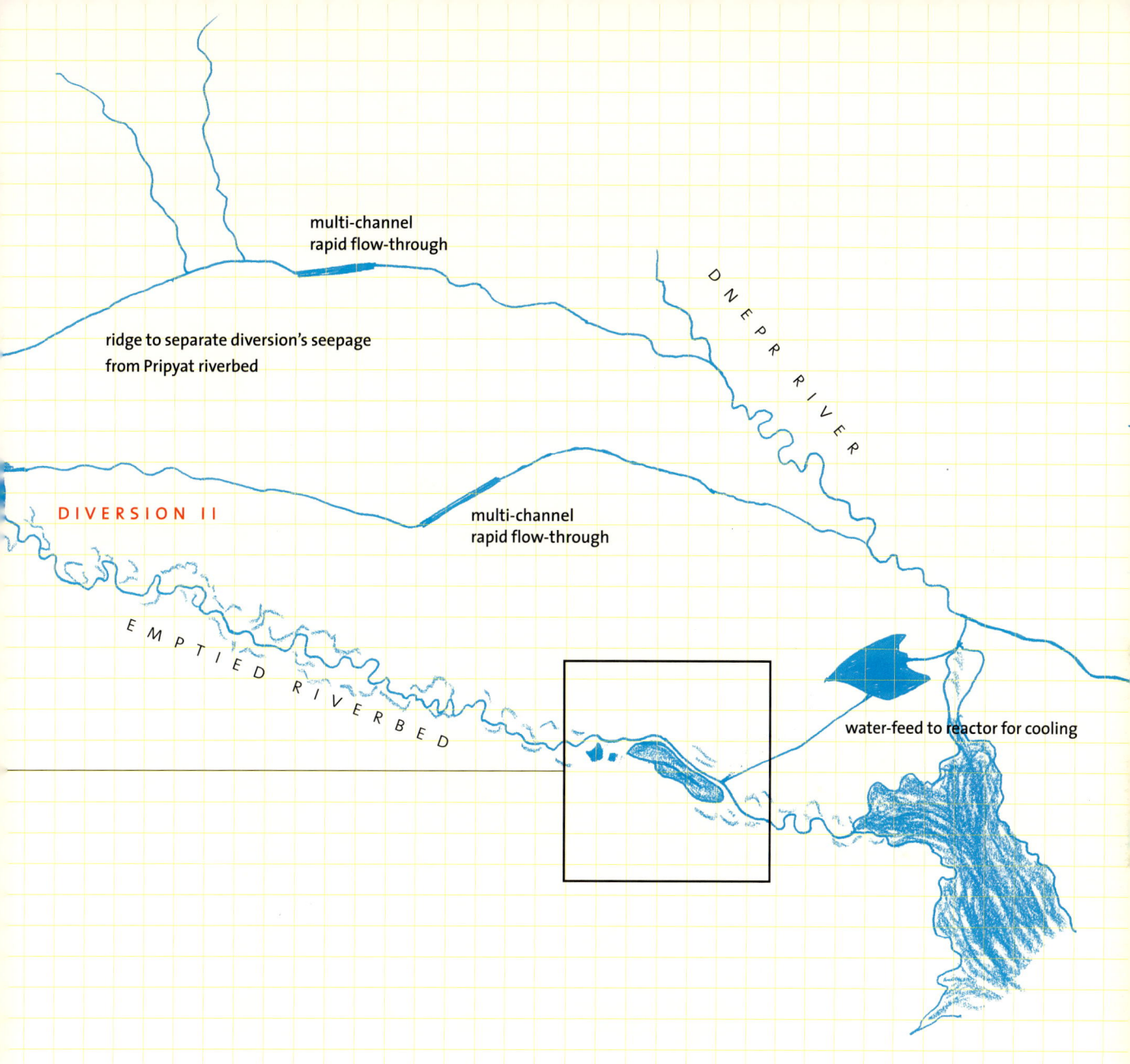

August 1986: Proposal for Pripyat River diversion, showing two possible routes for bypassing the Chernobyl reactor site.

PETER FEND

Contamination from the Chernobyl reactor complex continues to spread into the water of the Pripyat River basin, which flows into the Dnepr, and eventually to the Black Sea. Each spring, the snowmelt and shifting flow of mud and water bear down upon the reactor complex, increasing the levels of contamination and—more disturbing—the possibility of further break-up of the reactor. A shutdown of the entire reactor complex has been recommended for several years.

Peter Fend presents a series of engineering solutions, aimed at ending the spread of contamination and developing a new source of energy and electric power for the region, which would make possible the shutdown of the Chernobyl complex. His proposals, based on satellite surveys by Ocean Earth Development Corporation, the organization Fend founded in 1980, focus on three sites: 1. The Pripyat River upstream from Chernobyl, where Fend models a sixty-kilometer diversion of the river to the Dnepr River, and possibly also to the neighboring Desna River, in order to limit the mud and water pressure exerted on the reactor complex and to decrease the spread of contamination already existent in the surrounding soil. As the reactor complex, sitting on the middle of the river bed, is reported to be architecturally unstable, Fend believes that diverting the river is the only safe solution to the Pripyat pressures and attendant leakage. 2. The Don River, near Volgograd, where the channeled flow can be diverted into the Volga basin, away from the Black Sea, thus making the Black Sea more saline. This would allow greater bioproductivity and, according to some marine scientists, help in absorption of the radionucleides leaking into the sea. Any diversion here follows much discussion among scientists as to what strategies to adopt for improving the biochemistry of the three major southern seas of Russia and its neighbors: the Black Sea (not saline enough); the Caspian Sea (now swelling up with nutrient-poor waters); and the Aral Sea (rapidly disappearing). 3. The coastal waters of the Ukraine, which can be monitored and exploited to yield commercial quantities of brown or green algae that can in turn be harvested by the Ukraine state gas company, UKRGASPROM, for renewable, pollution-free fuel.

At all of these sites, Fend's designs take advantage of the new thinking in hydrological and ocean engineering embodied in 1970s and 1980s earthworks by American artists Michael Heizer and Dennis Oppenheim, and more recently used by Soviet military engineers to divert the Tigris and Euphrates Rivers for the Iran/Iraq war zone. He sees his work as a model *modus operandi* that uses a new conjunction of knowledge—of earth art, on one hand, and of catastrophes in large-scale terrain management, such as war, nuclear accidents, and floods, on the other—to find solutions to the problems caused by those catastrophic events.

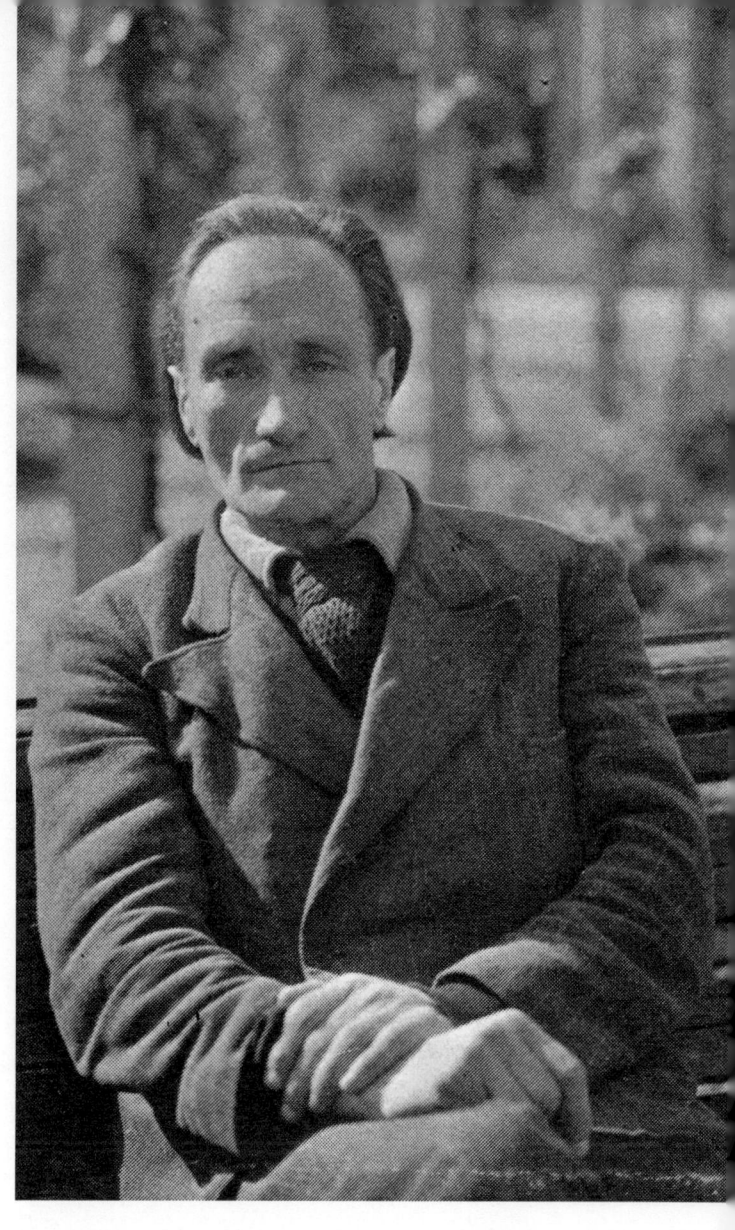

SPECTATOR, SPECTER, SITTER

CLAYTON ESHLEMAN

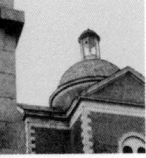

Antonin Artaud's final period (1945–48), which involved a complex interpenetration of drawing and writing, can be viewed as a successful culmination of his 1930s concept of a Theater of Cruelty. Eliminating playwright and script, the original Theater of Cruelty was to be directed "by a kind of unique Creator to whom will fall the double responsibility of the spectacle and the action." It was to be immediate (no spectacle was to be staged twice), gestural (physically articulated signs; actors as hieroglyphs), and dangerous—threatening the identities and bodies of both participants and spectators. Defining cruelty as a kind of charged rigor ("Everything arranged to a hair in a fulminating order"), Artaud proposed that the barrier between stage and performer should be obliterated, with the spectators placed at the center in a bare, undecorated building. Language, including screams, was to be used as percussive marking. The Theater of Cruelty was to evoke the plague, and be up to the forces of life at large, with the actor "an inspired ghost radiating affective powers."

Its evolution had three crucial stages. The first project failed to materialize because Artaud was dependent on the financial support of others for a spectacle that remained sketchy even for him. In the second stage, this theater abandoned its projected space in outer ceremony and took up residence in Artaud's own mind and body, becoming a psychotic shadow drama he could neither control nor share. Artaud completely cracked in the fall of 1937, becoming his own deliriously paranoid double, Antonéo Arlaud. He spent the next eight years and eight months in five insane asylums. At Ville Evrard, the interns recorded their amazement at the ferocious energy with which he would fight the demons he claimed surrounded him day and night. He believed that the interns as well as his friends in Paris were infested with Doubles, who were Initiates. They invaded him at night, attempted to steal his semen and excrement, dictated letters in his hand, and spied on him, possessing his thoughts before he could make them conscious.

This last complaint evokes Artaud's 1923 correspondence with Jacques Rivière, in which he protested against someone or something intercepting his thoughts. What had been invisible forces in 1923 had, by 1939, taken on identities in a Theater of Cruelty conceived and performed by and in the body and mind of Artaud/Arlaud. The beginning of Artaud's regeneration seemed to take place at this time. Although he still believed his thought was being robbed, he was identifying the robbers as fantasy formations and assigning them strategies and names—Astral, Flat-nosed Pliers, Those Born of Sweat, Cigul the Incarnation of Evil. At this time, Artaud was a savage parody of a creator/director/dancer, a one-man gestural theater, whirling about his intern-spectators, screaming, "an inspired ghost radiating affective powers."

After Artaud's 1943 transfer to the Rodez asylum, much of his demon-fighting energy was channeled into sound experiments: condensing syllables, grunting, humming, praying out loud while eating, and declaiming in a range of sonorous, monotonous, and full tones. His doctor, Gaston Ferdière, detested Artaud's "happenings" and, in a cruel attempt to redirect his energy, put him through fifty-one electro-shock sessions.

The third and final stage of the Theater of Cruelty began in 1945 when, after more than a year and a half of electroshock sessions, Artaud began to draw on large sheets of paper with pencils, crayons, and colored chalks. He also funneled his Ville Evrard cast of Doubles into a multi-prismed Catholic drama in the notebooks he began keeping. Near the end of 1945, he began to draw as well as to write in the notebooks, initially depicting bulbous, rigid, naked human figures tattooed with spots. Over the next several months, Artaud experimented with various layouts and ways of constructing figures. The drawings become playful at times, and include tiny figures strapped to tables, wheeled penis-cannons, cartoonish women holding huge scythes whose handles are penises, free-floating spread-eagled imps, envelopes turning into torso-like machines, and tubes, cylinders, and bubbles. Artaud's first fully articulated drawing, *The Totem* (December 1945), is an assertively reworked, smudged, mutilated, faceless, spindle-shaped female who will reappear in later writings as the "strangled totem" and the "innate totem."

From February 1946 on, until his release from Rodez the following May, Artaud's drawings became increasingly bold and slashing. His first self-portrait (the last drawing to be completed before his release) scathingly captures the asylum's assault in a face cut through with sores and scars, and measled with black spots. One eye is glazed, dead; the other starkly watchful and aware. This is probably the drawing that Artaud's one doctor friend, Jean Dequeker, watched him rework for several days, "shattering pencil after pencil, suffering the internal throes of his own exorcism."

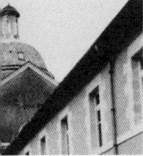

Once free of Rodez, and based in a clinic outside of Paris, Artaud turned a derelict pavilion into his workshop. By the end of his life (less than two years later, from intestinal cancer and possibly an overdose of chloral hydrate), the damp, dirty walls of this last "theater" were smeared with blood; his work table, his pounding stump, and the head of his bed were gouged with knife holes. Artaud would draw standing before a table, making noises, and often pressing his pencil point into the part of his head that corresponded to the part of the sitter's head that he was portraying. The sitter was forbidden to move, but allowed to talk. Artaud made dots by crushing his pencil lead into the paper; his strokes were so violent at times that he tore the paper, at others so insistent that the drawing took on an anthracitic gleam. Paule Thévenin—Artaud's dearest friend, sitter, and editor—said that sitting for Artaud was like being flayed alive. Thus he compressed the grandiosity of the original Theater of Cruelty into a one-on-one, face-to-face combat: the creator-director became a creator-drawer, the spectators a single, targeted sitter. Identities and bodies were still threatened, no performance was restaged, doubles were everywhere.

In Artaud's last period, every position taken to attack its opposite must, in turn, be rejected and attacked. Writing at once protects yet attacks the drawing, as drawing attacks yet protects the writing. In the texts the same ambivalence occurs between the incantations and the tirades. Based on nothing, a vertiginous, revolving movement cuts like a band saw through the paper as well as through Artaud's maternal language. The containing wall for these anti-positions is that they are at the mercy of a no longer repressed but still infantile unconscious. At the same time that Artaud sends out volleys of sparks, he regrinds his obsessions.

It had taken nearly two decades of rejection, abuse, and internal mayhem for Artaud to grasp that the only site at which he could exercise his faculties at large was one where he could completely control the unfolding of an event. He had tried to project an unrealizable Theater of Cruelty onto a new stage, but it boomeranged back at him and imploded. Rather than silencing or destroying him, the implosion populated his inner wasteland with saint-quality demons and willy-nilly placed him in the hands of the doctor who fried him alive for twenty months. Artaud's saga evokes Kenneth Rexroth's stanza about the knobcone pine, "whose cones / Endure unopened on the branches, at last / To grow imbedded in the wood, waiting for fire / To open them and reseed the burned forest." Opened by fire, Artaud revealed "being's disease, the syphilis of its infinity."

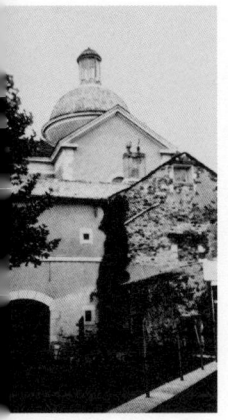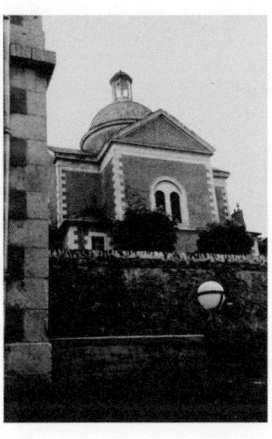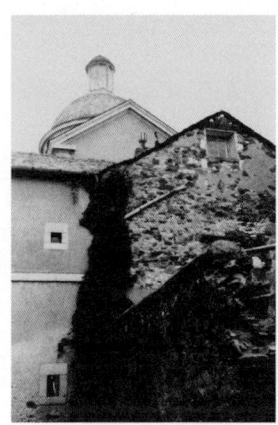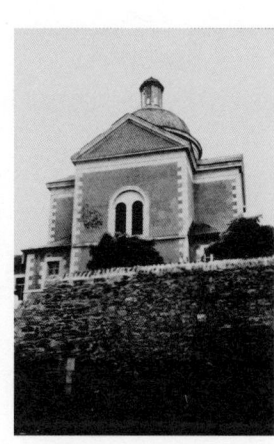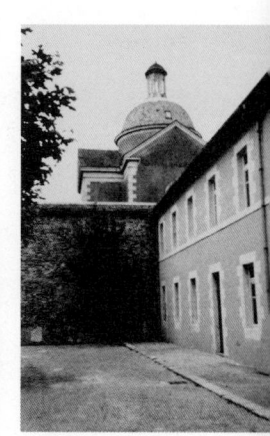

ANTONIN ARTAUD

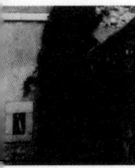

Ten years that the language is gone,
that there has entered in its place
this atmospheric thunder,
         this lightning,
facing the aristocratic pressuration of beings,
of all the noble beings
         of the butt,
cunt, of the prick,
of the lingouette,
of the plalouettee
         plaloulette
         pactoulette,
of the tegumentary trance,
of the pellicle,
racial nobles of the corporeal erotic,
against me, simple virgin of the body,
ten years that I once again blew up the Middle Ages,
with its nobles, its judges, its lookout,
         its priests above all,
         its churches,
         its cathedrals,
         its vicars,
         its white wafers.
How?
With an anti-logical,
         anti-philosophical,
         anti-intellectual,
         anti-*dialectical*
         blow of the tongue

with my black pencil pressed down
          and that's it.

Which means that I the madman and the mômo,
kept 9 years in a lunatic asylum for exorcistical and magical passes and because
    I supposedly imagined I'd found a magic and that it was crazy,
one must believe it was true,
since not a single day during my 3-year internment at Rodez, Aveyron, did the
    Dr. Ferdière fail at 10:30 A.M., the visiting hour, to come and tell me:
Mr. Artaud, as much as you may wish, Society cannot accept, and I am here the
    representative of Society.
If I was mad in my magical passes, what did it then matter to Society which
    could not feel attacked or injured and had only to despise and neglect me.
But the Dr. Ferdière presenting himself as a defender of that Society and
    entrusted to defend it must have recognized my so-called magical so-called
    passes since he was opposing me with Society,
I therefore say that the dismissed language is a lightning bolt that I was
    bringing forth now in the human fact of breathing, which my pencil strokes
    on paper sanction.
And since a certain day in October 1939 I have not written anymore without
    drawing anymore either.
But what I draw
are no longer subjects from Art transposed from imagination to paper, they are
    not affective figures,
they are gestures, a verb, a grammar, an arithmetic, a whole Kabala, and one
    that shits to the other, one that shits on the other,
no drawing done on paper is a drawing, the reintegration of a strayed sensibility,
it is a machine which has breath,
it was first a machine which at the same time has breath.
It is a search for a lost world
and one that no human tongue integrates
and the image of which on paper is even no more than a tracing, a sort of
    diminished
                    copy.
For the real work is in the clouds.

ANTONIN ARTAUD

Words, no,
arid patches of a breath which gives its full
but there where only the Last Judgment will be able to decide between values,
the *evidences*,
as far as the text is concerned,
in the moulted blood of what tide
will I be able to make heard
the corrosive structure,
I say hear
the constructive structure,
there where the drawing
point by point
is only the restitution of a drilling,
of the advance of a drill in the underworld of the sempiternal latent body.
But what a logomachy, no?
Couldn't you light up your lantern a bit more, Mr. Artaud.
My lantern?
I say
that look ten years with my breath
I've been breathing hard forms,
        compact,
        opaque,
        unbridled,
        without archings
in the limbo of my body not made
and which finds itself hence made
and that I find every time the 10,000 beings to criticize me,
to obturate the attempt of the edge of a pierced infinite.

Such are in any case the drawings with which I constellate all my notebooks.

In any case
the whore,
oh the whore,
it's not from this side of the world,

it's not in this gesture of the world,
it's not in a gesture of this very world
that I say
that I want and can indicate what I think,
and they will see it,
they will feel it,
they will take notice of it
through my clumsy drawings,
but so wily,
and so adroit,
which say SHIT to this very world.

What are they?
What do they mean?

The innate totem of man.

Gris-gris to come back to man.

All breaths in the hollow, sunken
        pesti-fering
        arcature
of my true teeth.

Not one which is not a breath thrown with all the strength
of my lungs,
with all the sieve
of my respiration,

not one which does not respond to a real physiological activity,
which is not,
not its figurative translation
but something like an efficacious sieve,
on the *materialized* paper.

I am, it seems, a *writer*.
But am I writing?
I make sentences.
Without subject, verb, attribute or complement.
I have learned words,
they taught me things.
In my turn I teach them a manner of new behavior.
May the pommel of your tuve patten
entrumene you a red ani bivilt,
at the lumestin of the utrin cadastre.
This means maybe that the woman's uterus turns red, when Van Gogh
    the mad protester of man dabbles with finding their march for the
    heavenly bodies of a too superb destiny.
And it means that it is time for a writer to close shop, and to leave
    the written letter for the letter.

April 1947

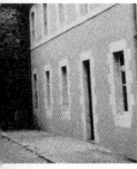

        Translated from the French by Clayton Eshleman, with Bernard Bador

I TALKED ABOUT GOD WITH ANTONIN ARTAUD

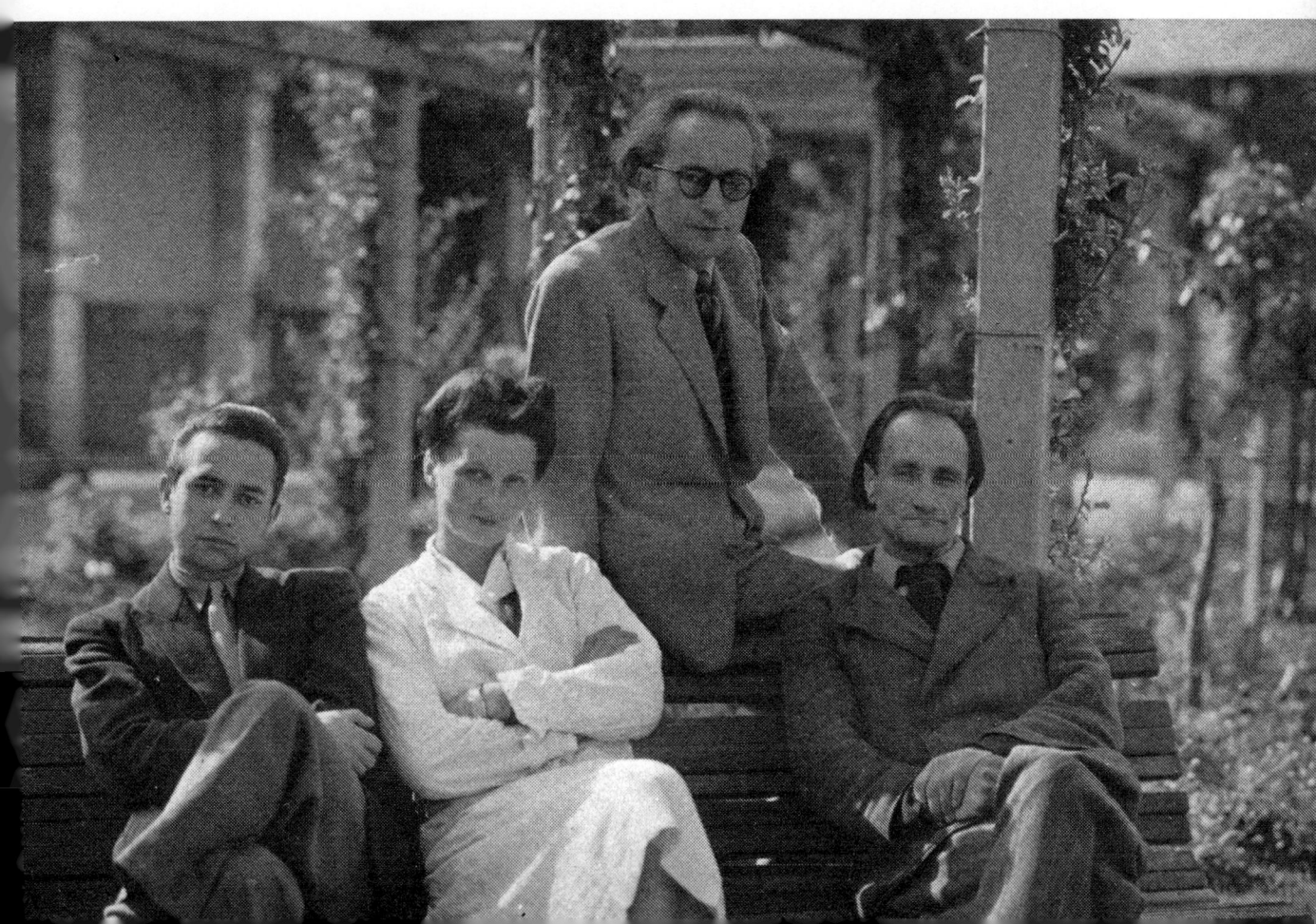

SYLVÈRE LOTRINGER / DR. JACQUES LATRÉMOLIÈRE

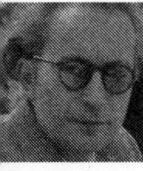

My dear friend, When I arrived here two years ago you received me with a great deal of kindness: Dr. Ferdière, who had known me for years, had told you of my odyssey and like him you wanted to make amends in your heart for the injustice that had been done me in treating me like a madman. . . . Electric shock, Mr. Latrémolière, reduces me to despair, it takes away my memory, it dulls my mind and my heart, it turns me into someone who is absent and who knows he is absent and sees himself for weeks in pursuit of his being, like a dead man alongside a living man who is no longer himself. . . . I have a great deal of affection for you and you know it, but if you do not stop these electric-shock treatments at once I shall no longer be able to keep you in my heart. . . . Personally, I believe, Mr. Latrémolière, that you have understood me very well and have accepted me in your heart, but that you are not always really there with your whole personal self and your whole representative consciousness.

—*from a letter from Antonin Artaud to Dr. Jacques Latrémolière,*
JANUARY 6, 1945

Fifty years after his death, Antonin Artaud remains at the center of a heated controversy that has pitted against each other his later friends and self-styled disciples, his publisher, Editions Gallimard, his psychiatrists at the Rodez hospital, and his family. During his lifetime, Artaud's family was extremely concerned about the blasphemous and anti-Catholic nature of many of his texts. Friends and family have repeatedly clashed over the nature of Artaud's beliefs, and the religious funeral arranged by his sister, Marie-Ange Malausséna, caused a heated debate.

On Artaud's death, his literary editor, Paule Thévenin, was notified first and, according to Thomas Maeder's 1978 biography, she and several other friends, apparently fearing that the family would destroy or suppress his work, took the notebooks and drawings that were left in his room. Litigation ensued, and the family, most recently, has accused Thévenin, who died three years ago, of having falsified Artaud's manuscripts. The publication of Artaud's last works has been suspended pending the result of ongoing litigation.

Meanwhile, the psychiatrists have accused Artaud's family of neglect and have blamed his death on his friends who procured him drugs after his move from the Rodez hospital to Ivry, near Paris. Artaud himself ignited the debate by publicly accusing Dr. Ferdière of having subjected him to a massive dose of electric shocks. Given the by now mythical stature of Antonin Artaud, the "Artaud Affair," as it is called, is not likely to be settled soon.

The following interview took place at Dr. Jacques Latrémolière's home in the small town of Figeac, near Rodez, in 1983. Dr. Latrémolière, who was Dr. Gaston Ferdière's intern during the Second World War and subjected Artaud to fifty-one electric shocks, died in the late 1980s.

SYLVÈRE LOTRINGER

DR. JACQUES LATRÉMOLIÈRE: I have to admit that when you called me to make an appointment, I wasn't all that enthusiastic. Rehashing Artaud's life, thirty years after the fact, seems a little ridiculous to me.

SYLVÈRE LOTRINGER: Weren't you personally in charge of Antonin Artaud while he was at the Rodez asylum?

LATRÉMOLIÈRE: I worked with Dr. Ferdière, who was the director of the asylum. I was Artaud's friend for two years. Have you read the article I wrote about him?[*] I said just about everything I could say about Artaud there. Since then, I think a little differently. The studies are multiplying and I think that's a pity. Artaud didn't have any message to communicate. He never had a message. He was a first-rate paranoiac, with absolutely extraordinary delusions of grandeur and persecution.

LOTRINGER: You were Artaud's friend?

LATRÉMOLIÈRE: He turned to his friends, that is, to the people he took advantage of, every time he needed opium—we never gave him opium, but he kept asking for it. We were his friends, but as soon as we disappeared from sight, we became his enemies. That was the case for many of the people who knew him. I consider his written work as something of a scream. A scream of horror, uttered by a man who had no sense of other people. He put himself at the center of the world. So I find the glory attributed to him a little overblown.

---

[*]Published in the second Artaud issue of the magazine La Tour de Feu, April 1961.

LOTRINGER: But isn't it precisely the horror of paranoia that makes what he says so important? Those emotions are what caused him to write as he did, and what he wrote triggered a kind of shock...

LATRÉMOLIÈRE: How was it possible for him to feel such different things almost simultaneously? It didn't have anything to do with the depth of his soul. I saw him cry out, I heard him cry out. And I don't think that there is anything to search for in Artaud's work. Nothing. It won't advance civilization. Just the opposite. He spent all his time shouting, and I don't believe that someone who cannot control himself has anything to offer to anyone else. I have Artaud's complete works, and in the entire body of his work, there is very little that is intelligible. I can guarantee you that he had no interest in civilization. What he was interested in was himself.

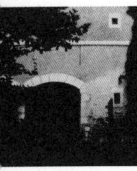

LOTRINGER: What was it like to be Artaud's friend?

LATRÉMOLIÈRE: We had long conversations that lasted for hours. Conversations about God, and, God knows, his thoughts on religion were debatable. It was a kind of myth to him, which circled around him.

LOTRINGER: Did Artaud believe he had a special relationship with God?

LATRÉMOLIÈRE: Special? He was the one who was going to take power before God's last appearance on the earth. So you see why I laugh when people talk about his message. There was nothing. How many people read him? No one. No one. A few intellectuals here and there.

LOTRINGER: His work has had a great influence on our culture. The major contemporary theater directors—Jerzy Grotowski, Peter Brook, the Living Theater—all over the world, in Poland, England, the United States, see him as a seminal figure.

LATRÉMOLIÈRE: He was incapable of having a proper relationship with anyone. He was no longer socially viable. And if we treated him— which we have been criticized for doing—it was because we had to protect him from himself. And we saw him improve. He became capable of writing again, of drawing, of chatting with us. We gave all that back to him. I will always remember my friend Ferdière saying, "If I had known, I wouldn't have let him leave Rodez. I truly regret it."

LOTRINGER: How did you first hear of Artaud?

LATRÉMOLIÈRE: I didn't hear of him. He arrived at Rodez because he was dying of hunger at Ville-Evrard.* Ferdière knew one of the psychiatrists there, who was able to send him to a psychiatric hospital on the border of the occupied and free

---

*Ville-Evrard, in Seine-et-Marne near Paris, was the fourth institution Artaud had been sent to since his return from Ireland in 1938. He arrived there in February 1939 and was admitted to the drug-addict ward. During his four-year stay, he was subjected to the starvation rations then allotted to asylum inmates by the German Occupation government and his physical health deteriorated drastically. In February 1943, his mother, along with the writers Robert Desnos and Paul Eluard, finally succeeded with Dr. Ferdière's help in having Artaud transferred to the more humane psychiatric hospital at Rodez, in Aveyron, on the border of the unoccupied zone.

zones. When he arrived he was very thin and in a bad state. I hadn't read anything by him at that point, and if I hadn't known him, I never would have read anything by him, that's clear enough.

LOTRINGER: How was he presented to you?

LATRÉMOLIÈRE: Ferdière told me about him. He told me that he'd been arrested on his way back from Ireland for creating a disturbance on the boat. He was talking about St. Patrick's walking stick when they locked him up, which is why he was taken to the closest psychiatric hospital, in Sotteville-lès-Rouen, if I remember correctly. It was immediately apparent that he was not behaving normally. All you had to do was spend a quarter of an hour with him. . . .

Psychiatrists are required to follow their patients closely, to talk to them as equals. I realize that I had against me the fact that I had absolute power over his freedom—although I wasn't the only one. That didn't make our relationship any simpler.

But when he needed me, he was charming. In those conversations he didn't make any of the declarations he made later. Later he could do anything. People hung on his every word. There are always people who, whenever they see anything extraordinary, will call it a miracle.

LOTRINGER: It's not so important to know whether Artaud deceived his friends. I'm sure he did, especially the friends his freedom depended on. . . . There's a whole controversy over whether Artaud did or didn't believe in God. What do you think?

LATRÉMOLIÈRE: I don't think that's of any interest. He believed at a certain point, and then he didn't believe anymore. When he believed, he believed badly, or strangely. I'm telling you that Artaud's religion was himself. He was at the center of the world.

LOTRINGER: So, when he went to church, he was God going to church? Or himself going to church?

LATRÉMOLIÈRE: That was just part of his general incoherence.

LOTRINGER: One of his texts on the Tarahumaras* was written at Rodez in 1943. It is strangely stuffed with saints and religious symbols, a delirium of Christ on the Cross that Artaud dismissed several years later, back in Paris, as a stupid spell placed on him by the clergy. The texts written in Mexico, on the other hand, are very beautiful, very clear. . . . They express an extremely serene vision of things, which is completely uncharacteristic of Artaud. Everything is in its place, the gods, men, the stones. Men are no longer the center of the universe, they are carved in stone and the stones are the gods. There is a kind of material harmony. Do you think it's strange that he continued to write like that, the mass of texts he produced . . .

LATRÉMOLIÈRE: He couldn't stop himself. He had notebooks everywhere. Here, this will

---

* The Tarahumara Indians, a tribal grouping in Chihuahua, Mexico, whom Artaud visited in 1936.

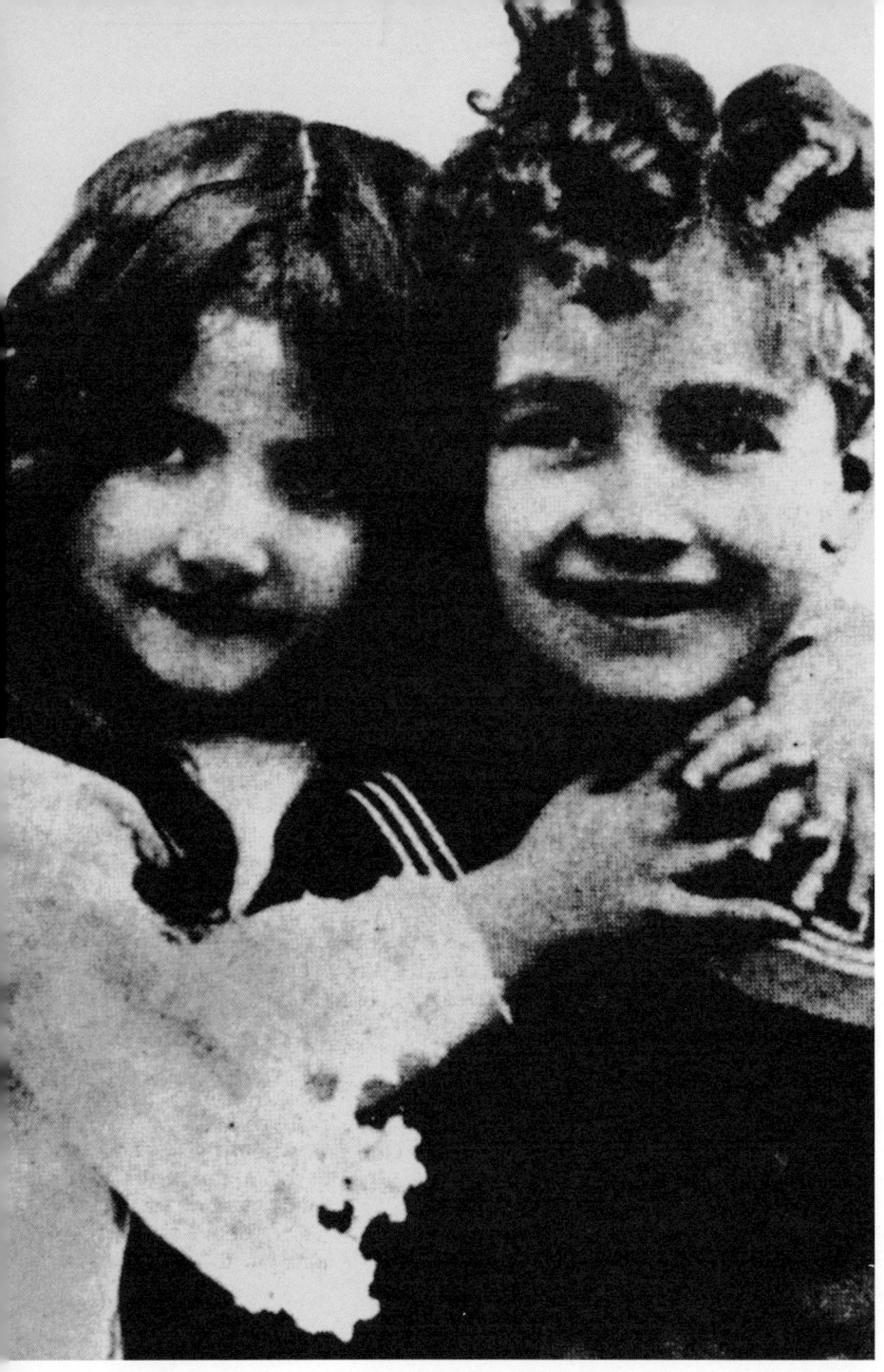

interest you. I taped a conversation with his sister, Marie-Ange Malausséna, at Rodez about ten years ago. She described her childhood with her brother and the bonds between them.*

*

LATRÉMOLIÈRE: It could be important if you would tell me about the quality of your brother's love for you.

MARIE-ANGE MALAUSSÉNA: Well, I don't want to exaggerate, but it seemed to me to be absolute, in terms of the kind of love that a brother can have for a sister. I always had the feeling that I was deeply loved by Antonin. When we walked together, he was always worried about where I was and always had to be next to me. He held my hand tightly so that I wouldn't get away from him.

LATRÉMOLIÈRE: Did he have the impression that people could get away from him?

MALAUSSÉNA: Yes, always.

LATRÉMOLIÈRE: Why do you think that was?

MALAUSSÉNA: I don't know. It was part of his character, his way of thinking. He was always terrified of losing what he loved. It was the same with our mother. He really adored my mother. I've told you about those little childhood scenes when I had to serve as interpreter and give my mother the letters Antonin had written to ask her forgiveness. And later, when he was a young man, he sometimes had differences with our mother—nothing serious—and then he would go and get her an immense bouquet of flowers so that she would forgive him.

LATRÉMOLIÈRE: Forgive him for what?

MALAUSSÉNA: The way he had behaved toward her. Which was sometimes really nothing to anyone else, but for him it took on enormous proportions. That was his personality. He was an extremist in everything, I think. I have the impression that he always lived in the absolute. As much in his emotional life as in his work, in his poetry, his writing, his plays.

LATRÉMOLIÈRE: Do you have the impression that the work he did when he was very young was already . . . marked . . . ?

MALAUSSÉNA: Yes, profoundly. It's difficult to define. It was his temperament, his character. He so badly wanted things to be done in a meticulous way, you see, that he looked for the absolute in the details themselves.

LATRÉMOLIÈRE: And how did he express the details when he was young? How did he work? I'm asking about the drawings he made.

MALAUSSÉNA: Well, his drawing was a little strange. I told you that on Thursdays and holidays he often went on the boat with Papa.

---

* Artaud was born in Marseille in 1896, to Antoine-Roi Artaud, a shipbuilder, and Euphrasie Artaud, who was descended from a Greek family that had settled in Smyrna. He moved to Paris in 1920, at the age of twenty-three, leaving behind both parents, his younger sister (by three years), Marie-Ange, and brother, Fernand. The following interview with Marie-Ange, who died in 1978, dates from the early '70s.

Then, when he got home, his first impulse was to pick up a notebook and immediately draw boats and boats and boats. He was very marked by this question of boats. And then, when he was thirteen, he started to make poems, and each time he'd written a poem, he'd come and read it to me, or to our mother.

LATRÉMOLIÈRE: What was his relationship with his father like?

MALAUSSÉNA: It was good. Papa was always very interested in . . . how shall I say it . . . his education. He was very much a humanist and he would work with Antonin on his Latin for long periods of time. Antonin always had good grades.

LATRÉMOLIÈRE: You spoke earlier about your holidays in Smyrna. He was very influenced by the Oriental style?

MALAUSSÉNA: Yes, yes. It was also the fact that our mother was a very good storyteller. And Antonin took after her. She told him Oriental legends, or French legends, of course, and he admired her, listened to her very closely. Later, when he would read aloud, he often had her inflections. Mother had a way not only of telling things, but of miming them, acting them out. I remember when she told us the story of Joseph being sold by his brothers. Or the story of Bluebeard. She had a lot of imagination and I think that Antonin resembled her. He'd get very excited when she told us frightening stories. He was always drawn to things that . . . how can I explain . . . were out of the ordinary or supernatural, you see.

LATRÉMOLIÈRE: At what point did you notice the anxiety that he so often developed in his work?

MALAUSSÉNA: Oh, I think that started when he was fourteen or fifteen. For example, when he was fifteen, he had a cousin—whom we liked very much—who often came to our house. One day Antonin staged a macabre greeting for him. He sent everybody away from the house—the maid, everyone—and he placed several skulls in his room, surrounded by candles. Then he disappeared. When my cousin rang the bell and came in, he went into Antonin's room to look for him, saw this terrifying scene, and was . . . how shall I say it . . . very scared. Then Antonin came in and they laughed about it together. . . .

LATRÉMOLIÈRE: Do you have the impression that he didn't feel loved?

MALAUSSÉNA: Yes, he probably had the impression that he wasn't loved as he would have liked to be. But, at home, he was always the most important person. Anything he wanted, my parents would give it to him. And when he wanted to come to Paris to be in the literary milieu he loved so much, no one stood in his way. Whatever he said, he was left alone.

And one thing is sure: my mother adored my brother, and my brother returned the feeling. She always protected him, or tried to, at least. Besides, she followed him step for step during his life. When Papa died, she sold everything in Marseille and came to live in Paris and let him stay with her. Even when he was in Paris and we lived in Marseille, Papa came to Paris every month to bring Antonin his monthly stipend. So

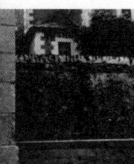

from a material point of view, he didn't have anything to worry about.

LATRÉMOLIÈRE: When he had gone to Ivry, after leaving Rodez, he continued to come home?

MALAUSSÉNA: Oh yes, of course. After he got back from Rodez, he was always at home. And sometimes, in the afternoon, he would lie down and ask me to wake him at whatever time he had to leave. He rested with us, and he wrote.

LATRÉMOLIÈRE: And he didn't disturb your family's life?

MALAUSSÉNA: Not at all. Quite the opposite. We were always so happy to have him with us. . . . The day before he died, I was with him.* He had asked me to help get his things in order. Then when the time came for me to leave, he wanted to come with me. I think I've already told you about how concerned he was to place in a corner, to hide, the last things he'd written. So, for a while, a long while, he paced around his room, and finally I said, "I think the best way to hide your things would be to put them under the new notebooks I brought you. In that pile of new notebooks, no one will go looking for the one that's been written in." And that completely . . . how can I explain . . . reassured him and he was calm again.

LATRÉMOLIÈRE: And the morning of his death,

---

* Shortly after his release from Rodez, Artaud went to live in a dilapidated, two-room pavilion on the edge of the property belonging to the clinic at Ivry. He lived there until his death from an overdose of chloral hydrate, which he was taking to lessen the pain of cancer.

did you have the impression that he knew it was going to happen? Did he say to you: if I take a few too many tranquilizers, there's a danger of . . . ?

MALAUSSÉNA: Yes. He was taking chloral hydrate then. The day before he died, because I was with him, he wanted to drink a glass of water with chloral hydrate. So he took out a soup spoon and said, "You see, if I take just a little more than this, I could just stay under, with a heart attack, or an embolism." And that's what must have happened in the night, because he was found dead of an embolism the following morning. I suppose that he must have raised the dosage without meaning to. And he stayed under.

*

LATRÉMOLIÈRE: It's an interesting document. I often heard Antonin Artaud talk complete nonsense. When he was with his friends in the cafés, he was always yelling at the top of his lungs. But when he went to his sister's house, he was as gentle as anything. That's what I wanted you to hear. You see, I didn't share literature with Artaud, I shared life.

LOTRINGER: He seems to have had a remarkable ability to adapt. Isn't that how we characterize normality? The ability to adapt to one's situation.

LATRÉMOLIÈRE: You can't judge a man by selected moments. I had to pass judgment on Artaud in order to care for him, in order to help him be normal again. After he left Rodez, he'd go to the cathedral and fall to his knees in the middle of the aisle, gesturing wildly with his arms. . . .

SYLVÈRE LOTRINGER / DR. JACQUES LATRÉMOLIÈRE

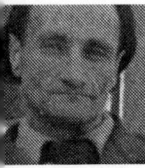

LOTRINGER: I've seen thousands of people walk up the aisle on their knees in the cathedral in Krakow. And they were excellent Catholics, I can assure you. If Artaud had crawled on the sidewalk in New York, no one would have stopped to watch him.

LATRÉMOLIÈRE: He wasn't fit, you know. He wasn't viable. The only thing that mattered for him was his personal purity.

LOTRINGER: That's very Christian. He was very influenced by the church, if you believe his sister.

LATRÉMOLIÈRE: Having spoken with him on the subject, I can tell you that it didn't really go very far.

LOTRINGER: Perhaps it went farther than with other people. Perhaps Artaud shows the extent to which, if one exaggerates "legitimate" things, they can become dangerous. What if the world proved him right?

LATRÉMOLIÈRE: Right about what? He was incoherent from start to finish.

LOTRINGER: Then how could he be a threat to society? Why was he given electric-shock treatments?

LATRÉMOLIÈRE: Oh, don't talk to me about electric shocks. I was the one who gave them to him. I can show you the letter from Ferdière.... It's a disgrace that he was criticized for administering electric shocks. It's ridiculous. I'm convinced that Artaud would be given electric-shock treatments even now.

LOTRINGER: So you don't believe that Artaud was capable of living in society?

LATRÉMOLIÈRE: No, if he hadn't been thrown back into it, he would have lived a lot longer. He was a patient like any other.

LOTRINGER: Were people aware, while he was at Rodez, that he was a, let's say, exceptional man?

LATRÉMOLIÈRE: No, absolutely not.

LOTRINGER: How do you react to Artaud, now, independently of all the noise that has been made about him?

LATRÉMOLIÈRE: I told you. He was one patient among many. One who interested us. He came to our home, he lunched with us and read us work by other writers, which was fascinating. And we spoke of other things. That's all.

LOTRINGER: So you were only witness to a small phenomenon?

LATRÉMOLIÈRE: Yes.

LOTRINGER: That's a shame.

LATRÉMOLIÈRE: No. It's not my fault, it's his. He didn't have a world-shattering effect on me. I pitied him, with all my heart. I tried to be close to him, in order to understand a way to help him out of his illness. And in three years, we just about managed to do it, but not quite.

Translated from the French by Deborah Treisman

CONTRIBUTORS

DANIEL LEE ANDERS was born on July 30, 1940. "A Haitian voodoo midwife prized me from the womb of a mother I would never meet. I never knew my dad either. My first bed was the top drawer of a chest of drawers, in the middle of my grandparents' living room in the shotgun shack I was raised in, in a long line of row houses arranged like dominoes along the bank of the Chocolate Bayou just northwest of Port Arthur, Texas. My schoolmaster-preacher Baine was also the Enlightened Cyclops of the Vidor, Texas, Illuminated Fraternity of the White Camellia, of which my Grandpa had been a card-carrying member for thirty years. It wasn't until I was in Korea that I was told convincingly that the United States wasn't a backwater suburb to Texas. I quit school when I was fourteen and got a job on the Houston Ship Channel unloading grain and cargo barges and ships. I met Carol Jean (CJ) Henning when she was six and I was seven, and married her when I was fifteen. I worked on the Houston Waterfront from fourteen to fifteen and a half, and was then sent to the Artesan Hall juvenile home for stealing hubcaps from 1953 Oldsmobiles. I went to Korea instead of the Gatesville Reformatory, and returned to the States in '59. My wife and I worked on the river-barge towboats out of Arkansas Pass, Texas. I spent a year on a Texas Department of Corrections prison farm, two years in Mexico in a Job Corps program with CJ, then lived in Phoenix until she died of cancer in 1978. I went on a two-year drinking binge and basically woke up in prison in 1980." Anders was convicted of mayhem assault and conspiracy to commit murder in 1980, and was sentenced to forty-years-to-life in the Arizona prison system. Verso will publish a selection of his letters to Mike Davis in 1998.

Anders can be contacted by mail at ADC #49750, Arizona State Prison Complex–Florence, Florence, AZ 85232.

ANTONIN ARTAUD was born in Marseille in 1896. Briefly associated with André Breton and the Surrealist movement, he rejected the group because of its political involvement. In 1926, he founded the Théâtre Alfred-Jarry, but it failed within two years. Tortured for much of his life by poverty, drug addiction, and mental and physical illness, he left a legacy of literary and dramatic work that reached fruition in the works of such dramatists as Samuel Beckett, Eugène Ionesco, Jean Genet, and Edward Albee. He died in Ivry, a suburb of Paris, in 1948.

BERNARD BADOR, a surrealist collagist, lives in Los Angeles. His books are published by the Saint-Germain Press in Paris. He is the author of *Sea Urchin Harakiri* (Panjandrum), translated by Clayton Eshleman.

SUSAN BROWNSBERGER has translated novels by Fazil Iskander, Yuz Aleshovsky, Vladimir Voinovich, and most recently Andrei Bitov's *The Monkey Link* (Farrar, Straus & Giroux). She is currently translating two of Bitov's short stories for Glas.

JEFF CLARK was born in southern California in 1971, and currently lives in San Francisco. His first book of poems, The Little Door Slides Back, will be published by Sun & Moon Press in 1997.

DAVID CRONENBERG was born in Toronto in 1943. While studying English Language and Literature at the University of Toronto, he produced two 16-mm shorts, Transfer and From the Drain. By 1970, he had also shot two independent 35-mm films, Stereo and Crimes of the Future. Cronenberg's first commercial feature film, Shivers (released in the United States as They Came from Within) was one of the fastest recouping movies in the history of Canadian film. Films written and directed by Cronenberg include Rabid (1977), Fast Company (1979), The Brood (1979), Scanners (1981), Videodrome (1983), The Fly (1986), Dead Ringers (1988), which won him the Los Angeles Film Critics' Society's Best Director Award, and Naked Lunch (1991). Naked Lunch won the Genie Awards for Best Picture, Best Director, and Best Screenplay. Cronenberg's screenplay for Naked Lunch was also judged the best of the year by the New York Film Critics' Circle and the Boston Society of Film Critics. In 1990, he was named a Chevalier de l'Ordre des Arts et des Lettres by the French Ministry of Culture. His new movie, Crash, will be released in March 1997.

SALVADOR DALÍ was born in Figueras, Spain, in 1904. In 1921, he enrolled at the San Fernando Royal Academy of Fine Arts in Madrid and joined an avant-garde circle of students that included filmmaker Luis Buñuel and poet-dramatist Federico García Lorca. Shortly afterward, he came under the influence of two forces that shaped his philosophy and his art: Sigmund Freud's theory of the unconscious and the French Surrealist movement. In 1929, Dalí settled in Paris and became in a short time one of the best-known members of the Surrealist movement. During the 1930s, his paintings were included in Surrealist shows in Europe and the United States. At this time, his style crystallized into the disturbing blend of precise realism and dream-like fantasy that became his hallmark. His works, which he described as "hand-painted dream photographs," were inspired by dreams, hallucinations, and other unconscious forces that the artist was unable to explain, and were produced by a creative method he called "paranoiac-critical activity." Dalí worked on two films with Buñuel, An Andalusian Dog (1928) and The Golden Age (1930). His writings include poetry, fiction, and an autobiography, The Secret Life of Salvador Dalí (1942). He died in Figueras in 1989. The Rotten Ass is an excerpt from his work, La Femme Visible, which was first published in French in 1930 by Editions Surréalistes.

LÁSZLÓ DARVASI was born in Hungary in 1962. He is the founder and coeditor of the Budapest-based weekly magazine Eles es Irodalom (Life and Literature) and the editor of the literary publication Pompeji. He is one of the most successful writers of his generation in Hungary and has received many grants and awards. His book, Das traurigster Orchester der Welt (The Saddest Orchestra in the World), was published in German by Rowohlt-Berlin in 1995. Darvasi is currently writing a novel. He lives in Szeged in southern Hungary.

MIKE DAVIS is finishing a new book on Los Angeles's recent trial by riot, flood, and earthquake titled *Ecology of Fear*. He is a contributing editor to *Grand Street*.

CLAYTON ESHLEMAN is currently working on a book on the origin of image-making in Upper Paleolithic cave art. In May 1997, he will lead a group to the French Dordogne, where they will visit some of the Ice Age decorated caves. In the spring of 1997, Marsilio will publish a new edition of his *Novices: A Study of Poetic Apprenticeship*, along with a bilingual edition of his cotranslation of Aimé Césaire's *Notebook of a Return to the Native Land*. Eshleman continues to teach at Eastern Michigan University, where he edits *Sulfur* magazine, now on its fortieth issue. *Spectator, Specter, Sitter* was excerpted from a paper originally presented as part of a panel discussion on Artaud's writing and drawing at The Drawing Center, New York, October 11, 1996. Organized by Sylvère Lotringer, the panel also included Jacques Derrida, Margit Rowell, Nancy Spero, and Gayatri Spivak.

PETER FEND was born in 1950. His most recent solo exhibitions were held at Galerie Metropol, Vienna, and the Marc Jancou Gallery, London. He is the founding president of the Ocean Earth Development Corporation, which maintains offices in New York and Paris. He is represented by American Fine Arts, Co., New York.

LAWRENCE FERLINGHETTI was born in Yonkers, New York, in 1919. He received a B.A. in Journalism from the University of North Carolina and an M.A. from Columbia University. After completing his Navy service in World War II, he moved to Paris, where he received a Doctorat de l'Université from the Sorbonne in 1949. On his return to the United States, he settled in San Francisco, where he and Peter D. Martin founded City Lights Books. Under the City Lights imprint, Ferlinghetti began the Pocket Poets Series, which included work by William Carlos Williams, Allen Ginsberg, Kenneth Patchen, Kenneth Rexroth, and Antonin Artaud. Ferlinghetti's second book of poems, *A Coney Island of the Mind* (New Directions), is one of the best-selling poetry books of our time. The poems published in this issue of *Grand Street* will appear in Ferlinghetti's collection, *A Far Rockaway of the Heart*, which New Directions will publish in May 1997.

COLA FRANZEN has translated a volume of selected poems by Jorge Guillén titled *Seen and Remembered*, as well as a group of poems by Federico García Lorca, *Selected Verse by García Lorca* (Farrar, Straus & Giroux). Her recent publications include *Mean Woman* (University of Nebraska Press), a novel by Alicia Borinksy, and *Si regreso / If I Go Back* (Cross-Cultural Communications) by Juan Cameron.

FORREST GANDER's recent books include a collection of poetry, *Deeds of Utmost Kindness* (Wesleyan University Press), and a bilingual anthology, *Mouth to Mouth: Poems by 12 Contemporary Mexican Women* (Milkweed Editions). He is currently spending a year in Iowa City.

ARTHUR GOLDHAMMER was recently awarded the French-American Foundation Translation Prize for his translation of *Realms of Memory*, edited by Pierre Nora and published by Columbia University Press.

EINAR MÁR GUDMUNDSSON won the Nordic Council Literature Prize in 1995 for his novel, *Angels of the Universe*, from which the selection published in this issue of *Grand Street* was excerpted. He is the author of three collections of poetry, short stories, screenplays, and a novel. He lives in Reykjavik, Iceland. *Angels of the Universe* will be published in English by St. Martin's Press in the spring of 1997.

JORGE GUILLÉN was born in Valladolid, Spain, in 1893. His first book of poems, *Cántico*, was published in 1928, while he was a lecturer at the Sorbonne in Paris. A member of the "Generation of 27," the poetry movement whose members included Federico García Lorca, Rafael Alberti, Pedro Salinas, and others, Guillén described his work as dedicated to "reality, not realism." At the outbreak of the Spanish Civil War, he was briefly detained in Pamplona as a political prisoner, and in 1938 he moved to the United States, where he remained until the death of Franco. He returned to Spain in 1978 and died in Malaga in 1984.

ALEX HALBERSTADT is a writer and coeditor of *Moscow Channel* (http://www.moscowchannel.com), a journal on the World Wide Web devoted to Russian culture, politics, and arts. In the fall of 1996, *Moscow Channel* presented the first retrospective of work by Vladimir Kovenatsky. Halberstadt lives in New York.

MICHAEL HOFMANN lives in London and teaches half the year at the University of Florida. His translation of Franz Kafka's novel, *The Man Who Disappeared* (Penguin), was published in February 1997. Faber and Faber will publish his fourth book of poems, *Approximately Nowhere*, and a collection of essays in 1998.

FANNY HOWE's most recent collection of poems is *O'Clock* (Reality Street Editions).

NORA OKJA KELLER, a Korean-American who lives in Hawaii, is a freelance journalist and fiction writer, and has published numerous stories and essays on Asian-Americans. After graduating from the University of Hawaii at Manoa with highest honors in English and Psychology, she went on to receive her Master's degree in American Literature from the University of California at Santa Cruz in 1990. At UCSC and later at the University of Hawaii, Keller taught classes in creative writing, composition, and American literature. Her fiction has appeared in *Hawaii Review*, *Honolulu Magazine*, and *Bamboo Ridge*, among other publications. The selection published in this issue of *Grand Street* was excerpted from her first novel, *Comfort Woman*, which will be published in April 1997 by Viking. She is currently working on her second novel.

DANIIL KHARMS was born Daniil Yuvachov, in St. Petersburg in 1905. In 1925, he assumed the pseudonym "Kharms" (a combination of the English words "charms" and "harms"), and began participating in poetry readings and literary gatherings in Leningrad. In 1926, he became a member of the Leningrad Union of Poets, and in 1927, he founded the literary group OBERIU (an acronym of the three Russian words for Union of Real Art). Kharms was arrested in 1931 and exiled to Vologda on his release in 1932. In the 1930s, Kharms restricted his publications to children's stories. He was arrested again in August 1941. When his wife came to leave a package for him at the prison hospital on February 4, 1942, she was told that he had died on February 2.

VLADIMIR KOVENATSKY was born in Kharkov, Russia, in 1938, and spent most of his life in Moscow. After graduating from art school in 1959, he made a living as a book illustrator and designer working at the Soviet Union's state-run publishing houses, magazines, and film studios. He left behind in his personal files, however, a diverse body of work including drawings, woodcuts, linocuts, prints, poems, short stories, essays, and an autobiography titled *The Way It Was*. During his lifetime, Kovenatsky made no attempt to show his work publicly. Mentally and physically ill, and on the verge of starvation, he died in his Moscow apartment in 1986. A small viewing of Kovenatsky's work, organized by the World Wide Web site *Moscow Channel* and Boris Kerdimun, the artist's executor, collaborator, and closest friend, was held in New York in 1996.

DAMON KRUKOWSKI's first book of poetry, *5000 Musical Terms*, was published by Burning Deck in 1995. He edits Exact Change Books in Boston, and is a sometime musician—formerly the drummer in the band Galaxie 500, now one-half of the duo Damon & Naomi. He is currently working on a collection of prose poems.

PAUL LAFFOLEY was born in Cambridge, Massachusetts, in 1940. He spoke his first word, "Constantinople" at six months, then remained silent until the age of four (having been diagnosed as slightly autistic), when he began to draw and paint. He has continued as a self-taught artist to the present. In his senior year at Brown University, he was given eight electric-shock treatments. He was dismissed from the Harvard Graduate School of Design, but managed to apprentice with the sculptor Mirko Baseldella, before going to New York to apprentice with the visionary architect Frederick Kiesler. He formed the Boston Visionary Cell, Inc. in 1971. He has participated in over two hundred exhibits, nationally and internationally. In 1990, he became a registered architect. In 1992, during a routine CAT scan on his head, a metallic implant, 3/8 of an inch long, was discovered in the occipital lobe of his brain. Local M.U.F.O.N. Investigators declared it to be an alien nanotechnological laboratory.

JAMES LAUGHLIN's most recent book of poetry, *The Secret Room*, will be published by New Directions in April 1997.

SYLVÈRE LOTRINGER is a Professor of French Literature at Columbia University and the General Editor of *Semiotext(e)*. He has published a monograph on *Antonin Artaud* (Scribner's), *Overexposed* (Pantheon), and books of interviews with Paul Virilio and Jean Baudrillard (both published by Semiotext(e)). He was a consultant for the recent *Antonin Artaud: Works on Paper* exhibition at the Museum of Modern Art, New York, and organized the concurrent Artaud events held at The Drawing Center, New York.

MICHAEL MADORE is an artist and writer living in New York City. He has written for *New Art*

Examiner, Poliester, and *Trans>arts.culture.media.* He shows with Bridges & Bodell and Cavin-Morris Galleries in New York.

JACKIE McALLISTER will participate in Smart Show, an international art fair, which will take place from March 20 to 23, 1997, on one of the world's largest cruise ships that will sail the Baltic Sea between Stockholm and Helsinki.

HEINRICH ANTON MÜLLER was born in Versailles, France, in 1869, and moved to the village of Corsier, near Bern, Switzerland, soon afterward. He was an agricultural and vineyard worker until 1906, when he was committed to a psychiatric hospital in Münsingen, where he would remain until his death in 1930. His drawings, paintings, and photographs of his sculptures were shown at a one-man exhibition in Paris in 1949, at Documenta 5 in Kassel in 1972, in 1981 in *Paris-Paris: Créations in France (1937–1957)* at the Centre Georges Pompidou, Paris, and in 1992 in the exhibition *Parallel Visions: Modern Artists & Outsider Art* at the Los Angeles County Museum.

D. NURKSE's most recent book, *Voices Over Water*, was reissued by Four Way Books in 1996. He is the recipient of a Whiting Writers' Award and two NEA Fellowships.

VICTOR PELEVIN was born in Moscow in 1962. He has received degrees from the Moscow Institute of Power Engineering and from the Russian Institute of Literature. His work has appeared widely in Russian magazines and has been translated into French, German, Japanese, and English. His collection of short stories, *The Blue Lantern* (to be published by New Directions), won the 1993 Russian Booker short-story prize, and his novel, *Omon Ra* (Farrar, Straus & Giroux), was among those nominated for the 1993 Russian Booker Prize.

ADRIAN PIPER is a conceptual artist whose work in a variety of media has focused on racism, racial stereotyping, and xenophobia for almost three decades. She exhibits her work internationally and at the John Weber and Paula Cooper Galleries in New York, and is the recipient of Guggenheim, AVA, and numerous NEA Fellowships, as well as the Skowhegan Medal for Sculptural Installation. Her collections, OUT OF ORDER, OUT OF SIGHT, *Volume I: Selected Writings in Meta-Art 1968–1992* and *Volume II: Selected Writings in Art Criticism 1967–1992*, were recently published by MIT Press. Piper is also Professor of Philosophy at Wellesley College. She has received Andrew Mellon and Woodrow Wilson Research Fellowships and her principal publications are in meta-ethics, Kant, and the history of ethics. She is currently working on a three-volume collection titled *Rationality and the Structure of the Self*. All of her texts published in this issue of *Grand Street* appeared in *Decide Who You Are: Texts* (Paula Cooper Gallery, 1992).

TOM SACHS was born in New York in 1966. He attended the Architectural Association in London in 1987 and received a B.A. from Bennington College in 1989. His firm, *Allied Cultural Prosthetics*, which generates his multi-cycle production, consults for NASA, Philip Morris, and the Rand Corporation, among others. *Cultural Prosthetics* was exhibited in 1996 at the Morris Healy Gallery, New York. An exhibition of his work will be held in March 1997 in Milan, Rome, and Turin, in conjunction with the Gian Enzo Sperone Gallery. His work is included in the public collections of the Jewish Museum, New York, and the San Francisco Museum of Modern Art. He is represented by the Morris Healy Gallery, New York.

IVAN SANDERS is Professor of English at Suffolk Community College and Adjunct Professor at the New School for Social Research. He has translated works by George Konrád, Milán Füst, Péter Esterbázy, and others. His translation of Péter Nádas's *Book of Memories* will be published in 1997 by Farrar, Straus & Giroux.

BERNARD SCUDDER was born in Canterbury, Kent, in 1954, and has lived in Iceland since 1977. He studied English at the University of York and Icelandic at the University of Iceland, and has been a full-time translator since 1990. In addition to work by Einar Már Gudmundsson, he has translated fiction by Thor Vilhjamsson, Olafur Olafsson, and Gudbergur Bergsson. He is currently part of an editorial team that is producing an English translation of the complete Icelandic sagas, scheduled for publication in 1997. His translation of Gudmundsson's *Angels of the Universe* will be published by St. Martin's Press in the spring of 1997.

FIONA SHAW was born in Cork, Ireland, and studied philosophy at Cork University, before moving to London to study at the Royal Academy of Dramatic Art, where she won the two top academy awards. She joined the Royal Shakespeare Company at Stratford in 1985, where she appeared in *As You Like It*, Gorky's *Philistines*, *Les Liaisons Dangereuses*, and *The Taming of the Shrew*. In 1986, she toured the United Kingdom with major roles in *Much Ado About Nothing* and *The Merchant of Venice*. She also performed in Ariane Mnouchkine's production of *Mephisto* at the Barbican Theatre in London. In 1993, she performed in Sophie Treadwell's *Machinal* at the National Theatre. Shaw's film appearances include roles in *My Left Foot*, *Jane Eyre*, *London Kills Me*, *Super Mario Bros.*, and *Undercover Blues*. Her first major collaboration with the director Deborah Warner was *Electra*, which was performed at the Barbican Theatre in 1990, and toured through the United Kingdom and France. Shaw also played the title role in Warner's *Hedda Gabler* at the Abbey Theatre in Dublin, and performed the role of Richard II in Warner's production of the Shakespeare play at the National Theatre, London. She recently completed an international tour of her dramatic performance of T. S. Eliot's poem, *The Waste Land*, also directed by Deborah Warner. She lives in London.

LARISSA SZPORLUK's poem, "Holy Ghost," is part of her book-length manuscript of poetry, *Dark Sky Question*. She teaches in the Women's Studies program at Bowling Green State University in Bowling Green, Ohio.

SURVIVAL RESEARCH LABORATORIES was conceived of and founded by Mark Pauline in November 1978. Since 1979, SRL has staged over fifty mechanized presentations in the United States and Europe. SRL recently signed a contract for a show at the Longhorn Speedway in Austin, Texas, on March 28, 1997.

CONTRIBUTORS

WILLIAM T. VOLLMANN is working on a study of the ethics of violence.

DAVID FOSTER WALLACE's most recent novel is *Infinite Jest* (Little, Brown). A collection of his nonfiction, *A Supposedly Fun Thing I'll Never Do Again*, was recently published by Little, Brown.

JOHN WATERS lives in Baltimore, Maryland, where he just finished writing his script, *Pecker*. *Director's Cut*, a show of his photography, was recently exhibited at American Fine Arts, Co., New York.

MELVIN WAY was born in South Carolina in 1943 and moved to New York with his family in the 1960s. Way played woodwinds and percussion in his high-school orchestra and later went on to play jazz and rhythm and blues in bands such as the East Coast Players, Bumble Bee Band, and BBB Sterlings. During the day, he worked as an industrial machinist and as a chauffeur. In the 1970s, 1980s, and 1990s, Way lived in single-resident dwellings and homeless shelters on Ward's Island, and participated in Andrew Castrucci's artists' workshops at Ward's Island and at a Bowery Residency in Spanish Harlem. Way currently lives at a shelter in Fort Washington, New York. He will have his first one-person show at the Bridges & Bodell Gallery in October 1997.

ROBERT McLIAM WILSON was born in West Belfast in 1964. His novel, *Ripley Bogle*, from which the selection published in this issue of *Grand Street* was excerpted, was first published by Andre Deutsch Ltd. in the United Kingdom in 1989. His second novel, *Eureka Street*, was published by Secker & Warburg in 1996. Wilson lives in Belfast.

JOHN YAU has published several books of poetry, including *Radiant Silhouette: New & Selected Writing, 1974–1988* and *Edificio Sayonara* (both Black Sparrow). He is also the author of a novel, *Hawaiian Cowboys* (Black Sparrow), and *In the Realm of Appearances: The Art of Andy Warhol* (Ecco Press). Both *Big City Primer*, which received the Brendan Gill Award, and *Berlin Diptychon* (both published by Timken Books) juxtapose poems and prose with photographs by Bill Barrette. Yau's latest books include *Forbidden Entries* (Black Sparrow), *Ed Moses: Paintings and Drawings, 1951–1996* (Museum of Contemporary Art, Los Angeles, and University of California Press) and *The United States of Jasper Johns* (Zoland Books). He and Arthur Sze guest-edited an issue of *The Asian Pacific American Journal* (Fall-Winter 1996). Yau lives in New York.

Grand Street would like to thank **DONNA LEONE HAMM**, Director of Middle Ground Prison Reform and Prisoner/Family Advocacy, Tempe, Arizona, for her invaluable help in researching Daniel Lee Anders's *Letters from the Hole*.

Grand Street would like to thank the following for their generous support:
EDWARD LEE CAVE
CATHY AND STEPHEN GRAHAM
BARBARA HOWARD
DOMINIC MAN-KIT LAM
THE NEW YORK STATE COUNCIL ON THE ARTS
SUZANNE AND SANFORD J. SCHLESINGER
BETTY AND STANLEY K. SHEINBAUM

American Short Fiction

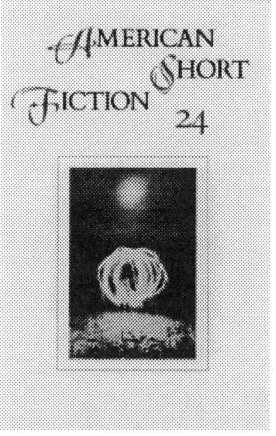

JOSEPH E. KRUPPA, Editor,
University of Texas at Austin

National Magazine Award for Fiction
1993 and 1995 Finalist

Stories you'll love to read.
Stories you'll remember.
Stories that will make you think.
Long stories. Short stories.
Short short stories. And nothing but stories.

American Short Fiction is published in
Spring (March), Summer (June), Fall (September), and
Winter (December)

Subscriptions: Individual $24, Institution $36
Canada/Mexico, add $6; other foreign, add $14(airmail)

Single Copy Rates:
Individual $9.95, Institution $12,
Canada/Mexico, add $2; other foreign, add $4(airmail)
Prepayment only, please.
Refunds available only on unshipped quantities of current subscriptions.

To subscribe, or for more information, write:
University of Texas Press
Journals Division
Box 7819, Austin, Texas 78713-7819
journals@uts.cc.utexas.edu

ILLUSTRATIONS

FRONT AND BACK COVER
Tom Sachs, 12 ga. @ 3 m 1/6/97 9:46 p.m., 1997. Duct tape and magazine, 9 1/2 x 7 3/4 x 1 in.

TITLE PAGE
Tom Sachs, *Glock Box*, 1996. Mixed media, 17 1/4 x 27 x 7 in.

TABLE OF CONTENTS
Film still from *Shivers* by David Cronenberg. Copyright © 1975, Cinepix Film Properties, Inc.

P. 12 In *Le surréalisme au service de la révolution*, Vol. XII, No. 3, Paris, 1931. Copyright © 1997, Artists' Rights Society (ARS), New York.

PP. 16–24 Tom Sachs, *Cultural Prosthetics*. Titles and dates appear with images. **P. 18** Mixed media, 13 x 38 x 14 in. **P. 19** Telephone books, duct tape, valise, and necktie, 24 x 30 x 9 1/4 in. **P. 20** Mixed media, dimensions unknown (destroyed). **P. 21** Mixed media, 12 x 7 1/2 x 1 3/4 in. **P. 22** Kitchen knives, broomsticks, mop handles, hardware, vinyl golf bag, and silk neckties, 62 x 15 x 8 1/2 in. **P. 23** Mixed media, 9 1/2 x 6 1/4 x 2 in. All photographs except **P. 18** copyright © Tom Powel. All images courtesy of the artist and Morris Healy Gallery, New York.

PP. 50–57 David Cronenberg, *Shivers*. Twenty-six film stills from *Shivers* (a.k.a. *They Came from Within* or *The Parasite Murders*), 1975. Eighty-seven minutes, 35 mm, color. Production company: DAL Productions, Ltd., with the participation of the Canadian Film Development Corporation. Executive producer: Alfred Pariser. Producers: Ivan Reitman, John Dunning, André Link. Director: David Cronenberg. Screenplay: David Cronenberg. Cinematography (color): Robert Saad. Sound: Michael Higgs. Editor: Patrick Dodd. Music: Ivan Reitman. Special make-up and creatures: Joe Blasco. Cast: Paul Hampton (*Roger St. Luc*), Joe Silver (*Rollo Linsky*), Lynn Lowry (*Forsythe*), Allan Migicovsky (*Nicholas Tudor*), Susan Petrie (*Janine Tudor*), Barbara Steele (*Betts*), Ronald Mlodzik (*Merrick*), Fred Doederlein (*Emil Hobbes*), and others. All images copyright © Cinepix Film Properties, Inc., Toronto. Courtesy of David Cronenberg.

PP. 76–81 Heinrich Anton Müller, *Mobiles and Machines*. Titles and dates appear with images. **PP. 76–77** Whereabouts unknown. Photograph courtesy of the Prinzhorn Collection, Heidelberg. **P. 78 (TOP AND BOTTOM) AND P. 79 (TOP)** Photographed in the courtyard of the Münsingen Asylum. Destroyed. Photographs courtesy of the Kunstmuseum, Bern. **P. 79 (BOTTOM)** Whereabouts unknown. Photograph courtesy of the Collection de l'Art Brut, Lausanne. **P. 80 AND p. 81** Photographs courtesy of the Prinzhorn Collection, Heidelberg. **P. 80 (TOP, RIGHT)** Chalk and pencil on pieced and sewn cardboard, 30 7/8 x 32 11/16 in. Collection Peter Lauri, Bern. **P. 81 (TOP)** Chalk over pencil on pieced cardboard, 20 1/8 x 33 7/16 in. Collection Peter Lauri, Bern. **P. 81 (BOTTOM, CENTER)** Gouache, chalk, and colored pen over pencil on cardboard, 29 11/16 x 17 11/16 in. Collection Peter Lauri, Bern. Whereabouts of other works unknown.

ILLUSTRATIONS

P. 84 Image of the Arizona State Prison Complex–Florence courtesy of the Arizona State Department of Corrections World Wide Web site at http://www.state.az.us/adc.

PP. 105–112 Vladimir Kovenatsky, *The Way It Was*. Titles and dates appear with images. **P. 105** Ink on paper, 15 1/4 x 10 5/8 in. **P. 106** Ink on paper, 11 5/8 x 8 1/4 in. **P. 107 (LEFT)** Ink on paper, 10 3/4 x 8 in. **P. 107 (RIGHT)** Ink on paper, 10 5/8 x 7 1/2 in. **P. 108** Ink on paper, 11 5/8 x 8 1/4 in. **P. 109 (LEFT)** Ink on paper, 7 1/2 x 5 1/16 in. **P. 109 (RIGHT)** Ink on paper, 7 1/4 x 5 11/16 in. **P. 110 (LEFT)** Linocut, 8 x 6 1/8 in. **P. 110 (RIGHT)** Linocut, 10 1/2 x 6 1/8 in. **P. 111** Linocut, image 8 7/8 x 7 1/4 in. **P. 112** Collage and ink on paper, 5 11/16 x 7 15/16 in. All works courtesy of Boris Kerdimun.

PP. 137–145 Adrian Piper, *Decisions, Decisions*. A project drawn from the series, *Decide Who You Are*, all 1992. **P. 137** Center panel from *Decide Who You Are #1: Skinned Alive*. **P. 138** Left-hand panel and **P. 139** Right-hand panel from *Decide Who You Are #28: Endless Loop, Record/Erase*. **P. 140** Left-hand panel and **P. 141** Center panel from *Decide Who You Are #2: Snakes on Stilts in Bags*. **P. 142** Left-hand panel, **P. 143** Center panel, and **P. 144** Right-hand panel from *Decide Who You Are # 13: Virtue*. **P. 145** Text from *Decide Who You Are #35: Hey, God!* All images courtesy of the artist and John Weber Gallery, New York.

P. 153 Courtesy of the Royal National Theatre, London. Photograph by Ivan Kyncl. **P. 158** Courtesy of the Royal National Theatre, London. Photograph by Neil Libbert. **P. 164** Courtesy of James L. L. Morrison Public Relations. Photograph by Neil Libbert.

PP. 171–176 Melvin Way, eight untitled works on paper, 1992–1996. **P. 171** Ink, crayon, and watercolor on paper, 12 x 9 in. All other works ink on paper. **P. 172** 7 1/2 x 8 1/2 in. **P. 173 (TOP)** 5 7/8 x 6 in. **P. 173 (BOTTOM)** 1 1/2 x 2 1/16 in. **P. 174** 4 1/2 x 8 1/2 in. **P. 175 (TOP)** 4 x 10 3/4 in. **P. 175 (BOTTOM)** 4 11/16 x 8 in. **P. 176** 10 7/8 x 8 3/8 in. All images courtesy of the artist, Margaret Bodell Gallery, New York, and Andrew Castrucci/Hospital Audiences, New York.

PP. 201–208 Paul Laffoley, *Speculations in Mind Physics: Work in the Visionary Genre*. Titles and dates appear with images. All works oil, acrylic, ink, and lettering on canvas, except **P. 202** silk-screen print. All works 73 1/2 x 73 1/2 in., except **P. 202** 28 x 28 in. and **P. 204** 51 x 51 in. All images courtesy of the artist and Kent Gallery, New York.

P. 210 AND P. 212 Denny Moers, two photographic monoprints. **P. 210** 20 x 24 in. **P. 212** 17 x 23 in.

PP. 214–217 Survival Research Laboratories, twenty-one images from SRL events. Images numbered 1, 3, 8, 9,10,18, 20, and 21: *Crime Wave*, in connection with William Linn, Blasthaus Gallery, November 26, 1995, San Francisco. Images numbered 2, 14, 15, and 19: *A Calculated Forecast of Ultimate Doom: Sickening Episodes of Widespread Devastation Accompanied by Sensations of Pleasurable Excitement*, May 28, 1994, San Francisco. Image numbered 7: *Europe*, 1988. Image numbered 13: *An Infestation of Peculiar Irregularities: Taking Place in a Disintegrating Landscape, Marked by Unsolved Entanglements*, August 28, 1992, Aurrillac, France. Images numbered 5, 12, and 17: Staged as part of the book-release party for RE/SEARCH #8/9: J. G. Ballard Issue, October 28, 1984, Fort Mason Center, San Francisco. Images numbered 11 and 16: *Mysteries of the Reactionary Mind*, April 5, 1981, San Francisco. Images numbered 4 and 6: *SRL Contemplates: A Million Inconsiderate Experiments in Phoenix, Arizona*, January 27, 1996, Phoenix, Arizona. All images courtesy of Mark Pauline/SRL.

PP. 233–239 Peter Fend, *Chernobyl Solutions*. Captions and dates appear with images. Images selected from a show of the same name installed at Steffany Martz Gallery, New York, in cooperation with American Fine Arts, Co., New York, on April 25, 1996, the tenth anniversary of the explosion at the Chernobyl reactor complex. All images copyright © Peter Fend/OEDC. Courtesy of the artist and Steffany Martz Gallery.

P. 241 Antonin Artaud on the grounds of the asylum in Rodez, France, May 1946. Photograph taken from Antonin Artaud, *Nouveaux écrits de Rodez* (Gallimard, 1977). **P. 245** Five black-and-white photographs of the Rodez asylum by Sylvère Lotringer (details of these photographs appear on **P. 242, P. 244, P. 246, P. 248, P. 250, P. 254 AND P. 258**). **P. 251** Artaud (far right) and Dr. Gaston Ferdière (second from right), with staff members, on the grounds of the Rodez asylum, May 1946. Photograph taken from Antonin Artaud, *Nouveaux écrits de Rodez* (Gallimard, 1977). Details of the photograph appear on **P. 252** and **P. 260. P. 256** Artaud at age five, with his younger sister Marie-Ange. Photograph taken from *Antonin Artaud: Selected Writings*, edited and with an introduction by Susan Sontag (Farrar, Straus & Giroux, 1976).

TriQuarterly
Fiction • Poetry • Art • Criticism

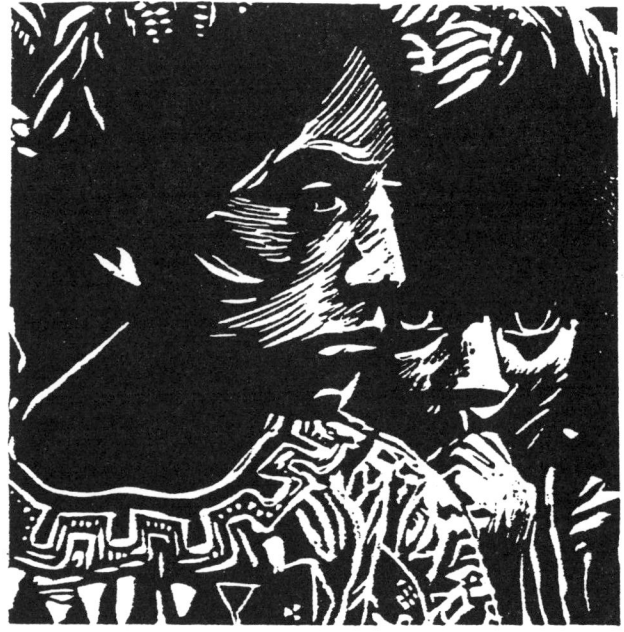

Réne Arceo: *Mujeres guatemaltecas* / From *TQ* #86

TriQuarterly publishes poetry—and fiction, translations and graphic art—of rare and consistent excellence. For nearly three decades, *TriQuarterly* has been noted for literary exploration and discovery—always lively, serious and varied. Subscribe now!

$24/year   2020 Ridge Avenue
$44/2 years   Evanston, IL 60208

CALL TOLL-FREE: 800-832-3615

BOOKFORUM

ARTFORUM'S BOOK REVIEW

BELLHOOKSDOUGLASCOUPLAND
WILLIAMBURROUGHSPETERSCHJELDAHL
QUARTERLY HAROLDBLOOMLINDA
NOCHLINLISALIEBMANNPAULBOWLES
GARYINDIANAPETERPLAGENSDAVID
WOJNAROWICZANDY **ART** WARHOL
DIDEROTJOHNASHANDREWSOLOMONBRUCE
HAINLEYMAN **ARCHITECTURE** RAY
ANDRÉBRETONRICHARDPRINCENANGOLDIN
GUYTREBAYBIGHAIREHGOMBRICHDIANE
ARBUSLOUISE **MUSIC** BOURGEOISWAYNE
KOESTENBAUMCHUCKCLOSEBARBARA
KRUGERANDREWHULTKRANSDAVID
RIMANELLIDENNISCOOPER **FASHION**
MAYAANGELOUYVEALAINBOISBRIANENO
FICTION PHILIPTAAFFERICHARDAVEDON
DAVEHICKEYJASPERJOHNSHILTONALS

2 YEARS • 8 ISSUES • $10.00
TO SUBSCRIBE CALL 1 800 966 2783
TO ADVERTISE CALL DANIELLE McCONNELL 212 475 4000

Ploughshares
a literary adventure

Known for its compelling fiction and poetry, *Ploughshares* is widely regarded as one of America's most influential literary journals. Each issue is guest-edited by a different writer for a fresh, provocative slant—exploring personal visions, aesthetics, and literary circles—and contributors include both well-known and emerging writers. In fact, *Ploughshares* has become a premier proving ground for new talent, showcasing the early works of Sue Miller, Mona Simpson, Robert Pinsky, and countless others. Past guest editors include Richard Ford, Derek Walcott, Tobias Wolff, Carolyn Forché, and Rosellen Brown. This unique editorial format has made *Ploughshares*, in effect, into a dynamic anthology series—one that has established a tradition of quality and prescience. *Ploughshares* is published in quality trade paperback in April, August, and December: usually a fiction issue in the Fall and mixed issues of poetry and fiction in the Spring and Winter. Inside each issue, you'll find not only great new stories and poems, but also a profile on the guest editor, book reviews, and miscellaneous notes about *Ploughshares*, its writers, and the literary world. Subscribe today.

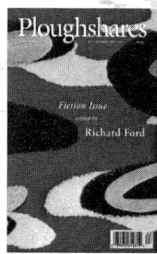

Sample *Ploughshares* on the Web: http://www.emerson.edu/ploughshares

----

❏ Send me a one-year subscription for $21.
  I save $8.85 off the cover price (3 issues).

❏ Send me a two-year subscription for $40.
  I save $19.70 off the cover price (6 issues).

Start with: ❏ Spring ❏ Fall ❏ Winter

Add $5 per year for international. Institutions: $24.

Name_____

Address_____

Mail with check to: Ploughshares · Emerson College
100 Beacon St. · Boston, MA 02116

AEXGSS97

GRAND STREET
BACK ISSUES
AN ESSENTIAL COLLECTION

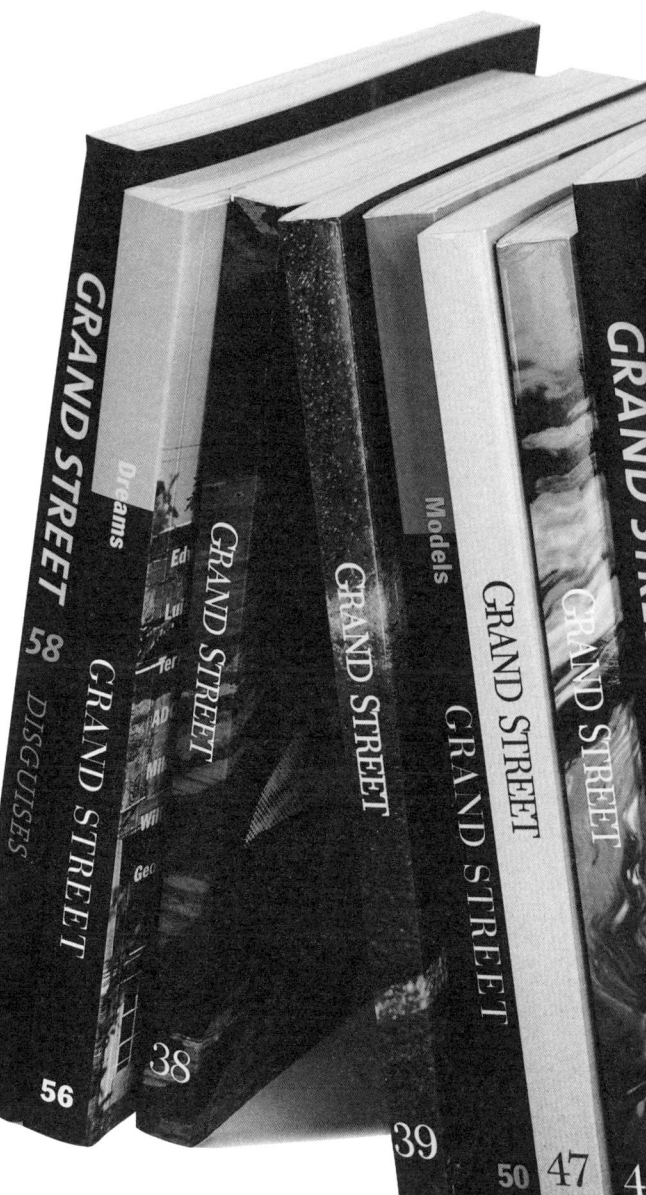

36 Edward Said on Jean Genet; Terry Southern & Dennis Hopper on Larry Flynt
STORIES: Elizabeth Bishop, William T. Vollmann; PORTFOLIOS: William Eggleston, Saul Steinberg; POEMS: John Ashbery, Bei Dao.

37 William S. Burroughs on guns; John Kenneth Galbraith on JFK's election
STORIES: Pierrette Fleutiaux, Eduardo Galeano; PORTFOLIOS: Blackboard Equations, John McIntosh; POEMS: Clark Coolidge, Suzanne Gardinier.

38 Kazuo Ishiguro & Kenzaburo Oe on Japanese literature; Julio Cortázar's HOPSCOTCH: A Lost Chapter
STORIES: Fernando Pessoa, Ben Sonnenberg; PORTFOLIOS: Linda Connor, Robert Rauschenberg; POEMS: Jimmy Santiago Baca, Charles Wright.

39 Nadine Gordimer: SAFE HOUSES; James Miller on Michel Foucault
STORIES: Hervé Guibert, Dubravka Ugrešić; PORTFOLIOS: Homicide: Bugsy Siegel, Mark di Suvero; POEMS: Amiri Baraka, Michael Palmer.

40 Gary Giddins on Dizzy Gillespie; Toni Morrison on race and literature
STORIES: Yehudit Katzir, Marcel Proust; PORTFOLIOS: Gretchen Bender, Brice Marden; POEMS: Arkadii Dragomoshchenko, Tom Paulin.

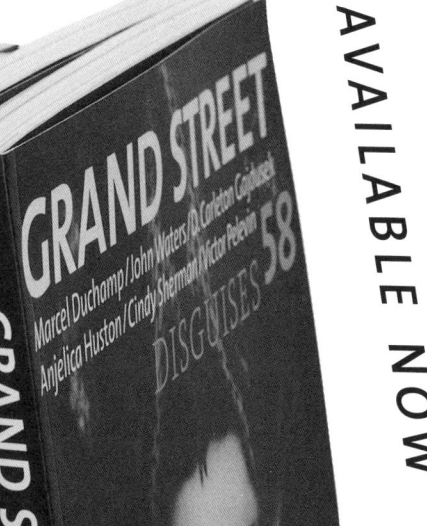

AVAILABLE NOW

41 Nina Berberova on the Turgenev Library; Mary-Claire King on tracing "the disappeared"
STORIES: Ben Okri, Kurt Schwitters; PORTFOLIOS: Louise Bourgeois, Jean Tinguely; POEMS: Rae Armantrout, Eugenio Montale.

42 David Foster Wallace: THREE PROTRUSIONS; Henry Green: An unfinished novel
STORIES: Félix de Azúa, Eduardo Galeano; PORTFOLIOS: Sherrie Levine, Ariane Mnouchkine & Ingmar Bergman — two productions of Euripides; POEMS: Jorie Graham, Gary Snyder.

43 Jamaica Kincaid on the biography of a dress; Stephen Trombley on designing death machines
STORIES: Victor Erofeyev, Christa Wolf; PORTFOLIOS: Joseph Cornell, Sue Williams; POEMS: Robert Creeley, Kabir.

44 Martin Duberman on Stonewall; Andrew Kopkind: Slacking Toward Bethlehem
STORIES: Georges Perec, Edmund White; PORTFOLIOS: William Christenberry, Fred Wilson; POEMS: Lyn Hejinian, Sharon Olds.

45 John Cage: Correspondence; Roberto Lovato: Down and Out in Central L.A.
STORIES: David Gates, Duong Thu Huong; PORTFOLIOS: Ecke Bonk, Gerhard Richter; POEMS: A. R. Ammons, C. H. Sisson.

46 William T. Vollmann on the Navajo-Hopi Land Dispute; Ice-T, Easy-E: L.A. rappers get open with Brian Cross
STORIES: David Foster Wallace, Italo Calvino; PORTFOLIOS: Nancy Rubins, Dennis Balk; POEMS: Michael Palmer, Martial.

ORDER WHILE THEY LAST.
CALL 1-800-807-6548

Please send name, address, issue number(s), and quantity. American Express, Mastercard, and Visa accepted; please send credit card number and expiration date. Back issues are $15.00 each ($18.00 overseas and Canada), including postage and handling, payable in U.S. dollars. Address orders to GRAND STREET, Back Issues, 131 Varick Street, Suite 906, New York, NY 10013

47
Louis Althusser's ZONES OF DARKNESS; Edward W. Said on intellectual exile
STORIES: Jean Genet, Junichiro Tanizaki; PORTFOLIOS: Barbara Bloom, Julio Galán; POEMS: John Ashbery, Ovid.

48 OBLIVION
William T. Vollmann: UNDER THE GRASS; Kip S. Thorne on black holes
STORIES: Heinrich Böll, Charles Palliser; PORTFOLIOS: Saul Steinberg, Lawrence Weiner; POEMS: Mahmoud Darwish, Antonin Artaud.

49 HOLLYWOOD
Dennis Hopper interviews Quentin Tarantino; Terry Southern on the making of DR. STRANGELOVE
STORIES: Paul Auster, Peter Handke; PORTFOLIOS: Edward Ruscha, William Eggleston; POEMS: John Ashbery, James Laughlin.

50 MODELS
Alexander Cockburn & Noam Chomsky on models in nature; Graham Greene's dream diary
STORIES: Cees Nooteboom, Rosario Castellanos; PORTFOLIOS: Paul McCarthy, Katharina Sieverding; POEMS: Nicholas Christopher, Robert Kelly.

51 NEW YORK
Terry Williams on life in the tunnels under NYC; William S. Burroughs: MY EDUCATION
STORIES: William T. Vollmann, Orhan Pamuk; PORTFOLIOS: Richard Prince, David Hammons; POEMS: Hilda Morley, Charles Simic.

52 GAMES
David Mamet: THE ROOM; Paul Virilio on cybersex and virtual reality
STORIES: Brooks Hansen, Walter Benjamin; PORTFOLIOS: Robert Williams, Chris Burden; POEMS: Miroslav Holub, Fanny Howe.

53 FETISHES
John Waters exposes his film fetishes; Samuel Beckett's ELEUTHÉRIA
STORIES: Georges Bataille, Colum McCann; PORTFOLIOS: Helmut Newton, Yayoi Kusama; POEMS: Taslima Nasrin, Simon Armitage.

54 SPACE
Born in Prison: an inmate survives the box; Jasper Johns's GALAXY WORKS
STORIES: Vladimir Nabokov, Irvine Welsh; PORTFOLIOS: Vito Acconci, James Turrell; POEMS: W. S. Merwin, John Ashbery.

55 EGOS
Julian Schnabel: THE CONVERSION OF ST. PAOLO MALFI; Suzan-Lori Parks on Josephine Baker
STORIES: Kenzaburo Oe, David Foster Wallace; PORTFOLIOS: Dennis Hopper, Brigid Berlin's Cock Book; POEMS: Amiri Baraka, Susie Mee.

56 DREAMS
Edward Ruscha: HOLLYWOOD BOULEVARD; Terry Southern and Other Tastes
STORIES: William T. Vollmann, Lydia Davis; PORTFOLIOS: Jim Shaw, ADOBE LA; POEMS: Bernadette Mayer, Saúl Yurkievich.

57 DIRT
John Waters & Mike Kelley: THE DIRTY BOYS; Rem Koolhaas on 42nd Street
STORIES: Mohammed Dib, Sandra Cisneros; PORTFOLIOS: Langdon Clay, Alexis Rockman; POEMS: Robert Creeley, Thomas Sayers Ellis.

58 DISGUISES
Anjelica Huston on life behind the camera; D. Carleton Gajdusek: THE NEW GUINEA FIELD JOURNALS
STORIES: Victor Pelevin, Arno Schmidt; PORTFOLIOS: Hannah Höch, Kara Walker; POEMS: Vittorio Sereni, Marjorie Welish.

59 TIME
Mike Davis on the destruction of L.A.; John Szarkowski: LOOKING AT PICTURES
STORIES: Naguib Mahfouz, Nina Berberova; PORTFOLIOS: Spain, Charles Ray; POEMS: Adonis, James Tate.

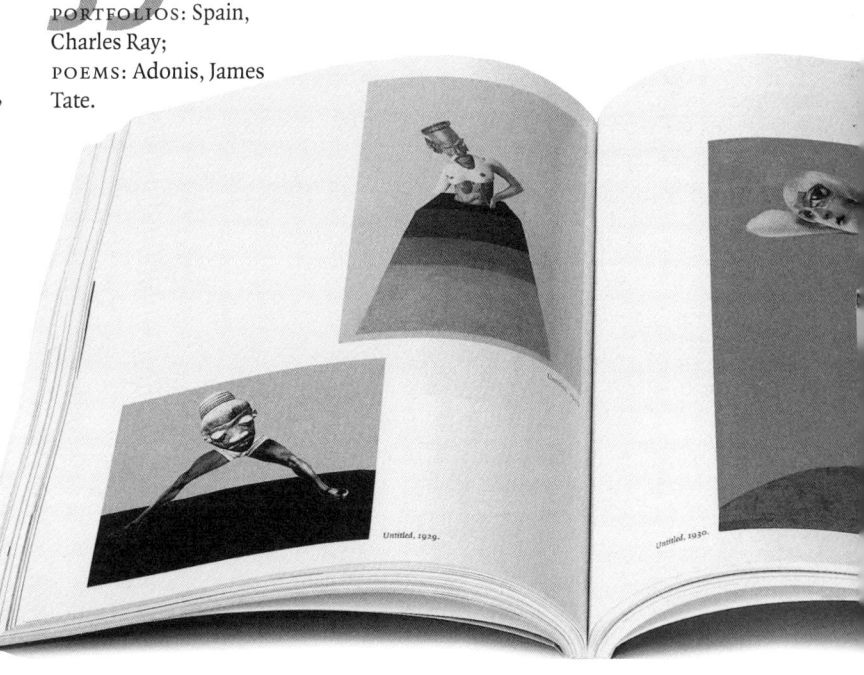

Some of the bookstores where you can find
GRAND STREET

Magpie Magazine Gallery, Vancouver, CANADA

Newsstand, Bellingham, WA
Bailey Coy Books, Seattle, WA
Hideki Ohmori, Seattle, WA

Looking Glass Bookstore, Portland, OR
Powell's Books, Portland, OR
Reading Frenzy, Portland, OR

...On Sundays, Tokyo, JAPAN

Baxter's Books, Minneapolis, MN
Minnesota Book Center, Minneapolis, MN
University of Minnesota Bookstore, Minneapolis, MN
Walker Art Center Bookshop, Minneapolis, MN
Hungry Mind Bookstore, St. Paul, MN
Odegard Books, St. Paul, MN

ASUC Bookstore, Berkeley, CA
Black Oak Books, Berkeley, CA
Cody's Books, Berkeley, CA
Bookstore Fiona, Carson, CA
Huntley Bookstore, Claremont, CA
Book Soup, Hollywood, CA
University Bookstore, Irvine, CA
Museum of Contemporary Art, La Jolla, CA
UCSD Bookstore, La Jolla, CA
A.R.T. Press, Los Angeles, CA
Museum of Contemporary Art, Los Angeles, CA
Occidental College Bookstore, Los Angeles, CA
Sun & Moon Press Bookstore, Los Angeles, CA
UCLA/Armand Hammer Museum, Los Angeles, CA
Stanford Bookstore, Newark, CA
Diesel, A Bookstore, Oakland, CA
Blue Door Bookstore, San Diego, CA
The Booksmith, San Francisco, CA
City Lights, San Francisco, CA
Green Apple Books, San Francisco, CA
Modern Times Bookstore, San Francisco, CA
San Francisco Camerawork, San Francisco, CA
Logos, Santa Cruz, CA
Arcana, Santa Monica, CA
Midnight Special Bookstore, Santa Monica, CA
Reader's Books, Sonoma, CA
Small World Books, Venice, CA
Ventura Bookstore, Ventura, CA

Asun Bookstore, Reno, NV

Chinook Bookshop, Colorado Springs, CO
The Bookies, Denver, CO
Newsstand Cafe, Denver, CO
Tattered Cover Bookstore, Denver, CO
Stone Lion Bookstore, Fort Collins, CO

Nebraska Bookstore, Lincoln, NE

Sam Weller's Zion Bookstore, Salt Lake City, UT

Kansas Union Bookstore, Lawrence, KS
Terra Nova Bookstore, Lawrence, KS

Bookman's, Tucson, AZ

Bookworks, Albuquerque, NM
Page One Bookstore, Albuquerque, NM
Salt of the Earth, Albuquerque, NM
Cafe Allegro, Los Alamos, NM
Collected Works, Santa Fe, NM

Honolulu Book Shop, Honolulu, HI

Page One, SINGAPORE

Book People, Austin, TX
Bookstop, Austin, TX
University Co-op Society, Austin, TX
McKinney Avenue Contemporary Gift Shop, Dallas, TX
Bookstop, Houston, TX
Brazos Bookstore, Houston, TX
Contemporary Arts Museum Shop, Houston, TX
Diversebooks, Houston, TX
Menil Collection Bookstore, Houston, TX
Museum of Fine Arts, Houston, TX
Texas Gallery, Houston, TX
Bookstop, Plano, TX

Bookland of Brunswick, Brunswick, ME
University of Maine Bookstore, Orono, ME
Books Etc., Portland, ME
Raffles Cafe Bookstore, Portland, ME

Pages, Toronto, CANADA

Dartmouth Bookstore, Hanover, NH
Toadstool Bookshop, Peterborough, NH

Wootton's Books, Amherst, MA
Boston University Bookstore, Boston, MA
Harvard Book Store, Cambridge, MA
M.I.T. Press Bookstore, Cambridge, MA
Cisco Harland Books, Marlborough, MA
Broadside Bookshop, Northampton, MA
Provincetown Bookshop, Provincetown, MA
Water Street Books, Williamstown, MA

Northshire Books, Manchester, VT

Main Street News, Ann Arbor, MI
Shaman Drum Bookshop, Ann Arbor, MI
Cranbrook Art Museum Books, Bloomfield Hills, MI
Book Beat, Oak Park, MI

Afterwords, Milwaukee, WI

Accident or Design, Providence, RI
Brown University Bookstore, Providence, RI
College Hill Store, Providence, RI

Farley's Bookshop, New Hope, PA
Faber Books, Philadelphia, PA
Waterstone's Booksellers, Philadelphia, PA
Andy Warhol Museum, Pittsburgh, PA
Encore Books, Mechanicsburg, PA
Encore Books, State College, PA

Rosetta News, Carbondale, IL
Pages for All Ages, Champaign, IL
Mayuba Bookstore, Chicago, IL
Museum of Contemporary Art, Chicago, IL
Seminary Co-op Bookstore, Chicago, IL

Yale Cooperative, New Haven, CT
UConn Co-op, Storrs, CT

Encore Books, Princeton, NJ
Micawber Books, Princeton, NJ

Community Bookstore, Brooklyn, NY
Talking Leaves, Buffalo, NY
Colgate University Bookstore, Hamilton, NY
Book Revue, Huntington, NY
The Bookery, Ithaca, NY
A Different Light, New York, NY
Art Market, New York, NY
B. Dalton, New York, NY
Books & Co., New York, NY
Coliseum Books, New York, NY
Collegiate Booksellers, New York, NY
Doubleday Bookshops, New York, NY
Exit Art/First World Store, New York, NY
Gold Kiosk, New York, NY
Gotham Book Mart, New York, NY
Museum of Modern Art Bookstore, New York, NY
New York University Book Center, New York, NY
Rizzoli Bookstores, New York, NY
St. Mark's Bookshop, New York, NY
Shakespeare & Co., New York, NY
Spring Street Books, New York, NY
Wendell's Books, New York, NY
Whitney Museum of Modern Art, New York, NY
Syracuse University Bookstore, Syracuse, NY

UC Bookstore, Cincinnati, OH
Bank News, Cleveland, OH
Ohio State University Bookstore, Columbus, OH
Student Book Exchange, Columbus, OH
Books & Co., Dayton, OH
Kenyon College Bookstore, Gambier, OH
Oberlin Consumers Cooperative, Oberlin, OH

Indiana University Bookstore, Bloomington, IN

Iowa Book & Supply, Iowa City, IA
Prairie Lights, Iowa City, IA
University Bookstore, Iowa City, IA

Box of Rocks, Bowling Green, KY
Carmichael's, Louisville, KY

Louie's Bookstore Cafe, Baltimore, MD

Xanadu Bookstore, Memphis, TN

Bridge Street Books, Washington, DC
Chapters, Washington, DC
Franz Bader Bookstore, Washington, DC
Olsson's, Washington, DC
Politics & Prose, Washington, DC

Library Ltd., Clayton, MO
Whistler's Books, Kansas City, MO
Left Bank Books, St. Louis, MO

Daedalus Used Bookshop, Charlottesville, VA
Studio Art Shop, Charlottesville, VA
Williams Corner, Charlottesville, VA

Paper Skyscraper, Charlotte, NC
Regulator Bookshop, Durham, NC

Chapter Two Bookstore, Charleston, SC
Intermezzo, Columbia, SC
Open Book, Greenville, SC

Square Books, Oxford, MS

Oxford Bookstore, Atlanta, GA

Books & Books, Coral Gables, FL
Goerings Book Center, Gainesville, FL
Bookstop, Miami, FL
Rex Art, Miami, FL
Inkwood Books, Tampa, FL

Lenny's News, New Orleans, LA

And at selected Barnes & Noble and Bookstar bookstores nationwide.

Subscribe to "the leading intellectual forum in the US"

—*New York* magazine

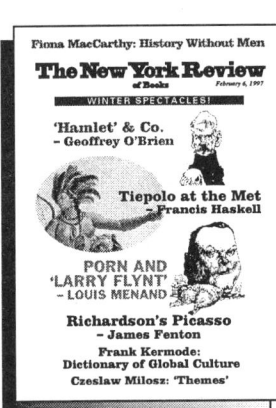

Since we began publishing in 1963, *The New York Review of Books* has provided remarkable variety and intellectual excitement. Twenty times a year, the world's best writers and scholars address themselves to 130,000 discerning readers worldwide...people who know that the widest range of subjects—literature, art, politics, science, history, music, education—will be discussed with wit, clarity, and brilliance.

In each issue subscribers of *The New York Review* enjoy articles by such celebrated writers as John Updike, Elizabeth Hardwick, Gore Vidal, Nadine Gordimer, Oliver Sacks, and countless others, as well as the literary bare-knuckle boxing of the Letters to the Editors section.

If you think you too might enjoy the penetrating insights and arguments found in each issue of *The New York Review*, subscribe now with this special introductory offer. You'll not only save over 60% ($42.50) from the newsstand price, but you'll also get a free copy of *Selections*. With this offer you'll receive:

➤ **20 Issues** A full year's subscription of 20 issues for just $27.50—a saving of 50% off the regular subscription rate of $55.00 and a saving of $42.50 (60%) off the newsstand price.

➤ **A Free Book:** *Selections* is a collection of 19 reviews and essays published verbatim from our first two issues. In it you'll discover how certain works such as *The Naked Lunch* or *The Fire Next Time*, now regarded as modern classics, were initially perceived by critics when they were first published and reviewed.

➤ **A Risk-Free Guarantee** If you are unhappy with your subscription at any time, you may cancel. We will refund the unused portion of the subscription cost. What's more, *Selections* is yours to keep as our gift to you for trying *The New York Review*.

The New York Review of Books

Return to: Subscriber Service Dept., PO Box 420382, Palm Coast, FL 32142-0382

❑ **Yes!** Please enter my one-year subscription (20 issues) to *The New York Review* at the special introductory rate of only $27.50 (a saving of 60% off the newsstand rate). With my paid subscription, I will also receive *Selections* at no extra charge and a no-risk guarantee.

❑ $27.50 enclosed*   Charge my: ❑ Am Ex ❑ MasterCard ❑ Visa ❑ Bill me. (US only)

Name

Address

City/State/Zip

A7C17G

Credit Card Number

Credit Card Expiration Date/Signature

SELECTIONS

FREE with this offer

☎ For faster service on credit card orders, fax to: (212) 586-8003. Please include your own phone and fax in case of questions. *If you fax this order, do not also mail it.*

*Make checks or US money orders payable to *The New York Review of Books*. We accept US Dollars drawn on a US bank or Canadian Dollars drawn on a Canadian bank. If paying by CDN$ return to Mike Johnson, *The New York Review of Books*, 250 West 57 St., Rm 1321, New York, NY 10107. *After May 1997*: 1755 Broadway, 5th Floor, New York, NY 10019-3780. We cannot accept international money orders. Rates outside the US: to Canada $53/$72.50CDN, Rest of World Regular Post $57, Rest of World Print Flow Air Post (recommended for Africa, Australia, the Far East, New Zealand, and South America) $84. Credit card orders will be charged at the US Dollar rates shown. Please allow 6 to 8 weeks for delivery of your first issue.